To Bjarnie Anderson:
With thanks
and apprecia...
your support.
Joan Jacoby

# The American Prosecutor:
# A Search for Identity

# The American Prosecutor: A Search for Identity

**Joan E. Jacoby**
Bureau of Social Science
Research, Inc.

**LexingtonBooks**
D.C. Heath and Company
Lexington, Massachusetts
Toronto

**Library of Congress Cataloging in Publication Data**

Jacoby, Joan E
   The American prosecutor

   Includes bibliographical references.
   1. Public prosecutors—United States. 2. Prosecution—United States.
I. Title
KF9640.J28      345'.73'01      79-2795
ISBN 0-669-03291-3

Prepared under Grant Number 76-NI-99-0128 from the National Institute of Law Enforcement and Criminal Justice Law Enforcement Assistance Administration, U.S. Department of Justice. Points of view or opinions stated in this document are those of the author and do not necessarily represent the official position or policies of the U.S. Department of Justice.

Published simultaneously in Canada

Printed in the United States of America

International Standard Book Number: 0-669-03291-3

Library of Congress Catalog Card Number: 79-2795

*To these who are the ties that bind,*

*my mother, Pearl McGrady*
*my daughters, Christina, Jennifer, and Erica*

# Contents

# List of Tables

# Acknowledgments

This book was written as part of the National Institute for Law Enforcement and Criminal Justice Visiting Fellow program with support from the Law Enforcement Assistance Administration, U.S. Department of Justice. The opportunity afforded by the existence of this program, combined with the support and encouragement of its principals, Blair Ewing, Richard Barnes, and Winifred Reed, and the fellowship of the other Visiting Fellows made this study both pleasurable and productive.

It is hard to imagine how this book could have been accomplished without the aid and dedication of Kevin J. Brosch: his willingness to dig into library files in search of often elusive materials; his ability to sort and compile them into meaningful units that could be written about; his keen insights and critical discussions about the major, and minor, issues; his capacity to edit and rewrite the many drafts that were produced and, finally, to endure the drudgery of checking citations all contributed to the existence of this report. In addition, Kevin deserves a special acknowledgment because of his major contribution to chapter 1.

Although the visiting fellowship program and the availability of Kevin Brosch were the keys to the happy completion of this book, its substance stems from another source—namely, the American prosecutors. This is their story—as told by them over the years and interpreted into this perspective.

Because my association with the American prosecutor extends over such a long period of time, it is impossible to individually acknowledge all who have contributed to this study. Instead, I wish to thank the three prosecutors whose offices became the case studies for this report: District Attorney Harry Connick, Orleans Parish, Louisiana; District Attorney Alexander M. Hunter, Boulder County, Colorado; and Prosecuting Attorney Ralph Martin, Jackson County, Missouri. These three prosecutors represent the highest levels of prosecutorial leadership. They demonstrate that model offices can exist despite some critics' claims to the contrary; that prosecution services can be provided using good management practices; and that the policy of the prosecutor is of critical importance to the quality and character of justice in a community. That these three offices are so distinctly different and yet so obviously successful in their delivery of services indicates that choices are available to the public with respect to the type of prosecution one can expect and that the locally elected status of the prosecutor holds him accountable to the community's expectations, standards, and values. To each of these prosecutors and their staffs, I extend my sincerest thanks for their generous assistance and support. In addition, I wish to acknowledge the invaluable contribution of Patrick F. Healy, executive director of the National District Attorneys Association, to my education about the prosecution.

I would also like to thank Robert Bower, director of the Bureau of Social Science Research (BSSR) for providing me with all the support that I requested and for his underlying interest in the successful completion of this study. Access to the research environment offered by BSSR and the professional and personal interactions with my colleagues are appreciated.

Finally, I would like to thank Francys Richardson for her patient and careful typing and editing services as she moved from one draft to another and Gayle McLeese for the final manuscript preparation.

# Introduction

The American prosecutor is a unique figure, not only in the American system of justice but in the criminal justice systems of the world. In no other country is there an official like the prosecuting attorney, who exercises a special hybrid of quasi-judicial and political power. The prosecutor is established as the representative of the state in criminal litigation, by either constitutional or statutory mandate, and yet is directly answerable to the local electorate at the ballot box. Although the American system of justice evolved from a wide mix of European predecessors, the office of the prosecuting attorney is a uniquely American institution; it has no exact counterpart in England or in any of the other European states.

The power and significance of the prosecutor is derived from the many roles that he plays daily in the administration of justice. He is the principal representative of the state before the courts, charged with the responsibility of upholding the laws and the constitution. He is the reviewing officer for all arrests made by the police and is therefore an interpreter of the laws, capable of influencing the character and quality of law enforcement through the decisions he makes in charging crimes. He takes active part in reviewing the functions of the criminal justice system and often makes suggestions about remedial legislation or alterations in the substance and procedures of the criminal law. He is a locally elected politician with an independent source of power—the local voters—and can exercise independent judgment and discretion by making key policy decisions for his community.

Despite the fact that the prosecutor has held a key position in the criminal justice system for over two hundred years, his role has been virtually ignored by the literature. Little has been written about the prosecutor; scant research has been conducted. As recently as 1971, the National Association of Attorneys General complained that "virtually no primary data on prosecutors are available from any source." Since then, three separate surveys have been conducted, but information is still indefinite and incomplete.

The lack of inquiry into the function of the prosecutor reflects the general limits of understanding about the nature of the office both among the general public and in academic and research communities. The prosecutor has a vague image in the public eye, and much of this arises because the prosecutor's own self-image is fuzzy. The concept of the proper role of the prosecuting attorney lacks uniformity; there is wide diversity of opinion about his proper role from jurisdiction to jurisdiction. The diversity of situations in which the prosecutor must operate perpetuates this vagueness. It is hoped that analysis of the role of prosecutor from a perspective that includes both environmental constraints and specific policy choices will begin to clear up this definition.

This study attempts to focus on all these dimensions to provide a better understanding of the prosecutor's functional responsibilities, his relationship with other agencies and systems, and the issues of prosecutorial power and its control. This analysis of the local prosecutor's identity will provide insights into what properly designed systems of prosecution are and what they mean. The general approach will be to conduct a broad and generalized examination of the prosecutive function in American society, to look at the origins of prosecution in America, the diverse situations in which it thrives, and the nature and character of different prosecutorial styles. This book is written for those who know little about prosecution or who have had only limited experience or contact in this area. The aim is to expand the reader's view by exposing him to the diversities and problems inherent to this uniquely American institution.

## Approach and Methodology

To describe the American local prosecutor as he functions in diverse environments, we have merged three approaches: (1) a historical overview of the prosecutor's origin in America and subsequent development; (2) an analysis of the effects of the diversified environmental and systemic characteristics on the more than three thousand prosecutors who operate in the counties and districts of the fifty states; and (3) an evaluation of the emerging role of the prosecutor with respect to the different prosecutorial policies that are most clearly exemplified in the charging function. Case studies of three different prosecutor's offices are presented to draw the important issues into a meaningful context.

### Historical Traces

An understanding of the past is important in studying any subject. It is certainly significant in examining the local prosecutor, both because of the scarcity of information about him and because of his institutional uniqueness. In the beginning chapters the historical factors bearing on the origin and develoment of the office of prosecutor and leading to his modern position as a locally elected official are traced. The approach taken was to follow the major issues that led to the present definition of the prosecutor as a "locally elected official": to see why his jurisdiction is local rather than state or federal; why he is elected rather than appointed; and why he exercises wide discretionary power rather than simply becoming a court or police functionary.

The locally elected prosecutor is unknown to either the English legal system or to any of the other major European systems of justice. The

English system was one of private prosecution, a system that was never adopted by the early American colonists. After early settlement, the responsibility for bringing criminal actions in each of the thirteen colonies was lodged in a centralized figure—the King's Attorney or Attorney General. But because this responsibility was not directly equivalent to the role that the King's Attorney had played in the English legal system, the role of the Attorney General remained undefined as to the extent of his involvement in criminal prosecution. Furthermore, as the nation gained its independence, and as expansion began in the ensuing movement west, centralization of this responsibility became impractical. Local prosecutors were appointed at first to represent various communities; later, as will be seen, they gained elective status. Today, forty-five of the fifty states elect prosecuting attorneys on a local level.

Decentralization of judicial and quasi-judicial power is the legal tradition within the United States. The basic structure of the American legal system was taken from the British common law system, of course, although some influence has been felt from various civil law systems, most notably the French influence in Louisiana and some Spanish influence in California and the southwestern states. But, overwhelmingly, American law is a direct descendant of the British common law tradition. America's own contributions to the development of this system have come, in a large measure, in its unique procedures and officers. Much of this alteration can be attributed to the different nature of the American continent—to the vast expanse of land and sparse population—which spawned stronger institutions of local government than were known in England or anywhere else in Europe.

Local government in America developed its strong traditions because its characteristics comported with the essentially rural and agrarian nature of American life and economy during the developing period of the late eighteenth and early nineteenth centuries. This may be the single most influential factor in the historical forces that shaped the prosecuting attorney. Local government certainly had been a factor in the English system of government—the sheriff and the coroner have long traditions in England. They were transferred into the American system. But the prosecuting attorney developed here because of the greater reliance of American society on settling local problems quickly and independently and because of the demand of the citizens of small towns and rural counties for autonomy and independence in decision making. There have been movements down through the years to establish state-controlled or state-administered systems of prosecution, but, for the large part, these have failed to make a dent in the strong tendency to preserve local prerogative.

In essence, the office of the locally elected prosecutor is the logical result of the forces and events that shaped the entire nature of American government. As will be seen, the characteristics of local prosecution have been somewhat inevitable. Attempts to change the nature of this political phenomenon run against the basic traditions and historical trends of the past three centuries.

*Diverse Environments*

Although early political trends did much to solidify the prosecutor as a locally elected official with primary responsibility for bringing criminal actions in the courts, more recent social and economic trends have placed him within a widely diverse and confusing system of external and environmental constraints. Modern industrial society, the advent of large urban areas, the increase in crime, and the new mobility of the American public have combined to place increased pressures on the individual who has been delegated the responsibility of enforcing the laws. Even the system of justice in which the prosecutor works has changed drastically. No longer can the prosecutor operate simply in the environs of the local county court, executing his office in the context of a small and closely related work-group.

There have been, of course, marked changes in the criminal justice system in the last half-century. Even the concept of a criminal justice system is new—a realization that the different agencies involved in the enforcement of the criminal laws—the prosecution, the courts, the police, the public defender, and the corrections agencies—have formed highly complex and interdependent relationships. The criminal justice system itself has been the subject of a number of studies, most notably those conducted by several national commissions during the past decade.

Many of these studies have pointed out the diversity that exists as a result of the complexity of modern life. Components of the system, in fact, have relationships that are more often symbiotic than systemic, and the actual interaction between the parts of the system has become difficult to describe and to predict because of the subtle differences that have developed in their goals and objectives. Each component has developed independently, and often it has different perspectives about crime and about the relative roles that it plays in the processing of a criminal case.

This fragmentation is aggravated by the operation of criminal justice services at different jurisdictional levels—across counties, at state or municipal levels. Traditionally the prosecutor's role has been less clear than that of some other components of the system, such as the police or corrections. The tendency has been to think of the prosecutor as a functionary of police or court power rather than to see him as an independent agent with his own discretionary power. Yet it is obvious that he has his own duties and his own independent goals. Measures of success for one agency will not necessarily be a measure of success for the prosecuting attorney. The police have traditionally been interested in "clearing" cases as an indicator of performance; a judge thinks of performance in terms of his ability to move the trial docket. Yet neither measure properly indicates success for the prosecutor, who, as will be seen, is interested in a combination of measures that indicate both his ability to deal with the case volume that he receives and his ability to make discrete choices about the charges that he levels in those cases.

Is there any one feature that is characteristic of the typical prosecutor? As has been suggested, little research has concentrated on this office. A Law Enforcement Assistance Administration (LEAA) census, taken in 1970, lists approximately 3,400 state and local prosecutors. Three other national surveys have collected data and information about the local prosecutor, but these provide only scant information about his characteristics or jurisdiction: The National Association of Attorneys General (NAAG) collected basic information about the office of the local prosecutor; a more comprehensive survey attempt to collect more information was conducted in 1972 by the National Center for Prosecution Management (NCPM) under the auspices of the National District Attorneys Association (NDAA); a follow-up to this survey was conducted by the NDAA in 1974-1975.

Of special interest to this study are the results of the NCPM survey, since its primary purpose was to investigate and identify the environmental factors that affect the prosecutor in the performance of his duties and characterize his operations. This was the only nationwide, research-oriented study of prosecutors ever to look at external influences. Statistically significant factors that influenced the prosecutor were identified, and these are reported in part II of this book. An examination of the effects of exogenous factors on prosecution permits the researcher to separate factors over which the prosecutor has little or no control from those for which he can be held accountable. The factors in the NCPM study results can be classified in two groups: (1) the demographic and population characteristics of the jurisdiction, and (2) the component activities within the criminal justice system itself. A major objective of this work is to highlight the diversity that exists, because of these factors, in the prosecution process and to show how and why different prosecutorial responses occur.

The overwhelming majority of local prosecutors are elected for a 4-year term, although the range of terms runs from 1 to 12 years. Despite the emphasis that is placed on the needs of urban prosecutors who must cope with case overloads and backlogged courts, the overwhelming proportion of local prosecutors are from rural counties or small towns. (Seventy-six percent of all prosecutors represent jurisdictions with populations of less than 100,000.) Furthermore, 74 percent of all prosecutors operate either as a "one-man" office or with fewer than four assistant prosecutors to aid them.

Although the general focus of the prosecuting attorney is on criminal case processing, he is not simply a criminal litigator. More and more the prosecutor has been assigned other duties by the legislature. Three out of four prosecutors have civil responsibility for representation of the county board of commissioners or for the local governing agency. The prosecutor's duties have been extended to include involvement in juvenile matters, in family and domestic-relations court, in answering or responding to citizen complaints, in conducting nonsupport programs, in handling traffic, consumer, or environmental protection projects, and in pursuing appeals. His interests and jurisdiction have been extended to cover a wider avenue of community problems. When attempting to analyze or evaluate the prosecutor's role in criminal case processing, one must consider the demands of these other activities and the effect that they have on his total effort.

The prosecution function is most effectively analyzed by viewing it as a highly discretionary decision-making system operating in a complex set of constraints. These constraints must be identified and analyzed thoroughly before a proper evaluation can be performed. Prosecution can only be evaluated in terms of what it can control. Thus, any search to establish the identity of the prosecutor must eliminate those factors over which the prosecutor has little or no control and focus on those on which he does have definite impact.

The office of the prosecutor is created by the state constitution or legislation and operates, first of all, within these constraints to his power. For example, modern and efficient charge review procedures in Michigan are made possible by a statutory requirement that complaint warrants be reviewed and their issuance recommended by the prosecutor before cases can be filed in court. This is a favorable environment for screening and contrasts significantly with other states where there are no such rules and where the assistant prosecutors may not even know of the existence of a case until days after it has been filed with a justice of the peace or a committing magistrate.

The external factors examined in this book can be grouped into four general areas. The first and most important is the geographic and demographic characteristics of the jurisdiction. This forms the primary descriptor of the prosecutor's role. Obviously the type, size, and population of the jurisdiction distinguishes the small-town or rural prosecutor from the large-city or suburban prosecutor. Second, the character and volume of the workload determines the size and composition of the office. As the people's lawyer, the prosecutor must respond to the work brought to his office by the police, sheriff, or citizens. The amount and type of crime in a jurisdiction forces certain prosecutorial responses and priorities.

The preceding factors also determine the resources that are made available to him (primarily through his budget) and that define the bounds of his activity. What programs are implemented may be more realistically determined by the level of local appropriations than by office policy. (Almost 60 percent of the offices responding to the NCPM survey reported that 90 percent or more of their funding was received from the county.) The resources that are available and how they are allocated within the office not only has a fundamental bearing on the prosecutor's ability to perform his duties as defined by the state but also sets performance priorities according to his personal policy. These policy implications are the basis for part III.

The last factor affecting prosecution is the type of criminal justice system in which the prosecutor must work, particularly the type of court system. From the prosecutor's perspective, the problems of intake, review, case preparation, and disposition are compounded or minimized by these systems. If many police agencies provide crime reports of varying quality, the quality of charging has to be affected. If lower courts are not "courts of record," the prosecutor must anticipate heavier caseloads resulting from *trial de novo* appeals. If courtroom capacity is not available to handle the existing caseload, the prosecutor may be forced into plea bargaining at levels he would not accept under more favorable circumstances. If judicial districts exist and the prosecutor has county jurisdiction only, more fragmentation occurs. The absence or presence of the use of a grand jury, the characteristics of the defense bar, and even the type of docketing system all temper the prosecutor's role and distinguish one prosecutor's office from another.

## Internalizing the Prosecution Function

A key characteristic of the American local prosecutor is the independent source of power he exercises as a result of his locally elected status. He enjoys an unreviewable discretionary power to prosecute, a power that has been consistently upheld by the courts. It is this dimension of his role that gives birth to the most problematical aspects of his existence and raises issues fundamental to our democratic form of government. As an elected official, his duty is to respond to the community's values and mores. His discretionary power, if exercised, reflects not only political influences but, more importantly, the social environment. The extent to which is charging policies and discretionary power color the character of prosecution and American criminal justice is the subject examined in part III.

Part III explores the most prevalent responses by the prosecutor to his environment: a traditional, conservative, legal response; a discretionary, interpretive response; and a policy-making response that extends the power derived from an elected status. These categories are not necessarily mutually exclusive but exist along a continuum of increased discretion. For purposes of this analysis, they will be treated separately, since each points up important distinctions.

In 1972, the NCPM surveyed a small group of prosecutors attending a National District Attorneys Association meeting to test their perceptions of their jobs. The results of that informal experiment were insightful. The survey revealed that the original expectations of newly elected prosecutors were to view their role as lawyers and their primary function as prosecuting criminal cases. As the elected prosecutors gained experience and time in office, they saw themselves assuming more administrative and management duties, and finally they begin to perceive their role as leaders in the community.

Varying interpretations of prosecutorial roles and responsibilities naturally occur. Depending on his experience or predilection, a prosecutor may view himself primarily as an officer of the court or, alternatively, as an agent of a law enforcement agency. It is not uncommon to find a prosecutor who is unaware of his discretionary authority and responsibility. This naiveté was exposed during a question-and-answer exchange between prosecutors attending a statewide seminar in the midwest. A small-office prosecutor complained about the quality of the reports he received from the sheriff. They were so poorly prepared that he did not have enough information to try the case. His question to the panel was, "What should I do?" Patrick Leahy, then State's Attorney from Burlington, Vermont (now a U.S. Senator), responded, "Have you considered not prosecuting?" With obvious surprise, the prosecutor asked, "Can I do that?"

A conservative legalistic approach to prosecution is, to a certain extent, the safest response the prosecutor can make to his environment. It is an approach that requires little effort to justify. This response is sanctioned by the standards of the American Bar Association (ABA), the ethics committee of the local legal society, the judiciary, and the law enforcement agencies. The weakness of this approach is that the prosecutor is not truly protecting the interests of the public or moving to improve the law. He is, rather, providing only a minimal level of service with respect to his inherent powers.

A more dynamic approach is the discretionary, interpretive response, wherein the prosecutor accepts the discretionary power inherent in his position. The amount of discretion and the extent of control of that discretion vary from office to office. The first and most important area of the prosecutor's discretionary power is the decision to charge a defendant with a crime. The policies concerned with that decision are the focus of attention in this book. In some offices, the charging policy is published and disseminated to all assistants, and the charging decisions are monitored. In other offices there are no articulated charging policies and no controls on the assistant's discretion. When the prosecutor responds in an interpretive manner, evaluating cases for prosecution, he broadens his authority and widens his role. For the evaluation of the case, the prosecutor assumes a quasi-judicial role. Once he has decided to accept the case for prosecution, he assumes an adversary role.

The exercise of discretionary power, particularly at intake, not only influences the quality and quantity of work flowing into the criminal courts but also requires that the prosecutor expand the perception of his role to include managerial or executive characteristics.

The prosecutor assumes his most powerful position when he uses the independence bestowed on him by his elected status to exercise leadership beyond processing the criminal case docket. This response is uniquely characteristic of the American prosecutor. The independent source of power given him as an elected official not only makes him responsive to the desires of his constituency but also permits him the opportunity to influence social, economic, legal, or political changes in his community. The advantages lie in the potential benefits for improving welfare in the community. These leadership activities can include giving drug-abuse lectures to schoolchildren, initiating basic consumer-protection programs, or operating diversion programs. However, this response is not without its drawbacks because it exposes the active prosecutor to criticism. It has both the greatest potential for exercise of political power and the greatest potential for partisan attack.

The approach followed in this book has been to integrate knowledge about the prosecutor—his genesis and historical development, the type of power and discretion that is unique to his office, and the external forces that affect his operation—to define his role in American criminal justice today. In many ways, the identity of the American prosecutor is only now beginning to be sorted out. The picture presented here represents not only the efforts expended by the author during this fellowship but also the results of almost ten years of work and research in this field.


**Structure of the Book**

The book's format reflects the developmental approach taken to describe the American prosecutor. Part I, which is quite extensive, chronicles the origins and development of the prosecutor in this country. It demonstrates that the office of the prosecutor is a logical and consistent outgrowth of the American concept of justice. Part II examines several of the external factors that affect the prosecutor and looks at how some of the major social and demographic trends in this country have also had specific impacts on prosecution. It specifies the large amount of diversity that exists in prosecution and destroys some of the more well-recognized stereotypes. Part II also focuses in on the internal functions of prosecution and examines the way in which the office operates within the criminal justice process. It examines the exercise of discretion at various processing points—intake, accusation, trial, and postconviction. It looks at the prosecutor's relationship with defense counsel and the effect that that relationship can have on case processing.

Part III includes an examination of prosecutorial policy and how the exercise of discretion affects the character and nature of the application of the law. It is derived, in large part, form research done during a National Evaluation Phase I Project on this topic. It sets out the typology that was developed during that project and expands on it through the use of three case studies of prosecutors whose styles and approaches to prosecution are vastly different from one another. These case studies should demonstrate the existing diversity in prosecution and the wide-ranging influence it has on the system of criminal justice. Part IV summarizes the issues raised in the preceding chapters, offers some preliminary findings, and suggests areas for further research.

# The American Prosecutor:
# A Search for Identity

*The Prosecutor, reviled, unloved, unknown—except for the occasional Tom Dewey or Frank Hogan. On television and in fiction generally he's the ruthless Cromwell to the defense attorney's dashing King Charles. In the movies most often he's the plodding Watson to the super-detective Holmes. In the press, the F. Lee Baileys and the Edward Bennett Williamses outscore him ten to one in paragraph space. . . . Yet though he and legions of experts he commands are the cornerstone of the democratic American system of justice and law enforcement—what the prosecutor does and how he does it are almost totally unknown to the vast majority of the American public.*

—Bill Davidson, *Indict and Convict*
(New York: Harper and Row, 1971), p. vii.

# Part I
# Origins and Development

# 1

# Origins and Development of American Prosecution

## Introduction

In recent years, there has been increased interest in the office of the American public prosecutor. Previously, the role and function of the prosecuting attorney largely have been overlooked in the bulk of legal literature. A few commentators have remarked on the irony that an office of such extreme power and importance in the American system of jurisprudence and government should have been so long and so shamefully ignored. But, whereas some attention has been focused on the prosecuting attorney's immense discretion in criminal matters, very little historical research has been conducted to determine the origins of this power or to chronicle the development of the office itself.

For the most part, historical references to the prosecuting attorney have pictured him as having descended from one of three European predecessors: either the English Attorney General, the french *procureur publique*, or the Dutch *schout*. All three of these officials were involved, in some fashion, with prosecuting crimes within their respective systems of criminal justice; all three nations had definite impact on the early history and development of the American nation. Convincing arguments can be developed for the influence of all three heritages in American criminal justice, yet no compelling theory has been forwarded that shows clearly a direct line from any one European precursor to the American prosecutor.

Although the local American prosecutor shares characteristics with all three of these European officers, he is very different in many respects. He has the power, like the *procureur*, to initiate all public prosecutions; he is a local official of regional government like the *schout*; he has the power to terminate all criminal prosecutions like the Attorney General. Yet, his powers and discretion are vastly greater than those of any European prosecutor. The American prosecutor enjoys an independence and discretionary privileges unmatched in the world.

One of the first attempts to describe the origins of the American prosecutor was a short summary published as part of the *Missouri Crime Survey* in 1926. The summary was not a detailed, scholarly work, but simply stated that the American public prosecutor was descended from a "chief prosecuting officer in England . . . whose duties for centuries have been the

---

Kevin J. Brosch assisted in the preparation of chapter 1.

3

prosecution of crimes and misdemeanors.''[1] This assertion was inaccurate, since England had only a prosecutor charged with public prosecution of crimes since 1879, less than fifty years prior to the publication of the report.[2]

The Wickersham *Report on Prosecution* in 1931 made a longer and more detailed attempt at a fair history. The commission noted that American criminal justice differed from the English tradition in that the British had developed a system of private prosecution whereby individual citizens hired lawyers to press prosecutions of crimes they had suffered, whereas Americans entrusted criminal prosecution to a single, elected public officer. The report concluded that the concept of a public officer to conduct prosecution had been borrowed from the French after the American Revolution, when French institutions were in favor and British institutions were unpopular, and that these public prosecutors had gained elective status during the democratization of the Jacksonian era.[3]

Although this theory had some merit, it overlooked the facts that appearance of public prosecution had preceded the American Revolution and that public officers were conducting prosecution 75 years before French influence was being felt in the young American republic. It also failed to account for crucial differences in the systems: The American prosecutor was an independent local official, whereas the French *procureur* was part of a national civil service hierarchy with very little freedom of action.

Another highly provocative theory was forwarded in 1952 by W. Scott Van Alstyne writing in the *Wisconsin Law Review*.[4] Van Alstyne argued that the prosecuting attorney was an office that resulted from Dutch influence. He wrote that the early Dutch settlers scattered along the American seaboard from Delaware to Connecticut had utilized a local prosecuting officer called the "*schout*." Although the Dutch settlements were very short lived, Van Alstyne showed that they were more numerous and widespread than had generally been believed and that the colonial records showed evidence of the existence and influence of the *schout* in at least five of the original colonies.

Van Alstyne attempted to undercut the arguments that supported British or French influence. He pointed out that the American tradition of public prosecution was clearly a break from the mainstream of British procedure, because the British Attorney General did not have the power to prosecute public crimes. He also pointed out the lack of French influence at the crucial time when public prosecution first appeared in the American colonies, thereby making any attribution of French influence spurious.

Other sources have offered less detailed and less helpful descriptions of the development. Martin wrote that the prosecutor developed from the English Attorney General, but he failed to produce any convincing line of reasoning or evidence to support his contentions.[5] The National Association of Attorneys General described the office of prosecutor as having been "carved out" of the office of the Attorney General, but its analysis overlooked the fact that the prosecutor has wider powers in criminal matters than those ever enjoyed by the British Attorney General.[6]

Other writers have relied heavily on earlier studies without adding significantly to the body of knowledge. Grossman echoed the Wickersham *Report*, whereas Friedman seemed heavily influenced by Van Alstyne's work.

The most comprehensive study of the possible historical origins of the American prosecutor was prepared in 1976 by Jack Kress of the State University of New York.[7] Kress discussed the strengths and weaknesses of the three major theories of development and concluded that the truth lay in a combination of factors and influences. Kress offered a unique perspective from which to study the development of the office. His analysis suggested that the development of the prosecutor could be traced by integrating the numerous and various factors that influenced the evolution of the office rather than by trying to force the modern prosecutor into a narrow historical framework.

Legal scholar Lawrence Friedman had suggested this more dynamic approach when he wrote that "the strongest ingredient in American law at any given time, is the present. . . . The history of law has meaning only if we assume that at any given time the vital portion is new and changing, form following function, not function following form. History of law is not—or should not be—a search for fossils, but a study of social development, unfolding through time."[8]

This more dynamic approach places the prosecutor and prosecution within their historical contexts. It begins with understanding the legal institutions and choices available to the first American colonists, documents the significant alterations in the office of the prosecutor, and analyzes the historical and social trends that brought them about. It ends with an accurate appraisal of the power and position of the modern prosecutor.

Before one starts examining the development of the American prosecutor it is necessary to note three crucial differences between the modern American prosecutor and his antecedents. Whereas the *procureur*, the Attorney General, and the *schout* all were involved in criminal prosecution, none was truly the primary law enforcement official in a specific jurisdiction. All three officers were essentially operatives of a national and centralized authority and drew their power from another official; the American prosecutor is an officer of local government with little or no supervision from other levels of government. The European officials were appointed to office and served at the pleasure of the appointer, whereas the American prosecutor is generally elected and answerable to his constituency.

Most of today's prosecutors represent a local jurisdiction. They are elected. They are the chief law enforcement official in their jurisdiction, exercising immense and almost unreviewable discretion. Historical attempts to locate a single predecessor, a single judicial officer with the same or comparable power from which the prosecutor descended have failed for the simplest reason: none ever existed.

This does not suggest that the local prosecutor materialized from some form of legal spontaneous generation. Quite the contrary. The office of the prosecutor is the natural and logical result of the legal, social, and political developments that shaped the United States' judicial system over the past 350 years. The prosecuting attorney is a distinctly American figure, and for distinctly American reasons.

The key to a successful inquiry in this direction may lie in subscribing to the view that the prosecuting attorney did not descend from any one particular institution at any one time or in any one place. It can be safely said that there was no figure like the prosecutor at Jamestown or Plymouth; that by the time of the Revolution an officer with some of his basic characteristics had appeared in various colonies; that by the civil war, there were District Attorneys quite like those we have in the present era functioning in a large number of the states; and that, at the present time, most states employ a single, locally elected officer with primary responsibility and discretion to prosecute all criminal matters within a defined political subdivision.

The most apt description of the process that has occurred in American criminal prosecution over the past 350 years is "evolution." Professor Kress stopped short in asserting that "whatever the derivation of the office, it rooted quickly and firmly into American life with remarkably few changes in form or function over the following two hundred years."[9] Accepting that statement excludes an examination of numerous subtle and essential changes that have occurred since the Revolution. The office of the prosecuting attorney did not root firmly and quickly. It has, rather, changed slowly and gradually in an evolutionary process that has taken 350 years, and that, in many ways, continues today.

Perhaps there is less irony than has been suspected in the fact that the prosecuting attorney has been paid so little attention historically. The neglect, indeed, may be an accurate reflection of the slow evolution of the office of the prosecuting attorney from one of little stature and power to one whose authority and discretion have grown so large that it commands notice. Evidence also points to the gradual change of the role of prosecutor from a weak and minor court official to a chief law enforcement official. This evolution seems to have roots in four identifiable political, legal, and social systems.

First, Americans adopted a system of public prosecution, thereby creating a need for a prosecutor to represent the state. This was in spite of the fact that the British common law system for prosecution was essentially litigation between private parties. Yet, because of other European influences and factors inherent in colonial America, the Americans chose public prosecution for their common law system.

Second, local governmental systems were created as the nation pursued democracy as a form of government. Because of this decentralization of power, towns and counties predominated early American government, and the American prosecutor, unlike his European cousins, became an officer of local government.

Third, the prosecutor gained independent elective status when a great tide of democratic sentiment swept America between 1830 and 1850. This elective nature gave the American prosecutor new responsibilities and independent, discretionary powers.

Fourth, by adopting the French principle of strict separation of judicial and executive power, the prosecutor's position as part of the executive branch of government was solidified. The unique combinations of powers that the prosecutor inherited from different traditions and the liberating influence of elective status made him a unique and powerful figure in American government. The prosecutor's influence spans both the executive and the judicial branches of government. His authority is locally derived, yet his power affects the state and the national levels. Implementing and enforcing state law permits the prosecutor to exert influence on changing these laws.

**Private versus Public Prosecution**

The fundamental, differentiating factor in American criminal law lies in our adoption of a system of public prosecution. The public prosecutor is not part of America's heritage from British common law. As Professor Kress has stated, the District Attorney seems to be "a distinctive and uniquely American contribution . . . whereas Americans typically describe their legal system as based upon English common law, in terms of both its procedural attributes and substantive state penal codes, the public prosecutor is a figure virtually unknown to the English system, which is primarily one of private prosecution to this day."[10] Still others have been even more emphatic, pointing out that the conceptual framework of public prosecution, as well as the office itself, is "largely an American invention."[11]

The origin of a public prosecution presents something of a historical and social puzzle. The English common law tradition is one of private prosecution. Not only is the procedure for bringing an action against an alleged criminal different in England from what it is in the United States, but the entire conceptual framework supporting the procedure is dissimilar. "In common law [in England], a crime is viewed not as an act against the state, but rather as a wrong inflicted upon a victim. The aggrieved victim, or an interested friend or relative, would personally arrest and prosecute the offender, after which the courts would adjudicate the matter much as they would a contract dispute or a tortious injury.''[12]

The English have, to the present, largely retained the private system with a few noteworthy changes. In 1879 the office of the Director of Public Prosecutions was created. This office, thought by some to be vaguely analogous to the American prosecutor, is in reality a shadow of its American cousin. The director's powers are far more limited than his impressive title suggests, more limited in fact than the average American county attorney. As recently as 1960, this office was prosecuting a mere 8 percent of the criminal cases in Great Britain, the remainder being handled by private individuals or the police.[13] Increasingly in the modern era, the police officer has become the privotal figure in prosecutions in England. He most often brings charges against the suspected criminal, although, in British theory, he is still acting as a ''private citizen interested in the maintenance of law and order'' but has slightly broader arrest powers than the average British citizen.[14]

There are clear differences between a system of private prosecution and a public one, both in conceptual framework and in working procedures. The English system of private prosecution was unlike the American system in its early stages of development as well as in its present status.

The British system developed from a social and governmental scheme that had its roots in medieval rather than modern social contracts. The monarch, in such a scheme, was not the symbol of popular governmental power that he later became, but rather a strong and independent individual who sat at the society's apogee. He was the first among all individuals of the realm. The court system that evolved was one that pitted individual against individual. English common law did not make the sharp division between civil wrongs and criminal wrongs in the sense that the American system does at present. All violations of law were wrongs committed by an individual against an individual. In certain cases, crimes that might be currently considered antisocietal were thought of as violations of an individual's prerogative, very often the King's. A violation of the King's rights were prosecuted by the King's Attorney. Violations of individual rights other than the King's were pursued through the courts by the victim or by his friends or relatives.

As a result, English justice, like the society in which it first evolved, was patently hierarchial. It was a system whereby the individual protected himself and avenged himself in the courts rather than being able to rely on the strength and security of societal protections. It was a system that was designed to protect property in a society based on property. The advantage was naturally with the men of property and position, with the rich and the affluent. In the main, it was a system of government ''of the rich and by the rich," but then, so too was the medieval English society in which it was first developed.[15]

With this basic conceptual framework, procedures developed that protected and extenuated the underlying assumption of the system. Until 1879, there was no public officer or officer of the court charged with the responsibility of prosecuting crimes. The King's Attorney or Attorney General became involved in litigation only to protect the King's interest, although the concept of the King's interest became more widely defined in later centuries.

As the legal system developed and became more complex, the professional bar grew and adapted, serving as prosecutors for individual clients. No lawyer was elected or appointed to serve as representative of the county, the court, the town, or the government. Rather individual soliciters and barristers were hired to prosecute individual cases in the same manner as they were for any other legal matter.

The rise of an organized police force did not significantly alter the method of prosecution. Arrests made by the police were referred to private members of the bar on a case-by-case basis. The conduct of the prosecution was never "in the hands of any special body of counsel dedicated to that particular class of work . . . there is nothing which corresponds to the District Attorney in the United States."[16]

There were, however, efforts beginning as early as the sixteenth century to alter methods of prosecution in England. Henry VIII proposed that local sergeants of the Commonwealth act as public prosecutors to enforce penal statutes throughout the country. This proposal was rejected by Parliament, and other similar suggestions were opposed until the passage of the Public Prosecutions Act in 1879. Much of the resistance to change was based on strict adherence to traditional legal methods and social and legal status. There was, however, also opposition from the legal profession, who felt that the development of a prosecutor position would be detrimental to private attorneys, many of whose practice included occasional prosecution.

The move to some form of public prosecution was favored by British legal reformers of the early nineteenth century. Sir Robert Peel proposed such an adjustment; Jeremy Bentham and Edwin Chadwick both favorably discussed the proposal. Several treatises on the subject were prepared and published by Patrick Colquhoun, the legal scholar and philanthropist, in 1805. Enactment of legislation, however, did not succeed for another 75 years.

Ultimately private prosecution was retained in England with only slight alteration because it was the established procedure, not because it was equitable. Private prosecution was heavily ingrained in the English common law practice and appealed to sectors of the British public on the strong grounds of tradition. Moreover, private prosecution favored the wealthy and the legal profession, and therefore had the support of both influential and powerful groups.

Still, the system was fraught with problems and inequities, most of which have been long recognized. "Among the defects of the system of private prosecution, the outstanding one is the impunity of a good many offenses where the complainant is either too weak or too poor to bring the action."[17] Even in cases where the rich and poor did not clash, there were serious imbalances. Offenders with past experience before the courts were at an advantage when charged by a victim who was unfamiliar with judicial practice, especially one who hired an inexperienced barrister. Coloquhoun complained that too many criminals were escaping punishment because of technicalities, that repeat offenders were favored under the system, that the innocent were not protected, and felonies were being compounded, lawyers and witnesses bribed, and perjury suborned.[18]

The French had operated under a similar system beginning in the twelfth century but had begun, in progressive stages, to adopt public prosecution within the following 300 years. They eventually abandoned the private system of prosecution, retaining private complaint only as a method of correcting a neglectful prosecutor. The Dutch and the Germans similarly adopted related forms of public prosecution. Only the British persisted with this medieval institution at the time of the colonization of the North American continent.

Private prosecution was inconsistent with the American concept of democratic process and had a short life span in the American colonies. By 1704 one colony, Connecticut, had adopted a system of public prosecutors, and all others would soon follow. Although the system of private prosecutions prevailed in the English world at the time of the establishment of the first American colonies at Jamestown and Plymouth, it quickly vanished in America. Today the idea of private prosecution is alien to modern America, as is its basic supposition that crime is essentially a private concern between the aggressor and the victim. The concept of criminal justice that has developed in the United States proclaims the opposite view; the American system conceives of the criminal act to be a public occurrence and of society as a whole the ultimate victim. The American concept is that all criminal acts, as the Vermont Constitution declared in 1796, violate the essential "peace and dignity of the state."

There are few vestiges of private prosecution in the United States today. The system failed to hold because it fit poorly with the concept that the new Americans had developed for their government. It also was less effective than other available European alternatives. Presently, few states allow the use of private prosecutors, and those that do restrict their participation to limited types of cases. The opposition to private prosecution has also been clearly and consistently demonstrated by court decisions. In several states, convictions were overturned in cases where private counsel was hired to pursue a prosecution. In the opinion of the Wisconsin courts in the *State* v.

*Peterson*, such practice was contrary to "state policy." The Connecticut courts made the definitive statement on opposing private prosecution in *Mallory* v. *Lane*, where the opinion of the court stated:

> In all criminal cases in Connecticut, the state is the prosecutor. The offenses are against the state. The victim of the offense is not a party to the prosecution, nor does he occupy any relation to it other than that of a witness, an interested witness mayhaps, but none the less, only a witness.
>
> It is not necessary for the injured party to make complaint nor is he required to give bond to prosecute. He is in no sense a relator. He cannot in any way control the prosecution and whether reluctant or not, he can be compelled like any other witness to appear and testify.
>
> The Peace is that state and sense of safety which is necessary to the comfort and happiness of every citizen and which government is instituted to secure.[19]

## The Colonial Period: The Public Prosecutor and Local Government

From the beginning, both the politics and geography of the American colonies severely strained the centralized nature of British government. The impetus for, and the method of, British colonization fostered independence and isolation within the early settlements. The first colonies were spread along the Eastern seaboard of North America for almost two thousand miles with only distant connections to the central government in England and with virtually no ties to one another. The British influence on the colonies was weakened by distance and poor communications. Although the basic forms and traditions were British and the system of jurisprudence was English common law, isolation from direct British control and authority encouraged the emergence of strong and independent forms of local government:

> Yet none of their institutions were quite like its English counterpart; the heritage of English ideas that went with the institutions was so rich and varied that Americans were able to select and develop those that best suited their situations and forget others that meanwhile were growing prominent in the mother country. Some differences were local: The New England town, for example . . . set New Englanders off not only from Englishmen, but from Virginians.[20]

From the first, locally autonomous government and regional innovations were marks of colonial America. And, although English royal power would increase the size of the colonies through the concerted efforts of the crown in the eighteenth century, a basic local populism remained the dominant force in the colonies until the American Revolution.[21]

Distance and isolation also served to reenforce many of the political positions of the first settlers. For the most part the colonists were dissenters, religious and political, whose tendencies were to question traditional points of view. Certainly the colonists were more conscious of individual rights than were their relatives who remained in England. They engendered the basic spirit that fostered American democracy. "Englishmen brought with them to the New World the political ideas that still give English and American governments a close resemblance. But Americans very early developed conceptions of representative government that differed from those prevailing in England during the colonial period."[22]

Their successes in independently establishing the colonies imbued the early settlers with a confidence in their abilities for self-rule. They were most comfortable with the closeness and intimacy of a local form of government in which they could actively participate and which they could closely regulate. This closeness to government, the daily experience that they enjoyed with self-government, helped to adjust their view of authority. The monarchy, so distant and so abstract across the ocean, became less necessary as a figure of authority. The American colonies were becoming an object lesson in the theory that authority could originate from the will of the governed.

In many ways, too, the rise of local independence was as much a result of the neglect by the British government as it was an exercise of the independent nature of the colonists. This was clearly illustrated by the methods in which the early court systems were established.

> The British government claimed the sole right to create courts, and the early courts except in the charter and proprietary colonies, were created by executive action. However, after the initial settlement, the judiciary received little attention from the King, and colonial courts were left to evolve without much thought, or consideration. England never tried to make the judicial system in the colonies uniform.[23]

These first courts were simple tribunals held by the governor of the newly formed colony with all procedure directly copied from the English common law. Prosecution of criminal offenses consisted of charges being brought to the attention of the courts by individuals who had been wronged and who sought redress. There was no formal system of advocacy, no trained bar, no public official to bring charges.

The first court was held in the Virginia colony, where, after 1619, the governor sat regularly with his council and the elected burgesses to decide criminal cases. This court system reflected the simple nature of colonial society with its small population. There was no separation of powers or function in government that would mark later American government. Again, this situation merely mirrored the British government, where there was substantial involvement by the executive and the legislative branches with the judicial branch of government.

Other colonies experimented for a short time with more novel and unorthodox alternatives to British law. In Rhode Island in 1639 there was a brief attempt at government by arbitration in the colony at Newport. This quickly gave way to a simple court system modelled after the British justice-of-the-peace courts when Newport City was founded in 1640.[24]

The same framework had been adopted in Massachusetts several years earlier.[25] The larger population of the Bay Colony in 1636 made it possible for the colony to support a professional judiciary, and it chose to pattern the courts after the rural justice-of-the-peace system that they had known in England.

> The colonists' substantial adaption of the machinery of criminal justice as administered by the English justices of the peace was apparently deliberate. It was what they were used to, and, as the system was developed initially in Massachusetts, it provided wide latitude for the exercise of magisterial discretion; consequently, it comported well with the leaders' ideas about the functions of government and law . . . indeed it worked even more successfully in the colonies partly because the community was small. . . .[26]

These simple courts with simple procedures required no officer to represent the government or to bring prosecution. The court itself represented the government; individuals brought charges against law breakers.

In 1643, an officer was appointed to the courts of the Virginia colonies as a representative of the King. He was Richard Lee, the first Attorney General of Virginia. Lee's position was ostensibly that of the King's Attorney in the Virginia courts. He represented the interests of the King, and, so far as it was in the royal interest, provided expert advice on points of law. It has been suggested that the King's Attorney or Attorney General was the predecessor of the modern prosecuting attorney. Closer scrutiny of the duties and powers of Richard Lee and his successors at the post of the Attorney General reveal that they were not to be adopted by the emerging local prosecutor.

Lee's primary responsibility in the court was advisory, and most of his formal duties were concerned with corresponding with legal authorities in England to get opinions on certain points of law. A lack of law books and of learned attorneys in the colonies made these duties all the more necessary. Lee became involved in criminal matters only where an alleged violation of the law directly involved the royal interest, which was infrequent. So strong was his advisory role that for the most part, he was not required to be at court. In fact, the Attorney General of Virginia was not even required to live at the capital in Williamsburg, where court was held, until 1670.

In the colonies of New York and New Jersey, the British common law methods of prosecution were altered early because of the influence of Dutch law and the duties of a Dutch judicial officer, the *schout*. New York and

New Jersey were first settled by the Dutch, who established the colonies' first courts at New Amsterdam[27] (now Manhattan) in 1653 and at Bergen[28] (now Elizabeth, New Jersey) in 1661. The Dutch legal system was different from the British and derived from the continental or civil system of law. The first courts in the Dutch colonies consisted of a director general, three magistrates, and a presiding officer, the *schout*, whose duties in the court were to present criminal charges against alleged criminals.

Again, the powers and duties of the *schout* were different from those associated with the modern American prosecutor but strikingly more similar than those of the King's Attorney. He was a combination constable and court officer with limited discretion in charging. His duties, however, included presenting the case against the defendant and notifying all accused of the charges being levelled against them. He had some powers of arrest and was involved in the collection of evidence. But he served more as a central figure who controlled access to the court than as an officer who initiated prosecutions. Citizens with complaints would go to the *schout*, provide him with statements and available evidence; he would notify the accused and make the presentation before the court.

Early records of the New Amsterdam court show that the first *schout*, Cornelius Van Tienhoven, appeared as plaintiff in a criminal trial for the first time on February 17, 1653, and consistently thereafter in most criminal matters until his replacement in 1665. *Schouts* remained in office for the next 20 years and even weathered the change of flags over the colony. In 1664, the English captured the settlement in the name of the British crown and the Duke of York. Under the interim code of law known as the "Duke's Law," the *schout* remained as an officer of the court. The Dutch retook the colony in 1673, but their second occupation lasted only a year before the English wrested final control.

English common law was established in 1674 in New York, in New Jersey, and in other former Dutch settlements in Delaware and Pennsylvania. Although the title of *schout* disappeared, his function as a police-prosecutor was carried on through the office of the sheriff. When the priopriety of this was questioned for lack of precedent in the English courts, "the Governors council issued a plainly-worded reply which stated that the sheriff was to put the law into execution, apprehend and prosecute violators."[29] The evolutionary process was well on its way in colonial America.

Records of the New Netherlands colony show that the office of the *schout* was also established in settlements in New Jersey, Delaware, and Pennsylvania. The Dutch had also established a colony in western Connecticut, but there is no positive record that the colony had a *schout*.

The influence of the *schout* may have had a lasting effect on the courts in these former Dutch possessions. Records exist of an ordinance established by the English governor of Newcastle, Delaware, in 1676 directing the sheriff to act as principal officer in the execution of the laws; and subsequent records show him acting as the prosecutor in a notorious murder case in the Newcastle courts. Other colonies went a step further. In 1686 the Quaker community of Burlington, New Jersey, established the position of county prosecutor, and, later the same year, the county of Philadelphia, Pennsylvania, did the same. Both towns were in close geographic proximity to former Dutch settlements in whose courts *schouts* had conducted prosecutions only 10 years earlier.

Still, the Dutch colonies did not have hegemony over the new form of public prosecution. Other evidence indicates that similar changes were also taking place in colonies in which the Dutch had never set foot and that adjustments were being made to a traditional English office, the Attorney General. In the same year, for example, that Philadelphia County appointed its own prosecuting officer, the English governor of Pennsylvania appointed David Lloyd Attorney General of the colony. Lloyd, in turn, appointed deputies for each county court, each of whom had some limited responsibility for criminal prosecution.[30]

In some colonies, the Attorney General had, from the first, a more active role in criminal matters than was traditional in England or had been the case in the first colony, Virginia. William Calvert, the first Attorney General of Maryland and the brother of the governor, assumed much more than advisory responsibility.[31] Calvert, appointed in 1666, was responsible for presenting criminal indictments to the grand jury and sat on the court as a member of the Governor's Council during all criminal trials.

In 1670, the Attorney General of Virginia was ordered to appear in the Court of Oyer and Terminar during all trials and to relocate his residency in the capital. By 1687 Virginia had deputy attorney generals for courts in the outlying counties, and by 1711 both the attorney general and his deputies were handling all serious criminal trials, although less serious matters were still being handled summarily by the magistrate of the court. New Hampshire, which existed for its first 45 years without an attorney general, created the post in 1683, and at once the attorney general was charged with the responsibility for presenting all cases before the grand jury.[32] In the Carolinas, the Attorney General was created by the Acts of 1738, which also allowed for deputies in all county courts. There, prosecutions were brought almost exclusively by these men. "There were important changes in the courts' procedures for exercising its criminal jurisdiction. For the first time the courts had a prosecuting attorney, a deputy appointed by the attorney general for each county."[33]

Once deputy attorneys general were assigned permanently to local county courts, it was not long before they were considered instruments of local, rather than central, government. As pointed out earlier, the movement toward local government and local control was rampant in the American colonies. By 1711, local men were being nominated from Virginia county courts to serve as deputy attorneys general.[34] In New York, other bodies of local government were working to strengthen local control of the courts, including local control of prosecution. At the beginning of the eighteenth century, the sheriff prosecutors had been replaced by deputy attorneys general, who had much the same power and responsibility. But, because of their status as assistants to the Attorney General, the deputies were paid a percentage of the court fees collected and thus were the victims of uncertain wages. By 1732, however, the counties began to pay these officials through relief granted by the county grand jury under its common law powers. Recognition of an obligation to pay for the services of the prosecuting officer without duress indicates that by 1732, the deputies had become an integral part of the local court structure. Again, this action resulted in many of the attorneys settling into the county and becoming permanent members of the local bar.[35]

Connecticut was the first colony to establish county attorneys as prosecutors. William Pitkin, the first such prosecutor, was appointed at Hartford in 1662. In 1704, Connecticut became the first colony to entirely eliminate the system of private prosecution and to establish public prosecutors as adjuncts to all county courts. The statute of 1704 states:

> Henceforth there shall be in every county a sober discreet and religious person appointed by the county court to be attorney for the Queen to prosecute and implead in the law all criminals and to do all other things necessary or convenient as an attorney to suppress vice and immorality.[36]

Throughout the colonial period there were two major trends in prosecution: the first was the change from private prosecution to public prosecution; the second was the shift from central power and authority to local government. These developments occurred in both the colonies that were first settled by the English and those first settled by the Dutch, and for this reason important influences of *schout* and Attorney General are overshadowed by the very nature of colonial politics and society that shaped the office of the prosecuting attorney.

Some of the forces of change were inherent in the way in which the colonies were settled. The spirit of self-government and independence dominated the life of the colonies. There were also new demands created by the vast new expanse of territory in North America that made central control increasingly difficult. Both the desire for more self-government and the isolation imposed by the expanding territory reinforced the local court concept and eventually supported the formation of the position of local prosecutor.

It is impossible to say exactly why the system of private prosecution failed to root in the American colonies, but the evolution of a public officer to initiate and present criminal cases suggests that private prosecution provided unsatisfactory remedies to colonial society. For the colonists, bound together by the overriding need to conquer a foreign and alien environment, the focus on the survival of the colony may have given rise to the concept of public protection. For the intelligensia, this concept would be consistent with a movement toward public prosecution on the European continent and a call for reform in Britain. For the egalitarians, the reformers had indicted the system of private prosecution, as historian Douglass Campbell points out, as "a part of a system of a government by the rich and for the rich."

> It has often been said that in England it (was) better to kill a man than a hare. The hare is probably belonging to some patrician, who will naturally hunt down the offender. Minor crimes against the person are in that country always prosecuted less vigorously and punished less severly than in other civilized countries, and with much less vigor than those committed against property. Something of this is due to other causes, but is it not partly explicable by the fact that in the former case, the sufferer is usually a poor man or woman unable to prosecute the offender and in the latter case a rich one who can employ his own counsel?[37]

The rejection of the general notion of a privileged class within society also resulted in the rejection of ideas and forms that tended to protect that privilege. In colonial America, public prosecution was an available and progressive remedy for a population dedicated to a more democratic society.

Connecticut, the first colony to appoint public prosecutors, made this feeling clear. The concept of a King's Attorney denoted more individual prerogative than the citizens of the colony intended for this new public office. In 1764, apparently to remove any doubt that the representatives of the crown also represented the sovereignty of the colony, the King's Attorneys in the several counties were empowered to appear in all cases concerning them or brought for or against the colony. This was a radical departure from the prior concept of a King's Attorney.

But radical departures were becoming commonplace in these rapidly changing times. The population grew quickly, and settlements sprung up in the west. To reach a dispersing population, in 1691 the New York colony reorganized its court system, providing a more complex two-tiered system with courts of original jurisdiction in all outlying counties and an appellate level court at New York. Maryland and Massachusetts made similar changes the following year, Pennsylvania in 1702, Virginia in 1705, and South Carolina in 1721.

Yet, even with the spread of lower courts to all counties, there still remained inadequate expertise to litigate serious cases at the local level. Even after court reorganization in Virginia, for example, it was not uncommon for a retinue of ten to twenty citizens from an outlying county to spend days on the road coming to Williamsburg for a serious trial. Without proper legal counsel and expert magistrates, the citizens were cautious about local trials where harsh punishment might be the result for the accused. So all serious cases were heard in Williamsburg; and the occasion of the trial required that the prisoner, his guards, the local sheriff, the accuser, all witnesses, and a jury of six or twelve men be sent from the rural counties to the capital.[38] Ultimately, the difficulty of the logistics favored local trials and supported the need for local legal expertise.

In some cases too, private prosecution had begun to lead to abuses. By 1710, the courts of Virginia were losing much of the revenue that they anticipated from fines levied at criminal trials. In a pretrial collaboration between the accused and accuser the matter would be settled out of court for a negotiated percentage of the penalty. This practice threatened both the system of law and order and the financial solvency of the courts. In 1711, the Attorney General ordered his deputies to become involved directly in prosecutions to insure that these practices would cease.[39]

A professional prosecutor was also seen as a buffer against other abuses, most specifically, the uneducated impulses of juries and grand juries. By 1680 the Attorney General of Rhode Island exercised more than a fair amount of discretion in determining which cases were truly worthy of the court's attention and which were exercises in personal hatred and vindication.[40]

Whereas the grand jury is often perceived as the common law guarantor against unwarranted prosecution, in the colonial era a professional prosecutor was often seen as professional protection against an unfettered grand jury. In most colonies, presentment by the grand jury was as common a method of bringing charges as was indictment or information. Presentment was a method by which members of a sitting grand jury could suggest individuals to be brought to trial for transgressions. Oftentimes, presentments were for simple public nuisance, but many times the grand jury members managed to inflict their personal biases and dislikes on the court. And, in some colonies, presentment or indictment by the grand jury began to carry such weight in the community that it resulted in de facto elimination of jury trial viability. The prosecutor became a professional buffer against such potential abuse. "At Plymouth Colony, presentment by the Grand Jury was tantamount to conviction, unless a traverse of the presentment was had and then there was trial by jury. In New York, the use of employed officials as accusers guaranteed an accusation but also a trial for the accused."[41]

There was a growing realization that the protection of personal liberties required additional legal expertise in the courts. In North Carolina, the rise of the local prosecutor coincided with the demand for jury trial and with the increased use of the grand jury. "With the addition of the Grand Jury, there was a clear need for a prosecuting attorney." Jury trials in North Carolina had not been "common in criminal cases before 1739. Prior to that time the justices handled criminal offenses in summary manner. Thereafter, the county court began to summon the grand jury, and to have criminal cases tried before a jury by a public prosecutor."[42]

Similarly in Virginia, as the technical requirements of court became more demanding, the courts began to rely more heavily on the Deputy Attorney General, and his responsibilities and powers increased. In 1751, the Virginia courts ordered that all witnesses and accusers, in even the most simple cases, confer with the Deputy Attorney General assigned to the court before filing complaints or affidavits. The penalty for failing to do so was the loss of any witness fee or reward. Thus, for the first time, the prosecutor in the Virginia courts had an opportunity to review charges prior to their being presented in court and to exercise his influence on the charging process.[43]

By the advent of the American Revolution, private prosecution had been virtually eliminated in the American colonies and had been replaced by series of public officers who were charged with handling criminal matters. The nature of these officials varied. Some were county officials appointed by the courts; some were deputies of the Attorney General but were nominated by the county court and operating with little supervision; some were deputies of the Attorney General operating directly under his view. In spite of these differences, the prosecuting attorneys in all the colonies held one thing in common—they were a new breed, unlike any judicial officer in England or Europe, created by the demands of a new society.

## From Appointed to Elected Status: 1776-1860

In the postrevolutionary United States, the first Congress established the office of the attorney general and created United States attorneys. There were no strictly American precedents for either a national office of attorney general or for local federal deputies to prosecute the federal statutes. There were European precedents for a national system or Department of Justice, but, as will be seen, they were not copied. Instead, the form of prosecution that was adopted drew from the existing forms that had evolved for local prosecutors in the thirteen original states. Thus, one of the best indicators of the status and nature of local prosecution at that time can be found in the description of the U.S. Attorney General.

The U.S. Attorney General was created by a statute of 1789. His duties were "to prosecute and conduct all suits within the Supreme Court of the United States in which the United States might be concerned" and to give advice and opinion upon questions of law when "required by the President of the United States or requested by the heads of the executive departments."

United States district attorneys were also created by the Judiciary Act of 1789. "The statute, in language in which one may trace an echo of the Connecticut Act of 1704, made provision for the appointment in each district of 'a meet person learned in the law to act as attorney for the United States' and made it his duty to 'prosecute in each district all delinquents for crimes and offenses cognizable under the authority of the United States.' But down to 1861, these district attorneys were legally and actually quite independent in the conduct of their office."[44]

Certainly this schema was not modeled after the British system. ". . . [T]he office [of U.S. Attorney General] was at first far more restricted in its scope than that of the English Attorney General. For example, the conduct and control of the Federal prosecution and litigation was confined to cases in the Supreme Court. . . . Indeed, until 1853 the Attorney General did not reside at the capital and was in private practice. There was nowhere any general, organized control of Federal prosecution."[45] The English furthermore had no equivalent of the U.S. district attorney; indeed, they were still locked into a system of private prosecution and would be for the following century.

The American federal prosecution system was also unlike the French system and its *procureur de roi*. Although there were some similarities of function, the French prosecutor was part of a rigid, hierarchical, and centralized structure, whereas the American federal prosecutor at first enjoyed almost unlimited independence.

The actual model was closest to the indigenous form of the local prosecutor as he had evolved in colonial America. By the time of the American Revolution the divergent traditions of the Dutch *schout*, the English Attorney General, and the French *procureur* had interacted with the emerging concepts of local government and public prosecution to shape, in every colony, a local prosecuting attorney function. The structure differed in various colonies. By 1789, most of the states were utilizing deputy attorneys general for prosecution. However, local control was being established over these nominally state officers in many cases. In Virginia, for example, all county officials were either chosen by the county court, or recommended by it to the state government. In Connecticut the prosecuting attorney was totally independent of the Attorney General and was considered an officer of the county, appointed by county judges.

Even where the Attorney General was nominal head of state prosecution, in reality the local prosecuting attorney was swiftly drifting toward his own island of localized power. Local courts and local appointments or recommendations hastened this trend, which was also marked by a concommitant decline in the centralized power of the Attorney General.[46] The position and power of the Attorney General had been uncertain from the beginning in colonial America. He was the "King's Attorney," a notion that fit poorly in isolated and independent America. The changes in criminal procedure and emphasis on local government only served to shake further the foundations of that office. One Attorney General had remarked as early as 1701 that he "never could know what was [his] duty . . . what [he] should do . . . all the other officers know their power, duty and dues by the law, but relating to the King's Attorney the law is silent."[47]

The federal system of prosecution established in 1789 provides a freeze-frame of the trends and philosophies that were predominant in criminal prosecution at the beginning of the American nation. The Attorney General was a weakened office relegated to vague supervisory power, advisory capacity, and limited appellate jurisdiction. Primary responsibility for prosecution was in the hands of local officials, whose power and independence would grow for the next 200 years.[48]

In the first 30 years of the new republic there were few changes in the duties and responsibilities of the prosecuting attorney, and there was little alteration in his base of power. The major reason for the stable but limited power of the prosecuting attorney was the fact that he was an appointed officer. As such, he could not make independent decisions or exercise choice and discretion without regard for the opinions and politics of those who appointed him. Whether the appointer was the governor, as in Pennsylvania, the attorney general, as in North Carolina, the local judge as in Connecticut, or the local court as in Virginia, the prosecutor was subordinate to another official within the political process on whom his tenure depended.

The limitation of appointive status was not exceptional during this period. In fact, few offices were elective, and few citizens were electors. The period of the early republic was one of strict limitations on the general franchise, and the nation was, by modern standards, a very limited democracy. Voting was regulated by age, sex, race, and property ownership. Those actually allowed to cast ballots in the general election constituted a small minority of the population. At the same time, very few offices were popularly elected, and, in the earliest years, the position of legislator was the only office that was elected by the people in all states.

Review of the first thirteen state constitutions indicates just how limited democracy was in the first 30 years of the nation's existence. Even though the state legislatures and assemblies were all popularly elected, the office of the governor was on the ballot in only six of the thirteen states— Massachusetts, Rhode Island, Connecticut, Pennsylvania, Delaware, and Maryland. In New York, New Jersey, New Hampshire, Virginia, North Carolina, South Carolina, and Georgia, the governor was either appointed or elected by the legislature in one manner or another.

Very few other offices were chosen by the voters. New Jersey and Pennsylvania elected their county sheriffs and coroners at large, and Maryland elected just the sheriff. North Carolina made provision for these county offices but declined in the constitution to say whether they would be elected or appointed. In fact, they were appointed. Virginia had no provision for election of local officers, but did say that they would continue, as had been the colonial custom, "to be nominated by their respective courts."

In the Southern states, Virginia, North Carolina, and South Carolina, county and local officers were elected indirectly by the legislature rather than being appointed by the governor with the consent of the legislature, as was the case in New York, Massachusetts, and New Jersey.

Only five of these first thirteen constitutions—Massachusetts, New Jersey, Maryland, Virginia, and Georgia—mention the office of the Attorney General. Significantly, as will be seen, all five list the office in the judicial article rather than the executive article of the constitution. Only one state, Connecticut, made mention of local prosecutors. Referring to the statute of 1704, its constitution states simply that "there is no attorney general, but there used to be a King's Attorney in each county; but since the King was abdicated, they are now attorneys to the Governor and company."

The increased stature and power of the prosecuting attorney arrived, not with the changes in the legal code in the first 30 years of the republic, but rather as an outgrowth of a wider and more dynamic movement that began about 1820, was highlighted by the presidency of Andrew Jackson, and culminated prior to the Civil War.[49] The period of Jacksonian Democracy saw increased democratization of the American political process. Its effects were to redefine the national political process to include greater numbers of citizens both as voters and as potential officeholders. As a result, greater numbers of public officials were popularly elected; local elections were held to elect local officials. These movements strengthened the concept of a decentralized government, which had been the hallmark of colonial government. They eventually established greater independence for elected officials, and defined positions that required exercise of discretion. Not the least affected by these changes was the prosecuting attorney. "In the colonial period, and for some decades thereafter, the prosecutor's office was in fact an appointive one, appointive being in some cases by the governor and in others by the judges. . . . As with judicial offices, however, appointment almost everywhere gave way to popular election in the democratic upsurge of the nineteenth century; and it became the universal pattern in the new states."[50]

This democratic upsurge reawakened the basic populist spirit that had operated in the colonial period. It was generated in the rural and western sectors of the country. As the nations expanded westward, the impetus for change and increasing democratization came from the new states, and the steady increase in the number of offices popularly elected is evident in the more progressive constitutions of these western states as they entered the union.

The first three additions were Vermont, Kentucky, and Tennessee, all of whom entered the Union during the Washington administration and before the turn of the century. Although Vermont (1791) and Tennessee (1796) adhered fairly rigidly to the pattern of the original states by providing for election of assemblymen only, Kentucky followed the more progressive example of the middle states and allowed that county officers, most notably the sheriff and coroner, be elected in its counties.

While none of these states mentioned the office of prosecuting attorney specifically, all included some mention of prosecution. Article 29 of the Vermont constitution required that all prosecutions be public and that indictments include the phrase "against the peace and dignity of the state." Kentucky provided for an attorney general, who would appear for the Commonwealth "in all criminal prosecutions and in all civil cases in which the Commonwealth shall be interested in any superior court." Tennessee mentioned neither prosecuting attorneys nor an Attorney General but did set limits on the amount of money to be paid for attorneys appearing "for the state in Superior Court."

The popular election of judges was a key element in the development of the locally elected prosecutor. Although the local prosecuting attorney is presently considered an executive officer, and the primary law enforcement official in his district, in the early republic he was clearly defined as a judicial figure. Georgia, which revised its constitution in May of 1798, made a significant innovation in the prevailing pattern of democratization by allowing its citizens to elect not only local executive officials but also local judges. "Five justices of the inferior court shall be elected by the voters in each county, to preside in the inferior courts of the county; and justices of the peace shall be elected annually by the voters in every militia captains district." We know that current descriptions of the prosecutor often refer to him as an executive officer with quasi-judicial functions. This most likely is based on a twist of historical fact. At the beginning of the nineteenth century in America, the district attorney was viewed as a minor figure in the court, an adjunct to the judge. His position was primarily judicial, and perhaps only quasi-executive.

A great deal of evidence supports this thesis. Most telling was the fact noted earlier, that the prosecuting attorney, whether district attorney, county attorney, or Attorney General, was mentioned in the judicial article of the constitution. Even in states where separate articles were written for local and county officers, the prosecuting attorney, for the first half-century at least, was relegated to a subsection of those articles establishing the structure and officers of the state court systems. Never was he listed as a member of the executive branch; never was he described as an officer of local government. He was, in the eyes of the earliest Americans, clearly a minor actor in the court's structure.

Much greater deference and attention was placed on two other officers of the county whose positions in the early American criminal justice system very clearly outstripped that of the prosecuting attorney. These were the county sheriff and county coroner; their importance is demonstrated by the fact that these were the first offices to gain independent status and to be locally elected.

The prosecuting attorney was largely ignored even by his contemporaries. As a subsidiary of the courts, he was considered merely an adjunct to the real powers of the courts, the judges. It was only after it became acceptable to elect judges that it became regular practice to elect the prosecuting attorney. As Professor Caldwell, a critic of judicial elections, states: "Most of the reasons that militate against the popular election of judges also stand opposed to the popular election of the administrative officers of our prosecutive system. Every thinking person knows that election by popular vote is determined not by merit or ability but by popularity and that popularity is not always based on merit."[51] When election of judges finally came, so did that of prosecuting attorneys.

The earliest literature and the proceedings of the courts indicate that the sheriff was the foremost member of the criminal justice system as it existed before the Civil War, and no other office was in even close competition. When a member of the New York bar, John Tappen, prepared a manual for junior and entering members of the bar describing the New York courts and government in 1816, he gave an extensive treatment of the sheriff's office and describes the duties of twenty other offices.[52] There is, however, no mention of the prosecuting attorney, although the office clearly existed at the time. New York had established a seven-district court system in 1796 and had placed an assistant attorney general in charge of prosecution in each district. In 1801, chapter 246 of the state laws provided for a district attorney for each district. Lack of even the most perfunctory attention leads to the conclusion that the position of district attorney at that time was certainly a minor role in the criminal justice hierarchy. Historians studying the Virginia courts in the early republic describe the sheriff's revered status but again make no mention of the prosecuting attorney.[53]

Louisiana failed to provide for the election of judges in its 1812 constitution and, quite expectedly, failed also to provide for elected district attorneys. It did, however, establish the office of prosecuting attorney as separate and apart from that of attorney general, another indication of the growing independence of the office from any semblence of formal centralized authority. Mississippi (1807) likewise created the offices of Attorney General and Prosecuting Attorney as separate entities. In Mississippi, though, Prosecuting Attorneys were elected in districts determined by indirect election; that is, they were elected by voice vote of the assembly in session. Alabama followed suit in 1819.

In the several states formed from the Northwest Territory, the widening democratization brought about election of governor and numerous local offices in Ohio (1802), Indiana (1816), and Illinois (1818). There was no mention of judicial election or of the prosecuting attorney in any constitution, but such alterations were possible if the legislature so desired. By 1821, the first prosecutor in Ohio, elected and serving Cuyahoga County, was provided by statute.[54]

After Andrew Jackson was elected in 1828, the trend toward more electable offices, toward wider franchise so long restrained, swept the United States and changes were made in almost every state. In the next 20 years, seven of the thirteen founding states altered their constitutions to accommodate this new spirit. Lower court judges and justices of the peace were elected in Rhode Island (1842), and New York (1846), and justices of the peace only, in Pennsylvania and Delaware. The Attorney General became an elected position in Rhode Island and New York. In Georgia, the state that had first provided for elected jurists, an amendment to the constitution in 1839 provided for Prosecuting Attorneys in each county elected by the General Assembly.

In 1832 Mississippi became the first state to include in its constitution a provision for the popular election of local district attorneys. It also allowed for the election of all judges on the circuit and appellate levels. Similarly Iowa decided to hold popular election for its judges and county attorneys in 1846. Massachusetts had created the office of District and County Attorney in a statute of 1817.[55] The law, however, had placed this under the nominal supervision of the Attorney General. By 1843, the position had become so independent that the Attorney General's office was abolished as being unnecessary. In New York the prosecuting attorney became a constitutional office in 1846. The District Attorney was established by the Pennsylvania legislature on May 3, 1850, a move that was motivated by "a wave of home rule sentiment in the country."[56]

By the time of the Civil War, there were other signs that public perception of the status and responsibilities of the public prosecutor had changed. In some of the new state constitutions prior to the war, the District Attorney had been listed, for the first time, in the executive article along with other county officers, the sheriff, the coroner, and the clerk. His new elective status and independence placed him in another light. The public had begun to perceive that his position was actually executive and that there should be a clear and distinct separation between the duties and powers of the prosecutor as an advocate for the public and those of the courts.

Roscoe Pound wrote about the influence of the French law and thought in the United States in the first half of the nineteenth century, and nowhere is the changing nature of the public prosecutor in more evidence. The public prosecutor's increasing independence during this period, his shift from appointive to elective, from judicial to executive status, exemplifies the French belief, dictated by Montesquieu, that there should be full and complete separation between the branches of government. In this respect, at least, the American local prosecutor is much more clearly descended from the *procureur publique* than from the King's Attorney.[57]

By 1850 the trend was clear and irreversible. For the most part, the new states thereafter provided for a prosecuting attorney in their constitution; those that did not provided for one by law; and by 1912, when New Mexico and Arizona were admitted, all forty-eight states had such an officer, thirty-eight by constitution and ten by law.[58] In only five states were prosecutors still not elected—Connecticut, New Jersey, Delaware, Rhode Island, and Florida. Florida later altered its procedures, and the prosecuting attorney is now elected in that state also.

It is interesting to note that all four states in which the prosecuting attorneys are not elected officials were original states of the Union, suggesting that they have preserved the original forms of early prosecution. Two of those states—Rhode Island and Delaware—are so small that it has been possible from the first to run a statewide system of prosecution. In both these states the Attorney General has evolved as the principal officer of prosecution. The limited size of the state, however, makes it possible to argue that the Attorney General in both states is still local in character. In the other two states, New Jersey and Connecticut, the prosecutor is local but appointed: by the Governor in New Jersey, by the local court in Connecticut. Notably, in neither state were judges ever placed on the ballot, which, as has been mentioned earlier, seems to have been an essential step in the transition to locally elected and independent prosecuting attorneys.

Even though the vitality of Jacksonian Democracy was a major force shaping the development of the local prosecutor, the organization of the prosecutive system also was affected by other political and social currents. One of these was the pattern of local government developed prior to the Civil War. In general, there were two fundamental organizational structures for local government in early America. The first was based on the county as the basic unit. This form of government developed in the more rural sections of the country, dominated the South and West, and was modeled after the Virginia governmental system. The other was based on the township as the basic unit. It began in New England, took root in the more urban sections of the country, and dominated the development of the Midwest, in particular those states formed from the Northwest Territory.[59]

Because of the sharp regionalism that developed in the pre-Civil War period, all development, including governmental procedure and innovation, tended to follow regional lines. It is not surprising then to see that the jurisdiction of the local prosecutor developed in two patterns—northern township and southern county. We noted earlier that the constitutional development of the office occurred in the South, in Georgia and Mississippi particularly. In the North the office developed largely through changes in statutory law rather than through changes in the constitution.

Much of the change that increased the power of the prosecutor and made him an officer in the criminal justice system independent of the courts occurred in the South. This was partly a result of the dominance of the county unit in that section of the country, and subsequently through most of the United States.[60] "Virginia county government played a very important role in the history of the South up to 1860, for it served as a model for local political organization for the entire South. It was largely through the county organization that not only the local, but also the state and national policies of the South were controlled."[61] The South believed that the country was the fundamental unit of government and that all power in government should begin at the local level and most of it should remain there. The officers of Virginia government were appointed by the local courts and recommended to the governor for appointment until the Civil War.[62] While most southern states followed the basic framework that Virginia invented, the newer western states, less dominated by tradition and more democratically minded, instituted popular elections for almost all offices including the prosecuting attorney.

Although modern observers have lamented the fact that the prosecutor has become more and more burdened by his noncriminal duties, the fact is that the prosecutor has traditionally worn two hats. The colonial prosecutor in New York, the deputy District Attorney, handled land transfers and patent applications. The Attorney General of Maryland was given numerous noncriminal duties. The prosecutor established in Massachusetts in 1817 was entitled "District and County Attorney" to emphasize that he had both civil and criminal responsibilities. And so it was with the first elected prosecutor in the South, who is still called soliciter despite the fact that he is the chief of prosecution.[63]

Some states attempted to deal with this problem by creating two offices.[64] Once again the pattern of the county government in the South is evident in that those states that created separate offices for civil and criminal matters have been by and large southern states—Kentucky, Georgia, Mississippi, Florida, Texas, and Utah. Nevertheless both offices represented the same basic governmental unit until more recent times.

The northern pattern of development tended to be less uniform and less pronounced. In many instances, a dual level of prosecution grew up with a town or township prosecutor created to enforce ordinance violations, and a district or county prosecutor enforced state law within the same geographic jurisdiction. For example, the city of Cleveland created the post of municipal prosecutor in the city police courts as early as 1854 despite the fact that Cuyahoga County had had its own county prosecutor since 1821.

This dual level of prosecution still exists in many of the large northern industrial areas. In some cases, such as Baltimore and St. Louis, the city prosecutor has become the primary and sole agent of prosecution for the state within the city limits.[66]

It is interesting to note that in those states where the system of county government is weakest, particularly in the New England area, the position of the prosecutor remains relatively weak. Massachusetts still retains some form of the police-prosecutor apparatus that has been largely eliminated in the rest of the country. County government is virtually nonexistent in Rhode Island and Connecticut, and, as has been mentioned, neither state has developed a typical locally elected prosecuting attorney.[67]

Yet, in both the northern and southern experiences, the dominant themes of local government and local election ring clear. Despite particular or procedural differences, the overriding spirit remained uniform. Tocqueville, that fascinating French observer of American democracy, commented:

> The laws differ, and their outward features change, but their character does not vary. If the township and the county are not everywhere constituted in the same manner, it is at least true that in the United States the county and the township are always based on the same principle, namely, that everyone is the best judge of what concerns himself alone and the most proper person to supply his private wants. The township and the county are therefore bound to take care of their special interests; the state governs, but it does not interfere with their administration. Exceptions to this rule may be met with, but not a contrary principle.[68]

### Discretionary Power as the Chief Law Enforcement Official

By 1912, when Arizona and New Mexico were admitted to the Union, the process of consolidating prosecutorial power and discretion in the local prosecuting attorneys had been completed. The local prosecutor was the primary representative of the public in the area of criminal law. "In every way the Prosecutor has more power over the administration of justice than the judges, with much less public appreciation of his power. We have been jealous of the power of the trial judge, but careless of the continual growth of the power of the prosecuting attorney."[69] His position was secure, according to Professor Newman Baker, because "the permanence of the prosecutor as he exists at present, is substantially buttressed by constitutional provisions in most of the forty-eight states and revision of such constitutional provisions come slowly."[70] Nearly half a century later, the National Association for Attorneys General would comment that "there is little probability that the basic pattern (of increased power and prestige for local prosecutors) will be changed; there is every indication that it will be strengthened."[71]

The prosecutor had become a unique amalgam of the offices and historical influences that had preceded him. Like the private citizen in the English system, or the *procureur* or the *schout*, he could initiate those prosecutions he chose. Like the English Attorney General, he could terminate prosecutions by informing the courts that the state was unwilling to proceed further. Because he was a local offficer, he was free to apply the laws to his jurisdiction as he felt best served his constituency. And, because he was an elected official given these discretionary powers by the constitution or by state statute, his decisions were virtually unreviewable. Although his common law and European legal inheritances were important, it was really these last two characteristics that set him free and made him a center of power in the American criminal justice system. He is an independent and locally-elected official.

This freedom to "make a choice among possible courses of action or in-action"—unreviewable prosecutorial discretion—was, in the end, what truly set the American prosecuting attorney apart from all other members of the criminal justice system.[72] The discretionary power of the American prosecuting attorney had become indisputable in three crucial areas. He alone had the power to decide whether criminal action would be brought; he alone would decide the level at which an individual would be charged; he could not be prevented from terminating prosecution where he deemed it appropriate and necessary.

The effects of Jacksonian democratization on the once minor court figure are no more telling than in case law. By 1883, in an Illinois decision, *People* v. *Wabash, St. Louis and Pacific Railway*, the Illinois Court of Appeals voiced their strong interpretation of the powers of the prosecuting attorney: "He is charged by law with large discretion in prosecuting offenders against the law. He may commence public prosecution in his capacity by information and he may discontinue them when, in his judgment the ends of justice are satisfied."[73]

This use of discretionary power has been consistently upheld. Attempts to compel the prosecuting attorney to proceed in cases where he felt criminal prosecution was not warranted have persistently failed. In *Wilson* v. *County of Marshall*, the prosecutor was said to have "absolute control of the criminal prosecution."[74] In cases in New York (*People* v. *Berlin*),[75] New Jersey,[76] and California (*People* v. *Adams*),[77] the state courts have declared that they lack the power to compel the prosecuting attorney to enforce the penal code. "The remedy for the inactivity of the prosecutor is with the executive and ultimately with the people."[78]

To further buttress this discretionary power, the prosecutor has the right to determine what crimes he will investigate, and under what circumstances. In a Wisconsin case, *State ex. rel. Kurkierewicz* v. *Cannon*, the family of an 18 year old who had been shot by a policeman under suspicious circumstances sought a write of *mandamus* from the courts to compel the prosecutor to order an inquest into the causes of death.[79] The family cited an earlier Wisconsin case, *State* v. *Corbal* in which the court had held that although the prosecutors' duties are discretionary, they remained subordinate to the will of the legislature.[80] Again, the court refused to interfere with the discretion of the prosecuting attorney in this case. In *Wilson* v. *State*, a 1949 Oklahoma court decision defended the prosecutor's right to charge a defendant with a charge that was less than the evidence would support.[81] In several federal cases, including *Howell* v. *Brown, Milliken* v. *Stone*, and *Pugach* v. *Klein*, the courts ruled that similar unfettered discretion exists at the federal level.[82]

This series of court cases, beginning in 1883 and continuing to the present, has almost unanimously affirmed the prosecutor's unshared and unreviewable power in this aspect of the criminal law.[83] Yet this growth has not been without public apprehensiveness, and the long slow evolution to power culminated in the public's belated recognition of this power.

By the 1920s, the prosecuting attorney was to become the subject of a number of studies and reports focusing on his central role in the criminal trial process. Many of these studies were instituted by various localities, cities, and states that had experienced increasing difficulty with rising crime rates after World War I. Crime emerged as one of a complex series of problems that followed the war—new technology, rising expectations, increasing populations, new immigration, Prohibition, and general changes in social and moral outlooks. Most of the commission studies were attempts to define the current state of the local criminal justice system and to assess its abilities to cope with the additional stresses of that turbulent period.

Crime commissions were formed in Baltimore and Chicago in 1921, in Cleveland in 1922, and for the state of Missouri in 1926. Commissions also met in Georgia, New York, Illinois, Minnesota, Pennsylvania, and California before the end of the decade.[84] Almost all of them took a long hard look at the prosecutor. Most were shocked by the extent of his power and dismayed by his inability to control the crime situation.

Some of the commission reports were politically motivated as was the Chicago report of 1921, which was prepared by a political opponent of the Cook County States Attorney.[85] The report offered as a solution to the crime problem "election of an efficient, incorruptible, and industrious lawyer" to replace the incumbent and attributed the sorry state of Chicago's law enforcement to direct underworld influence in the office of the States Attorney.

Most of the reports, however, were earnest attempts to remedy the then-decaying law enforcement structure. The Cleveland survey included a complete description of the duties and responsibilities of the office of the prosecutor and included an attempt to statistically describe the functions of the office.[86] The Missouri crime survey devoted a large section to the history, development, and then-current status of the Missouri prosecuting attorney. It published a long list of findings and recommended numerous changes including offering specific suggestions for improving salary and for insuring the highest level of professional conduct in the office.[87] The California Crime Commission (1929) called for more attention to the "unsupervised area of plea-bargaining" and suggested that the power of the prosecutor in this area be diluted.[88]

In 1934, a national commission was formed to study the status of criminal justice in the United States under the leadership of legal scholar, George W. Wickersham. The Wickersham Commission included some of the more notable legal minds of the day, including Wickersham (who had previously authored voluminous legal texts and articles), Roscoe Pound of Harvard University, Newman Baker of Northwestern, and Clarles Bettman, the author of the *Cleveland Crime Commission Study*. The Commission concentrated an entire volume of its report on the duties and functions of the prosecuting attorney.

There is a tone of shock to the report that is highly critical of the situation in the criminal courts. The commission felt that the political nature of the prosecutor was detrimental to the best administration of justice and that direct election of prosecuting attorneys provided neither qualified candidates nor a proper check on the prosecutor's discretionary practices. The report was especially disturbing on the issue of plea bargaining, which was constantly referred to as an "abuse" of the process. The report expressed the opinion that the prosecuting attorney had gained too much power and too many responsibilities, recommending that the states institute a "systemized control of prosecutions under a director of public prosecutions or some equivalent official with secure tenure and concentrated and defined responsibility."[89]

Prosecution also began to draw the attention of independent legal scholars. One of the first to write on this topic was Franklin C. Davidson who commented on modern crime and its affects on the duties of the prosecutor. Davidson wrote, in a 1929 article in the *Indiana Law Journal*, that the prosecutor was faced with an entirely new set of problems unlike those that had faced his predecessors. He was especially concerned with the change in the patterns of crime that had emerged with the invention and proliferation of the automobile and suggested that mobilized crime would require strong and determined response from the criminal justice system, in which, Davidson felt, the prosecuting attorney played a key role.

Davidson also commented that "law has not kept up with the social sciences." He pointed to yet another area of controversy that would provide special problems for the prosecutor: the treatment of special classes of offenders, especially juveniles and adolescents. He suggested the need to develop specialized procedures and programs to cope with social needs. He also recognized the needs for prosecutors to keep statistics and the more general need to develop uniform methods for keeping those statistics.

Other authors in the 1930s were interested in the growth of the prosecutor's power in the area of criminal accusation. Although the criminal complaint had originated as an indictment or presentment by the grand jury, or as an information filed on behalf of a complainant, the shift from private to public prosecution and the increased statutory duties of the prosecuting attorney had modified the process to the point that the prosecutor had commanding authority in its issue. The grand jury, the common-law body governing criminal accusation, was losing ground to the prosecutor who had come to "dominate the grand jury process" in his position of advisor and presenter of evidence. "The Grand Jury" said political scientist Austin MacDonald, "is poorly fitted to perform its allotted tasks—it is virtually compelled to rely on the prosecutor for its facts, witnesses and opinions."[90]

By 1930, twenty-four states had by-passed the grand jury process, and almost all criminal cases were being filed by means of prosecutor information.[91] In other states, there was movement for similar change, for a procedural recognition of a legal fact of life—that the power to charge no longer was controlled by the grand jury; it was, in fact, a function of the locally elected prosecutor. Raymond Moley, writing the following year in the *University of Michigan Law Review*, recorded the sentiment of the times: "In many states in which indictment is still required there has been a distant agitation for change. The New York Crime Commission favored it. The Illinois Crime Commission made it a definite issue. The Pennsylvania Crime Commission considered it seriously. On the other hand, no commission in states where the information is used has recommended a return to the indictment system."[92] Moley argued that the use of the information rather than the indictment system "properly centers responsibility upon the prosecutor for actions which are apparently largely under his control even when indictments only are used. He seems to dominate the grand jury to such a degree that its actions are in reality his own, and for that reason they should be his nominally as well as actually."[93]

Justin Miller, in a study published by the *University of Minnesota Law Review* agreed with Moley and added that the use of informations was a fiscal boon to criminal justice administration. His study showed that informations were more expeditious, less expensive, and more efficient, resulting in the initiation of fewer unsuccessful prosecutions.[94]

Opponents of the grand jury system often remarked on the symbolic character of its powers with derision. Ernst Puttkammer, writing in 1953, dismissed the grand jury indictment as a "de facto power of the prosecutor."[95] Even those who favored its existence often did so because it was a useful tool for the prosecutor, rather than an instrument for the defense of civil liberty. Lester Orfield suggested that the grand jury was helpful because it provided the prosecutor with another method of investigation, especially for what he called "modern crimes"—antitrust or organized crime conspiracies. Even so, Orfield himself was vague in his defense of the grand jury, slaying that "doubtless, because of some merit, [it] has survived the campaigns waged against it."[96]

From 1930 to the present the grand jury system has continued to erode, and this trend seems likely to continue. One reason why the grand jury did not completely disappear was that many prosecutors desired to keep the institution. In states where the grand jury was still convened, prosecuting attorneys found it useful to take politically explosive or socially controversial cases before the grand jury. Although the prosecutor controlled the flow of information and evidence to the members of the grand jury, he escaped the political consequences of an unpopular decision, since he could claim that the power to indict or not to indict in that specific case had been in the grand jury's hands and not his.[97]

Despite these few mitigating circumstances in its favor, the grand jury's impotence became evident to the legal reformers of this century. By 1964, MacDonald wrote that "the present trend seems to be toward the further expansion of the powers of the prosecuting attorney and the virtual abandonment of the Grand Jury system in ordinary criminal proceedings."

The most comprehensive series of articles written on the topic of the public prosecutor was published between 1933 and 1935 in the *Journal of Criminal Law and Criminology* at Northwestern University. The series was coauthored by Newman Baker, a professor of law, and Earl DeLong, an instructor in the Department of Political Science. Baker and DeLong were the first to describe the paradoxes that were embodied in the development of the local prosecutor. "The people of the United States have traditionally feared concentration of great power in the hands of one person and it is surprising that the power of the prosecuting attorney has been left intact as it is today."[98] Baker and DeLong were especially impressed with the power that the prosecuting attorney had attained. "Nowhere," they proclaimed, "is it more apparent that our government is a government of men, not of laws."[99] They pointed out that the prosecutor was shaped only by those who elected him and that popular election had meant that local standards had come to determine how the law was applied. And this, they argued was the crucial factor in the effectiveness of the criminal laws. "The law is written by legislators, interpreted occasionally by appellate courts, but applied by countless individuals acting largely for himself. How it is applied outweighs in importance its enactment or its interpretation. . . ."[100]

Other commentators had been wary of a power that was only checked at the ballot box and warned that it would lead to abuses. Judge William

B. Quinlin of Wisconsin, speaking before a meeting of the state's district attorneys in 1921, exhorted them "not to legislate."[101] He pointed out that, in his opinion, the district attorney was duty bound to equitably prosecute all crimes brought to his attention. He feared that the voter was not likely to provide diligent check on unlimited discretion. As another author has said: "To some extent [the Prosecutor] derives his authority from statute, but more largely he relies on custom. The people look to him for results in the unending war of society on crime, and, if he produces results they are not likely to ask whether he has stayed within the exact limits of his powers."[102]

Baker and DeLong, however, recognized that it was no accident that the prosecutor was allowed to exercise wide discretion and that he often enforced the laws as a direct expression of local custom and sentiment. They knew that the system characteristically produced satisfactory prosecutors for the majority of American jurisdictions and that there was too direct a connection between the voters and the officeholder for any crime that was genuinely perceived as dangerous to the community to go unprosecuted. At the same time, they noted that the rise of crime would force the prosecutor to "steer a middle course" between initiating all actions and following only his personal preferences.[103]

Baker and DeLong recognized the need for professionalization of the public prosecution and anticipated in their articles in 1934 a movement toward training and advanced education in that specialty. In one of their early articles in the series, Newman and Baker pointed out, for example, that only half of the states at that time required the prosecuting attorney to be a licensed lawyer. In the first three decades of the twentieth century a number of court cases had dealt with this issue, and the trend was toward requiring legal training for all prosecutors. A Wisconsin court held, in *State* v. *Russell* that the district attorney had to be a licensed attorney because of the court's interpretation of the intent of the statute.[104] The pivotal case, however, was an Illinois decision in the case of the *People* v. *Munson* in 1926.[105] The court declared that the duties of the prosecuting attorney were such that he would have to be an attorney to be able to perform them. It also declared erroneous the notion that election to the office would automatically grant to the layman the privileged position of attorney-at-law. In the subsequent decades, almost every state has made provisions through either statute or court rules requiring a degree of law for those who hold the office.

The influence of Baker and DeLong's writings on the prosecutor, and the notoriety gained through their series of articles, made Northwestern University Law School a center in the field of prosecution. The interest spilled over into the development of Northwestern's famous "Short Course for Prosecutors," which was begun before World War II. The course was offered to help those recently elected prosecutors or recently appointed deputy prosecutors to familiarize themselves quickly with the specific problems connected with the daily practice of the prosecuting attorney. The course attempted to give its students both theoretical and technical knowledge, preparing them in the case law and the practical and management problems of the office.

The Northwestern short course was discontinued during the war and was not reconvened until 1949. Since then, it has been offered every year.[106]

A controversy that has arisen on numerous occasions since the 1920s concerns another aspect of professionalization in the office of the prosecutor. Some of the early crime commission reports criticized the fact that prosecutors in small towns and rural counties were employed on a part-time basis. The Missouri crime survey pointed to the dangers of allowing prosecuting attorneys to serve less than full-time and made the switch to full-time service its first recommendation.[107]

Many states have resisted a change to full-time prosecutors because such a change would lead either to large increases in the cost of criminal justice, or to a switch to nontraditional methods of defining jurisdictional boundaries.[108] Colorado, which had always maintained a district system, adopted a full-time rule in 1970, as did New Mexico in 1975.[109] Oklahoma changed from a county to a district system in 1965, when candidates failed to file for the office in a number of counties that had previously employed prosecutors on a part-time basis.[110] Even though a large number of experts have favored the district system, the traditional strengths of the county government system have resisted this effort, and, to the present, the controversy remains heated.

The expertise of the prosecuting attorney has long been a serious problem. In the nineteenth century, the lesser demands and lower status of the prosecutor resulted in low pay, which made the position unattractive for qualified attorneys. Justice William Evans of the Iowa Supreme Court reminisced in 1914 on the condition that led him to be elected county attorney in Iowa as his first job out of law school. "I was nominated and elected as the first county attorney in my county and only because I was then the youngest practitioner at our bar."[111] Judge Quinlin of Wisconsin, speaking in 1922 to a graduating class of law students at Marquette University, stated that he expected that many of the graduating class would become either assistant district attorneys or would run for the office right out of law school. This seemed to be the course of the day.[112]

Justice Evans commented further that "the office has largely become the prerequisite of the young attorney. It is the first arena."[113] For many, it was also the first arena in a political career. The position of prosecuting attorneys in Indiana for the prior 80 years revealed that the office was a tremendous springboard into politics during the period from 1880 to 1920; and that, although the trend had diminished in the period from 1920 to 1960, it still remained a viable method for a young lawyer to gain political experience and reputation.[114]

In recent years, the prosecutor's office has been perceived by young attorneys as the quickest method of gaining invaluable litigation experience. Young attorneys in private practice may spend their early years preparing briefs and processing paperwork, but the assistant prosecutor is immediately thrown into the fray. The pressure generated by the low levels of staffing and the increasing demands of the criminal courts provides the novice lawyer with almost immediate exposure to the courtroom. "A recent survey of selected offices across the nation found that the major problem was not recruiting prosecutors, but keeping them; prosecutors' offices were, in effect, training grounds for private and corporate practice."[115] The National Association of Attorney Generals reported that "rapid turnover among prosecutors is a problem that limits the development of expertise."[116]

**Summary and Conclusions**

The remarkable emergence and development of the American prosecutor mirrors the emergence and development of the United States. The office developed as it did because factors and forces—political, social, and legal—combined to generate a need for public prosecution and then shaped an office to meet these needs. In perspective, the American prosecutor is logically derived and historically consistent.

We have seen that the concept of public prosecution had to be adopted by the Americans before the prosecutor could emerge. The rejection of the British common law system of private prosecution was quickly achieved. By 1704, Connecticut became the first colony to entirely eliminate the system of private prosecution and to establish public prosecutors as adjuncts to all county courts. Soon other colonies adopted similar stances.

Our system of public prosecution was created in an environment conducive to defining the prosecutor as representative of local government rather than a centralized authority. The spirit of self-government and independence that dominated the life of the colonies, the demands created by the vastness of the territory being colonized, and the benign neglect of the courts by the British made centralized control immensely difficult. Although the first Attorney General was appointed in 1643 in Virginia and the other colonies followed suit in the period between then and the early 1700s, his existence could not curb the desire for more self-government and local control. Coupled with the isolation resulting from expanding territories, the local court concept was reinforced. This eventually led to defining the prosecutor as a local official. When local control over recommendations for appointments to deputy attorneys general was demanded, the relatively weak central government acceded.

The growth of the country produced a growing demand for legal expertise, and, in the courts, the role of the lawyer began to take shape. In addition to advising the court, he also was to prevent abuses to the court system and to act as a buffer against the uneducated impulses of juries or grand juries. Later, as the technical requirements of the court became more demanding, the court's reliance on the deputy attorney general increased along with his powers and responsibilities. Thus, by 1751, the Virginia courts ordered that all witnesses and accused, in even the most simple cases, confer with the deputy attorney general assigned to the court before filing complaints or affidavits. The penalty for failing to do so was the loss of any witness fee or reward.

By the advent of the American revolution, private prosecution had been virtually eliminated in the colonies, and a new breed, the local prosecutor, had been created. It was, therefore, not surprising to see states, after the Revolution, adopting the form of prosecution that already existed in the colonies and not that imposed by their German, Dutch, or British antecedents.

Even though the Attorney General was the nominal head of state prosecution, in reality, the local deputy Attorney General was swiftly establishing his own local power base. Local courts, local appointments and recommendations solidified this trend. By 1789, the primary responsibility for prosecution was in the hands of local officials whose power and independence would continue to grow.

It was not until some 40 years after the Revolution that another nationwide trend would arise to change the nature of American prosecution and thrust the prosecutor into a position of eminence. Highlighted by the presidency of Andrew Jackson, the country entered a period of democratization that was to stop only with the Civil War. The national political process was redefined to include greater numbers of citizens, both as voters and as potential officeholders. The result was that more public officials were popularly elected, and more of the elections were for local officials. The prosecutor's role (now thoroughly defined as local) had undergone a strengthening and expansion as the needs for legal expertise continued to grow.

The steps can be seen through the early state constitutions, where the Attorney General was first defined in the judicial articles. In states where separate articles were written for local and county officers, the prosecuting attorney for the first half of the nineteenth century at least was relegated to a subsection of those articles establishing the structure and officers of the state systems. But the shift was there. By 1821, the first prosecutor to be elected was in Ohio, serving Cuyahoga County.

After Andrew Jackson was elected in 1828, the expansion of democracy in the form of elected positions swept the country. Hanging on the coattails of the movement to elect local judges was the prosecutor. In 1832, Mississippi became the first state to include in its constitution a provision for the popular election of local district attorneys. By 1859 the trend was clear and irreversible—the prosecutor was a locally elected position.

The final authority was conferred by the courts, which upheld his discretionary power. This completed his development because it made him the chief law enforcement official in his community. As a local official he was free to apply the laws of his jurisdiction as he felt best served his constituency. As an elected official given discretionary power by the constitution or by state statutes, his decisions were virtually unreviewable. This freedom of choice was, in the end, what truly set him apart from all other members of the criminal justice system. In 1883, the Illinois Court of Appeals stated that his authority to commence public prosecutions and to discontinue them is not questionable. His authority has been upheld consistently by the courts, which have almost unanimously affirmed the prosecutor's unshared and unreviewable power in this aspect of criminal law.

The growth of the prosecutor in duties and responsibilities continued after the Civil War. In this 50-year period between 1865 and 1914, the country entered the modern age. Urbanization started with the building and rebuilding of cities, the opening of the West sparked a frontier philosophy of independence and innovation, the railroads were built, new waves of immigrants combined with the monied class to industrialize the post-Civil War society. As expansion and industrialization occurred the courts became extremely active, and the Supreme Court was called on to define issues basic to the country. Not overlooked by the prosecutor were the attendant problems of crime and the demands of an industrializing society.

By the 1920s what America had created and produced over the past 200 years became the focus of studies and reports for the first time. Increasingly troubled by the rising crime rate that appeared after World War I, the intensifying complexities of modern urban life and the adverse effects of prohibition, studies were undertaken by various localities, cities, and states. The crime commissions formed in Baltimore and Chicago in 1921, in Cleveland in 1922, and for the state of Missouri in 1926 set the stage for a series of similar studies in many other jurisdictions. Almost all took a hard look at the prosecutor. Most were disturbed by the extent of his power and dismayed by his inability to control the crime situation. Ironically, the very personage that had evolved so naturally in our society was viewed askance when he was finally introduced to society. There is a tone of shock from the Wickersham Commission (1934) as it considered the political stature of the prosecutor, his discretionary power, and especially his plea-bargaining practices. Yet these embodied the very concepts sought by the original colonists: local representation applying local standards to the enforcement of essentially local laws.

The importance of these commissions and studies extended beyond the examination of the role of the prosecutor in the conduct of criminal trials.

Their value was to broaden the concept of criminal justice to the consideration of its system and structural aspects. As attention focused on the prosecutor, weakenesses in his role and functions were also identified. In the 1930s the first calls for professionalism were presaged. The need was obvious. As recent as 1934, only one-half of the states required the prosecuting attorney to be a licensed lawyer. The courts through their appellate powers supported this movement, and the academic world, sparked by Northwestern University, recognized the training needs. As the demands for legal training, specialized training, full-time employment, and other matters multiplied, the office of the prosecutor became institutionalized and more firmly woven into our system of criminal justice. By the time World War II arrived, the office of the prosecutor was part of a modern and urbanized society.

In tracing the origins and development of the American prosecutor we can identify some of the factors that created and shaped him into a form unique to America. Perhaps the essential explanation for his emergence can be found in an America colonized and inhabited by a myriad of cultures—English, French, Spanish, German, and Dutch, to name a few. Each had systems of justice and laws as part of their heritage from which the Americans could draw. Hence, nothing was truly new or alien to all persons. The amalgam of these many different alternatives and procedures fostered an environment in which people were not afraid to try out new ideas, to adopt or to modify. The very diversity that existed nurtured innovation and change. Out of this rich soil emerged the American prosecutor.

**Notes**

1. *Missouri Crime Commission* (New York: McMillan, 1926).

2. Patrick Devlin, *Criminal Prosecution in England* (New Haven, Conn.: Yale University Press, 1958).

3. National Commission on Law Observance and Enforcement (NCLOE), *Report on Prosecution* (Washington, D.C.: U.S. Government Printing Office, 1931).

4. W. Scott Van Alstyne, "The District Attorney—A Historical Puzzle," 1952 Wisconsin Law Review 125 (1952). See also, Douglass Campbell, *The Puritan in Holland, England and America* (1899), pp. 438-467.

5. Frank Morten, *Diary of a D.A.* (New York: Henry Holt, 1960).

6. National Association of Attorneys General (NAAG), *Report on the Office of the Attorney General* (Raleigh, N.C.: The National Association of Attorneys General, 1971).

7. Jack M. Kress, "Progress and Prosecution," *Annals of the American Academy of Political and Social Sciences* 423 (January 1976):99-116.

8. Lawrence Friedman, *A History of American Law* (New York: Simon and Schuster, 1973).

9. Kress, "Progress and Prosecution," p. 105.

10. Ibid., p. 100.

11. Ibid., pp. 100-101. see also, Frank Miller, *Prosecution: The Decision to Charge a Subject with a Crime* (Boston: Little, Brown, 1969), p. 54.

12. Kress, "Progress and Prosecution," p. 100.

13. Ibid.

14. Compare Kress, "Progress and Prosecution" with Glanville Williams, "The Power to Prosecute," *Criminal Law Review* (1955):601.

15. See A.C. Wright, "French Criminal Procedure," 44 Law Quarterly Review 324 (1928).

16. Devlin, *Criminal Prosecution in England*, p. 25.

17. Wright, "French Criminal Procedure," p. 324.

18. Leon Radzinowicz, *A History of English Criminal Law: Reform of the Police* (London: 1956), p. 258. Compare with Campbell, *The Puritan*, pp. 438-467.

19. State v. Peterson, 195 Wis. 351, 218 N.W. 367 (1928); Mallery v. Lane, 97 Conn. 132, 138 (1921). Compare with views of Baker cited in note 46.

20. John Blum et al., *The National Experience* (Harcourt, Brace and World, 1968), p. 59.

21. Charles A. Beard and Mary R. Beard, *New Basic History of the United States* (Doubleday, 1968), p. 84.

22. Blum et al., *National Experience*, p. 59.

23. Edwin Surrency, "The Courts in the American Colonies," 11 American Journal of Legal History 253 (1967).

24. John T. Farrell, "The Early History of Rhode Island's Court System," in *Rhode Island History*, vol. 9, p. 65.

25. George Lee Haskins, *Law and Authority in Early Massachusetts* (New York: McMillan, 1960), p. 177.

26. Oliver P. Chitwood, *Justice in Colonial Virginia* (New York: DeCapo Press, 1971), p. 120. A different view is taken by Arthur P. Scott, *Criminal Law in Colonial Virginia* (Chicago: University of Chicago Press, 1930).

27. See generally, Julius Goebel and Raymond T. Naughton, *Law Enforcement in Colonial New York* (New York: 1944).

28. Harry B. Weiss and Grace M. Weiss, *An Introduction to Crime and Punishment in Colonial New Jersey* (Trenton, N.J.: 1960), pp. 8-9.

29. Van Alstyne, "The District Attorney," p. 137.

30. John J. Poserina, "Appointed Attorney General's Power to Supercede an Elected District Attorney," 33 Temple Law Quarterly 78, 83 (1959).

31. Raphael Semmes, *Crime and Punishment in Early Maryland* (Baltimore: Johns Hopkins Press, 1938).

32. Edwin L. Page, *Judicial Beginnings in New Hampshire* (Concord, N.H.: 1959), p. 60.

33. Paul M. McCain, *The County Court in North Carolina before 1750* (Durham, N.C.: Duke University Press, 1954), p. 18.

34. Chitwood, *Justice in Colonial Virginia*, p. 120.

35. Goebel and Naughton, *Law Enforcement*, pp. 332-334.

36. Compare Van Alstyne, "The District Attorney," p. 1125, with Kress, "Progress and Prosecution," generally.

37. Campbell, *The Puritan*, p. 444.

38. Scott, *Criminal Law*, pp. 48-49.

39. Chitwood, *Justice in Colonial Virginia*, p. 120.

40. Farrell, "Rhode Island's Court System," p. 14.

41. Goebel and Naughton, *Law Enforcement*, p. 334.

42. McCain, *County Court*, p. 33.

43. Scott, *Criminal Law*, p. 66.

44. NCLOE, *Report on Prosecution*, p. 15.

45. Ibid., p. 8.

46. Newman Baker, "The Prosecuting Attorney—Provisions of Organizing a Law Office," 23 Journal of Criminal Law and Criminology 926, 957-959 (1932).

47. Walter Pickett, "The Office of the Public Prosecutor in Connecticut." 17 Journal of Criminal Law and Criminology 348 (1926).

48. William E. Nelson, "Emerging Notions of Modern Criminal Law in the Revolutionary Era: An Historical Perspective," in *Criminal Justice in America*, ed. R. Quinney (Boston: Little, Brown, 1974), p. 101.

49. NAAG, *Report*, p. 19.

50. Lewis Mayers, *The American Legal System* (New York: Harper and Row, 1964), p. 413.

51. Baker, "Prosecuting Attorney," p. 962.

52. Tappen, *The County and Town Officer* (Kingston, N.Y.: 1816).

53. Isabel Ferguson, "County Courts in Virginia, 1700-1830," 8 North Carolina Historical Review 14 (0000).

54. Alfred Bettman, *Prosecution* (Cleveland, Ohio: Cleveland Foundation, 1921).

55. NAAG, *Report*, p. 15. See also Elliot Richardson, "The Office of the Attorney General: Continuity and Change," 53 Massachusetts Law Quarterly 6 (1968).

56. Poserina, "Appointed Attorney General's Power," p. 83.

57. See Roscoe Pound, "The Influence of the French in America," 3 Illinois Law Review 354 (1908). On independence of the U.S. attorney, see 85 F. Supp. 537, 540 (D. Nebraska, 1949).

58. See Baker, "Prosecuting Attorney," pp. 955-959. The ten states are Connecticut, Delaware, Maine, Rhode Island, Ohio, Missouri, Kansas, Nebraska, Wyoming, and Minnesota.

59. Beard and Beard, *New Basic History*, p. 88.

60. Baker, "The Prosecuting Attorney," p. 928.

61. Ferguson, "County Courts," p. 14.

62. Ibid., p. 39. See also McCain, *The County Court*, p. 25.

63. A.L. Gilbert, *County Attorneys* (Mayfield, Kentucky, 1914).

64. Baker, "Prosecuting Attorney," p. 945.

65. Bettman, *Prosecution*, p. 56.

66. NCLOE, *Report on Prosecution*, p. 10.

67. NAAG, *Report*, p. 107.

68. Alexis de Tocqueville, *Democracy in America* (New York: Schocken Books, 1961), pp. 79-80.

69. NCLOE, *Report on Prosecution*, p. 11.

70. Baker, "Prosecuting Attorney," p. 927.

71. NAAG, *Report*, p. 103.

72. Kenneth Culp Davis cited in Kress, "Progress and Prosecution," p. 100. See People v. Newcomer, 284 Ill. 315, 120 N.E. 244 (1918).

73. 12 Ill. App. 263 (1883).

74. 257 Ill. App. 220 (1930).

75. 361 N.Y.S. 2d 114 (1974).

76. See State v. LeVien, 44 N.J. 323, 209 A.2d 97 (1965). See also State in the Interest of F.W., 26 N.J.Super. 513, 327 A.2d 697 (1974).

77. 117 Cal. Rptr. 905 (1974).

78. Milliken v. Stone, 7 F.2d 397, 399 (S.D.N.Y. 1925).

79. 52 Wis.2d. 368, 166 N.W.2d 255 (1969).

80. 248 Wis. 247, 21 N.W.2d 381 (1946).

81. 209 P.2d 512, 514 (Okla. 1949).

82. Howell v. Brown, 85 F. Supp. 537 (D. Neb. 1949); Milliken v. Stone, 7 F.2d 397 (S.D.N.Y. 1925); Pugach v. Klein, 193 F. Supp. 630 (S.D.N.Y. 1961).

83. But see, People v. Newcomer, 284 Ill. 315, 120 N.E. 244 (1918) (*mandamus* denied to states attorney seeking to compel trial judge to accept *nolle prosequi*).

84. See NCLOE, *Report on Prosecution*.

85. John J. Healy, *The Prosecutor in Chicago in Felony Cases* (Chicago, 1921), p. 307.

86. See Bettman, *Prosecution*, pp. 56-60.

87. *Missouri Crime Commission*, pp. 159-160.

88. Baker, "Prosecuting Attorney," pp. 788-789.

89. NCLOE, *Report on Prosecution*, p. 38. See also Kress, "Progress and Prosecution," pp. 110-111; Roscoe Pound, *Criminal Justice in America*, American Constitutional and Legal History Series (New York:

DeCapo, 1972); Compare with views of Raymond Moley, "The Initiation of Criminal Prosecution by Indictment or Information," 29 Michigan Law Review 403 (1931).

90. Austin F. MacDonald, *American State Government and Administration*, 6th ed. (New York: Thomas Crowell, 1961), pp. 474-475. Notable exceptions to this are North Carolina and Connecticut.

91. Moley, "Initiation," p. 403.

92. Ibid.

93. Ibid.

94. Ibid. See Justin Miller, "Information or Indictment in Criminal Cases," 8 Minnesota Law Review 379-408 (1924).

95. Ernst W. Puttkammer, *Administration of the Criminal Law* (Chicago: University of Chicago Press, 1953), p. 191.

96. Lester B. Orfield, *Criminal Procedure from Arrest to Appeal* (New York, 1947), p. 191.

97. See Moley, "Initiation," p. 403.

98. Baker, "Prosecuting Attorney," p. 934.

99. Newman F. Baker, "The Prosecutor—Initiation of Prosecution," 23 Journal of Criminal Law and Criminology 770, 771 (1933).

100. Ibid., p. 796.

101. William B. Quinlin, "The District Attorney," 5 Marquette Law Review 190, 194 (1921).

102. MacDonald, *American State Government*, p. 474.

103. Baker, "The Prosecutor," p. 771.

104. 83 Wis. 330 (1892).

105. 219 Ill. 596, 150 N.E. 280 (1926).

106. See "One Hundred and One Prosecuting Attorneys from Thirty-one States Attend Short Course for Prosecutors at Northwestern University School of Law," 40 Journal of Criminal Law and Criminology 223 (1949).

107. *Missouri Crime Survey*, p. 159.

108. Mayers, *American Legal System*, p. 412.

109. Colorado Legislative Council, "Report on Salaries of District Attorneys," *Reports to the General Assembley*, 152 (November 1970).

110. NAAG, *Report,* p. 109.

111. William Evans, "The County Attorney: What Shall He Do to Be Saved?" 9 Iowa Law Bulletin 1 (1914).

112. Quinlin, "District Attorney," p. 190.

113. Evans, "The County Attorney," p. 9.

114. Kan Ori, "The Politicized Nature of the County Prosecutor's Office—Fact or Fancy: The Case in Indiana." 40 *Notre Dame Lawyer* 289 (1964).

115. *U.S. News and World Report*, 29 December 1969, p. 34. See also NAAG, *Report*, p. 114.

116. NAAG, *Report*, p. 107.

**Part II
External Factors Affecting
Prosecution**

# 2

# The Power of Population on the Prosecutive Function

## Introduction

Although the social sciences have developed complex methodologies since the 1920s and 1930s to examine population growth, mobility, and their attendant effects on society, little systematic attention has been given the role of the prosecutor within this social ecology.[1] Yet the single most powerful influence on the prosecutor, his role, and the operations of his office is the nature of the population he represents, its resources, and the consequent social and cultural patterns it develops. The primary reason for this profound effect stems from the elective status of the prosecutor's office. In most instances, the prosecutor is a locally elected official and, as such, must reflect the values and norms of the community if he is to attain (and retain) office.

The ecology in which prosecution functions is a variegated universe where the size of the population defines the basic social forms. Just as the size of jurisdictions vary, so do the social environments. Prosecution as a part of this environment also tends to mirror the image of the community, its values, and its cultural biases. The problems and issues faced by the 6 cities having populations of over one million hardly are comparable to those of the 13,706 communities defined in 1970 by the Census Bureau as "rural territories" and having a population of less than 2,500.

Although a community colors the style of prosecution, its own composition and character may be shaped by other societal forces beyond its control. Changes in population trends, the establishment of different patterns of mobility, and the broad social forces of urbanization and suburbanization have either an immediate or delayed effect on the community and ultimately on the type or volume of work coming into the prosecutor's office. Understanding the effect of population on prosecution includes the necessity of noting the effects of these changes or shifts well.

This chapter focuses on the more significant effects of population groupings on the prosecutive function. It examines the impact of the size of the jurisdiction and the characteristics of the community on the role and function of the prosecutor. Also, since population trends and shifts may change the nature of prosecution, both locally and nationally, the more important of these are discussed to lend perspective to the analysis. Of special interest will be two trends that have matured in the last 25 years: suburbanization and the increasingly stronger relationship between population and crime.

Inspecting the prosecutive function from a population perspective hopefully will destroy the stereotype that prosecution is an urban function. On the contrary, crime is the urban function. Prosecution is predominantly a small-town rural function. The vast majority of prosecutors are local officials operating mostly in rural or small-town environments. At the risk of overgeneralization, three classes of prosecutors can be described: the rural or small-town prosecutor, the urban, and the suburban. Using these categories spotlights the basic differences and issues generated by the type of population being served and shows the power of population on the prosecutive function.

## Population Growth and Trends

The population statistics for the past century show an astonishing picture of rapid growth and accelerating change in our society. In retrospect, these trends and shifts seem obvious, but it was not until the 1920s that the study of population and demography gained stature and recognition as a legitimate social science. Today, we are far more acutely aware of the importance of demographic data than we were 100 years ago, and we have developed the ability to predict from present population statistics with a fair degree of reliability. We see very clearly the effects of changing from a rural society to an urban one and, more recently, a suburban one. For some this shift has occurred within a single life span. By 1920, the United States had crossed the line from rural to urban when less than 50 percent of its population resided in rural areas. In the following 5 decades, almost 75 percent of the population resided in urban areas.[2] Table 2-1 summarizes this changing pattern of urbanization from 1880.

Table 2-1
Distribution of U.S. Population by Rural and Urban Areas, 1880-1970
*(percent)*

| Year | Rural | Urban |
|---|---|---|
| 1880 | 73.7 | 26.3 |
| 1900 | 62.7 | 37.3 |
| 1920 | 48.6 | 51.4 |
| 1940 | 43.5 | 56.5 |
| 1960 | 30.1 | 69.9 |
| 1970 | 26.5 | 73.5 |

Source: U.S. Department of Commerce, Bureau of the Census, *Historical Statistics of the United States, Colonial Times to 1970*, part 1, series A 73-81 (Washington, D.C.), p. 12.

As the population quadrupled from 50 million in 1880 to 203 million by 1970 and the industrial technology advanced to levels capable of sustaining ever-larger population groups, the urbanization of America flourished. Not only did the cities increase in size, but they increased in number. The local, fragmented, and often isolated communities of the eighteenth and nineteenth centuries bear little resemblance to the megalopolises of the twentieth century. In 1890, the Census Bureau reported 1,348 urban territories and 6,490 rural territories with less than 2,500 residents. This 1-to-5 ratio had narrowed to almost 1 to 2 in less than one hundred years when in 1970 there were 7,062 urban territories as compared to 13,706 rural. Table 2-2 illustrates the growth of our society both in size and degree of urbanization. This fact is especially important in the study of local government and local government officials. Table 2-3 illustrates the increasing population density as the growth of the cities expanded. Yet, despite this massive urbanization, America still has numerically more rural and small towns than it does cities. Even though, in 1970, almost 75 percent of the population lived in urban areas, of all the 7,062 places classified by Census Bureau as urban, almost 80 percent had populations of 10,000 or less. For all places, almost two-thirds were classified as rural territories. From a local government perspective, America is still rural or small town in structure if not in outlook.

For those who migrated into the cities, and for those who were denied the opportunity because of scarce resources and materials, the end of World War II started a new population movement that was to have a profound effect on prosecution, namely, suburbanization. As Skogan so aptly stated, "Perhaps the single most important force in American life since the second World War is suburbanization—the selective movement of people and jobs from the central city to the suburban fringe and the impact of that movement upon those left behind."[3]

Table 2-2
**Urban and Rural Territories by Population, 1890-1970**

|                   | 1970   | 1950   | 1930   | 1910   | 1890   |
|-------------------|--------|--------|--------|--------|--------|
| Urban territory   | 7,062  | 4,471  | 3,165  | 2,262  | 1,348  |
| 1,000,000 or more | 6      | 5      | 5      | 3      | 3      |
| 500,000-999,000   | 20     | 13     | 8      | 5      | 1      |
| 250,000-499,999   | 30     | 23     | 24     | 11     | 7      |
| 100,000-249,999   | 100    | 65     | 56     | 31     | 17     |
| 50,000-99,999     | 240    | 126    | 98     | 59     | 30     |
| Less than 50,000  | 6,666  | 4,509  | 2,974  | 2,153  | 1,290  |
| Rural territory   | 13,706 | 13,807 | 13,433 | 11,830 | 6,490  |
| 1,000-2,499       | 4,191  | 4,158  | 3,087  | 2,717  | 1,603  |
| Less than 1,000   | 9,515  | 9,649  | 10,346 | 9,113  | 4,887  |

Source: U.S. Department of Commerce, Bureau of the Census, *Historical Statistics of the United States*, part 1, series A43-56 (Washington, D.C., 1975), p. 11.

Table 2-3
Distribution of Urban and Rural Territories by Population, 1970 and 1890
*(percent)*

|  | *1970* | *1890* |
|---|---|---|
| Urban territories | 34.0 | 17.2 |
| 1,000,000 or more | a | a |
| 500,000-999,999 | 0.1 | a |
| 250,000-499,999 | 0.1 | a |
| 100,000-249,999 | 0.5 | 0.2 |
| 50,000-99,999 | 1.2 | 0.4 |
| 25,000-49,999 | 2.5 | |
| 10,000-24,999 | 6.7 | |
| 5,000-9,999 | 8.9 | |
| 2,500-4,999 | 11.1 | |
| Less than 2,500 | 3.0 | |
| Rural territories | | |
| 1,000-2,499 | 65.7 | 82.8 |
| Less than 1,000 | 45.8 | 62.4 |
| Total | 100.0 | 100.0 |

Source: U.S. Department of Commerce, Bureau of the Census, *Historical Statistics of the United States*, part 1, Series A43-56 (Washington, D.C., 1975), p. 11.
aLess than 0.1 percent.

In 1940, 74 million people lived in the cities. By 1970, the figure had doubled to 149 million. But this massive urbanization did not quite produce the satisfactions expected from the "American dream." The social problems of the city, the density, the anonymity and impersonality, the standardization of behavior, the increased opportunity for deviance, the crumbling standards of living, slums, congestion, and social disorders finally gave push first to "urban sprawl" and then to the development of suburbia.

The price of urban sprawl, the unplanned expansion of the city, was bad aesthetics and bad economics.[4] Anxious to cope with post-World War II housing needs and supported by federal lending policies that encouraged standardized housing design, landscaping, and placement on lots,[5] the builders leapfrogged over the countryside building poorly designed developments at excessive distances and costs for utilization by paved roads.[6]

Eventually some reason and planning prevailed, and urban sprawl gave way to the systematic development of suburbia. The extent of suburbanization can be measured by the percent of each Standard Metropolitan Statistical Area (SMSA) population that lives outside the central city. Table 2-4 illustrates the shifting balance between central cities and suburbia since 1950. This major shift of population from central city to suburbia had significant and not always beneficial effects. As Skogan notes: "The ecology

Table 2-4

SMSA Population Living Outside Central Cities, 1950-1970

|  | 1950 | 1960 | 1970 |
|---|---|---|---|
| SMSA total population (millions) | 94.6 | 119.6 | 139.5 |
| Percentage in central cities | 56.8 | 50.1 | 46.1 |
| Percentage in outside central cities | 43.2 | 49.8 | 53.9 |

Source: U.S. Department of Commerce, Bureau of the Census, *Statistical Abstract of the United States, 1977*, no. 15 (Washington, D.C., 1977), p. 16.

of American society has been altered drastically by the process of sub-urbanization. It has sorted the population along race and class lines, concentrating in large cities the poor and the unemployed. It has left large, dense central cities, a deteriorated physicial plant which is cheaper to abandon than repair, peopled by working class whites and blacks and Latins of various classes who are unable to escape."[7]

In an analysis of the twelve largest metropolitan areas, the Taeubers found that both white and black immigrants into the city had higher educational and occupational levels than did the whites who did not leave the central city. The lowering of these levels of central city people is attributed almost entirely to the extensive out-migration of whites of higher status.[8]

As the oportunities of suburbia attracted the middle class, it exacerbated the social overhead needs of the city and reduced the tax base by the lure of labor, cheap land, and good transportation at the edge of the metropolitan area. Thus the growth of the suburban fringes at the expense of the cities further increased the burdens borne by the central cities, which itself stimulated selected outward migration.

How this self-supporting cycle relates to crime and prosecution is summed up by Skogan: "While earlier social stratification and geographic segregation by race, class and culture was a neighborhood-level process, the massive flight of the white middle class beyond the jurisdictional grasp of the schools, courts, police and governments in many central cities has turned city boundaries into the relevant lines of cleavage."[9]

**Population and Crime**

Crime has long been considered one unenviable product of urbanization and life in the city. In fact, one of the best known statements on social organization can be found in Louis Wirth's theory of urbanism published in 1938.[10] Wirth hypothesized that crime rates and expenditures for policing should be highest in the most urbanized communities. He hypothesized that crime should appear in conjunction with the forces that shape city life: size, density, and heterogeneity.

In his analysis, he reasoned that each of these characteristics affected the social life within a community. At the urban end of the continuum, individual insecurity and anomie should be high; the strength of traditional mechanisms for social control weakened; and the potential for instability and conflict enhanced. Large size lends an impersonal, anonymous, and transitory character to relationships. Density demands the standardization of behavior, the establishment of rules, and the development of complex and specialized roles and structures. Heterogeneity in the population precluded common understandings, fostered competition and conflict, and could produce violent collective behavior. As a result, it is not surprising to find most of the formal social control concentrated in large cities.

Wirth was not alone in these hypotheses. The empirical work of the Chicago School linked crime rates to life in "zones" that more-or-less varied along Wirth's three dimensions. The President's Crime Commission on Law Enforcement and the Administration of Justice attributed more than one-half of the increase in reported crime during the early 1960s to changes in the levels of similar variables.[11]

Skogan, while recognizing the "ideal" validity of Wirth's thesis and the ecological studies of others, examined the relationship between crime, population size, density, and racial heterogeneity. Using time series data from a sample of cities, he found that the true relationship between urbanization and crime did not exist until the mid-sixties. "Before the early 1950s, the correlation between the crime rate and measures of the level of urbanization of American communities was low or negative; crime was not clearly concentrated in the most urban places." By the mid-1960s, the overlap of crime and urbanization was high, and "the official figures on crime now support a pessimism about the plight of our largest cities which earlier they could not."[12]

To the extent to which this strengthening of the urban-crime relationship is due to suburbanization (which may leave the future shape of the city as a doughnut with the peripheral areas holding the bulk of the jobs) has been the subject of much analysis.[13] It has been noted that when the middle class leave their downtown residences, the major land users in central city become commercial and industrial enterprises, government centers, and slums. The latter siphon off municipal expenditures without contributing to the revenue. Under these conditions of large populations, high densities, deteriorated environments, and a fragmented network of interpersonal relationships, there is good evidence that the flight to the suburbs has indeed increased the crime problems of the city.

Skogan found that: "Parsimonious interpretation of the data, . . . is that a fundamental shift is occurring in the social ecology of urban systems. . . . The selective movement of people and jobs from the central city to the suburban fringe, and the impact of that movement upon those left behind, may have produced the changes observed."[14]

A comparison of the 1970 Census data with the Uniform Crime Report (UCR) data furnished by the FBI, despite some definitional problems, show the present strength of this relationship. Not only are more than half the reported crimes occurring in cities with populations of 100,000 or more, but the rate of crime (the number of crimes per 1,000 population) is also highest for the largest cities (7,035) and lowest for the smallest communities (1,271).

What this means is that, today, crime is an urban disorder. Simply speaking, for whatever causes, one can claim with little chance of error that increasing population size leads to increasing crime. Conversely, the smaller the community, the safer it is likely to be. Because population size and crime rates are so highly correlated, it is not surprising to find the public's perception and image of the criminal justice system, including the prosecutor, to be an urban one. Yet, nothing could be farther from the truth.

**Characteristics of Prosecution**

The effects of urbanization largely have by-passed the vast majority of prosecutor offices and left them structurally intact. Because they overwhelmingly represent local government jurisdictions, the actual number of prosecutor offices remains relatively constant, and the size of the office is predominantly small.[15] Of the fifty states, twenty-eight provide for representation at the county level, and fourteen on a district basis. In three states, mixed representation at either a county or district level exists; in another two states, the county or city is the basis for representation. One state, Maine, has recently formed eight prosecutorial districts. Delaware and Rhode Island, our two smallest states, and Alaska, our largest state, have no local prosecutors; that function is performed by the Attorney General. Finally, in the District of Columbia, local prosecution is carried out by the federal government through the Office of the United States Attorney for the District of Columbia. In general, though, the office of the prosecutor has jurisdiction for either a county or a judicial district. These two entities are in themselves not subject to rapid or frequent boundary changes. Hence the relative constancy of the number of prosecutor offices. If change does occur, it usually is a state action consolidating county prosecutor offices into districts justified by providing better service to the public and eliminating part-time prosecution.

A survey conducted by the National Association of Attorneys General (NAAG) in 1972 showed that the median population served by county prosecutors was between 20,000 and 30,000 persons.[16] For prosecutors representing more than one county or district, the median rose to between 60,000 and 100,000. Only 5 percent of all prosecutors represented jurisdictions with populations between 250,000 and 500,000. About the same percentage served areas with populations over 500,000. These figures are substantiated by the membership distribution of the National District Attorneys Association (NDAA) for the same year and by the results of a survey conducted by the National Center for Prosecution Management (NCPM) in 1972.[17] Both these sources reported that approximately three out of every four prosecutors represented jurisdictions with a population of less than 100,000.

Because prosecution in the United States is typically found in small jurisdictions with relatively small populations, it is not surprising to find that office size is small and often operates on a part-time basis. The NAAG survey reported that "most prosecutors" (68 percent) do not have full-time staff attorneys, and, of the 32 percent who do, 35 percent have only one assistant and 56 percent has less than four.[18] The NCPM study found that 37 percent of the prosecutors reported that they operated "solo" (no assistants) and another 37 percent reported having staffs with one to three assistants. Nationally the average staff size was six persons. As Skoler points out in his work on the consolidation of these functions, prosecution even aggregated to a state level operates within a relatively small bureaucratic setting.[19] Certainly, in contrast to the state departments of transportation, education, and welfare, the few hundreds of individuals involved in prosecution do not produce what is commonly recognized as a large, unwieldly bureaucracy.

In addition to typically small local offices, prosecution is typically a part-time or partially compensated job. As NAAG reported, "Whether a prosecutor works full-time or part-time is directly related to the population the area which he serves. In population areas of less than 60,000, part-time prosecutors constitute a greater percentage. Where the population is over 60,000 people, the majority of prosecutors are full-time."[20] (See table 2-5.)

Part-time prosecution exists when the prosecutor or his assistants maintain a private practice in addition to prosecutorial duties. The origins of this practice are rather obvious. Historically many of the smaller, isolated communities simply could not provide enough work to support full-time prosecution; or they did not have a tax base capable of providing this service delivery on a full-time basis. This practice continues today for essentially the same reasons, but, now, its retention is buttressed by the solid supports of tradition. Although the reformers have consistently called for full-time prosecution, the goal has met with only limited success. As shown in table 2-5, without an adequate population base (variously estimated between 30,000 or 60,000) part-time prosecution is almost inevitable. The lack of volume, the power of tradition, and the opportunity for additional income through a private practice are strong incentives to the retention of part-time prosecutive systems.

The latest standards of the National District Attorneys Association address this problem in a realistic manner by calling for full-time prosecution:

> The office of the prosecutor shall be a full-time profession. The prosecutor shall neither maintain nor profit from a private legal practice. In those

Table 2-5
Comparison of Urban and Rural Places by Crime and Crime Rates, 1970

| | Number of Places | Number of Crimes | Crime Rate | Ranking by Crime Rate | Percent Distribution | |
|---|---|---|---|---|---|---|
| | | | | | Number of Places | Number of Crimes |
| Urban areas | 4,481 | 6,346,537 | 5,234.1 | | 53.0 | 74.4 |
| 1,000,000 or more | 6 | 1,318,597 | 7,035.0 | 2 | .01 | 15.4 |
| 500,000-999,999 | 20 | 988,273 | 7,618.8 | 1 | 0.2 | 11.6 |
| 250,000-499,999 | 30 | 710,128 | 6,785.0 | 3 | 0.4 | 8.3 |
| 100,000-249,999 | 98 | 876,429 | 6,237.5 | 5 | 1.2 | 10.6 |
| 50,000-99,999 | 252 | 817,711 | 4,692.7 | 4 | 3.0 | 9.5 |
| 25,000-49,999 | 504 | 701,308 | 4,030.9 | 6 | 6.0 | 8.2 |
| 10,000-24,999 | 1,177 | 619,420 | 3,354.3 | 7 | 13.9 | 7.2 |
| under 10,000 | 2,394 | 314,671 | 2,682.0 | 9 | 28.3 | 3.6 |
| Suburban areas | 2,415[a] | 1,864,242 | 3,150.3 | 8 | 28.5 | 21.9 |
| Rural areas | 1,563[a] | 318,002 | 1,271.4 | 10 | 18.5 | 3.7 |
| Total | 8,459 | 8,528,781 | | | 100.0 | 100.0 |

Source: Federal Bureau of Investigation, *Crime in the United States, Uniform Crime Reports, 1970* (Washington, D.C., 1971), table 9, pp. 104-107.
[a]Agencies

jurisdictions unable to justify the employment of a full-time prosecutor, the prosecutor may serve part-time until the state determines that the merger of jurisdictions or growth of caseload necessitates a full-time prosecutor. The prosecutor shall devote primary effort to his office, and shall have no outside financial interests which could conflict with that duty. . . .[21]

Ironically, unless the crime rate can be increased either by natural population growth, or by artificial jurisdictional mergers, the problems of part-time prosecution may never be resolved.

It is only in the larger urban areas that one begins to find some consistency in approaching full-time employment of prosecutors. Yet even here anachronisms exist. In Massachusetts, for example, with the exception of the District Attorney representing the district including Boston, all the other eight District Attorneys are considered part-time. In Jackson County (Kansas City) Missouri, of the thirty-seven assistants thirteen are part-time.

If one is to make any statement about prosecution, no matter how broad, it contains an exception. Yet the wide diversity in public prosecution systems as they exist today is rarely recognized by the public and often not even by an individual prosecutor. The latter often views his office as representative of most other offices. The public views the office almost entirely as an urban phenomenon. The fact that crime and prosecution are equated and that crime is predominantly an urban disorder supports this stereotype. In reality, hidden behind this single image are vastly different types of offices dealing with vastly different issues and offering services distinctly different from each other. Population size, as a broad indicator of the social and economic characteristics of a community, also serves as an indicator of different types of prosecution.

## Differentiating Effects of Population on Prosecution

When population is considered as a differentiator between prosecutive systems, three basic images can be examined: the rural, urban, and suburban offices. Admittedly, one may criticize the use of three stereotypical images as a means of destroying an urban stereotype of prosecution. And the criticism is so noted. But for the purpose of showing the effect of population size on prosecution, this offers a simple approach. The issues addressed by each of these systems of prosecution are so different that they are best presented according to this classification.

By broadly grouping prosecutors into rural, urban, and suburban categories the fundamental differences in focus and priorities can be observed. In our ever-changing environment, one should not assume that these differential effects of population will remain constant in a prosecutor's community. Even today we are seeing the problems common to the urban prosecutor shifting to the suburban areas. In addition, the exurbanization of America is bringing to the rural and small-town prosecutor an increasingly complex set of duties. Thus the snapshots presented here may represent only a moment of time for the local prosecutor.

### The Rural or Small-Office Prosecutor

Prosecution in a small-town or rural environment is characterized by a low criminal caseload, a small budget, and a lack of institutionalization. Because the least amount of reported crime is found in rural America, one can conclude that for most small-town or rural prosecutors, there is very little criminal work.

An analysis of the prosecutor's caseload by the NCPM showed that a logarithmic relationship existed between census resident population and felony caseload leading them to conclude that "despite all the definitional and procedural variations, however, the relationship between population and felony caseload is remarkably stable and strong."[22] In fact, in this same study, 45 percent of the offices responding stated that they processed less than 200 felonies in a 12-month period. With a felony caseload of less than two per month, one may envy the crimeless environment and wonder what the prosecutor does in these jurisdictions.

There are basically two prosecutive responses to this situation. One response is that the prosecutor functions on a part-time basis, supplementing his income with a private practice. The second is that the prosecutor's criminal responsibilities are supplemented with civil duties. It is not unusual to see both conditions existing in some offices. However, for purposes of this examination, we will consider the responses separately.

Part-time prosecution is predominantly a small-office function. As table 2-5 indicated, there is a high correlation between full-time employment and population size. One would expect also that part-time prosecutors would also receive a lesser salary than their full-time equivalents, since they supplement their partial income from prosecution with private practice income. And data confirm this. The NAAG survey found that the hourly median income of part-time prosecutors was reported to be between $6.50 and $7.50, which is hardly comparable to the median hourly salary of $11.74 for full-time prosecutors.

This is not viewed as a desirable solution. The American Bar Association in its report on *The Prosecution Function* warns that ". . . there is a great risk that the part-time prosecutor will not give sufficient energy and attention to his official duties. Since his salary is a fixed amount, and his total earnings depend on what he can derive from his private practice, there is continuing temptation to give priority to private clients."[23]

A practical illustration of this concern can be heard in the common complaint of the sheriffs or their deputies about sitting in the waiting room of the prosecutor's private office and taking their turn along with the private clients.

Since private practice presents a controversial solution to the low income produced by partially compensated public employment, some jurisdictions supplement the low level of criminal activity by giving the prosecutor civil responsibilities. This is not an unusual practice; its precedents can be traced to the colonial days when the local attorney, who would later be known as prosecutor, assumed the role of civil advisor to the local government body. Today, only thirteen states charge the prosecutor solely with criminal jurisdiction. In all the other states, with a few minor variations, the prosecutor assumes both roles.

The most common activities of the prosecutor in civil matters include advising the county board on contracts, arbitration of disputes, sewer development matters, zoning, education, parks, and recreation matters. The prosecutor also may be assigned specific responsibilities in statutes dealing with other areas such as: adoption, collection, and disposition of fines and forfeitures, mental commitments, narcotics control, paternity proceedings, public improvements, health rules, and so forth. In Illinois, for example, there are at least twenty-six other specific areas in addition to the previous listing in which the prosecutor is legally required to act, ranging from adoption matters, to water rights.[24] In Michigan, a search of the statutes identified fifty additional areas of obligation directly involving the Michigan prosecuting attorney.[25]

Some prosecutors react favorably to the comingling of civil and criminal jurisdictions. They view the alternative of civil lawsuits to criminal processing as an advantageous procedure. As the California District Attorneys Association stated: ". . . Civil lawsuits give the prosecutor certain major advantages . . . , civil suits may lead to faster correction of the problem and resolution. . . . The prosecutor is not limited to the dictates of the Fifth Amendment . . . and the lawsuit is more easily won."[26] For the small-office prosecutor such activities may not necessarily be a solution to a low-volume criminal caseload. Indeed, it may pose additional problems in the form of processing priorities or assigning available attorney manpower. The NCPM manual for the rural and small-office prosecutor cautioned that "although 50-60 percent of all matters coming to him will be civil in nature, it should be clearly recognized that the district attorney is primarily concerned with the prosecution of *criminal* matters."[27]

The National District Attorneys Association also gives priority to criminal case work and hints at the potential problem of not enough attorney power in a community when it calls for provisions for alternative representation in case of conflict: "The prosecutor shall represent the case of the people as to both civil and criminal jurisdiction. The criminal representation shall be the primary responsibility. In jurisdictions where civil and criminal responsibilities are invested in the prosecuting attorney, provision for alternative representation in the case of conflicts should be made."[28]

In the smaller jurisdictions, many resources normally accessible to larger jurisdictions are not available. The small-office prosecutor working as a solo or with fewer than four assistants, operates in jurisdictions that generally have limited tax bases. The public funds available to this office are meager and may even result in severe underfunding of the prosecutive function. Confirming this is the National Association of Attorneys General's study, which reported that the median annual budget for all prosecutors is in the $20,000-$30,000 range.[29]

Since the county unit is the major source of fundings (only 9 percent of the offices are totally funded by the state), the small-office prosecutor competes for a share of the money with other services such as education, trash collection, sewage disposal, road repair, and law enforcement. In communities with limited tax dollars, prosecution services rarely receive priority attention and funding. Thus the capacity of the office to expand or acquire additional resources is narrowly constrained by the size of the county's budget.

Even with appropriated funds, the prosecutor in the small jurisdiction faces resource problems so basic that their larger-office brethren can only react with shock when they hear the problems, and they are, most often, incapable of suggesting workable solutions. In the small-office environment the county appropriations for prosecution services may buy only an electric typewriter to replace the manual one. It may pay the salary or partially compensate a secretary who is presently being paid out of the prosecutor's pocket. It may pay for the printing of complaint forms, or file folders, or the file cabinets needed to hold them. In some instances, it may even pay rent for the office.

Small-office prosecutors live very close to the basics. The cutting edge of their existence sometimes depends on the lucrativeness of their own private practice. If successful in private practice, they can afford to share the same electric typewriter, personnel, and equipment between public and private duties, thereby supplementing the county's appropriation. This reduced funding level often produces more energetic or ingenious attorneys, who quickly learn how to tap other public agency resources. For example, processing of nonsupport cases is transferred to the welfare agency, and drug abuse and alcohol cases are referred to the health department.

Partly because of the low level of funding, but more as a function of the relatively low crime rate, the third characteristic of small office prosecution systems is their lack of institutionalization. When criminal matters are received, they are handled in an atmosphere of relative informality. In the small-town community, it is likely that the participants in the processing system are know to each other socially as well as professionally. Even the defendants are likely to be known to the criminal justice community. The low volume of crime, the small budget, and the small office create little demand for the highly organized structures and procedures needed by the larger offices. Thus such institutionalized procedures and programs as diversion, pretrial release; pretrial conferences, motions, hearings, and presentence investigations all may be performed within the criminal justice process but without the trappings of organizational or special programs developed specifically for one of these purposes. One could scarcely imagine a diversion program staffed by a director and counselors funded and operating for one or two cases a year. In the small-town environment, the informal sanctions of the community are more easily imposed and may be even more effective than the anonymous and impersonal organizations developed for these same purposes in the cities.

Within this small office world, the prosecutor faces two issues that rarely trouble his larger-office brethren. They are conflict of interest and flexibility. Conflict of interest can arise in two ways. Either as a result of the prosecutor's private practice or from his civil advisory function. The latter we have seen addressed by the NDAA standard that calls for the priority processing of criminal matters.

The President's Commission on Law Enforcement and the Administration of Justice also addressed the issue of conflict of interest and stated:

> While direct conflicts of interest between the prosecutor's public office and his private practice are clearly unlawful and, we may assume, rare, there are many indirect conflicts that almost invariably arise. The attorneys he deals with as a public officer are the same ones with whom he is expected to maintain a less formal and more accommodating relationship as counsel to private clients. Similar problems may arise in the prosecutor's dealings with his private clients whose activities may come to his official attention. It is undesirable to place a prosecutor in a position in which he must always be conscious of this potential for conflict and be careful to avoid improprieties or appearance of conflict.[30]

It may be undesirable to place a prosecutor in such a position, but, within the small-office environment, it may also be inevitable. It is often difficult to predict when a divorce proceeding will result in the filing of an assault charge, when a county commissioner who votes on the prosecutor's budget will be placed under grand jury investigation for fraud or when a contract being considered by the commissioners will affect the prosecutor's or his family's property. Conflict of interest, whether arising from the fruits of private practice or from the civil advisory function is a major issue in a numerically small legal community.

The second issue affecting the small office prosecutor is that of flexibility, or more appropriately, a lack of flexibility. Because so few resources are available to tap in case of an emergency or under special conditions, the prosecutor is not as maneuverable as are his large-office peers. The threat of an emergency is continuous and takes on greater significance than in the more urbanized areas. Most common are personal emergencies. For example, if the solo prosecutor is stricken ill, there is little choice but to request continuances for the active docket. In jurisdictions where criminal trials are infrequently set, if this means carrying it over to the next setting, or term, the effect on all participants is deleterious. Limited flexibility is an issue not only to the prosecutor but to the judge and to some extent even defense counsel. In the rural and small towns of America, the criminal justice system is more heavily dependent on the health of the participants than one often realizes.

In addition to these personal emergencies, the criminal justice system in rural America is not geared to handle extraordinary crimes or complex crimes that demand a disproportionately large amount of system processing time. One can wonder how many of the publicized problems stemming from town justice systems are aggravated by inadequate case-handling techniques or inadequate resources. It is difficult to imagine how a prosecutor in a small-office environment without access to investigative staff and modern laboratories can prosecute a complex case based on evidence supplied by an inadequately trained sheriff's department. It is even more difficult to imagine where the resources are that will permit the prosecution of a complicated murder, public corruption, or consumer fraud. These cases typically require an extraordinary amount of time, complex and sophisticated investigations, and the delicate development of evidentiary materials.

Although the preceding are exceptional events in the routine life of small town prosecution, they do deserve attention. Many proposals have been made to minimize conflict of interest and the need for additional resources. The most common proposal has been a call for districting the office. The President's Commission on Law Enforcement and the Administration of Justice said that "in the smaller jurisdictions, where the caseload does not justify a full-time prosecutor, consideration should be given to the use of prosecutors representing larger districts."[31] The standards of the American Bar Association agree with this position. But districting alone may not solve the issue of the partially compensated lawyer.

In 1967 Oklahoma reorganized its prosecutive system into a number of multicounty districts each with a full-time district attorney, a first assistant district attorney, and a district prosecutor, all salaried by the state. Prior to this legislation, the salaries of the part-time prosecutors were based on county assessments and were so unattractive that in one year, of the seventy-seven counties in the state, there were thirteen in which no lawyer would run for the job. The Oklahoma system is still only a partial solution. The legislation did not otherwise affect the existing county governments and county court systems. So while it minimized the conflict of interest problems, it only partially increased the flexibility needed to deliver prosecutive services. The prosecutor still copes with a separate court system for each county. His total budget is the sum of the individual appropriations approved by each county board of commissioners and that portion supplied by the state.

The use of districting in addition to state supplements to county funding, the establishment of state prosecutor associations with staff capable of providing technical assistance, and, in some instances, the availability of assistance from the Attorney General all have been offered and sometimes tested with varying degrees of success in an effort to resolve these major problems confronting the rural prosecutor. Unfortunately, too little systematic attention has been given to the special problems and issues facing this group.

*The Urban Prosecutor*

Crime is an urban phenomenon. It thrives in the largest cities, spawns law enforcement agencies, and produces complex prosecutor offices and court systems in addition to other necessary functions and services. In 1970, six cities with populations over 1 million, accounted for 17.5 percent of all known offenses reported to the FBI. Fifty-six cities with populations over 250,000 reported 40 percent of all known offenses and the 50 percent mark was reached by including ninety-eight cities with populations between 100,000 and 200,000. The sheer volume and variety of cases submitted for prosecution coupled with complex law enforcement systems have produced highly complex and structured organizations.

Los Angeles County, with the largest population in the United States (7.1 million), had an office budgeted in 1975-1976 for $28 million which, in part supported 605 assistant prosecutors. The second largest prosecutor's office is in Cook County (Chicago), Illinois. Here a staff of 341 assistants was supported by a budget of $5.5 million in 1975.[32] Table 2-6 shows the ten largest jurisdictions responding to the 1975-1976 NDAA survey by population, budget, and number of assistants to illustrate how large an office may become in contrast to the previously described rural or small-town prosecutor's office.

The urban prosecutor's office is usually staffed by attorneys on a full-time basis; that is, no private practice is allowed. As such, their salaries tend

Table 2-6
Ten Large Urban Prosecutors' Offices by Population Served, Budget, and Number of Assistants

| Jurisdiction | Population | Budget 1975-76 | Number of Assistants |
|---|---|---|---|
| Los Angeles County (Calif.) | 7,100,000 | $28,014,818 | 605 |
| Cook County (Chicago, Ill.) | 5,493,529 | 11,465,986 | 341 |
| Harris County (Houston, Texas) | 2,000,000 | 4,191,426 | 109 |
| Santa Clara County (San Jose, Calif.) | 1,665,000 | 4,537,589 | 69 |
| Orange County (Calif.) | 1,646,300 | 5,459,896 | 94 |
| Nassau County (N.Y.) | 1,500,000 | 4,053,500 | 96 |
| Bronx County (N.Y.) | 1,478,000 | 6,032,230 | 151 |
| Dade County (Miami, Fla.) | 1,389,400 | 3,638,422 | 80 |
| King County (Seattle, Wash.) | 1,444,000 | 2,300,000 | 60 |
| Erie County (Buffalo, N.Y.) | 1,127,000 | 1,838,601 | 62 |

Source: National District Attorneys Association, *National Prosecution Standards* (Chicago: National District Attorneys Association, 1977), app. 1-11, p. 19.

to be higher than their part-time equivalents. The NAAG study in 1973 reported a median hourly salary of $11.74 as compared to the $6.50 to $7.50 range for the part-time attorneys. The selected offices that responded to the NDAA survey, a sample of which were included in table 2-5, reported a starting assistant's salary range from a low of $10,680 in Erie County, New York, to a high of $15,516 in Los Angeles County. The chief prosecutor's salary in these ten jurisdictions also ranged from a low of $30,300 in Seattle, Washington, to a high of $48,998 in Buffalo, New York. In an urban area prosecution assumes the trappings of big business including higher pay and more expenses.

The bureaucratic trappings of the office include a vast array of support personnel to assist in the administration and operations. While the small-office prosecutor bemoaned the fact that he only had a part-time secretary and perhaps a part-time assistant, the large office contains an array of skills and talents. They range from clerical support staff to librarians, files and records control clerks to budget and accounting personnel. If the office is large enough to support automation, one may find computer programmers, systems analysts, and statisticians. Most of these offices employ either public information personnel or public relations officers to communicate the work and performance of the office to the electorate. Finally, from an operational perspective, the large volume of work is handled by a wide array of technicians in addition to the attorneys. Common to large offices are investigators and detectives, paralegals, and third-year law students. Although less frequent, one may also find forensic scientists, chemists, and photographers.

This prosecutorial panoply is the result of one thing—crime. Research performed by the National Center for Prosecution Management not only supported the relationship existing between population and crime but also uncovered a very strong relationship between the number of assistants in the office and the volume of its felony caseload.[33] Thus, as the population increases, crime increases, and the size of the prosecutors's office grows in a remarkably predictable manner. Unless there are some extraordinary circumstances, due to either understaffing or overstaffing, one can broadly approximate the size of the annual felony caseload by multiplying the number of assistants by 100. For example, Orleans Parish with sixty assistants handles a felony caseload that annually approximates 6,000. Similarly, Kansas City, with an assistant staff size of thirty-seven, processes about 3,850 felonies annually.

This large volume of cases typically is processed by what is known as "assembly-line justice." Cases flow in an orderly fashion from the complaint room, where the police charges are reviewed and a complaint prepared by an assistant, to the magistrate court, where the defendant is advised of his rights, bail is set, and defense counsel appointed, if necessary.

If the case is a felony, usually the next court appearance is the probable cause hearing, which may result in either a filing of a bill of information or a bind over to the grand jury for indictment. After filing or indictment, the defendant is arraigned, a motions hearing may be set, a pretrial conference may also take place, and ultimately the case, if it is still alive, may be set for trial. Prior research has designated the flow and delays encountered in a large urban court system as "spin arounds" at process points.[34]

Although variations do occur, the assembly-line process is designed to process large volumes of cases. As a result, size and controlling for the effects of size are the two overriding concerns in an urban prosecutor's office. The conflict of interest issue facing the small-office prosecutor is rarely an issue in the large urban office. Most of the prosecutors are full-time, and almost all are involved in processing criminal matters for the great proportion of their time.

Thirteen states assign the prosecutor solely with criminal duties. The ACIR study reported that ". . . in at least four others—California, Hawaii, Kansas, and Michigan—prosecutors in urban areas are divested of civil responsibilities which become the province of county or city corporation counsel." Expanding on the large criminal caseload handled by prosecutors, Morgan and Alexander in their survey of local prosecutors stated that "prosecutors devote most of their time to criminal matters; 78 percent reported they spend over one-half of their time on criminal work. The median percentage of time on criminal matters is 75 percent. In contrast, only 2 percent spend over one half of their time on civil matters."[35]

The major issues confronted by the urban prosecutor, differentiating his office from both the small and the suburban prosecutor's offices, are all size related: (1) reducing workload; (2) allocating resources, and (3) processing a massive caseload uniformly.

**Reducing Workload.** Of primary concern to the large office prosecutor are techniques available to cope with a volume of cases that usually is larger than the capacity of the court. If one thinks of the criminal process as an assembly line attempting to force more cases into a fixed pipeline than the pipe can accept, then the sense of urgency behind efforts to find new programs and alternative processing techniques becomes understandable. If one adds to the fixed court capacity, a time limit as is imposed by speedy trial rules, then one can also understand why in some cases urgency can turn into panic.

The prosecutor has two basic methods for reducing workload. He may impose tighter controls on what he accepts for prosecution or he may use other prosecutorial strategies to dispose of these cases without a trial, including alternatives to the formal adjudicative process.

Pretrial screening in the late sixties and early seventies was originally hailed for its instant reduction in caseloads. Rejection rates of 20-25 percent were quoted so often that they took on the mantle of being a standard without verification. One function of the screening process is to remove unwanted cases from the criminal justice system. Another function is to accept only those cases with prosecutorial merit. In justifying NDAA's standards on screening, the commentary lists reasons for allowing prosecutorial discretion in the charging process and states that "in the first area one primary justification cited for the existence of prosecutorial screening is that of simple expediency."[36] In a study of the New Orleans District Attorney's office, almost 50 percent of the cases were rejected at intake through the screening process. Regardless of other considerations—policy, quality, or external constraints—screening is an effective start on the road to caseload reduction.

Other techniques used by the prosecutor to reduce caseload come into play after the charging decision to go forward has been made. The most powerful of these are plea bargaining or negotiation, and diversion. Whenever a case can be disposed of by a negotiated plea before the day of trial, court processing time is significantly reduced.

Diversion, broadly defined to include the many alternative forms of adjudication and types of deferred prosecution, can be a valuable ally to the prosecutor seeking to reduce his caseload by using options other than criminal justice processing. Diversion programs exist in many forms and styles.[37] Essentially designed to provide alternatives to adjudication, or incarceration, and to eliminate the stigma of a criminal record, they have only recently gained in popularity and acceptance. A survey in 1974 showed that thirty-five major urban areas had active formal diversion programs with more than 10,000 defendants being diverted annually.[38] Other formal programs dealing in the treatment mode are also spreading. Most commonly known is TASC (Treatment Alternative to Street Crime), a drug abuse diversion program, which in 1975 was operating in twenty-two urban areas. Nontreatment diversion programs can be found in deferred prosecution programs or "stet" files as they are sometimes called. In these programs, prosecution is deferred for a specified period of time (usually six months to a year) or until restitution is made to the victim. If, at the end of the period, no further problems have been encountered by the defendant, the prosecutor will either dismiss the case or drop the charges.

Not all prosecutors believe in pretrial diversion; its adoption varies by community attitudes and prosecutorial policy. Needless to say, diversion and other procedures used as alternatives to adjudication are observable primarily in heavily populated jurisdictions. The informal avenues through which cases can be disposed of in smaller jurisdictions are difficult to adopt in the anonymous and high-volume processes in the city. Although the existence of many of these programs may be a direct response to community or prosecutorial values, the institutionalization of their purposes and functions is an urban phenomenon not a rural one.

**Resource Allocation**. The second issue facing the urban prosecutor and emanating from the size of his office is that of resource allocation. The organization of the office, and the management techniques employed, will color the quality and character of prosecution. A large office must employ the structure and controls inherent in bureaucracies. Yet establishing an effective organization often is difficult. Few prosecutors have had training in management and organization. Indeed their legal training, if at all important in this area, usually conflicts with management principles. A legal education focuses on the handling of an individual unit of work (cases) not all work; a search for exceptions (precedents), not the average. With this training the tools needed for management are not necessarily provided nor is there an easy acceptance of the concept of a systems approach to management. As a result the quality of management received little priority until the mid-1970s, and the organization of the office suffered from inattention as well. Tradition has reigned supreme.

The present organizational forms existing in prosecutors' offices vary according to the court system, tradition, whim, or any combination of these. Yet they are not totally irrational. Most are reflective of the court's operating system, narrowing the type of docketing system employed by the court. They can be classed into two basic organizational models. One is the assembly-line or process model; the other is the integrated or trial team model. The process model organizes the office around each process step in the justice system. Assistants are assigned to each processing point and supported by other staff personnel as necessary. In this model assistants may be assigned to the lower misdemeanor and felony intake courts, the complaint room, the intake screening and review unit, the arraignment court, grand jury, preliminary hearing, trials, and appeals. Assignments to each of these divisions may be rotated after a certain amount of time, when an expected competence level is attained. Usually, the newest assistants are assigned to either the appellate division or the lower misdemeanor courts before they take on criminal trials and other proceedings.

This model exists because the case moves assembly-line fashion from one court proceeding to another and from one courtroom to another. The advantage of this organizational model is that it permits a stable assignment procedure for assistants. Proper manpower levels for each court can be estimated and tested over a period of time without sacrificing flexibility. For predictable peak loads, such as the Monday morning intake crush, adjustments to staff assignments can be planned to accommodate these peaks. The major weakness of the model is that it requires extensive bureaucratic controls to ensure uniformity in processing and decision making. Since each unit tends to operate independently of the others, breakdowns in the uniform processing of cases are enhanced. For example, the preliminary hearing assistant, with little or no responsibility for anything other than conducting preliminary hearings, may rarely be held accountable for the decisions made at this hearing even though they were faulty. If he does not dismiss a case, it will merely survive to be disposed of later by another part of the system. The result of these independent operations and decision-making activities at each of the process points is to produce inconsistencies in the quality of case processing and a lack of accountability, unless extensive management controls are employed on a regular basis.

This model is not without value. Minimal uniformity in case processing is usually assured by a complaint process. When decision making is clearly and often faulty, complaints originate from the next process unit receiving the case. For example, poor charging decisions have to be processed by preliminary hearing assistants. In this sense, management by exception or complaint may be a common problem, unless it is recognized and abated by using stringent and extensive control measures that fix accountability and maximize uniform case processing.

The second model, the integrated or trial team model, flourishes best in those court environments where individual docketing to either a judge or a court-room is the practice. With few exceptions, a case, once assigned to either stays there. In response to this type of docketing system, the prosecutor is able to assign either an assistant or a team of assistants to the judge or the courtroom. As a result, assistants are able to handle not only a single case from assignment to disposition but also a variety of types of cases if they are randomly assigned to the court.

In some offices, the intake and screening function may be incorporated into the integrated case-processing system. This is especially likely to occur if the court docket assigns the case to a courtroom immediately on filing. In Baton Rouge, Louisiana, for example the cases were assigned to courts by date of arrest, and the prosecutor's office had ten days from the date of arrest to file charges. Since the office was organized into divisions, each handling a courtroom's caseload, the charging decision was made by the division that would have to prosecute the case.

The advantages of this organizational model are that it tends to improve job satisfaction, since the assistants handle the case from beginning to end; increase on-the-job training opportunities and establishes a career ladder; within the courtroom setting, fix accountability and increase uniformity in decision making. There are, of course, weaknesses in this model that require bureaucratic and management controls, although not for the same purposes as those required by the process model. With this model resource flexibility is limited. This is not a problem in a stable court environment, where the individual courts process caseloads in steady and predictable volumes. But in unstable environments, where one courtroom jams up while another remains idle, the prosecutor has little opportunity to shift resources from one courtroom to another. Since cases have been assigned to assistants who are attached to individual judges or courtrooms, the courtroom whose docket has "gone down" by 10:00 A.M. may well remain empty for the rest of the day. This does not mean that an idle courtroom means an idle assistant. He usually has other duties that can be performed on these occasions. Familiar examples are case preparation, interviewing investigators or witnesses, case law research, answering correspondence, and catching up on paperwork. Thus, although there is little case flow flexibility in responding to court processing, there are usually other alternative work tasks available to the assistants.

The major danger of this organizational model is its inability to ensure uniformity in decision making among the trail teams. Although accountability is more easily fixed within one court division, since supervision is over a small control span, there may be significant differences in philosophy and even policy among the different trial teams or courtrooms.

The urban prosecutor, with many assistants, has the unique ability to form various combinations and permutations within these two basic models. Some organizational arrangements reflect earnest attempts to cope with large volumes of work; others are a result of eclectic adoption of procedures that appeared to work well in other offices. A common modification to the basic organizational models described here is the creation of special units that process special cases. At the risk of oversimplification, the units may be divided into two broad categories: (1) Those that prosecute specialized crimes (for example, narcotics, rackets, organized crime, fraud) usually characterized by complexity and a need for prosecutorial expertise or the public's sensitivity to certain types of crimes and (2) those that prosecute selected criminals (for example, career criminals or major offenders). Both of these units may operate within the two basic organizational models and serve different prosecutorial purposes. The establishment of specialized crime divisions is a logical adaptation to the assembly-line or process model, which minimizes case preparation activities. Since this model transfers cases from one processing point to another, the continuity needed for investigating, preparing, and developing highly complex cases such as fraud, narcotics, or rackets is difficult to obtain. Hence, the establishment of special trial units to provide a trial team approach to these selected cases is justified and superimposed on the model. In some instances, even the court supports such approaches by designating special court rooms for specialized crimes (a good example are the narcotics courts in New York City).

The selective prosecution of defendants under such programs as Career Criminal, Major Offense Bureau, or Felony Tracking Units also imposes part of the integrated organizational model on the process model. By designating criteria for the selective prosecution of defendants, the prosecutor is able to give a small group of assistants a select set of cases for processing from beginning to end. In this way, the assembly-line process system can be modified to capture some of the benefits of the integrated, trial team system. Even when this program is established within the trial team organizational model, it enhances the prosecutor's assignment capacity by letting him assign more experienced assistants to these priority prosecution programs, thereby giving the assistants access to more than a single court room or division.

Thus in the urban environment, characterized by a large staff of assistants and supporting personnel prosecuting a large volume of crime, the prosecutor has a number of approaches available to him. Although constrained to some extent by the structure of the court system, how he allocates his resources in an effective and efficient manner is an issue that grows in complexity as the size of the office grows.

**Uniform Processing of Large Caseloads.** The final issue addressed here that distinguishes the large-office prosecutor from his colleagues in smaller offices again is size related. It is the issue of uniform and consistent case processing. This issue is particularly appropriate to large offices (even though differential prosecution standards may be found in other offices) because the larger offices have more opportunities for breakdowns.

Ideally, uniformity is achieved when the prosecutor and his assistants all agree on the same method of handling a case so that it reaches the same desired outcome. This ideal state is rarely attained even in the smallest offices, if only because of personal preferences and individual opinions. But it can be approached. In the smaller offices the prosecutor, as chief policy maker, is aware of any decisions that deviate from his policy position and can take corrective action if he thinks it is necessary.

As the office grows in size, direct line authority disperses. Its delegation to an ever-increasing number of assistants only underscores the potential for breakdowns in the uniform processing of cases. Georgetown University's nationwide study on plea bargaining recognized the dimensions of this problem and laid the primary cause to a lack of "internal accountability."[39] Based on their work they found that "there are few office policies relating to accountability of assistants. There are few enforced systematic procedures for internal review of decisions [that is, written documentation as to who authorized the decision and the grounds for it]." They worry about the procedures available for developing and ensuring uniformity in decision making, and they express their concern thusly: "If office policies are to have meaning and the chief prosecutor is to be the chief policy setter for the office, such internal accountability is a necessity. . . . By and large this type of internal accountability does not exist in many prosecutors' offices."[40]

Uniformity in case processing cannot be achieved unless there is a degree of accountability imposed on the prosecutor's system. We have seen that of the two basic organizational models, the process model has the greatest need for this because cases pass from one process point of responsibility to another. The integrated, trial team model needs more assurance of uniformity among the courtroom teams than within the teams.

The larger the office is, the higher is the probability of problems with the uniform processing of cases. Indeed, many prosecutors feel that if they can make uniform charging decisions, that by itself is a success. A symptomatic indicator of this unevenness is "assistant shopping," a practice whereby the arresting police office or the detective will wait until an assistant who agrees with or is amenable to his arresting philosophy is free to review his case for a charging decision. Instead of going to any assistant for review and screening, he shops around for the "hardest," "most liberal," the "softest" or any other superlatives that will suit his biases. For example, one assistant may be adverse to prosecuting homosexual cases, another one may not be.

Just as judge shopping is frowned on, so too is assistant shopping. Strangely the attempts to control this abuse have not been directed at the knotty problem of ensuring uniformity and consistency in decision making, rather they have been directed at minimizing its occurrence. This is frequently achieved by designating access to the charging assistants on a first-come, first-serve basis. The corridor to the assistant's cubicles may be guarded by a clerk who directs traffic to the assistants. This may ensure a random distribution of any potential charging bias, but it does not exclude bias or ensure the uniform handling of cases or charging decisions.

Decisions regarding the processing of cases are made a number of times as cases travel through the system. Without clearly stated policy and guidelines for implementing policy and articulated priorities, the decisions made by assistants operating in a large-office environment may not necessarily conform to prosecutorial policy.

Uniformity becomes an issue in this environment because it presupposes that not all cases will go to trial and that other methods of disposition are both available and desirable. Indeed, if all cases were to go to trial the community could not bear the costs of this procedure. The recent New York City Bar Association study of the state's narcotics law that imposed mandatory sentences and no plea reduction concluded in part that: "certain types of narcotics use have increased and that criminal court systems have become hopelessly clogged with prolonged trials that might have been avoided without the drug law."[41]

Because the prosecutor's discretionary power encompasses the right to prosecute as much as the right not to prosecute, and because discretionary power may be delegated to a number of assistants at different points in the processing system, the charging decision is not the only decision that needs attention. Selective prosecution policies have been endorsed by many prosecutors, sometimes to alleviate volume, sometimes to protect the community. For example, it is common to question whether a youthful defendant caught joy riding in a stolen car should receive full prosecutorial attention in contrast to a youthful defendant operating with an organized auto theft ring.

At the other extreme is the aggressive stance taken by prosecutors with regard to certain heinous crimes, crimes that threaten public safety and notorious criminals. The most publicized program addressing these problems today is the career criminal program. Viewed from a caseload perspective, the career criminal program directs scarce prosecutorial resources to those defendants who are considered to be most dangerous to the community because of either their current actions or their past history. In the largest offices, where not all cases can be handled with the same degree of expertise or attention and where the court system is so jammed that only a fixed number of cases can be processed, the need to apply a selection strategy that is fair is clear.

The aim of uniformity in case processing is not one of equality. It is one of distributing justice fairly. In a large office with a high staff turnover rate, uniformity is a never-ending issue of concern. The NAAG report noted that "turnover is one of the major problems which limits the development of prosecutorial expertise."[42] We can carry this statement a step farther by stating that it also limits the implementation of a uniform policy. Uniformity in decision making is the primary issue forced to the front for the urban prosecutor, even though it may not be recognized as such by the prosecutor himself.

*The Suburban Prosecutor*

The recipient of the changing population patterns in the United States was suburbia. About thirty years ago (1946) the so-called flight to the suburbs began. The suburbs in those days were not the economically and socially identifiable groupings of the mid-seventies. Whyte described them as, "urban sprawl and created because of a traditional American nostalgia for the small provincial town as the natural home of democracy."[43] Poorly designed, with bad aesthetics, the sprawl imposed single-family housing on subdivided farmland and pasture. Suburban housing shared common boundaries with the treeless fields and grazing cows.

The transformation of sprawl into suburbia occurred slowly. Supporting the movement was the federal government with its 90/10 highway funding that developed thruways, freeways, highways, and beltways, that ultimately turned bedroom communities into economically self-sufficient jurisdictions. The improved communications and transportation systems, and the desire for homeownership contrasted with the crowded living of the city, its anonymity and impersonality, all led to the development of a middle-class way of life in the suburbs.

In the 1950s and 1960s the stereotype of suburbia was flourishing:

> There are images of winding streets, two-car garages, bicycles, ranch type schools, much "neighboring," evening bridge, child-raising by Spock, the morning stationwagon race of commuters for the 7:12 train, active participation in local civic affairs. . . . Residents are supposed to be similar in age, income, occupation, education, position in the family cycle, and type of housing. These similarities are supposed to bind the residents together to strengthen a sense of community.[44]

Studies of suburban societies showed that, although they combined some parts of both urban and rural societies, they tended to combine into fairly homogenous groups and could be classified into models differentiated by social class, age, occupation, education, place in family cycle, and so forth.[45] This effect was not irrelevant to crime distributions. The socioeconomic homogeniety of the suburban community produced crime patterns that distinguished it from other suburban communities with different socioeconomic environments. For example, crime in an affluent community is typically characterized by crimes against property. These involve burglary, breaking and entering, and other offenses related to obtaining valuable property. In the poorer communities, crime assumes a more personal face. The violence associated with poverty results in a marked increase in armed robberies, assaults, weapons charges, and the like. Quinney reports higher murder and aggravated assault rates are associated with lower levels of schooling, family income, and the proportion of males in occupations other than white-collar.[46] Where communities are still primarily homogenous in socioeconomic status, the type of prevalent crime is rather predictable.

There are indications that this situation is changing. As the services provided by the suburbs become more attractive than those offered by a poverty-stricken inner city, as industry moves to the beltway fringes, the bedroom community for the urban area becomes economically viable and self-sufficient. It was only in the 1970s, for example, that enough industry and services had shifted to Montgomery County, Maryland (a suburb of Washington, D.C.) that for the first time more than 50 percent of the population resided in the same county that it worked in. With such relocations comes a heterogeneity in population mix as well as crime. In Skogan's study spanning 25 years, he found that "crime 'relocated' itself to the same areas where suburbs grew."[47]

The growth in population and the effects of suburbanization took their toll on prosecution. The once rural prosecutor, who knew most of the county-folk by name and farm, without much preparation and sometimes within a 4-year term of office, become a suburban prosecutor. The biggest result of this population shift was a growth in the size of his office. Between 1970 and 1975 the prosecutor in Howard County, Maryland, saw the population grow from 63,394 to 97,994 when the new town of Columbia was developed. During this period, the size of his office tripled from two to six assistants.

The suburban prosecutors have the shortest history of all the different types of prosecutive systems. Their 25- to 30-year existence has been primarily involved with change. Much of this is related to the multidimensional effects associated with growth. The suburban prosecutor operates within an environment of change that is generally supportive because the increasing population brought about expanding tax bases that were able to provide expanded services—schools, roads, trash collection, parks, and finally prosecution.

The community support provided by the ample tax base permitted experimentation and innovation. The concept of change was embraced by the prosecutor as well as the community, resulting in new forms for the delivery of prosecution services and the evaluation of the effectiveness of these programs. Improved training courses were developed, and funds were made available for the suburban prosecutor and his staff to attend conferences and serve as members of task forces. His perception of his role became less parochial, less wedded to the traditional way of doing things (his rural tradition was vanishing), and, in this financially and socially supportive environment, he became the innovator in the prosecutorial universe.

The role of the suburban prosecutor is emerging as one of the most important of all the groups we have examined. Since his development and roots are enmeshed in change, his acceptance of his responsibility as a leader in improving the criminal justice system is often not even due to a conscious effort on his part. Because the suburban prosecutor still operates within a relatively homogenous society, his policy about the nature and purpose of prosecution is rather easily established. A community composed of affluent, well-educated, high-income residents generally expects more of a defendant-oriented, treatment approach to prosecution, than do the residents of a blue-collar, working community.

A major distinguishing characteristic of the suburban prosecutor is his ability to be flexible within a socially stable environment. Yet the very stability of his community may paradoxically inhibit his ability to respond to changes in the community's population mix. One can worry, if crime does indeed "relocate," whether the suburban prosecutor will be able to adapt. It should be that, of all the prosecutive types considered here, the years of experimentation, evaluation, growth, and changes endured should provide a strong base for adjustment.

Yet not all prosecutors survived the change from the halcyon days of rural America to suburban growth. As the workload increased, so too did the staff. No longer were the assistants social friends. The emerging bureaucracy meant that the informal daily contacts lessened. Staff meetings became a necessity (although it was still not uncommon to be able to discuss the entire case docket for any given day with personal knowledge of each case). Assembly-line processing was yet to emerge—but its foreshadowing was clear. Often the cutting line between small-office informality and the need for organizational and management structure was articulated when the complaint by the prosecutor was simply stated as "it isn't any fun any more." Yet those prosecutors who were able to move ahead, who could delegate authority while controlling for uniformity, and who could structure their office more formally are now the recipients of the most enviable positions in the prosecution world.

Unlike the urban prosecutor, he does not deal with an endless array of the poor, unemployed, and undereducated who pass anonymously through the overloaded court system. Unlike the rural prosecutor, he does not operate in a community where all its members are known to him and its history a part of him. Straddling both extremes, the suburban prosecutor reflects the widest ranges of policy and value systems. For the time being the homogeneity of the socioeconomic structure in suburbia presents a good social laboratory for observing the effects of population on prosecution. It is unfortunate that the role of the suburban prosecutor has not been systematically examined since it may shed light on the power of community to shape prosecutorial priorities.

## The Effect of Special Population Groups

While there has been little systematic attention paid to the effect of population on prosecution, there has been even less paid to the effect of special population groups on crime and consequently prosecution. Conversations with the prosecutors give recognition to the problems caused by special population groups. Some early unpublished work of the Michigan Prosecuting Attorneys Association (1972) led investigators to suspect that there were differential effects emanating from these groups.[48] As a result, in 1972, the National Center for Prosecution Management incorporated into its study a question probing for further substantiation of these factors. The question was very generally posed:

Is your office affected (either by increased workload or increased population) through the existence of:
1. a resident college or university
2. military base
3. significant recreation or resort population
4. state hospital or prison
5. significant migrant worker population; or
6. significant welfare population?

The NCPM analysis showed that there was a significant relationship between some of these groups and the prosecutors' caseloads. The presence of military bases and welfare populations contributed to an increase in the prosecutors workload, whereas the presence of recreation/resort populations and resident colleges decreased the average felony caseload. Table 2-7 summarizes the findings. As table 2-7 shows, if a military base is present in a prosecutor's jurisdiction, he could expect, on the average, an increase in his felony caseload by approximately 366 cases a year more than would be predicted by the census resident population. Similarly, if there was a significantly large welfare population in the jurisdiction, the felony caseload would increase over the expected average by an average of 214 cases a year.

On the other hand, if the jurisdiction had a significant recreation or resort population, then the felony caseload would tend to be less than expected by an average of 289 felonies a year. The reason for this expected decrease is unclear. It may be that a recreation or resort area attracts a more monied (hence law-abiding) class of persons than the census resident population. On the other hand, it may be that the youth attracted to these areas create a different set of law enforcement standards.

Table 2-7
Average Change to Felony Caseload Due to Special Population Groups

| Population Groups | Average Change over Average Annual Felony Workload |
|---|---|
| Military base | +366 |
| Welfare population | +214 |
| Recreation/resort | −289 |
| Resident college or university | −217 |
| State hospitals or prisons[a] | |
| Migrant workers[a] | |

Source: National Center for Prosecution Management, *First Annual Report* (Washington, D.C.: National Center for Prosecution Management, 1972), p. 43.
[a]No significant change.

If the prosecutor's jurisdiction includes a resident college or university, then on the average, a decrease of 217 felonies per year can be expected. Again, reasons for this decrease may vary by other factors: one of which may be that the colleges tend to internalize their own affairs using college police rather than the local police department along with other forms of administrative and disciplinary control. A second factor may be that the social class of persons attending college would tend to have a higher income than the general average census resident population for the particular area.

The two other areas examined for impact, state hospital or prisons and migrant worker populations, did not produce any significant effect on the felony workload as predicted by the census resident population. Therefore, preliminary analysis indicates that the population can be used to predict felony workload in the prosecutor's office and that the existence of special population groups can cause the expected workload to change significantly.

## Conclusion

What we have attempted to show is the overpowering effect of population and the demographic characteristics of the community on the nature and character of prosecution in the United States. These, more than any other factors over which the prosecutor has no control, influence the type of prosecutive system established in a community. This can be most clearly demonstrated by examining the differences in the issues that face three broad categories of prosecution: the rural or small-town prosecutive systems, urban, and suburban.

The rural or small-town prosecutive system operates with an extremely small criminal caseload, usually not enough to support full-time prosecutors or assistants. As a result the system has responded by either permitting the prosecutor to maintain a private practice or by expanding the prosecutor's duties into the civil area. Because of these situations the basic concerns of prosecutors in small office environments are conflict of interest and a lack of system flexibility resulting from limited resources.

The urban prosecutor, in contrast, processes large volumes of assorted crimes by means of complex organizations and institutionalized procedures. Because authority and decision making are delegated throughout the process, the primary issue of ensuring uniformity in decision making is created. Secondary considerations confronting the urban prosecutor focus on how best to allocate the resources in the office and how to use alternatives to adjudication to reduce the workload.

The suburban prosecutor presents a most interesting role, since he is a new phenomenon who has already seen, sometimes in less than a generation, the office shift from small-town, to bedroom community, to an economically viable unit of government (generally county). The primary issue facing the suburban prosecutor is that of coping with change. As the urbanization of the suburbs continues, and with increasing population growth, one can expect to see this prosecutor emerge as a dominant force among the three. With a supportive and growing tax base and a relatively homogenous socioeconomic community, the prosecutor in suburbia offers a fortunate opportunity to study the role of the American prosecutor within a social context.

The real impact of demographic characteristics on the prosecutive systems and the need for further exploration of demography as it may predict criminal prosecution behavior is clearly demonstrated. Finally, it is now essential that before any study is made of the prosecutor and prosecutive systems the effect of population be taken into consideration. Without this consideration, a complete analysis is simply not possible.

**Notes**

1. Compare various approaches in Lane W. Lancaster, *Government in Rural America*, 2d ed. (Princeton, N.J.: D. Van Norstand, 1952); Frank W. Martin *Diary of a D.A.* (New York: Henry Holt, 1960); David Neubauer, *Criminal Justice in Middle America* (Morristown, N.J.: General Learning Press, 1974) with respect to treatment of the effects of population on local government institutions.

2. Definitions of rural and urban were taken from the U.S. Bureau of the Census, *Historical Statistics of the United States, Colonial Times to 1970*, bicentennial ed., part 2 (Washington, D.C.: U.S. Government Printing Office, 1975).

3. This discussion is drawn extensively from Wesley G. Skogan, "The Changing Distribution of Big-City Crime: A Multi-City Times-Series Analysis," *Urban Affairs Quarterly* 13, no. 1 (September 1977):43.

4. William H. Whyte, Jr., "Urban Sprawl," in *The Exploding Metropolis*, ed. Fortune Editorial Staff (Garden City, N.Y.: Doubleday, 1958), pp. 117-124.

5. Peter Blake, *God's Own Junkyard* (New York: Holt, Rhinehart and Winston, 1974), p. 17.

6. Whyte, "Urban Sprawl," pp. 117-124.

7. Skogan, "Changing Distribution," p. 43.

8. Karl E. Taueber and Alma F. Taueber, "White Migration and Socioeconomic Differences between Cities and Suburbs," *American Sociological Review* 29 (October 1964):718-729.

9. Skogan, "Changing Distribution," p. 47.

10. Louis Wirth, "Urbanism as a Way of Life," *American Journal of Sociology* 44 (July 1938):1-24.

11. President's Commission on Law Enforcement and the Administration of Criminal Justice, *Task Force Report: The Courts* (Washington, D.C.: U.S. Government Printing Office, 1967), p. 73.

12. Skogan, "Changing Distribution," p. 934.

13. James F. Kain, "The Distribution and Movement of Jobs and Industry," in *The Metropolitan Enigma*, ed. James Q. Wilson (Cambridge, Mass.: Harvard University Press, 1968), pp. 27-29.

14. Ibid., p. 943.

15. National District Attorneys Association (NDAA), *National Prosecution Standards* (Chicago: National District Attorneys Association, 1977), p. 12.

16. National Association of Attorneys General (NAAG), *The Prosecution Function: Local Prosecutors and the Attorney General* (Raleigh, N.C.: The National Association of Attorneys General, 1974), p. 8.

17. National Center for Prosecution Management (NCPM), *First Annual Report* (Washington, D.C.: National Center for Prosecution Management, 1972).

18. NAAG, *Prosecution Function*, p. 10.

19. Daniel L. Skoler, *Organizing the Non-System* (Lexington, Mass.: Lexington Books, D.C. Heath, 1977), chap. 5.

20. NAAG, *Prosecution Function*, p. 6.

21. NDAA, *National Prosecution Standards*, Standard 1.3, p. 9.

22. NCPM, *First Annual Report*, p. 40.

23. American Bar Association Project on Standards for the Criminal Justice System, *The Prosecution Function* (New York: The American Bar Association, 1970), approved draft, p. 60.

24. *Constitution of the State of Illinois*, art. 6, sec. 19; *Statutes of the State of Illinois* (1970), chap. 14, sec. 5.

25. John T. Hammond, "Other Duties of the Prosecutor," *Michigan State Bar Journal* (January 1972):40-45.

26. California District Attorneys Association, *Uniform Crime Charging Standards* (Sacramento, Calif., 1974), p. 54.

27. National Center for Prosecution Management, *Handbook of the Rural and Small Office Prosecutor* (Washington, D.C.: National Center for Prosecution Management, 1974).

28. NDAA, *National Prosecution Standards*, p. 9.

29. NAAG, *Prosecution Function*, p. 10.

30. President's Commission, *Courts*, p. 73.

31. NAAG, *Prosecution Function*, n. 22, p. 8.

32. NDAA, *National Prosecution Standards*, app. 1-11, p. 19.

33. NCPM, *First Annual Report*, p. 54.

34. See Joan E. Jacoby, *Snapshot Spin Around: A Technique to Measure Capacity in a Prosecutor's Office* (Washington, D.C.: National Center for Prosecution Management, 1973), p. 5.

35. Robert B. Morgan and C. Edward Alexander, "A Survey of Local Prosecutors," *State Government* 47 (1974):42-43.

36. NDAA, *National Prosecution Standards*, p. 126.

37. American Bar Association, Commission on Correction Facilities and Services, "Legal Issues and Characteristics of Pretrial Intervention Programs" 4 Capital University Law Review 37, 38 (1975).

38. American Bar Association, Commission on Correction Facilities and Services, *Sourcebook in Pretrial Criminal Justice Intervention Techniques and Action Programs* (Washington, D.C.: The American Bar Association, 1974).

39. Georgetown University Institute of Criminal Law and Procedure, *Plea Bargaining in the United States, Phase 1 Report* (Washington, D.C.: April 1977), p. 3.

40. Ibid., p. 12.

41. "N.Y. Drug Crackdown Called a Failure," *The Washington Post*, 22 June 1977, p. a-3.

42. NAAG, *Prosecution Function*, pp. 12-13.

43. Elmer H. Johnson, *Social Problems of Urban Man* (Homewood, Ill: Dorsey Press, 1973), p. 83.

44. Ibid., pp. 84-86.

45. S.D. Clark, *The Suburban Society* (Toronto: University of Toronto Press, 1966), pp. 8-13.

46. Richard Quinney, "Structural Characteristics, Population, Area and Crime Rates in the United States," 57 Journal of Criminal Law, Criminology and Police Science 49 (1966).

47. Skogan, "Changing Distribution," p. 16.

48. NCPM, *First Annual Report*, p. 50.

# 3 The Effect of Defense Systems on Prosecution

## The Changing Requirements for Defense Representation

The U.S. Supreme Court has consistently increased the scope of the right to counsel afforded indigents by the Sixth Amendment when read in conjunction with the due process clause of the Fourteenth Amendment. In a long series of cases beginning with *Powell* v. *Alabama*[1] in 1932 and climaxing with *Argersinger* v. *Hamlin*[2] in 1972 the right to counsel has been extended from a narrow federal court requirement to cover practically all state and local misdemeanor prosecution. Starting in 1932, *Powell* dictated that there was an inherent right to counsel in all capital cases tried in federal courts. In 1938, the court extended that right to federal felonies by its decision in *Johnson* v. *Zerbst*.[3] This situation was to remain virtually unchanged for almost twenty-five years until the 1960s when the Warren Court issued a wave of decisions that were to have profound effect on the extent of defense representation and substantially alter our American system of criminal justice.

In 1960, in *McNeal* v. *Culver*, the Court extended the right to counsel to cases less than capital that were "complex" and where the defendant requested the assistance of counsel.[4] *Carnley* v. *Cochran*, in the following year, obviated the need for the defendant to make the request for assistance in those complex cases defined in *McNeal*.[5]

The true landmark decision in the area of an indigent's right to counsel was made in 1963 when the Court held in *Gideon* v. *Wainwright*[6] that the defendant had a right to counsel in all felony cases, including state crimes. Although many states had preceded *Gideon* by providing counsel to those citizens who could not afford private counsel, the *Gideon* decision guaranteed the participation of counsel as a right of all citizens who were accused of serious crimes: "any person hailed into court, who is too poor to hire a lawyer."[7]

The extension of the coverage provided by the *Gideon* decision from felonies to misdemeanors did not occur until almost ten years later when the Court held, in *Argersinger* v. *Hamlin* that "absent a knowing and intelligent waiver, no person may be imprisoned for any offense, whether classified as petty, misdeameanor or felony, unless he was represented by counsel at his trial."[8] With this ruling the right to counsel was extended to all cases that were punishable by imprisonment. Right to counsel was no longer limited to statutory definitions such as "misdemeanor," "felony," "petty," "major," "minor," or the like. In the course of implementation, the generally accepted criterion for determining right to counsel became whether the defendant was placed in jeopardy of imprisonment for a period of 6 months or more.

While the Court, from *Gideon* through *Argersinger* defined the rights of the accused, rich or poor, to representation by counsel at trial, it also considered the various processing steps in the criminal justice system and made decisions that specified these same rights at "critical stages" of the criminal process. The right to counsel was mandated at preliminary hearings where the defendant's admissions were used against him by *White* v. *Maryland*[9] and then extended to cover all preliminary hearings in *Coleman* v. *Alabama*.[10]

Counsel was also guaranteed at police investigation (*Escobedo* v. *Illinois*)[11] at police questioning (*Miranda* v. *Arizona*)[12], at postindictment police lineups (*United States* v. *Wade*)[13], on appeal (*Douglas* v. *California*)[14], and at probation revocation proceedings (*Mempa* v. *Ray*).[15] Counsel was also guaranteed for juvenile defendants in certain types of cases and situations, (*In re Gault*).[16]

The holding by the Supreme Court that indigents had a right to representation in all cases and at all critical stages did not, however, immediately or necessarily insure that all defendants would receive aggressive or even adequate defense representation. First, there were very few criminal defense lawyers to provide these services. A survey conducted in 1966 showed that of the better than 313,000 lawyers licensed nationally (of whom two-thirds were engaged in private practice), only about 2,500 to 5,000 could be considered criminal lawyers.[17] Yet, at the same time, 2,750 countries in the United States were appointing lawyers from the private bar to provide indigent defense services. Obviously, the supply of experienced criminal defense lawyers was inadequate, and this raised serious doubts as to the quality and uniformity of publicly provided defense counsel. A second problem that arose concerned the types of defense systems that were created or modified to respond to the court's rulings. Different jurisdictions developed their own distinctive configuration, a situation that has produced ambiguous, if not ambivalent, results. To this day, no ideal system has been identified. A diversity of operational and structural types pervade the defense function, making it as disparate as the prosecution.

## Types of Defense Systems in the United States

As a result of the Supreme Court's mandates, publicly provided defense services for the indigent are a reality. They have taken two basic organizational forms, a defender organization or an assigned counsel system. Within each of these there are a number of operational variations employed by different localities.

In its pure form, the defender organization, like its counterpart the prosecutor's office, functions as a public law firm with a single mission—to provide defense services to indigents within the jurisdiction. As an organizational entity, it provides these services under policy direction from an administrator and within a bureaucratic framework of operating procedures, administrative support, and management review. Its size generally varies, depending on local volume of work and on the amount of money budgeted for operation.

The assigned counsel system, on the other hand, is a system in concept only, composed of unrelated individual members of the private bar, who are assigned indigent clients on an ad hoc basis by the court. Assigned cases may be distributed among the entire private bar or only to those members with a willingness to defend criminal cases. Since the system does not require an organization, there generally are no centralized policy makers nor centralized support services. Each lawyer assigned to defend an indigent client operates by himself, drawing on the resources of his private practice as necessary. His services are reimbursed according to some predetermined rate or schedule, usually from a part of the county's appropriation (normally a lump sum amount to the court).

Within these two basic forms, the various permutations that exist bear noting. The fact that so many configurations have come into existence provides a solid indication that neither system is ideal.

*Defender Organizations*

Although defender organizations are structurally similar, they may differ by type of funding source and the amount of independence they exercise. The most common defender organization is the public defender office, headed by a public official and supported by public funds. In some cases the public defender is an elected official (as in the city of Omaha, Nebraska, or in the judicial circuits of Florida). In other cases, he is appointed, very often by the judges of the circuit court, (as in Illinois). Some jurisdictions, believing that appointment by the court presents a conflict, specify that the members of the county commission appoint the public defender (as in California). Other states, seeking to minimize local control and its attendant problems, created a statewide defender system operating under a central statewide executive. In Colorado and New Jersey, for example, the state public defender has deputies assigned to each of the jurisdictions within the state.

Not all defender organizations are public bodies. Some are private agencies operating as private, nonprofit corporations, their basic financing provided by individual contributions or as part of a community fund. The executive officer of these private defender offices is appointed by the corporation's board of directors.

In other jurisdictions, the private nonprofit defender organizations receive their funding from such traditional public sources as the county and state budget. Akron Ohio's corporation is organized through the Akron Bar Association. The District of Columbia's private corporation, the Public Defender Service, receives public funds to perform local defense functions.

As an alternative to establishing a defender organization, other jurisdictions, such as Boise, Idaho, and Kalamazoo, Michigan, contract with law firms to provide indigent defense. These contracts are let on a one-time competitive bid for a predetermined period. The law firm or firms with the most acceptable bid enters into a contract with the city or county government.

Because of the organizational requirements for full-time employment, and the associated high costs of maintaining a full-time operation that characterizes a defender organization, defender offices have generally taken root only in the larger, metropolitan areas. Early studies concluded that such organizations would only be cost effective in jurisdictions with populations exceeding 400,000, although this assumption has recently been challenged.[18]

By 1974, there were approximately 650 various defender organizations operating in the United States. Their urbanized, large-office character is demonstrated by the fact that they provide indigent defense in only about 28 percent of all local jurisdictions, mostly the most populous areas of the country. Because they tend to operate in urbanized areas, the percentage of the total number of indigents handled by defender organizations is much higher than those handled under assigned counsel systems, even though assigned counsel systems are numerically more prevalent.[19]

*Assigned Counsel Systems*

Under the traditional assigned counsel procedure, the trial court appoints individual private attorneys to represent individual defendants as the need arises. This type of defense representation is most frequently used in the less populated areas of the United States, where the local government is financially less able to support and maintain defender organizations and where there is less pressing need for such an organization because of the relatively small criminal caseload in these jurisdictions. Under these circumstances using the private bar to occasionally defend a criminal case becomes a logical and reasonable way of providing for indigent defense services.

The differences in assigned counsel systems can be attributed largely to the different methods used to select the attorneys, which carry with them certain implications about the type of service. In some jurisdictions, the judge of the trial court chooses the attorney from a list of all private attorneys within the jurisdiction. Assignments are rotated so each attorney participates in the process. The rationale for this assignment procedure is the court's belief that it is in the general public interest to engage all members of the local bar in the process of providing indigent defense services. By this procedure, a more equitable distribution of legal resources is realized. This also minimizes the need to use only younger and less experienced members of the bar to provide criminal defense for the poor while the older, more experienced busy themselves with private practice.

A second prevalent assignment procedure used by the court is based on selection from a more limited list of those attorneys with criminal experience. Under certain circumstances this system has a number of drawbacks. In a high-volume court, it puts immense pressure on a small number of attorneys to shoulder the entire load of criminal indigent defense work. Because it requires criminal trial experience, it also limits the involvement of younger members of the bar, who may be eager to do the work but are effectively precluded from doing so.

To overcome the experience barrier and widen the available pool of legal talent, a third method of assignment is used. Based on a survey of the local bar, attorneys expressing an interest in being assigned these cases are listed. This procedure is generally popular with the bar, insuring good bench-bar relations, and is widely used, but it also has definite weaknesses. Most problematically, it supports the criticism that most indigent defense work will be performed by the least experienced or least successful members of the bar. Yet, in many areas, this procedure is viewed as a strong incentive for bringing young lawyers into rural or less populated areas. Without the monetary base provided by indigent defense work while they were establishing their private practice, many could not afford to move into these areas. Not surprisingly, however, this method is often opposed by individuals and groups who are concerned with the quality of defense services available to indigent citizens.

The method of assigning counsel that has proved popular with both the private bar and judicial reformers is the coordinated assigned counsel system. Here, the power to assign counsel is taken away from the judge of the trial court and placed in the hands of an administrator who assigns from a list of capable criminal lawyers in the local bar. The administrator exercises discretionary authority. He can limit his assignment to those attorneys with criminal experience or broaden it to include ones with less experience. In this way, the administrator can strike a balance between providing good legal defense while encouraging young attorneys to participate in the process.

By distributing cases based on their degree of seriousness and complexity, the younger attorneys may be included in the pool of legal talent available and gain experience over time.

Although these same options are open to the judge of the trial court, there are more advantages if an administrator performs them. First, an administrator has more time to monitor the flow of cases and to schedule the attorneys. Second, any possible conflicts that might arise when the judge who assigns counsel must hear the subsequent litigation are avoided. Third, by funneling all assignments through one administrator, the caseloads of all attorneys can be viewed as a totality. This last advantage supports the development of standards for criminal defense and creates a mechanism for evaluating defense attorney performance.

Unfortunately, for all its advantages the coordinated assigned counsel system usually does not succeed in very small jurisdictions. The very cost of hiring an administrator out of local government funds may well be a barrier. Coupled with a low demand for defense representation because of low crime rates and even a limited supply of attorneys, the small jurisdictions must rely on the other forms of assignment. Because of these factors, assigned counsel systems can be found in the vast majority of the American local jurisdictions. Yet, the percentage of total indigents serviced by these systems is smaller than defender organizations because the jurisdictions employing this approach are generally rural or more sparsely populated.

## Public Funding of Defense Systems

Since the 1963 *Gideon* decision, the inherent right of counsel for the indigent accused established a policy of public financing for defense services. However, the adoption and implementation of funding procedures have been both slow and erratic. As late as 1975 a study showed that proportionately very little money was allocated for the defense of the indigent population.[20] The largest proportions of the monies available are gleaned from state or local sources. Local sources provided nearly 73 percent of the money used to provide indigent defense services in the state courts with states contributing about 20 percent and various federal monies accounting for the other 7 percent. Despite the predominantly local funding procedure, the level of funding is very low. Less than 1 percent (0.7) of all monies spent by local governments on criminal justice programs were directed for defense services. The state's 20 percent contribution actually represents less than 0.4 percent of the monies spent by the state on criminal justice programs.

Another study conducted by Dr. Paul Wice examined the sources of funding available for public defender programs. Wice's survey of defender programs in cities with populations greater than 50,000 reported that the majority of funds (about 55 percent) come directly from local funding sources. On the average, the federal government provided approximately 17 percent of the funds for these programs, while the state contributed about 28 percent.[21]

It seems to make little difference whether defender offices are funded directly from the county treasury, or through a statewide, centrally directed and appropriated system. In either situation, the newly created offices have to compete with other agencies for the public dollar. Thus, it is not surprising to see limited funding in this area. Nevertheless, despite this handicap the mere fact that an organization has been created, provides the defense function with a flexibility not necessarily available to assigned counsel systems. This flexibility permits the adjustment of costs through the addition or deletion of support staff, the use of part-time versus full-time legal staff, and adjustments to space and equipment costs. In some cases, too, the public defender may obtain low-cost or free assistance from law school students and college interns as part of work-study training programs. Additionally, within the bureaucratic structure of the organization, an office has the ability to plan and the capacity to implement differential levels of service.

If funding has been difficult to obtain for defender offices, its availability for assigned counsel systems has been even more constrained. Generally speaking county funds for court-appointed counsel are appropriated as a lump sum budget item. Authority to disperse these funds is usually delegated to the court's presiding judge, generally under a predetermined payment plan. Under this arrangement, the presiding judge often assumes a control function by presenting the proposed budget for the next fiscal year, usually extrapolated from the prior year's budget.

If there is one constant to be found in examining compensation procedures among the states, it is that there is no uniformity. The closest one can come to making a generalized statement is that twenty-two states dictate that the fees be "reasonable" and the compensation be determined by the court. In Wisconsin reasonable is defined further as "comparable to fees of the private bar." Most of the remaining states have specified compensation in terms of hourly rates ranging from as low as $15 for work performed in court and $10 for work performed out of court to a high of $30 for in-court work and $20 for work out of court. Even the authority to establish fee schedules varies. To briefly illustrate, Connecticut's fee schedule is established by a state public defender service commission, whereas Ohio allows the county commissioners to establish the rates. Indiana's rate schedule is established by the state public defender with approval of the Supreme Court.

A number of states have attempted to control expenditures and abuses in individual billings by setting maximum payments allowable for various situations. Some states like Oklahoma and New Mexico make a distinction among rates with respect to whether the case goes to trial or not. Nevada's rates vary according to whether or not the crime charged is a misdemeanor or a felony. New Hampshire distinguishes between both the seriousness of the charge and the level of court where the case is heard. Those states that establish statutory maximums generally also make special provisions for additional payments for capital cases and for appeals to the Supreme Court. Some states stipulate maximum fees for special types of actions such as postconviction proceedings, juvenile cases, or mental health cases.

Currently, six states make no provision for reimbursement of appointed attorneys. Rhode Island does not need such a provision, since all indigent cases are handled by a statewide public defender system. Missouri, on the other hand, does not compensate appointed attorneys because it considers defense of the indigent as the rightful burden of the members of the bar. In *State ex. rel. Gentry* v. *Becker*, the Missouri courts held that an attorney could not decline an appointment to defend an indigent, and could not receive compensation if there was no statutory provision to compensate for such services.[22]

In general, it has been recognized that the appointed counsel system is one that uses the coercive powers of the court to force private attorneys to work for less than they are generally compensated. Most state case law has declared that attorneys cannot claim compensation above the established statutory limits even when they can show that they merit more payment. This detrimental effect on encouraging the participation of effective defense counsel has been recognized by many commentators.[23] The Supreme Court of New Jersey became so alarmed with the paltry compensations being offered in that state that it declared that assigned counsel had to be reimbursed at least 60 percent of actual expenses.[24] This is not a unique situation nor is it extravagant. A recent nationwide survey showed that assigned counsel generally received reimbursements totaling only 40 percent of reimbursements received by retained counsel.[25] A cautionary note must be interjected here, the fact the statutes specify compensation does not guarantee that funds have been appropriated to this service. In Orleans Parish, Louisiana, for example, statutory authority exists but, to date, money has never been appropriated to pay for the service.

In addition to compensation for assigned counsel, a few states recognizing the broader defense needs made provisions for compensating investigators, expert witnesses, and other special defense services. Presently seventeen states make some provision for payments of this type, the most common maximum limit being $300 per case. Some states restrict these services to capital cases, and almost all require prior approval of the court. Although Colorado has no direct statutory provision for payment of expert witnesses, the Colorado Revised Statutes, sec. 16-8-119, which dictates the reimbursement of court appointed counsel, have been interpreted by the courts to supply such a payment. In those states without specific provisions, the funds available for all these services in addition to legal representation can be drawn from the general assigned counsel fund, although they may be extremely difficult to get and only for the most unusual circumstances.

While various modes of compensation have been developed to control expenditures and minimize overcharging, other attempts have been made to control abuse of the indigent defense system by nonindigents. Even here, variation not uniformity is the rule although the circumstances are usually similar. These controls would by themselves not necessarily be a matter of concern here. Yet their effect on the private bar is such that they may become a major consideration in examining barriers to the degree of voluntary participation or the quality of representation. There are times when a court discovers that a defendant who has claimed indigency status does not, in fact, qualify under the standards set by the court for assigned counsel. If this is discovered before assigned counsel performs any work, then little is lost. However, where the discovery is made after services have been provided yet prior to payment of the attorney by the court, it is common practice for the court to instruct the lawyer to attempt to recoup his fees from the defendant through normal civil channels. This places additional hardship on the attorney who was assigned to represent the client and now must invest additional time to recoup any payment.

Some states such as South Dakota have a lien recoupment provision whereby the state, on designation of indigency, automatically places a lien against any property that the defendant might possess. In the case of fraud, the state has an established and recorded lien and is in the position to take action to recoup the amount of money that it cost to provide public counsel. However, there are weaknesses in many of these types of procedures. When the defendant has been assisted by the public defender, it is difficult to establish an independent case cost as the office is not geared to keep these types of financial figures. Also the enforcement of the lien falls to the responsibility of the county—most often, to the prosecuting attorney.

The fact that there is little recourse but to expend even more time and work to recoup expenses from nonindigents adds yet another barrier to the ability of a community or court system to recruit able defense counsel for the indigent. The quality of representation is greatly affected by the type of system used in a locality as is the nature of the criminal prosecution.

### Criminal Prosecution with Public Defender or Court-Assigned Systems

Despite wide variations that occur in structure and procedure among both public defender organization and assigned counsel systems, all forms of defense services can be examined for their functional impact. This impact can be measured in terms of the type of services offered as well as the type of prosecution response. One can hardly attribute any differences that exist between the two systems to differences among the personnel making up the system. Indeed, both systems draw from the legal profession, using attorneys produced from the same educational process. Given this similar professional base the differences that occur occur between the two types are a result of fundamental differences in system form and capabilities.

*Differences in Delivery of Services*

Each system has characteristically been thought to have its own particular set of strengths and weaknesses. Most jurisdictions, in selecting a system from the available alternatives, have tended to use system cost as the primary consideration; this has been particularly true for smaller jurisdictions. Still, much of the common wisdom about the relative strengths and weaknesses of each system has been questioned, pointing to a substantial need for additional study in this area.

The defender organization approach is most often justified by four key considerations:

1. In large jurisdictions, it is more economical.
2. The permanent staff of the public defender has more experience and competence in criminal matters than does assigned counsel.
3. Public defenders can enter the case processing at an earlier stage.
4. Public defenders have built in support services.

Even though these conditions exist in concept, they may not always be found in the real world. For example, the economic justification is supported by numerous studies showing that the public defender system costs less per case than an assigned counsel system. One national survey estimated that the public defender could provide defense at one-third the cost of the assigned system, another as high as 50 percent.[26] A New Jersey study estimated the public defender's cost at $178 per case, $103 lower than the assigned counsel cost.[27] A statewide public defender system for Maine was estimated to be able to save the state $200,000.[28]

A fundamental problem with these estimates is that they are based on current manpower allocations with the present public defender systems. Since no one yet has been able to develop a scientific standard for caseload for public defenders, public defenders may be handling more cases than they are capable of handling. If one uses the standards suggested by the National Advisory Commission and the Airlie House Conference of approximately

150 felonies or 400 misdemeanors per year per defender, it appears that the national average at the present time is 16 to 20 percent higher than those standards. To justify selecting a defender organization on the low cost per case data may be misleading, since the data may reflect an overload thereby reducing its ability to provide effective counsel.

Similar problems exist in the other areas. Although the defender organization is composed of assistants who handle only criminal cases, they may indeed be neither experienced nor competent. Studies have shown that the problems most commonly plaguing defender programs are the lack of experience and training among staff members. Most defender programs are low paying, attract young, inexperienced attorneys, and have very high turnover rates. Many programs employ attorneys on a part-time basis, forcing these assistants into developing private practices concurrent with their criminal defense duties.[29]

Similarly, the fact that defender organizations can enter the process earlier than assigned counsel is touted as a benefit of a public defender system. And indeed, such a procedure, used properly, provides added protection to the defendant especially with regard to bond or bail decisions. The earlier the involvement by defense counsel the better the likelihood for speedy dispositions. If defense counsel are present even when charging decisions are made, an alibi or other salient facts may be presented to change the nature of the prosecutorial decision. With court-appointed defense counsel, however, it is obvious that until a court hearing has been held no such presentation can be made. Not all systems are so ideal, however. In many instances, the public defender does not get involved as early as he might because of inability to represent an indigent client until official appointment from the bench. Thus, they lose the initiative in the same way as court-appointed attorneys.

Under ideal conditions, the defender organization is provided with substantial clerical and investigative support. In reality 83 percent of all public defenders have no investigators.[30] This finding reflects the reality that while there are a number of good and effective defender programs, they are, on the whole, underfinanced. This has led to serious and sometimes ludicrous results. In 1974, the federal court in the District of Columbia, appalled by the onerous caseloads being shouldered by the assistant public defenders, established maximum caseloads. It was not long thereafter that the court had to stop assigning cases because every public defender already had reached the quota.[31]

Paul Ligda, writing on the problems of defender caseloads, decried the fact that defender budgets were so low that staff attorneys were forced to take more cases than they could reasonably be expected to handle.[32] Paul Wice has commented that, despite the establishment of standards, "the nation's public defender programs are falling short."[33] Until funding levels

reach a degree of reality, reducing attorney caseload as well as providing increased support in the clerical and investigative areas, this advantage over
assigned counsel system may be more myth and hope than reality.

The assigned counsel system is also attributed with its own advantages.
Those most often mentioned are:

1.  It is cheaper in smaller jurisdictions.
2.  The court can appoint experienced criminal lawyers from the bar, and
    therefore there is no training at the expense of the defendant.
3.  Assigned attorneys handle fewer cases than public defenders and
    therefore can give more individual attention to each case.
4.  The participation of the private bar in indigent cases provides for a
    watch dog for the interests of the indigents.
5.  The privately assigned counsel are more independent from government
    control than public defenders.

Once again there is great variation in how the actual systems conform to
this idealized characterization. Almost without exception, it is a less expensive way to operate in small jurisdictions with a limited pool of attorneys.
However, the other claims are not necessarily automatically achieved. A
study of assigned counsel systems in Indiana showed that in one county they
performed extremely well, whereas in a second county they did not. The difference in performance seemed to be due to selection procedures. The first
county restricted appointments to experienced members of the bar; the second appointed at random.[34] There is no guarantee that appointed counsel
are experienced. For the most part, it does not appear that assigned counsel
systems provide top flight criminal trial attorneys. One cannot ignore the
simple fact that even today there is a conspicuous lack of criminal trial attorneys in the country.[35] From this group, few can be found practicing in
the predominantly rural areas where most assigned counsel systems exist.

A national survey of defender systems conducted in 1974 produced
some ominous facts about the state of assigned counsel systems in this country. Very few of those assigned considered themselves criminal lawyers or
had criminal trial experience or training. Only 1 percent of all assigned
counsel identified themselves as criminal lawyers; 20 percent had never
handled a single criminal jury trial; 75 percent had never attended a training
session or seminar in criminal defense.[36] In fact, there is strong evidence to
suggest that judges tend to appoint those lawyers with the least experience
to handle indigent cases rather than experienced counsel.

This action is not without a rationale. In many areas, the indigent
defense caseload is seen as the province of the new attorney who needs support while he develops his own practice. An Oregon study showed that the
lawyers who were most often retained privately were the least assigned, and

those with the fewest private clients were assigned most often. The "indigent bar" had almost ten years less experience than the general bar average. Those lawyers rated most competent by the local judges were the same lawyers who were least often appointed to indigent cases; those rated least competent were most often appointed.[37]

In general, these statistics and studies place in doubt the assumptions that assigned counsel are more experienced, or perform a watchdog function, or are more independent than the public defender. Nor do they substantiate claims for lower caseloads or more individual attention to cases. In fact it appears that the overriding reasons for utilizing assigned counsel systems are economic rather than qualitative concerns about the better delivery of services.

This raises the very serious problem of a lack of control over the quality of defense representation created under the court-assigned system. In the private sector, few organizational controls exist to monitor defense counsel's work, to review and evaluate his performance, and to provide sanctions for poor performance. Without a centralized process available to perform these functions, evaluation is based on an individual judge's assessment of the defense counsel's worth or on the attorney's reputation. It is clear that sanctions, in addition to complaints to the local bar association, need to be devised to identify the clearly incompetent or inexperienced attorney.

*Differences in Structure*

The differentiating characteristics between the defender organization and court-assigned systems for defense representation are structural. The structure and composition of these two basic defense delivery systems force special responses in the criminal justice system. Since defense services interact with the other components of the justice system, the effect of the structural differences can be observed most clearly in terms of these interactions and the underlying motivations and goals that are pursued within the two structures.

The assigned counsel system by definition uses attorneys on a part-time, sporadic basis in contrast to the generally full-time representation provided by defender organizations. With few exceptions, the occasional use of court-assigned counsel is a result of basically two conditions. Either the criminal caseload is not large enough to financially support ongoing activity (this is true in the less populated areas) or the court-appointed lawyer is used in conjunction with the public defender system. In Washington, D.C., for example, 15 percent of the cases are represented by the Public Defender Service and the remaining 85 percent by assigned counsel.

Unless the caseload is large enough to support assigned counsel on a continuous almost full-time equivalent basis, then one can reasonably assume that these assignments are imposed on other ongoing activities. For the attorney with a private practice focusing on torts or wills, contracts or patents, his civil practice represents his major source of income and, of course, dictates the priorities of his activity. Thus when a criminal case is imposed on ongoing civil practice, certain effects are predictable.

The primary effect is the economic impact of the assignment on the attorney. We have seen that the criminal case is billable at about 60 percent or less of the attorney's normal rate. Under these circumstances, one cannot expect the representation to be given higher priority than other cases in the office. Where the law office is sizable, it is not unusual to find cases passed on to younger, less experienced attorneys for preparation simply because his time is billable at a lower rate. The economics of case preparation and trial dictate that where defense services are handled on an occasional basis by attorneys not necessarily experienced in criminal matters and compensated at a lower rate, a trial-supportive environment is unlikely to exist. The lack of support is particularly aggravated in the largest firms, where even the overhead costs cannot be met by the assigned case compensation. Even where the attorney works alone or in a two- or three-man firm, with the low billing rates authorized by the courts, the primary concern becomes one of not losing money.

Whereas the economics of the system direct certain organizational responses in terms of case assignment and processing priorities, the addition of criminal court involvement to the ongoing court business may complicate case scheduling. The business of a law firm or an attorney may involve dealing with a number of courts or agencies representing varied jurisdictions. With a civil practice an attorney may be found in civil courts, appellate courts, or regulatory agencies. Each of these courts maintains its own schedule in which the lawyer must work. As the number of court systems increases so too does the potential for conflicts of schedules. A firm with an ongoing civil practice has to adjust its schedule to include the docketing of criminal cases. The more complicated these scheduling processes become, the greater is the chance for delay or system breakdown. It is not uncommon in most jurisdictions to continue a criminal case because the lawyer has to be in another court on another case.

If the criminal caseload is large enough to support a full-time ongoing activity in criminal defense representations and if the public defender system is not used or does not absorb a large amount of work in a jurisdiction, law firms specializing in criminal matters are formed. These firms tend to represent a mix of both privately retained cases and court assigned. They may even take on all the organizational aspects of a public defender system with one difference: they are private and profit making. In addition to the creation of the criminal law firm, the court-appointed system may be supported by the solo practitioners. Described as "lawyer regulars" by Abraham Blumberg, they are "those defense lawyers who by nature of their continuous appearances in behalf of defendants, tend to represent the bulk of a criminal court's nonindigent case workload. . . . Some of the 'lawyer regulars' are highly visible as one moves about major urban centers of the nation, their offices line the back streets of the courthouses, at times sharing space with bondsmen."[38] In Washington, D.C., they are known as "Fifth Streeters," and in Detroit as "Clinton Streeters." They make their living by roaming the halls of the courthouse looking for likely clients who may have some money or sitting in assignment court or at the first appearance hearing waiting for assignment from the bench. In many ways, the existence of the "lawyer regular" reflects the reality of crime in America—unspectacular, and woven in the fabric of poverty. Ordinarily, the criminal is poor. His defense needs are ordinary and short-lived. Although one may remember the exceptional cases, the complicated and expensive ones, it is the ordinary, relatively simple case that makes up the vast proportion of criminal defense work, and it is handled in a similar fashion by these attorneys.

This type of full-time criminal defense representation—supplementing a private criminal practice with court-assigned cases—is not without its advantages. An ongoing practice of this sort minimizes the very problems confronting the sporadic or part-time criminal defense systems. Inexperience quickly disappears with ongoing exposure to the system. Scheduling difficulties arising from operating in two or more court systems are minimized. Only as the caseload increases does scheduling become problematic. One criminal defense lawyer in Philadelphia had so many criminal cases that he created his own backlog. When the situation was finally recognized, the court assigned him his own courtroom, a judge to hear only his cases until the backlog was cleaned up, and then imposed a limit on the number of cases he could have at any one time. This is an extreme case but it points to the problem of case overload and its impact on scheduling.

There is another characteristic inherent in this system that distinguishes it from the defender organization and profoundly affects the justice system. The characteristic is the diminished capacity of court-assigned systems to exercise control over the quality of representation provided. We have noted earlier the different alternatives that have been proposed to control the quality of assignments. In addition, however, the lack of any centralized control mechanism also reduces the effectiveness of the defense in changing or improving procedures. Without leadership or policy-making authority, without procedures or controls, the potential ability of the defense component to affect the criminal justice system is severely restricted. Thus from an organizational perspective it is little wonder that we find the justice system shaped and dominated by the court and the prosecutor.

This is not necessarily the case where the defender organization is the prevailing form of defense representation. Clearly a product of the urbanized areas, its influence and power may make it an equal force in the justice system if not a respected adversary in its quest for power.

Unlike the court-assigned attorney, who is often an isolated individual dealing with criminal cases, the defender organization assumes the attributes and power of an organizational entity. Although it may perform its duties with part-time staff, as in DuPage County, Illinois, or on a full-time basis as in Washington, D.C., it nevertheless has organizational goals, identifiable leaders, and procedures to be implemented within the organizational structure. As an organization it delegates authority, power, and responsibility to perform essential tasks. It has management functions that among others relate to records and paperwork management, personnel systems, financial and budgetary systems; and it has a planning capability to provide for its maintenance and ongoing support.

More importantly, it has the ability to make policy about defense representation, the type of services to be provided, the quality of the service and the resources to be allocated to various cases; and, to change policy, if it so desires. It assumes the same organizational characteristics as the prosecutors office. It functions, as the ABA states, "as advocacy within the framework of the adversary system."[39]

The lack of centralized control or authority present in the private court-assigned systems is not inherent to the defender organization. To be sure problems may exist with respect to control or authority for a number of reasons, but not because there is no mechanism to provide for such centralized direction. Additional sanctions on performance are also available. The review and evaluation of an assistant public defender's work is possible, and, under good operating conditions, it is performed. Thus the quality of an attorney's work can be monitored and hopefully adjusted where necessary.

Enough has been written so far about the prosecutor's office and function; the mirror image reflected by the public defender's office needs little expansion here. The basic principles of organization and management apply equally to the public defender as well as the prosecutor. Yet the differing goals of each produce some management procedures that are not necessarily comparable or compatible if they were transferred from one office to another.

The basic philosophy of the defense system is to view the defendant as a client and to provide him with individualized legal services. The prosecutor, on the other hand, has no client as such. The prosecutor views a case in terms of strength factors—the severity of the offense, the seriousness of the defendant's record, and the evidentiary strength of the case. The defender's office, following private practice procedures, usually assigns one lawyer to each client. In recent years, with increasing crime and more system emphasis, there has been a tendency to criticize this procedure as unproductive and time consuming and to provide defense services on a system process basis, with one assistant handling all arraignments, another handling all pretrial conferences or motions, and finally assignment to an assistant for trial. Curiously, despite the movement toward assembly-line processing by the defense, the prosecutor has pushed for the integrated trial team approach. Today, the predominant form of defense services is still to provide a lawyer-client relationship.

*Differences in Goals*

In this adversary system of justice, goals of the different agencies vary often in subtle ways. The prosecutor's ideal goal is to dispose of cases according to their merits in a manner most favorable to the state. Ideally, this means that even losses at a trial level are better than having a case dismissed or nolled because of lack of merit, insufficient evidence, or system breakdowns. In practice, since trial courts usually cannot process all cases by trial, this means that other alternative methods of disposition are sought and used, including the more familiar ones of screening, diversion, plea bargaining, and deferred prosecution.

In contrast, the defense seldom wishes for adjudication but prefers early dismissals or other quick dispositions. The vigorous defense challenge to the prosecution is a luxury few can afford and only then under exceptional circumstances or within the umbrella of a defender organization. The court-assigned attorney has little incentive to perform such a service, especially on a regular basis.

The private court-appointed lawyer is guided by a practical concern: the profit motive. To incur no loss, he must bill to the maximum allowed. This means that each case is judged by the amount of time it will require for preparation and presentation and by the amount of money allowed for these tasks. These are not necessarily negative considerations. Such an attitude in the private sector of any other business would be considered "responsible." Unfortunately, the ideals presented as realistic goals for criminal justice do not necessarily mesh with practical renumerations. The operational constraint of obtaining payment for work is the underlying factor in characterizing the handling of a criminal defense. As Blumberg noted, fee setting and collection is inherently more difficult in the legal profession than others because "much legal work is intangible."[40] In addition not only must the assigned counsel justify his fee, he must also assume the burden of collecting it.

The office of the public defender does not suffer from these constraints. Because it is an appropriated body, its overhead and operating costs are subsidized and the personnel costs funded regardless of volume, manhours spent per case, productivity, or other potential constraints to the private counsellor. Operationally, the defender's office may bear little resemblance to a private attorney. The public defender office's primary concern is how to process workload in the most efficient and effective manner. Since there is a hierarchical power structure, work can be distributed and allocated in an efficient and effective manner. The resources of the office can be marshalled to do the job as effectively as possible. This situation is often impossible for private, court-assigned attorneys who act alone.

The operational goals of both types of defense systems produce almost the same desired outcomes and in the same order of preference. They are:

1. dismissals early in the process
2. early alternative dispositions, for example, diversion
3. plea bargains
4. acquittals by trial
5. reversals on appeal

The reasons for this ranking vary between defender organizations and court-assigned systems. The court-assigned counsel attempts to minimize costs. The fewer the number of court appearances, the less time spent on case preparation, the greater the chance of not losing money on a case. On the other hand, the public defender, although recognizing the economies of these outcomes, views the above order of preferred dispositions as a reflection of the efficient and effective case processing. The value of his performance is measured by his ability to control workload and volume and reduce backlog. Money is not necessarily the overriding concern.

The cutting edge is that defender organizations can afford to put up a vigorous defense challenge if necessary; the court-appointed attorney cannot. The organizational support provided by the agency to the assistant public defender affects the prosecution function in a number of ways, and the court-appointed lawyer is not without influence in other ways as well.

*Differences in Quality of Defense*

Although no definitive or particular standards have yet been devised to measure the effectiveness of counsel in a particular case, numerous cases and various studies have suggested that the quality of indigent defense can be compared to the quality of defense available to those who can afford to retain private counsel. The Supreme Court in *Douglas* v. *California*[41] and in

*Griffen* v. *Illinois*[42] mandated that there be parity between private and publically provided counsel. The standards of both the American Bar Association and the Model Defender Act suggest the need for support investigatory services that would provide parity with that which is available to clients of private attorneys. In reality, however, there is great variation with many procedures and rules that pose "significant handicaps not encountered by the wealthy client."[43]

Very often, as will be seen, the standard set among the local bar for defense of an indigent is much lower than that set for a private client. In *Walker* v. *Caldwell*, the attorney for an indigent client testified that he "followed a substantially different practice when representing fee clients rather than appointed clients."[44] In *Wallace* v. *Kern* the court criticized a Legal Aid Society because its quality of defense was substantially lower than that of private counsel that worked in the same court.[45]

In reviewing the literature available on this subject, at least two possible areas of measurement suggest themselves as fruitful indicators of similarity of treatment between methods of defense. The first is the promptness with which each system makes legal counsel available to the defendant. The assumption is that the earlier that the defense counsel is able to enter the case, the more options are opened to the client. The second area is the comparison of dispositions. The theory is that equality of representation will manifest itself statistically throughout a particular court system in similar dispositions for similar types of crime.

Studies conducted based on these assumptions have shown the wide disparity of effective defense services available. A *Harvard Law Review* study of various U.S. District Courts showed that substantially more guilty pleas were entered for indigent defendants than were entered for clients with retained counsel.[46] Similar results of studies were reported in studies conducted in Indiana.[47] Still, a study cosponsored by LEAA and Ohio State University in the Los Angeles courts showed that the dispositions for public defenders were not significantly different from those for privately retained counsel.[48] Another study attempted to compare the dispositions between the assigned counsel system operating in Milwaukee and the public defender systems in the Minneapolis area.[49] Even though studies tend to show that the effectiveness of publicly provided counsel is lower than that of the privately retained bar, this area is still relatively undefined and in need of further definition and study.

Even the courts are unprepared to address the problems of quality and effectiveness of representation. One commentator has noted that "neither the courts nor the legislatures have addressed the essential administrative rule-making tasks of defining caseload, counsel assignments and qualifications, service eligibility or procedures. . . . More than a decade after *Gideon* the question still remains whether [the system] can indeed render effective assistance of counsel.''[50] Nevertheless, though the procedures may be lacking, the workload and pressures on the prosecution are affected by the type of defender system operating in the jurisdiction and the adequacy of the system.

## Effects on Prosecution

Despite the basic structural and functional differences between the assigned counsel systems and the defender system, both have effects on prosecution, generally and specifically. These effects are not one-sided, since each system produces advantages as well as disadvantages for the prosecution.

### General Effects

The case law requiring the assistance of counsel at most stages of the criminal justice process and guaranteeing this assistance to indigent defendants has had a direct and substantial impact on the workload of the criminal prosecutor.

First, and perhaps most important, the prosecutor now must prepare himself to deal with defense counsel in almost every case. Prior to 1960 this was not always so. In fact, assignment of counsel prior to 1960 was mandatory in only about half the states. In fifteen states, including a major portion of the South, and four major northeastern industrial states, the courts did not assign compensated counsel. In seven others, it was discretionary. The presence of defense counsel now means that the prosecutor has to prepare each case more carefully and more thoroughly than was necessary before *Gideon* and *Argersinger*. The number of cases that were affected by these decisions is staggering. Of the 350,000 persons charged with felonies in 1971, for example, fully 60 percent or 210,000 were indigent. Although no absolute figures are available, Leo Silverstein projected that between 1967 and 1977 there would be an average of 400,000 felonies per year, and at least half would require free counsel.[51] He felt that perhaps as many as an additional 25 percent would require partial subsidy. Foreseeing the *Argersinger* decision, Silverstein also predicted that the number of indigent defendants accused of misdemeanors covered under that decision would approach two million per year. Similar figures were predicted by the Federal Bureau of Investigation. A third survey showed that 30 to 70 percent of all defendants qualified for indigency status.[52]

The immense increase in the number of cases handled by the defense bar affected the amount of work that had to be performed by the prosecution. Clearly, minimal case preparation that was possible in many thousands of instances prior to *Gideon* and *Argersinger* was insufficient once the defendants were provided counsel.

Secondly, the Court's mandate that defense counsel be present at numerous critical stages in the process again placed additional pressure on the prosecutor to appear at these critical stages. Once again, these decisions, by their very nature, increased the amount of litigation as well as appearances, making the average criminal case longer and procedurally more complex. Defendants were more likely to file motions, to demand rather than waive preliminary hearing, and to institute postconviction proceedings and appeals.

Thirdly, the demands of decisions like *Miranda* and *Wade* and the development of speedy trial rules put greater time constraints on the prosecution. The prosecutor had to be concerned with properly training and educating his staff and local police on the requirement of the law occasioned by these decisions. Greater care had to be taken to provide prompt and suitable protection of the rights of indigent defendants, both by informing them of their rights at all stages of the process and by insuring that the state's case was instituted before the proper deadlines. Having defense counsel in all cases would now exert pressure on the police and prosecution to perform to the letter of the law.

## Operational Effects

The flurry of legal activity generated by the increased presence of the defense bar forced the prosecution to find operational alternatives to the increased workload. As the type of defense system varied, so did the prosecutor's ability to work with each.

Generally, the prosecutor likes dealing with assigned counsel. He may not have much respect for their lack of criminal trial experience, but this very weakness coupled with the lower remuneration rates works to the advantage of the prosecutor. It places the prosecutor in a very strong position to drive a bargain favorable to his office. Even if the bargain is not struck and for some rare reason the case proceeds to trial, the resources and training of the prosecutor and his office usually give him an advantage over the independent court-appointed lawyer. The balance is clearly in favor of the prosecutor when one weighs his operating system against the assigned counsel system.

On the other hand, the circumstances are not quite so predictable with the defender system. Now the organizational entity of the prosecutor's office must compete with the organizational entity of the defender's office for the favorable disposition. The nature and character of the defender's office allows for a more vigorous defense challenge. The number of times that the public defender appears in court, or the length of time spent in case preparation, is relatively inconsequential in light of their positions as full-time employees. Additionally, although the public defender's office is usually staffed to a lesser degree than the prosecutor's, it does have the ability as an organizational entity to shift resources in special cases. The result is the establishment of two essentially comparable (and sometimes equal) systems that can take action in an adversary proceeding.

Although the prosecutor may prefer to have an upper hand in dealing with a less effective assigned counsel, the fact is that from a management and operational perspective, the prosecutor receives many benefits from the defender system that he could not receive from assigned counsel systems of defense. This is due to the existence of an organization that serves as a locus for communication, complaints and the development of procedures. The key to all this, of course, is that there is an organization with a specific authority responsible for providing defense services.

These organizational benefits may be offset if conflicts arise from policy differences. Like the prosecutor, the defender office has the ability to state and implement policy. Where this is in conflict with prosecutorial policy, the turmoil may create some devastating conditions. Imagine the drain on defender resources if the prosecutor decided to implement a no-plea-bargaining policy, and the defender's office found its cases being disposed of much later in the criminal justice process. Conversely, imagine the workload pressures forced on the prosecutor if the defender's office increases its filing of motions and appeals. It is obvious that clear recognition must be given to the power of the policies of these two organizational structures to improve or debilitate the system.

It seems clear that, although the impact on prosecutive systems will vary according to the type of defense representation, the assigned counsel system generally produces legal adversaries that the prosecutor finds easier to deal with. The potential of a vigorous defense challenge may generate unfavorable reactions from the prosecution. In the long run, however, the centralized control and organization of the defense function, when it is capable of being sustained by a jurisdiction, greatly improves the ability of the system to improve itself and be capable of monitoring itself.

Finally, however, the demands and needs of the court should not be ignored. An interesting analysis by Blumberg of one court system indicated the power of the court in defining a role for the defense counsel in criminal cases as an "agent-mediator," helping the accused "redefine his situation and restructure his perceptions concommitant with a plea of guilty."[53] The minimizing of the adversary situation of daily operating contacts within the same closed environment, with its own goals and procedures to process workload is further substantiated by David Sudnow's description of a court room where the public defender "takes his station" while the private attorneys come and go.[54] The working relations between all three principals, court, public defender, prosecutor assume bureaucratic proportion where each case is identified as a unit of production.

In fact, Sudnow described an office that demonstrates the provocative and disturbing conclusion reached by Blumberg in his expert study. Blumberg noted that "Recent Supreme Court criminal law decisions overlook . . . (1) the nature of the courts as formal organization; (2) the relationship that the lawyer-regular actually has with the court organization, and (3) the character of the lawyer-client relationship in the criminal court. . . ."[55]

The recent work of Eisenstein and Jacob explores in detail the relationships that exist among the members of the courtroom workgroup.[56] One of the most valuable insights reached by the study of three court systems is that the modes of operation differ markedly when the defense counsel are known to the courtroom workgroup in contrast to when they are not. In the former instance, a dispositional mode of behavior is exhibited as all members work to dispose of the daily docket. In the latter, as the degree of uncertainty in the relationship increases, greater reliance is placed on a formal adversarial system of cases processing.

It is very important, in viewing the prosecutor and his relations with defense counsel, that their interaction as members of formal organizations with different goals and priorities be separated from their interaction within the courtroom workgroup, where their roles become more informal and the goals are operationalized to dispose of the daily docket. To the extent that both the prosecutor and the defense assume the operational goals of the court (docket dispositions), one can expect a lack of conflict and even an increased opportunity for abuses in reaching mutually agreeable dispostions. The reward for this position is increased efficiency and productivity. On the other hand, to impose the American ideal of an adversary system of justice on the individual courtroom holds few rewards for the courtroom workgroup as it heightens antagonisms and debilitates the very relationships needed to process cases. For most court systems, one suspects that a balance has been struck that permits dispositional behavior as long as it conforms first with the formal policy of the prosecutor and, perhaps in some instances, secondarily with the defense counsel's priorities.

## Notes

1. 287 U.S. 45 (1932).
2. 407 U.S. 25 (1972).
3. 304 U.S. 458 (1938).
4. 365 U.S. 109 (1960).
5. 369 U.S. 506 (1961).
6. 372 U.S. 335 (1963).
7. Ibid.
8. 407 U.S. 25 (1972).

9. 373 U.S. 59 (1963).

10. 399 U.S. 1 (1970).

11. 378 U.S. 478 (1964).

12. 384 U.S. 436 (1966).

13. 388 U.S. 218 (1967).

14. 372 U.S. 353 (1963).

15. 389 U.S. 128 (1967).

16. 387 U.S. 1 (1967).

17. "Note: Dollars and Sense of the Right to Counsel," 55 Iowa Law Review 1249, 1259 (1970).

18. See, for example, Lawrence Benner), *The Other Face of Justice* (Washington, D.C.: National Legal Aid and Defenders Association, 1973), chap. 1; Special Committee of the Association of the Bar of the City of New York, *Equal Justice for the Accused* (New York: Doubleday, 1959), pp. 62-71; Peter Avery Anderson, "Defense of Indigents in Maine: The Need for Public Defenders," 25 Maine Law Review 1 (1973). See also "Note: Dollars and Sense."

19. Lawrence Benner, "The Other Face of Justice: A Summary," 32 NLADA Briefcase 12 (1974).

20. Lawrence Benner, "Tokenism and the American Indigent: Some Perspectives on Defense Systems." 12 American Criminal Law Review 667 (1975).

21. Paul B. Wice and Mark Pilgrim, "Meeting the Gideon Mandate: A Survey of Public Defender Programs," 58 Judicature 400 (1975).

22. 351 Mo. 769, 174 S.W.2d 181 (1943). See comments in 1964 Washington University Law Quarterly 370 (1964) and 19 Journal of the Missouri Bar 412 (1964).

23. Norman G. Kittel, "Defense of the Poor: A Study in Public Parsimony and Private Poverty," 45 Indiana Law Journal 90 (1970).

24. State v. Rush, 46 N.J. 399, 217 A.2d 441 (1966).

25. Kittel, "Defense of the Poor," p. 98.

26. Partman, "The Necessity for an Organized Defender Office," *Defender Conference Report*, quoted in Arthur B. LaFrance, "Criminal Defense Systems for the Poor," 50 Notre Dame Lawyer 41, 60.

27. See also Benner's study, quoted in LaFrance, "Criminal Defense Systems," p. 60.

28. See 25 Maine Law Review 1 (1973).

29. Benner, "Other Face of Justice," points out that less than 50 percent are employed full-time.

30. Ibid., pp. 70-77.

31. See United States v. Chatman, 42 U.S.L.W. 2593 (D.C. Superior Court, May 7, 1974).

32. Paul Ligda, "Defender's Workloads: The Numbers Game," 34 NLADA Briefcase 22, 25.

33. Wice and Pilgrim, "Meeting Gideon Mandate," n. 19 on p. 409.

34. Kittel, "Defense of the Poor," p. 90.

35. Fewer than 5,000 lawyers consider themselves to be "criminal lawyers." See 55 Iowa Law Review 1249 (1970).

36. Benner, "Summary," p. 12; See also, Pilgrim and Wice, "Meeting Gideon Mandate," p. 400.

37. Michael Moore, "The Right to Counsel for Indigents in Oregon," 44 Oregon Law Review 255 (1965).

38. Abraham S. Blumberg, "The Practice of Law as Confidence Game: Organizational Cooptation of a Profession," in *Criminal Justice: Law and Politics*, ed. George F. Cole (North Scituate, Mass: Duxbury Press, 1972), pp. 213-235.

39. American Bar Association Project on Standards for Criminal Justice, *Standards Relating to the Administration of Criminal Justice* (New York: The American Bar Association, 1974), pp. 56-58, 141-145.

40. Blumberg, "Practice of Law" p. 219.

41. 372 U.S. 353 (1963).

42. 351 U.S. 12 (1956).

43. LaFrance, "Criminal Defense Systems," p. 53. Compare provisions of ABA Standards or Model Defenders Act with provisions in Criminal Justice Act, 18 U.S.C. Sec. 3006(A)(e) (1970).

44. 476 F.2d 213 (5th Cir. 1973).

45. No. 72-C-898 (S.D.N.Y., filed May 10, 1973).

46. "Note: The Representative of Indigent Criminal Defendants in the Federal District Courts," 76 Harvard Law Review 579, 586 (1963).

47. Kittel, "Defense of the Poor," p. 90.

48. Marlene Lehtman and Gerald Smith, "The Relative Effectiveness of Public Defenders and Private Attorneys," 32 NLADA Briefcase 13.

49. See also David, "Institutional or Private Counsel: A Judge's View of the Public Defender System," 45 Minnesota Law Review 753 (1961).

50. LaFrance, "Criminal Defense Systems," p. 43.

51. Leo Silverstein, *Defense of the Poor in Criminal Cases in American State Courts* (1965), pp. 8-9, quoted in "Note: Argersinger v. Hamlin," 27 Southwestern Law Journal 406, 410 (1973), at n. 31.

52. LaFrance, "Criminal Defense Systems," p. 51, n. 28.

53. Blumberg, "Practice," p. 215, n. 35.

54. See Sudnow's article in *Criminal Justice in America*, ed. Richard Quinney (Little, Brown, 1974).

55. Blumberg, "Practice of Law," pp. 215-216.

56. See James Eisenstein and Herbert Jacob, *Felony Justice: An Organizational Analysis of Criminal Courts* (Boston: Little, Brown, 1977).

# 4 The Intake Process

## Introduction

Intake is the first stage of prosecution and probably the most important with respect to the prosecutor's discretionary power. It is during this stage that the prosecutor is notified of the occurrence of a crime and the arrest of a defendant. He reviews the facts and/or the evidence available, evaluates the case, and ends the process with a charging decision. Not all these events occur in the same sequence in all jurisdictions, nor do all prosecutors perform all of them. The variations that the intake process assumes—and their effect on prosecution—will be the subject of our examination here.

Cases presented for prosecution generally originate from four sources: the police, citizen complaints, grand jury investigations, and investigations initiated by the prosecutor. Since our focus here is on the intake process as it is affected by sources over which prosecution has little control, grand jury-originated and prosecutor-initiated investigations (consistituting a relatively small proportion of the total intake) will be excluded from this discussion.

Our attention will be on cases that originate from police activity and citizen complaints. The latter are generally domestic in nature, usually the result of a family dispute. In some jurisdictions, they are reviewed first by law enforcement agencies or other quasi-legal agencies such as citizen complaint centers or domestic relations councils. In others, the prosecutor performs this function. If these cases are distinguishable, it is only in the intake process, where they may be subject to different procedures. Once a decision to charge has been made, they are indistinguishable from the other criminal cases being processed.

The largest proportion of prosecutorial work at intake is generated by police activity. Therefore, our examination will focus, first and most extensively, on the intake processes used between the police and the prosecutor.

Optimally, an efficient and effective intake process is one where all relevant information reaches the prosecutor as quickly as possible after an arrest or criminal event so that the facts of the case can be properly reviewed and analyzed prior to a charging decision or the initiation of any court proceeding. Of all the areas of prosecutorial activity, the screening and charging functions at the intake stage have generated the most interest.[1] It is here that the prosecutor's discretionary power is first utilized in the charging decision, that prosecutorial policy is first implemented, and that the character of the justice system is first set by this gatekeeper. The quality of the decisions made here often set the course for justice in a community. Independent of any study perspective or personal values, from all quarters there emerges a single call for timely, accurate, and complete information to support the charging decision.

Recent criminal justice movements have pushed for increased prosecutorial activity in the review and screening of cases; the crime commissions of the sixties and seventies have called for uniform procedures and developed standards in support of this activity. More recently the National Center for Prosecution Management (NCPM) and the National District Attorneys Association (NDAA) have attempted to implement these standards through the development and dissemination of forms and procedures manuals.[2]

Despite the emphasis on standardization of procedures, little attention has been given to the structure of the intake process, its variations throughout the country, and the barriers (or supports) that they produce for standardizing or upgrading intake procedures. Nevertheless, there are some intake processing problems that can be directly attributed to the differences in local criminal justice system structures and processing procedures. These problems are not necessarily insurmountable. Too often, tradition, rather than thoughtful planning, has dictated the methods by which case information passed through the many local criminal justice systems. Nevertheless, the variations profoundly affect the prosecutor's charging procedures.

Structural differences, alone, of course do not provide the complete causative list of problems that may exist in the intake process. The interaction between the police and prosecutor must also be considered.[3] The roots of the law enforcement agencies are set in the principles of autonomy of operation and localism. As such their policies and goals may not necessarily be consistent with those of the prosecutor. Additionally, the caliber of the police force, its ability to preserve the chain of evidence or conduct proper investigations, all affect this intake process. Nowhere else in the criminal justice system is such a highly interactive area as visible as here. The result of this process, produced by a symbiotic relationship between police and prosecutor, reaches its tentacles into every other processing stage. How the police respond and transmit the information to the prosecutor is a critical area for examination. By following the routes taken for the transmittal of information, one can observe the functions of the actors in the system and can reach some conclusions about their effect on either improving the quality of the evidence or producing unnecessary impediments.

This chapter will examine the intake process for prosecution with respect to its ability to produce timely, accurate, and complete information for review by the prosecutor prior to making a charging decision. It will discuss the basic differences in roles and perception between the police and the prosecutor; examine the different universes in which the intake process operates; and describe the limitations and benefits of various transmittal procedures.

The effect of various intake procedures on the prosecutor's ability and opportunity to review a case before charging is the central focus of this section. The prosecutor's charging decision itself is not a factor in this examination, only his ability to make the decision based on timely, accurate, and complete information. The charging decision as the first measure of prosecutorial policy will be examined later for its policy implications. The difference between examining an intake process as contrasted with a charging decision (the culmination of the intake process) is that the intake process identifies the effect of environmental constraints on the prosecutor's charging decision, and the charging decision reflects the inherent power of the prosecutor. Although a prosecutor may exercise his free choice in making policy decisions, the external world of reality limits his choices among alternatives. The intake process represents a rugged terrain to which the prosecutor is forced to adapt.

**Prosecution and Police—A Difference**

The evolution of the American criminal justice system has separated the responsibilities of the police from the prosecutor and has moved toward clearer divisions of responsibility. As we saw, the emergence of the American prosecutor evolved from roots in a number of different sources, including the constable and sheriff and, in the early Dutch colonies, the *schout*, a type of police-prosecutor. The American police tradition, however, evolved essentially from English traditions that were transferred to this country during the colonial period.[4] "It was the sheriff-constable-watchman system that the colonists transplanted to the American shores. . . ."[5] In 1636, the first formal night watch was established in the city of Boston; New York, while under Dutch rule, formed a similar system in 1654; Philadelphia appointed a single night watchman to take charge of maintaining the peace in 1700. But the need for greater numbers came quickly, and by 1762 Boston had a force of thirty watchmen. After the American revolution, most towns had developed two separate police forces, a day patrol and the night watch. It was not until almost the Civil War that these two separate forces became integrated into a single unit.

At the beginning of the nineteenth century the district attorney was still a minor court official; the most important figures were the sheriff and the coroner. Great deference and attention was given to these two figures during these early years of our country's development. They were the first local offices, usually on the county level, to gain independent status and to be locally elected. But their elective status soon gave way to the tugs of local politics and the struggle between state and local government control. Beginning in 1861 there were a series of attempted takeovers of local police authorities, and as late as 1920 such major cities as Baltimore, Boston, Kansas City, and St. Louis still had forces that were under state control. Although sheriffs in the more rural settings have been able to maintain their elective status, police chiefs have come under the direct control of other elected city officials, mayors, councils, or boards. As a result their duties too have more of the central functions of the executive branch of government and less of the quasi-judicial duties performed by what we now know as prosecution.

The prosecutive duties once performed by sheriffs and police, including the presentation of the facts to the court, gradually were transferred to the prosecutor as his power, stature, and responsibilities took shape. Today few vestiges of police involvement in this function remain; although police prosecutors can still be found in Massachusetts trying cases in the lower courts, and the sheriff presents cases to local grand juries in North Carolina in a procedure that excludes the entrance of the local prosecution.

The separation of these roles and division of responsibilities has been a slow evolutionary process that one can expect to continue. In its commentary, the National Advisory Commission of Criminal Justice Standards and Goals (NAC) held fast to the traditional roles for both parties in the intake process and emphasized strict hegemony for each in its own sphere: "The decision to take a person into custody should be a police decision. . . . The decision to charge, to screen, or not to charge, should, however, be made by the prosecutor. . . . Although a police officer should have the authority to arrest and book a person, . . . without prior prosecutorial approval, the process should go no further than that without formal involvement of the prosecutor's office."[6] The NAC continued to reinforce these positive interpretations of responsibilities by disapproving those practices and procedures that would subvert these standards. Specifically they cited instances wherein the prosecutor was not made aware of the existence of a case until its presentation at grand jury by the sheriff and instances in which the decision to pursue formal charges was made by persons not on the prosecutor's staff (such as the police and magistrates).

Even though police and prosecutors are at least nominally on the same side in pursuing criminal prosecutions, this theoretically shared interest is belied by a lack of cooperation between the two more often than should be expected under these circumstances. Police are often disappointed with and wary of the prosecutor's decisions; the prosecutor often distrusts and questions the actions and motives of the police. In many instances, the two work together more in an atmosphere of sullen resignation than in one of trust and cooperation.

The obvious reason for the uneasy working relationship that often exists between the police and prosecutor is simply that they do not share the same interests, responsibilities, or goals in their respective pursuits of law violators. The police must keep the peace and apprehend the law breaker; the prosecutor must bring the case of the state in a court of law. The police arrest on the basis of probable cause to believe that an individual has broken the law; the prosecutor must produce a higher quality of evidence to convict the same man in the courtroom. The police are faced with the responsibility of keeping the streets safe by placing wrong-doers in the judicial system; the prosecutor is faced with the task of representing the community in all actions, of keeping the court process moving, and of eliminating those cases that are inappropriate or insufficient for the attentions of the court. As the division of work has separated the two agencies, the goals of each have become more divergent, thereby creating some problems that assume more significance as the criminal justice system becomes more procedure-bound and complex.

Each of the two agencies are endowed with discretionary powers that reflect agency goals and policies. For the police, "These policies reflect the proclivities of the police chief and indirectly the city administration and possibly the populace."[7] James Q. Wilson[8] has characterized three distinctive styles used in police discretion: the watchman style,[9] the legalistic style,[10] and the service style.[11]

The watchman style leads police to be most concerned with the maintenance of order. Arrests are made when an incident threatens to become uncontrollable. But if a violation occurs that does not threaten public order, the policeman is likely to dismiss the offender with a warning. Order is emphasized over enforcement.

The legalistic style calls for the enforcement of laws to take precedence over maintaining order. In this narrower view, if the behavior violates a provision of the criminal code, the police tend to arrest. Enforcement occurs even when the public order is not disturbed.

The service style emphasizes the responsibility of the department to provide a variety of services to the public. Police are responsive to calls in the legalistic style but may dispose of them more informally in the watchman style. The emphasis is on public relations and service.

Jacoby has identified four prosecutorial policies that govern decision making: legal sufficiency, system efficiency, defendant rehabilitation, and trial sufficiency.[12] In legal sufficiency, the charging decision is based on the presence of the legal elements of the case. Constitutional issues such as bad search and seizures are not part of the review at this time. Review and charging are cursory and brief.

The system efficiency policy aims at disposing of cases as quickly as possible by as many means as possible. This is a front-ended policy that requires intensive screening and review, good police cooperation, and the extensive use of plea bargaining.

The defendant rehabilitation policy opts for concern about the interests of the defendant vis a vis prosecution. The stigma of a felony conviction is avoided as much as possible. There is extensive use of diversion, deferred prosecution programs, and alternatives to adjudication.

The trial sufficiency policy states that what is charged is what will be tried and convicted. Plea bargaining is prohibited, dismissals are rare, the screening and charging decisions are considered to be the most important ones in the office.

If one attempts to match police styles with prosecutor policies, it becomes immediately clear that some will not mesh. For example, the defendant rehabilitation orientation conflicts with the legalistic police style. On the other hand, some seem clearly compatible; for example, the legalistic style with legal sufficiency. Where the goals conflict, harmonious police-prosecutor relationships are unlikely. The growing complexity of court procedures and constitutional protection has increased, not decreased, the need for cooperative working relationships between the two agencies.

Other differences emerge because of the changing roles of the police and the prosecutor during the course of the intake as well as the entire criminal justice process. Because police involvement does not end with arrest but extends into and through the judicial process (and sometimes into the postconviction area), the role of the police changes from one of authority, having great discretionary power over investigations and arrests, to one of justifier in the intake stage and one of being merely a coordinator of witnesses and evidences as well as being an expert witness in the courtroom. These changes may not be comfortable ones. The prosecutor during the intake process assumes a nonadversarial review and investigative role, judging and evaluating the policeman's work, until the charging decision is made. From that point on, as the representative of the state, his role is one of advocacy. When these role changes cannot be perceived or understood by either the police or the prosecutor, or when the differences in each agencies goals are not recognized, the development of uncertainty or distrust in the relationship is not surprising.

The dysfunctions that may appear during the intake process cannot be explained solely by the short-sightedness of the police or prosecutor in defining their roles and responsibilities. Although these effects should be recognized, much of the present confusion may be ascribed to the changing perception of the modern day prosecutor and his ever-widening assumption of discretionary responsibility. If one visualizes the continuum of increasing discretionary power available to a prosecutor, on the far left are those prosecutors who interpret their role simply as an arm of the law enforcement agency and who unquestioningly prosecute all police arrests. As the prosecutor begins to use his discretionary power, the decisions of the police are more apt to be overturned or modified. At the far right on the continuum are the prosecutors who have assumed a policy-making role in the community. Not only are police arrests subject to change under these circumstances, but more directly, the arrest policies and procedures in the community may be affected by the prosecutorial policies and standards. Thus as the prosecutor increases his use of discretionary power and assumes more of a policy-making stance, the opportunities for conflict become almost inevitable if the two agencies are not philosophically attuned.

The dysfunctions that exist between these two agencies have been well documented. Reiss's and Bordua's study points out that although the police make arrests that the prosecutor's caseload depends on, it is the prosecutor who decides the effectiveness of police arrest performance through screening policy and prioritization of cases.[13]

It is not always easy to accept reversal. This is particularly true at intake where police arrest decisions may be reversed for a number of reasons. As the President's Commission on Law Enforcement and the Administration of Criminal Justice pointed out:

> The police decision whether to arrest must usually be made hastily, without relevant background information, and often under pressure of a pending disturbance. . . . In some places particularly when less serious offenses are involved, the decision to press charges is made by the police or a magistrate rather than by a prosecutor. The better practice is for the prosecutor to make this decision for the choice involves such factors as the sentencing alternative available under the various possible charges, the substantiality of the case for prosecution and limitations on prosecution resources—factors that the policeman often cannot consider and the magistrate cannot deal with fully while maintaining a judicial role.[14]

The application of a different set of standards (the prosecutor's) to judge the effectiveness of a police action creates a fertile soil for conflict and distrust.

Because police are not trained as lawyers (and sometimes not trained at all), the development and protection of the evidence essential for the prosecutor's work may be sloppy, incomplete, or defective. The study on rape performed by Battelle pointed out that a common complaint by the prosecutors was that the police tended to be sloppy in their investigations, missed important evidence, and improperly seized or marked items that were gathered.[15] This finding was seconded and expanded on by the Rand study on criminal investigations.[16] They found that the quality of police investigation did indeed have a bearing on the prosecutor's actions but that the prosecutor also influenced the quality by his own expectations. Finally, in the development of its *Model Prosecution Report*, the NCPM staff noted that the major emphasis of the prosecutor was placed on techniques for capturing and recording information that established the chain of evidence.[17] All this points to the widely divergent measures of performance between the two agencies and the conflicts that are certain to arise if the goals and objectives of each of the two components are not understood and respected.

Other conflicts may be created by a lack of understanding of the universe of responsibility. As Miller[18] pointed out in his major study on prosecutorial discretion and as the ABA standards dictate,[19] individuals who are either not convictable or whose conviction would not be in the community interest should not be prosecuted. Here the standards for the violation of the law as implemented by the police stand in direct opposition to the prosecutor's responsibility to the court and the community. The Vera study points up this aspect by showing that the cases most likely to fall apart were those that contained elements of personal relationships.[20] Here, the responsibility of noncriminal justice processing seems to warrant further investigation. Finally Katz warns of the danger of the prosecutor assuming the responsibilities of the police: "The prosecutor who institutes felony charges against all defendants arrested by the police fails to make the necessary choices at this stage of the proceedings. Although he may be mollifying the public and the police, he is not adequately doing his job. He is shifting attention away from his office and focusing it on the inability of the courts to cope with their responsibility."[21]

Despite the probability of increasing system breakdowns, most prosecutors recognize the necessity of maintaining distance from the police action so that their review will result in independent decisions believed necessary to preserve the integrity of the process. Grosman noted that prosecutors who view themselves as extensions of the law enforcement process do so not because of police influence but because they tend to confuse the distinction between a law enforcement officer's decision to arrest based on the sufficiency of the evidence and the prosecutor's decision to charge.[22] The Court Standards of the NAC paid close attention to the division of responsibility and the distance necessary between the two agencies. In Standard 1.2 they state:

> Police, in consultation with the prosecutor, should develop guidelines for the taking of persons into custody. After a person has been taken into custody, the decision to proceed with formal prosecution should rest with the prosecutor. No complaint should be filed or arrest warrant issued without the formal approval of the prosecutor. . . . Final responsibility for making a screening decision should be placed specifically upon an experienced member of the prosecutor's staff.[23]

This very distance placed between the police and the prosecutor in the intake process contributes to the inability of the police to realize the scope of other systemic demands on the prosecutor. As a result, the whole question of charging is too often described as a game of wits between the police and prosecutor—the police overcharging because of their feeling that the courts are too lenient, and the prosecutor reducing because he feels the police often overreact and overcharge. Blumberg's study of the New York courts commented on this occurrence:

> Justice Sobel of the court who collected the data, did so largely to demonstrate that relatively few persons who are initially charged with a crime are indeed found to have committed the original version of the crime charged. It is a not uncommon administrative device of the police to couch the original version of their charge in the most extreme form possible within the confines of a given set of facts. Thus, very often, an original charge of a felonious assault (with a weapon) is reduced at the initial hearing to a more realistic one of simple assault, or even to disorderly conduct.[24]

But this conclusion is too simplistic. Not all such results can be explained away as "administrative devices" employed by the police. Courts, police, and prosecutors all may have to accept a part of the responsibility for this practice. Since police are not allowed to arrest for probable cause unless a felony has been committed, then one can expect the incentives for charging at the high end to be very strong. Add to this the practice of some police agencies to base merit promotions on this measure, and we can see that the law enforcement organization itself contributes to this practice. Finally, prosecution itself does not escape its share of responsibility particularly if the policy of the office is to dispose of cases as quickly as possible by extensive use of plea bargaining.

Other systemic demands on the prosecutor also may operate without police recognition. In a high-volume court the prosecutor may "serve as a regulator of case loads not only for his own office, but for the rest of the legal system. Constitutional and statutory time limits prevent him and the courts from building a backlog of untried cases."[25] These demands translate into operational considerations when the prosecutor is reviewing a case with possible weaknesses, realizes the court backlog and the plethora of delaying tactics available to an astute and hopeful defense attorney.[26] Pressures to alleviate the backlog in criminal trials are immense, and the prosecutor hears the echoes of demand from the courts and the public each time he reviews a case. The *U.S. News and World Report* summed up the situation when they reported "High court officials said that delay in criminal trials is the biggest complaint they receive from the public."[27]

Despite the environment within which it operates, the importance of the intake process lies in its ability to capture and describe the dimensions of the symbiotic relationship between police and prosecutor. Whereas the previous discussion has presented insights into the dysfunctional aspects of the process, the reader should be aware that for the most part, the parties have adjusted to one another's operations and objectives and operate in a state of relative harmony and accommodation. This is possible simply because the state of symbiosis demands it. As so accurately stated by Cole in his study of the King County (Seattle) Washington criminal justice system,

> Although the prosecuting attorney has discretionary power to determine the disposition of cases, this power is limited by the fact that usually he is dependent upon the police for inputs to the system of cases and evidence. The prosecutor does not have the investigative resources necessary to exercise the kind of affirmative control over the types of cases that are brought to him. In this relationship, the prosecutor is not without countervailing power. His main check on the police is his ability to return cases to them for further investigation and to refuse to approve arrest warrants . . . the police, in turn, are dependent upon the prosecutor to accept the output of their system: rejection of too many cases can have serious repercussions affecting the moral, discipline and workload of the force.[28]

Echoing the same general theme with respect to the symbiotic relationship, Katz notes,

> In most cities, a fine relationship exists between the police and the prosecutor's office. Since both are working towards the same general goals, each is dependent upon the other's labors to facilitate its own work. As a result, prosecutors are fully aware that they cannot pressure for prosecution in too many questionable cases, for it is the prosecutor who ultimately must justify that decision in court. For the most part, a mutuality of interests and limitations upon each agency's prerogatives tend to maintain cooperative that is based upon a healthy respect.[29]

## The Elements of Intake

Within this interactive environment of competing system demands, the prosecutor needs accurate, timely, and complete information if he is to perform the review and charging functions. There is no one set standard for the amount of information necessary to support these functions, but all commentators agree that it is critically important to determine the strength of the evidence and the legality of the arrest at this process point. To properly evaluate the case, the prosecutor must have adequate information, even though the definition of adequacy varies. Grosman limits his discussion to information provided by the police: the facts of the case, and the arrest record or "rap sheet."[30] Miller includes interviews with witnesses, the victim, and the defendant, and reports from other criminal justice system components.[31] He notes that the information generally available to the prosecutor when making his decision is from the police officer, the police report, or the summary of the alleged crime—occasionally witnesses, the suspect and the victim. What is available at case review is largely dependent on the prosecutor's policy or on the decision of the reporting police officer.[32] In some cases, but by no means routinely, reports of medical examiners, results of polygraph tests, physical evidence either of the crime or the condition of the victim are examined by the prosecutor.[33] Occasionally, defense attorneys are permitted to present arguments about the sufficiency of evidence and even to call the prosecutor's attention to additional evidence.[34]

Katz advocates the use of attorney-prosecutor charging conferences as a means of moving negotiations between the prosecutor and defense attorney to the earliest stage, to screen out weak cases, to revise unrealistic police charges and to develop a charge that the defense attorney knew the prosecution would either go to trial on or accept a plea to.[35] Katz concluded that "the charging conference, then, will result in the emergence of convictable charges rather than in the existing reducible charge."

The American Bar Association (ABA) standards materially extend the basic conceptualization of Miller.[36] Like Miller, the ABA recognizes that intake is a process that results in placing cases with sufficient evidence to support a conviction before the courts. But the ABA standards go further by directing attention to the decision itself as a critical point in the process and then by elaborating factors other than the weight of the evidence in terms of applicable law that have a bearing on the decision. Other considerations include: (1) the prosecutor's reasonable doubt that the accused is in fact guilty; (2) the extent of the harm caused by the offense; (3) the disproportion of the authorized punishment in relation to the particular offense or the offender; (4) possible improper motives for a complainant; (5) prolonged nonenforcement of a statute, with community acquiescence; (6) the reluctance of the victim to testify; (7) cooperation of the accused in the apprehension or conviction of others; and (8) availability and likelihood of prosecution by another jurisdiction. The ABA standards, like the works of Miller, Grosman, and others, is an elaboration and substantiation of the belief that for proper charging what is needed is a careful and rational review of the information available to the prosecutor.

In addition to the availability of facts necessary to make proper decisions or implement proper intake procedures, time constraints also are a consideration, especially since the timing of police reports and the timing of court appearances vary creating thereby varying effects. We will examine some of these subsequently, and explore the implications they pose. Unfortunately, although many case studies of single offices exist, and some researchers (Katz, Cole, Eisenstein, and Jacob, to name a few) have examined clusters of offices in which this facet of prosecutorial activity is examined, no systematic study of this aspect of police prosecutor relationships has been undertaken with respect to the time constraints and how they affect charging.

Gathering and collecting evidence may span a number of days or sometimes weeks, yet many jurisdictions require the defendant to be brought before a court within 24 hours or "without undue delay." It is at this time that the defendant is notified of the police charges, of his right to remain silent, of his right to be represented by counsel, of his right to be assigned counsel if he is indigent, of his right to a preliminary hearing, and of his possible release on bail. The first appearance, preliminary examination, or arraignment, as it is variously known, does not necessarily require the filing of prosecutorial charges nor the taking of a plea from the defendant. It serves primarily as a means for setting bail and assigning counsel, if needed.

The distinction between this court hearing and a preliminary hearing to determine probable cause is an important one, because it separates the requirement for reviewing the justification of restricting a person's liberty as soon as possible from the requirement of the prosecutor to review the evidence and make a charging decision. In too many jurisdictions the distinction is blurred, both are treated as one and the same, resulting in charges being filed in this abbreviated time span. To achieve this, police are under intense pressure to forward reports to the prosecutor as soon as possible even though they may be incomplete and based on the barest facts or observations.

Where the distinction between first appearance, for bond setting and assignment of counsel, and preliminary hearing for determining probable cause is made, most states require that the hearing be held within a reasonable time, some specifying a period within 10 days or 2 weeks.[37] Sometime within this period after arrest the prosecutor then can file charges. The advantage, of course, is that additional time for evidence gathering and review is possible.

If timing is a key factor in the intake process, the length of time between the arrest and the receipt of the police report should be crucial to the prosecution. One might expect that this is one procedure that operates smoothly between the two agencies because of its day-to-day repetitiveness. But the contrary is more often the case. The NCPM survey, for example, found that a surprising one-third of the prosecutors reported that they had to ask the police for the report instead of it automatically being filed with them.

One would expect that in addition to the automatic transmittal of police reports to the prosecutor that this would be done promptly. Yet, again, the results contradict the assumption. The NCPM survey showed wide variation in the timing of the receipt of these reports, as summarized in table 4-1.

**Table 4-1**
**Distribution of Offices Responding by Time from Arrest to Receipt of Police Reports**
*(percent)*

| Reports Received | Offices Responding *(N = 539)* |
|---|---|
| Immediately | 6.1 |
| Within 24 hours | 41.3 |
| Within 1 week | 35.6 |
| More than 1 week | 16.9 |

Fewer than half of the offices (47 percent) responded that they received the police reports within 24 hours after the arrest. If one sets a goal of swift reporting, one could conclude from these figures that the majority of prosecutors operate under what could be considered less than favorable conditions. Fifty-three percent receive the reports within a week or more. However, the delay is more understandable if these statistics are examined and interpreted in terms of other factors, one of which is detective and investigative resources. Although nationwide data are not available, field visits indicate that such delays are most common where detectives or investigators conduct extensive case preparations before referring the case to the prosecutor. These activities may include, for example, obtaining supplemental reports from the chemist, coroner, or other expert witnesses; taking witness testimony and statements as well as defendant statements; and the development and building of the chain of evidence. This procedure is in stark contrast to other law enforcement agencies where these activities are minimal because the initial report, and sometimes the arrest record, are forwarded immediately.

It is interesting to note that, although the extensive case preparation performed by detectives may create delay by increasing the time between arrest and prosecutorial review, in the long run, it may be far more effective for its ability to develop a better quality case and support a better quality review. The early review of the facts for a charging decision may, in fact, be counterproductive if it diminishes the extent to which the detectives have time available to work up the case. Coupled with the tendency for the police to "close the books" with an arrest, the value of a speedy transmittal of police reports for speedy prosecutorial decision making may be seriously questioned.

Not all delays in receiving police reports can be attributed to the modes of transmittal. Far too many simply reflect inefficient procedures or actual breakdowns in the intake process. As an indication of this, 33 percent of the prosecutors reported in the NCPM survey that they had to request the police report, rap sheet, or other evidentiary investigative materials rather than having them automatically forwarded. Breakdowns are also more likely when a prosecutor deals with more than one law enforcement agency. Without coordination, even the determination of which agency to contact may be problematical. When the police file complaints directly with the magistrate, bypassing the prosecutor, other breakdowns may be sparked. Under these conditions, the case may be presented to the magistrate, a bail decision made about the suspect, and the complaint and/or warrant signed by the magistrate without the participation of the prosecutor. When the paperwork reaches the prosecutor (the time will vary according to court procedures) it may or may not have a police report attached. Clearly, the prosecutor is stymied in his work until adequate information can be obtained. In some jurisdictions, unless the sheriff notifies the prosecutor by a "jail list," the prosecutor may be unaware of an arrest and subsequently surprised by a docketed case. Even where jail lists are maintained and routinely forwarded, the prosecutor still must coordinate the arrest information, the rap sheet, and the witnesses.

Paperflow between two different agencies, between police and prosecutor, for example, can present management problems that are capable of producing complete system dysfunction, even though the process for remedying the solution might be quite simple. One prosecutor's office, to illustrate the point, had been experiencing great difficulty in filing cases because of a police practice of batching all cases over a week's time and filing them with the prosecutor en masse. The result had been the creation of "peakloads," days in which the prosecutor was deluged with cases whereas the rest of the week's input was rather light. The prosecutor was also experiencing difficulty, because of this police practice, in meeting his jurisdiction's requirements of filing all charges within 10 days of the original arrest or complaint. The problem was eventually resolved after a conversation with the chief of police revealed that no one in the prosecutor's office had taken the time to explain that "batching" created problems that would be eliminated if each day's work were sent out daily.

Many prosecutors seek to increase their intake effectiveness by adding their own investigative resources to those of the police. Both parties admit to the need for better coordination and education, but the existence of both activities results in a less than clear understanding or agreement on the division of responsibilities between police detectives and prosecutor investigators.

NDAA offers an extensive discussion of these roles in *National Prosecution Standards*.[38] Their standards recognize that "investigation is primarily a police function" and "question . . . the prosecutor/investigator relationship with the police" with respect to maintaining autonomy and distance.[39] But they espouse the maintenance of an investigative staff in the office of the prosecutor to supplement the police activity (standard 7.1). Leonard and Saxe, quoted in the commentary on this standard, attempt to shed light on the distinction between the roles and the inappropriateness of speedy charging decisions. They state: "A prosecutor who bases his estimate of the probability of a case on a one-page police report can easily dismiss strong cases and press cases that ultimately prove to have little foundation. A prosecutor with no background information about an offender can easily mistake a dangerous person with plausible manner or story for a marginal offender."[40] With regard to the respective roles of the two agencies, they state, "although the information and evidence which the police gather is useful to the prosecutor, the difference in purpose between police and prosecutorial investigation should be noted: while the police gather evidence for the purpose of arrest, the prosecutor's sights are geared toward conviction."[41] Yet this distinction becomes blurred when the investigators in the police agencies are trained to have the same "conviction sights."

The juxtaposition of these two requirements—the need for adequate police information and the need for prosecutorial investigators—does not resolve the dilemma created by conflicting goals. But it does move in a direction that should reduce the problems created by inadequate information or poor investigations.

### The Transmission of Reports—Different Routes

One cannot examine the effects of the police reporting procedures on the intake process of prosecution without taking into account the case-processing procedure and transmittal route from the police to the prosecutor. We have noted that the adequacy of the information and the timeliness of the information has great bearing on the ability of the prosecutor to review and screen cases. We will now examine the way these cases and reports come to him and the implications each of the different routes has on his ability to screen and make charging decisions.

There are potentially five actors in the police intake transmittal process: the arresting police officer (APO), the detective, the police (or court) liaison officer, the magistrate, and the prosecutor. Each performs separate and distinct functions, but the effect on the prosecutor varies according to how many participate and according to the order of participation.

A police officer may arrest any person who commits a crime in his presence.[42] Even though the officer has not witnessed the crime, if the crime is a felony, he is permitted to arrest if there is probable cause to believe that a crime has been committed and that the suspect is the guilty party. If the crime is not a felony, the police officer may arrest only on the basis of a duly authorized complaint signed by the complaining witness and an arrest warrant.

The role of the arresting police officer does not end with the arrest of a suspect. Although his decision-making power may be transferred to either a detective or the prosecutor, he still must serve as witness and sometimes, the coordinator of other witnesses. His involvement in the case extends through the entire justice system.

If the case is transferred to a detective unit within the law enforcement agency, the detective on the case "has almost total discretion as to whether to proceed with the prosecution. He can simply release the suspect if he does not believe that the evidence warrants prosecution, or he can initiate formal proceedings."[43] In the latter decision, the detective may work independent of the prosecutor's office in developing the evidence, taking statements and witness testimony; or he may work in conjunction with the prosecutor. If the last, the detective becomes more responsive to the prosecutor's needs and with continuous association, absorbs the prosecutor's perception of what evidence is necessary for successful processing. Examples of such cooperative efforts can be found in the Philadelphia District Attorney's office where the homicide division works with the police department's homicide detectives; in Kansas City, Missouri, where the Jackson County Prosecuting Attorney's office works closely with the Kansas City Police Department detectives whose interest spans all felonies; and in Washington, D.C., where "Operation Doorstop" was formulated by the Metropolitan Police Department and the U.S. Attorneys office to stop the "revolving door" career criminal so effectively.

If the prosecutor has his own investigative resources, the extent of the detective's participation in case preparation may be determined by the adequacy of the detective's work and skills. The National Advisory Commission (NAC) alluded to this problem: "The prosecutor's primary function should be to represent the State in court. He should cooperate with the police in their investigation of crime. Each prosecutor also should have investigatorial resources at his disposal to assist him in case preparation, to supplement the results of police investigation when the police lack adequate resources for such investigation."[44] In general, one can assume that the detective, representing a higher level of achievement, brings more professionalism and experience into the intake process.

The third actor in the intake transmittal process is the police liaison officer, also known in jurisdictions variously as court liaison officer, duty or watch officer. His duties vary almost as much as his title. Perhaps the best list of his duties was compiled by the NAC: to maintain lines of communication; to discuss and identify mutual administrative problems and develop solutions; to limit unnecessary court appearances by police officers; to inform officers of the disposition of their cases and reasons for unfavorable dispositions; to obtain the assistance of offices in the preparation of cases for trial; and to insure police reports are forwarded promptly to the prosecutor's office.[45]

This last activity will be the subject of our attention. In some jurisdictions, the liaison officer merely acts as a courier, bringing batches of police reports to the prosecutor's office. In other jurisdictions, he assumes more of the other duties listed. As courier, he has little knowledge of the content of the cases he carries.

The magistrate, justice of the peace, municipal court judge, or police court judge is the principal judicial officer, usually presiding over a court of limited or inferior jurisdiction, and has the authority to authorize a search or arrest warrant, hold a preliminary examination and a probable cause hearing for felony arrests. His warrant issuance power, exercised without prosecutorial approval, has spawned a maelstrom of controversy over his power to control the intake process. Adding more fuel to this fire is the fact that, sometimes, it is not even the magistrate who issues complaints and warrants but the court clerk. For example, in Massachusetts the police (or civilians) approach the District Court Clerk for a complaint. Usually within 1 day, the defendant is brought into District Court for arraignment and bail setting, and, if a felony is involved, a probable cause hearing is scheduled in a period of 10 days to 2 weeks. The Massachusetts Assistant District Attorney is given little if any opportunity to review the facts and no opportunity to approve the complaint or warrant. It is of little wonder that this practice is roundly condemned by the prosecutors. Nor is it surprising to see them adopt a strong stance with regard to warrant review that states in part: "A. The office of the prosecutor should review all applications for search warrants whenever practical and all complaints for felonies to be executed within the prosecutor's jurisdiction. B. No application for an arrest warrant should be submitted to a judge without the prior review and approval by the prosecutor's office."[46] They argue that "Whether lawyers or laymen, magistrates do not have the investigational facilities available to prosecutors. . . ."[47] Where magistrate intervention precedes that of the prosecutors, the system accommodates such a practice, invoking neither police nor prosecution sanctions, since the ultimate control rests with the prosecutor's power to *nolle prosequi* the case.

Finally, the prosecutor himself, with the sole responsibility for the charging decision is called on to "see that the charge selected adequately describes the offense or offenses committed"[48] and that "the decision to initiate or pursue criminal charges should be within the discretion of the prosecutor excepting only the grand jury."[49] As LaFave indicated, the decision to prosecute may not differ substantially from the consideration of the same factors that led to the decision of arrest.[50] However, it is the prosecutor who has the sole responsibility for charging or not charging.

With this cast of actors, it is now possible to examine the impact of various transmittal routes on initiating the prosecutor's work and affecting either the quantity and quality of his workload. We will consider first police-generated complaints, then citizen complaints. Table 4-2 illustrates

**Table 4-2**
**Order of Transmittal, Police-Originated Complaints**

| Actors | Case Transmittal Modes | | | | | | |
|---|---|---|---|---|---|---|---|
| | With Review Function | | | | No Review Function | | |
| | 1 | 2 | 3 | 4 | 5 | 6 | 7 |
| APO | 1 | 1 | 1 | 1 | 1 | 1 | 1 |
| Detective | | 2 | | 2 | | | 2 |
| Police liaison | | | 2 | 3 | | 2 | |
| Prosecutor | 2 | 3 | 3 | 4 | 3 | 4 | 4 |
| Magistrate | 3 | 4 | 4 | 5 | 2 | 3 | 3 |

the variety of information flow routes that are possible in the processing of a criminal complaint. The initiator (in this case the Arresting Police Officer, APO) is designated as number 1. The next person or agency to whom he transmits the information is number 2, the third person or agency number 3, and so forth. By discussing these transmittal modes one can briefly highlight the different external conditions facing the prosecutor during the intake process.

Mode 1 accounts for a large proportion of prosecutorial intake procedures. Coupled with mode 2, which introduces a detective function into the process, it represents the majority of intake routes. In mode 1, the arresting police officer brings the police report of the event directly to the prosecutor for review before the charge is filed in court. As we have noted, although the information contained in the report may be minimal, one could expect it to be timely and as complete as possible under the circumstances. Since these reports are most likely to be completed prior to the end of the police officer's duty shift and reviewed for accuracy by a senior watch officer, they usually are available within 24 hours of the arrest. However, the arresting officer is limited in the amount of time he can spend on investigations and is not necessarily trained in the detective function. As a result, his report to the prosecutor may very likely be judged insufficient.

The expected prosecutorial responses to cases judged insufficient include ordering additional police investigation for the missing elements of the case, assuming the responsibility for strengthening the case himself if he has the investigative resources, or declining to prosecute on the basis of insufficient evidence and data. The decision to order additional investigation depends on the resources of the police department, the value of the case to the prosecutor, and the resources of the prosecutor. Obviously, the specific mix of these factors limits the options of the prosecutor.

When the arresting police officer (APO) is the primary source of information, to order additional investigation results in one of two police activities: either the APO performs this in addition to his ordinary routine duties or the case is transferred to a detective squad. If the responsibility is given to the APO, the daily, ongoing duties and assignments of the police officers leave little time for such additional activities, and the police system itself offers few incentives or rewards for performing them. The latter course of action (using police investigators or detectives) also produces no guarantees that the needed work will be done on time. Without initial involvement in the case, and an intimate knowledge of the facts, the detective is less likely to identify with the prosecutor's priorities and requests, especially if these interfere with his other ongoing investigations. Even if the investigation is performed, the uncertainty of whether the police agency can meet a court-imposed time schedule is a factor to be measured and evaluated in the decision to order additional investigation. Clearly the workload of the investigative units is a consideration in the prosecutor's decision. The net results are to decrease the amount of additional investigation ordered for valuable cases to minimum acceptable levels; to decline prosecution of marginal cases needing complex investigations; and to call for more investigative resources. "The facts are counsel's most important assets and the investigation is the instrument for getting the facts."[51] The recognition that "evidence gathering or the task of reconstructing accurately past events is so difficult and carries such serious consequences" plays a strong part in the desire of the prosecutors to have their own investigative staff.[52] It also may reflect levels of dissatisfaction with police investigative procedures.

Because of all these limitations, the prosecutor's intake environment can be characterized generally as one that gives only cursory review to the facts presented by the police officer and bases charging decisions more on the existence of the legal elements in the case than on its sufficiency for trial. The weakness of this position is clearly pointed out by Katz: "Aside from the importance of the alleged crime, the most significant criterion is whether the case provides enough admissible evidence to secure a conviction. It is a waste of time for the court, prosecutor, police, and witnesses to involve themselves in a case where the evidence will not support a conviction of the charge."[53] Nevertheless, one must not overlook an important benefit that accrues to the prosecutor in this mode. He, at least, has the opportunity to review the case before the charges are filed and reject it outright or order more work if its value warrants.

It seems obvious after this discussion that a more valuable intake environment is created when the detective is interjected into the transmittal route (mode 2). In this transmittal mode, with a professionally trained detective force, one would expect to find most of the complaints about inadequate investigations disappearing and opportunities for the prosecutor to make more than a cursory review of the facts increasing.

With urbanization, the emergence of large, bureaucratic law enforcement agencies and more sophisticated technology for developing evidence, specialized units or detective units have expanded in law enforcement. Some units are trained and equipped to handle specific crimes such as robbery, vice, homicide, narcotics, rackets, and so forth. Others assume more general duties; their training is broader and their assignment to cases is determined more by what occurs during the shift than by specific crime. Some jurisdictions assign detectives on the basis of other factors such as the severity or frequency of the crime or the seriousness of the defendant. New York City, for example, grouped some of its detectives into a Major Offense unit to work in conjunction with the prosecutors in getting "career criminals" off the streets.[54] Regardless of how they are structured, where detective forces are available as a resource, one can expect to find routine and simpler crimes flowing directly from the arresting police officer to the prosecutor, whereas the more serious or more complicated are developed and prepared by detectives.

When the detective function meets the prosecutor's intake process, three issues emerge: the extent to which the detectives are trained and qualified to develop the evidence and meet prosecutorial needs; the degree of cooperation between the detectives and the assistant prosecutors; and the timing of the reports. Vitally important to the prosecutor is the support of a professional and highly trained detective force. Yet this is not easy to achieve. As Uviller stated: "To our police we have assigned the task of identifying, locating and apprehending the criminals among us while carefully assembling the evidence of their guilt from a variety of sources. It is a demanding assignment under the best of circumstances. And the circumstances are rarely of the best."[55] The abilities of the detective forces to develop the evidence, preserve the chain of evidence that might be destroyed otherwise by a less skilled police officer on the scene, take statements of witness testimony, ensure constitutional protections, and produce well-documented cases plays a significant part in expanding the number of choices as available to the prosecutor at the intake stage. With sufficient information, the prosecutor is able to make more considered and realistic decisions, which in subtle forms have profound effects on defendants. More options open up for the prosecutor as a result of more substantial information: the prosecutor who has a complete criminal history available may be able to invoke the habitual offenders statute rather than simply filing on the instant offense; the prosecutor who is aware of mitigating circumstances may choose deferred prosecution rather than insisting on participation in a diversion program. When the detective force is inadequate or poorly trained, the prosecutor not only receives little benefit from their work, but in addition, may have to deal with problems arising from a lack of investigative time. Time spent by the detective force in producing imperfect results is time wasted if it means that the prosecutor must salvage the case himself at a later date.

The second issue characteristic of this transmittal route is the extent and type of cooperation between the detectives and the prosecutors. In some jurisdictions, as noted earlier, where the detectives work closely with the prosecutors in developing the case, they are more likely to absorb the prosecutor's goals and value system as well as gain a deeper appreciation of the legal requirements needed for conviction. Their activity and success measures tend to be conviction oriented rather than arrest oriented.

There is a major difference between the intake procedures that involve the detectives' preparation of the case report and those where only the arresting police officer is involved; it can be found in the timing of the receipt of the report. If only an APO is involved in preparing a report, it usually can be completed by the end of his shift. But if detectives are involved, one can expect a properly investigated and prepared case to consume a number of detective hours, if not days. The detective function is best supported by court environments that do not expect immediate prosecutorial charging decisions or preliminary hearings. If preliminary hearings to determine probable cause are held from 20 hours to 20 days after the arrest or the defendant's initial appearance, the prosecutor (and the detectives) are able to extend their evidence collection and review process time. If by court rule, interpretation, or tradition, the defendant is charged within 24 hours after arrest by the prosecutor, one would not expect to find an active or involved detective/prosecutor relationship especially with respect to on-the-scene arrests. Regardless of the consequences we still must remember that these variations occur in an environment permitting prosecutorial review before charging.

Modes 3 and 4 inject a police liaison officer into the previously described procedures. Depending on the role of this actor, the effects on prosecution intake vary. If the liaison officer is merely a courier, collecting batches of cases prepared by the police officers and bringing them to the prosecutor for review, it is obvious that the intake assistant's opportunity for questioning someone with on-the-scene knowledge of the event before he makes a charging decision is almost nonexistent, hence his charging decision of questionable quality. Even if he has time before the decision is made, his scheduling of interviews with the police officer is complicated and subject to breakdowns. Of all information routes, these two appear to offer the most hazards to the prosecutor's intake review process. If on the other hand, the liaison officer acts as a courier for detective-developed cases, these problems are reduced because most of the information needed by the prosecutor should be contained in the reports. Communication between the prosecutor and the detective would operate more on an exceptional basis than as an ongoing daily routine.

When the liaison officer's role expands from courier to coordinator, it affects other stages of prosecution, such as assembling witnesses and evidence and coordinating police appearances in the court. This coordination and liaison function may also serve as a vital link between the prosecutor and the police in the areas of "additional investigation." Thus, one should first specify what this actor does and within what processing environment before evaluating its effect.

The NAC states, in part, in standard 1.2, "No complaint should be filed or arrest warrant issued without the formal approval of the prosecutor."[56] Yet despite this admonition, these procedures exist in Chicago, Illinois, Brooklyn, New York, and Baltimore, Maryland.[57] The standards adamantly call for prosecutorial review and approval, justifying such a review by noting the distinction between a judicial review on the sufficiency of the evidence to convict and the accused's right to obtain a judicial determination of whether "adequate evidence is available to justify trial."[58] In addition, they recognize the unreviewable authority of the prosecutor to refuse to charge and state that "there should be no judicial involvement in the decision not to screen."[59]

In those jurisdictions where the prosecutor is the recipient of court papers after complaints have been filed by police or citizens (Modes 5-7 in table 4-2), the consequences are so overwhelming that the transmittal route to the prosecutor has little effect on his intake procedures. The latter are dependent on the amount of information received from the court, the difficulties in obtaining basic documentation from the police or complaining witness, the degree to which the details of the case can be reconstructed at a later time, the ability to identify witnesses, and the timing of the receipt of documents and reports with respect to the next court date.

Some of these problems may exist also in intake environments affording prosecutorial reviews and, once corrected, produce a desirable situation. Where prior review and approval are not part of the prosecutive function the situation is more difficult to correct. Since the early 1900s and the first crime commission reports and until the current publication of standards by the ABA and the NDAA, the case has repeatedly been made for the prosecutor's review and charging authority. Where prior review is not the practice, the prosecutor has generally been forced to resort to the use of other corrective procedures such as *nolles* or dismissals, deferred prosecution, or treatment programs.

Besides his inability to review cases prior to acceptance, the prosecutor is afforded no opportunity to correct or control police arrest policy. He can only respond to police activity rather than shape police performance to meet prosecutorial needs. The traditional aim of creating separate spheres of responsibility for each agency is encumbered by this type of court action. In other words, the direct feedback loop between police and prosecutor has been disturbed. By intervening in the charging process, the court may be placed in the awkward position either of assuming some of the prosecutor's charging authority or, if it wishes to maintain its judicial distance, of becoming a simple assentor to police activity.

In sum, the process of prosecutorial review subsequent to court filings produces unnecessary delays and takes in unnecessary cases. As Katz pointed out,

> the key to reversing the trend of greater and greater delays in the criminal justice system lies in its preliminary stages. If the proposed time line for disposition of criminal cases is to become a reality, the process must be reconstructed at its earliest stage. The number of preliminary steps must be cut, and those that are retained must be redeveloped so that the goals of charging and screening are fulfilled within the concepts of equitable and speedy justice. Each step of the procedure must become a meaningful judicial exercise, not just a formalistic, court-clogging requirement.[60]

## Citizen Complaints

Despite the extensive literature devoted to the intake process of the prosecutor, his screening procedures, and discretionary charging authority, little attention has been devoted to the special needs of the citizen complainants and their relation to prosecution. Perhaps part of the reason for the low visibility of citizen complaints is because of the diverse ways they are handled by the criminal justice system or shunted into other governmental agencies. The many different ways tend to dilute their identification as an element in the intake process. Since complaints are ultimately translated into a police report and subsquently handled as a police-arrest procedure, citizen-initiated complaints, as an entity, become indistinguishable from the police-initiated cases. Citizen complaints may constitute a numerically large proportion of the prosecutor's intake process. For example, in 1972, the State's Attorney's office in Dade County (Miami), Florida, reviewed approximately one hundred citizen complaints a day, although it accepted only five or six for prosecution.[61]

Citizen complaints are those that arise from either the citizen's observance of the commission of a crime or from his victimization. The vast majority of complaints are domestic in nature. Although there are a growing number of complaints involving consumer issues, the most common ones revolve around assaults, abusive treatment, and other interpersonal breakdowns.

Many jurisdictions have responded to citizen-initiated complaints and to the need for domestic relations assistance by creating specialized institutions, courts, or agencies. About half of the prosecutors responding to the NCPM survey stated they had specialized citizen complaint sections, some with intake centers like that which exists in Washington, D.C. These intake centers are equipped to handle the myriad of problems facing the troubled citizens, some of which might eventually result in being referred for criminal prosecution.

Other jurisdictions provide few specialized services to the citizen. They are forced to sit in the waiting room in the prosecutor's office with lawyers, police officers, defendants, and witnesses until their complaint can be handled by an assistant. Some offices assign paralegals for initial screening; others use the office's assistant prosecutors, scheduling all citizen complaints for the evening hearings, thus accommodating both the citizen's and the prosecutor's work schedule.

It is a delicate task to handle the problems of emotionally wrought and angry citizens and to ferret out the correct legal determination. The assistant must ascertain whether a crime has been committed, whether there is sufficient evidence to convict, and whether a prosecution is in the best interests of the parties and the community. The assistant tries to strike a delicate balance. Often complaints are only domestic squabbles, where the complainant will be unwilling to testify by the time the case comes to court. Yet, domestic problems can, at times, erupt into violence, and assistants are aware that failure to act in those cases may result in further injury or death to the citizen who is seeking assistance. Citizen complaints are difficult to assess because of the lack of prior case evaluation by the police, which is available in most other cases. This area is unpredictable—most cases are simple enough, but some have tremendous potential for destruction.

This, perhaps more than any other reason, is why the citizen complainant receives the biggest "run-around" in the criminal justice system. Table 4-3 illustrates the variety of procedures used in processing a citizen complaint.

If the citizen (1) first approaches the prosecutor, the reviewing assistant, or paralegal, briefly determines whether there is indeed a crime and whether the victim or complaining witness will be willing to go forward with the accusations and testimony after a period of time that constitutes a "cooling off" period. If these conditions seem to be satisfied, the prosecutor may issue a complaint and warrant (Mode 1) or, more likely, may refer the citizen to the police so that a police report of the offense can be prepared before the warrant is issued (Mode 2). A variation occurs when the pros-

Table 4-3
Orders of Referral for Citizen Complaints

| Actors | Mode | | | |
|---|---|---|---|---|
| | *1* | *2* | *3* | *4* |
| Citizen | 1 | 1 | 1 | 1 |
| Police department | | 3 | 2 | |
| Prosecutor | 2 | 2 | 3 | 3 |
| Magistrate | 3 | 4 | 4 | 2 |

ecutor does not make the decision but tells the citizen to go to the police with the complaint. If the police believe a crime has been committed, then they submit a police report for prosecutorial review and charging (Mode 3).

When the citizen first approaches the police, three events may occur. First the police may agree to file a complaint and submit the paperwork for prosecutorial or magisterial review and approval. Or the police may refer the case to the prosecutor for his evaluation before taking any further action. Or, in some jurisdictions, the complaint may be sent to the magistrate for the issuance of a warrant.

In some jurisdictions the citizen may directly approach the magistrate for relief. After review the magistrate may issue the complaint and warrant directly, refer the case to the prosecutor for review before issuing, or send the applicant to the police for formal processing (Mode 4).

What is obvious about all these processing routes is that there is little opportunity to fix responsibility for decision making or to establish any accountability for decisions or actions. Therefore the potential for abuse, indifference, or inaction is great.

Reiss has pointed to the paradoxical treatment of citizens as law enforcers and victims or complainants.[62] He describes the former by noting that the criminal justice system is loosely organized and highly discretionary with the first discretionary powers being wielded by the citizens. "The *citizen law-enforcement system* is made up of private citizens and their corporate bodies in their role as enforcers of the law. Citizens control much of the input into the criminal justice system by making discretionary decisions to mobilize the police or to seek warrants from the prosecutor. Citizens also crucially control the information that is input for processing the system by being the main source of evidence in criminal events. Their oral testimony often is the sole evidence for deciding criminal matters."[63] Despite this great power, Reiss also comments that the "bureaucratization of justice increasing denies citizens their formal roles in the system and relegates them to informal control within the citizen system."[64] This impact is evident not only in the citizen's well-publicized, formal role as witness or juror, but also in the less obvious intake process where the citizen is an initiator of the action. Yet as Reiss so aptly foresaw: "Fewer and fewer citizens enter the role of formal witness or juror; their main status is that of complainant."[65] When their role as complainant is processed initially outside of the law enforcement environment, through the vehicle known as citizen complaint, their status as a complainant is undermined, and the review and approval functions exercised by the prosecutor during the intake stages may never occur. Clearly this is an area requiring further examination when one considers the overall power of the citizen to control much of the input into the criminal justice system and the disturbing trend to decrease his importance in the criminal justice system by the prosecutor's reliance on nontrial dispositions. This trend itself may be the reason for such an absence of concern in this area.


## Conclusion

The intake process of prosecution is dominated by two issues: the ability to review and approve charges before they are filed in court and the extent to which the evidence is available for review and charging. The different types of intake procedures result, as we have observed, in vastly different prosecutorial responses. Some of these point up the absence of these issues, others simply demonstrate a need for change or more efficient procedures. Of critical importance is the amount of time given to case preparation prior to prosecutorial review. This is one of the few areas in the prosecutive process where delay favors the prosecutor. The simple separation of the first appearance to set bond and appoint counsel from a preliminary hearing to determine probable cause may produce, in many instances, the time needed to properly review a case. A well-trained detective force, as an adjunct during these initial proceedings, maximizes the review function. There is little evidence or logic to support the existence of procedures that deny the prosecutor review before filing a case in court or present him with hastily compiled information. The need for "deliberate speed" at this point in the process is most critical.


## Notes

1. A good bibliography on this subject is W. Randolph Teslik, *Prosecutorial Discretion: The Decision to Charge—An Annotated Bibliography* (Washington, D.C.: National Criminal Justice Reference Service, Law Enforcement Assistance Administration, 1975).

2. National Center for Prosecution Management, *Model Prosecution Report and Model Casefile* (Washington, D.C.: National Center for Prosecution Management, 1974).

3. See George F. Cole, "The Decision to Prosecute," *Law and Society Review* 4, no. 3 (February 1970):331-343.

4. A short but thorough discussion of the evolution of American policing can be found in William Lineberry, ed., *Justice in America* (New York: W. Wilson, 1972), pp. 12-26.

5. Ibid., p. 13.

6. National Advisory Commission on Criminal Justice Standards and Goals (NAC), *Courts* (Washington, D.C.: U.S. Government Printing Office, 1975), p. 25.

7. Herbert Jacob, *Urban Justice: Law and Order in American Cities* (Englewood Cliffs, N.J.: Prentice-Hall, 1973).

8. James Q. Wilson, *Varieties of Police Behavior* (Cambridge, Mass.: Harvard University Press, 1968).

9. Ibid., pp. 140-171.

10. Ibid., pp. 171-199.

11. Ibid., pp. 200-226.

12. Joan E. Jacoby, *The Prosecutor's Charging Decision: A Policy Perspective* (Washington, D.C.: Law Enforcement Assistance Administration, 1977), pp. 13-32.

13. Albert J. Reiss, Jr. and David J. Bordua, "Environment and Organization: A Perspective on the Police," in *The Police: Six Sociological Essays*, ed. David Bordua (New York: John Wiley and Sons, 1976), pp. 25-55.

14. President's Commission on Law Enforcement and the Administration of Criminal Justice, *Task Force Report: The Courts* (Washington, D.C.: U.S. Government Printing Office, 1967), p. 5.

15. Battelle Law and Justice Study Center, *Forcible Rape: A National Survey of the Responses of Prosecutors* (Washington, D.C.: National Institute of Law Enforcement and Criminal Justice, Law Enforcement Assistance Administration, 1977), pp. 2, 21.

16. Peter W. Greenwood et al., *Prosecutions of Adult Felony Defendants in Los Angeles County: A Policy Perspective* (Santa Monica, Calif.: The Rand Corporation, 1973), pp. 84-86.

17. National Center for Prosecution Management, *Model Prosecution Report* (Washington, D.C.: National Center for Prosecution Management, 1973).

18. Frank W. Miller, *Prosecution: The Decision to Charge a Suspect with a Crime* (Boston: Little, Brown, 1969), pp. 21-23.

19. American Bar Association, *Standards Relating to the Prosecution Function and the Defense Function* (New York: American Bar Association, 1971), pp. 43-46.

20. The Vera Institute, *Felony Arrests: Their Prosecution and Disposition in New York City Courts* (New York: The Vera Institute of Justice, 1977).

21. Lewis R. Katz, *Justice Is the Crime: Pretrial Delay in Felony Cases* (Cleveland, Ohio: Case Western Reserve University Press, 1972), p. 105.

22. Brian Grosman, *The Prosecutor: An Inquiry into the Exercise of Discretion* (Toronto: University of Toronto Press, 1969), pp. 20-23.

23. NAC, *Courts*, p. 24.

24. Abraham Blumberg, *Criminal Justice* (Chicago: Quadrangle Press, 1970), p. 53.

25. George Cole, *Criminal Justice: Law and Politics* (North Scituate, Massachusetts: Duxbury Press, 1972), pp. 173-174.

26. See Martin Fleming, *The Price of Perfect Justice* (New York: Basic Books, 1974), pp. 54-55, for his discussion of delaying tactics and their effects.

27. *U.S. News and World Report*, 11 January 1971, p. 65.

28. Cole, *Criminal Justice*, pp. 173-174.

29. Katz, *Justice Is the Crime*, p. 104.

30. Grosman, *The Prosecutor*, pp. 20-21.

31. Miller, *Prosecution: Decision to Charge*, p. 19.

32. Grosman, *The Prosecutor*, p. 25, and Miller, *Prosecution: Decision to Charge*, p. 17.

33. Miller, *Prosecution: Decision to Charge*, p. 19.

34. Ibid., p. 16.

35. Katz, *Justice Is the Crime*, pp. 130-132.

36. American Bar Association, *Standards*, pp. 92-98.

37. See Katz, *Justice Is the Crime*, app. B.

38. National District Attorneys Association (NDAA), *National Prosecution Standards* (Chicago: The National District Attorneys Association, 1977), pp. 108-111.

39. Ibid., p. 110.

40. Robert F. Leonard and Joel B. Saxe, *Screening of Criminal Cases* (Chicago: The National District Attorneys Association, 1973), p. 22.

41. NDAA, *Standards*, p. 110.

42. See Delmar Karlen, *Anglo-American Criminal Justice* (1967), pp. 111-112.

43. Katz, *Justice Is the Crime*, p. 103.

44. NAC, *Courts*, p. 244.

45. Ibid., p. 248.

46. NDAA, *Standards*, p. 115.

47. Frank W. Miller and Lawrence P. Tiffany, "Prosecutor Dominance of the Warrant Decision: A Study of Current Practices," 1 Washington University Law Quarterly 6 (1970).

48. NDAA, *Standards*, p. 131.

49. Ibid., p. 125.

50. Wayne LaFave, "The Prosecutor in the United States," 18 American Journal of Comparative Law, 532, 536, and n. 25 (1970).

51. J. Gramenos, "Investigation and Discovery in Criminal Cases," 49 Chicago Bar Record 386 (1968).

52. NDAA, *Standards*, p. 110.

53. Katz, *Justice Is the Crime*, p. 113.

54. NAC, *Courts*, p. 245.

55. H. Richard Uviller, *The Process of Criminal Justice: Investigation and Adjudication* (St. Paul, Minnesota: West Publishing Co., 1974), p. 1.

56. NAC, *Courts*, p. 24.

57. Ibid., p. 25.

58. Ibid., p. 26.

59. Ibid., p. 26.

60. Katz, *Justice Is the Crime*, p. 126.

61. Joan E. Jacoby, "A Study of the Dade County Prosecutor's Office," (Paper, 1973).

62. Albert J. Reiss, Jr., "Discretionary Justice," in *Handbook of Criminology*, ed. Daniel Glaser (Chicago: Rand-McNally, 1974).

63. Ibid., p. 680.

64. Ibid., p. 695.

65. Ibid., p. 695.

# 5 The Accusatory Process

## Introduction

The accusatory process is a critical stage of the prosecution function that profoundly affects both the future of an individual defendant and the overall operations of the criminal justice system. It is during this process that the prosecutor first establishes strategic control over a case. The short time span occupied by the accusatory process, beginning with the decision to charge and ending with the arraignment on an accusatory instrument in the court, belies the power of its ability to limit the defense's knowledge of the evidentiary strength of the case, to change the processing time, and to enhance the investigative function of the prosecutor.

There are two major forms of criminal accusation in the United States: the grand jury indictment and the prosecutor's bill of information showing probable cause (ruled on at a preliminary hearing). Both procedures are deeply ingrained in the American system of justice, but they are so different from one another that they raise profoundly different legal and management issues. Each has a unique operational impact on prosecution.

This chapter will examine the dimensions of the accusatory process and the forms it most commonly takes. Understanding the variations in these processes helps explain corresponding variations in prosecutorial policy decisions. To set the stage, we will trace, first, the origins and growth of the grand jury, its composition, and the degree to which it is influenced by the prosecutor. We will discuss the introduction of the prosecutor's bill of information in the mid-1800s as an alternative accusatory procedure and the controversy it sparked as it grew in importance and use. As the effect of the recent Supreme Court decision in *Gerstein* v. *Pugh*[1] became known and as increasing emphasis was placed on system efficiencies, the popularity of preliminary hearings as the primary accusatory process increased.

There are four commonly used accusatory processes that can be altered or changed to meet special needs. Integral to some is the grand jury. We will examine the essential powers of this body, and discuss whether alternative institutions are sufficient to justify abolishing the grand jury.

All this is preparatory to a discussion of the effect of various accusatory forms as they foster different prosecutorial attitudes, favor different prosecution strategies, and create structural barriers or environments.

*The Origin and Growth of the Grand Jury*

The grand jury was first conceived in England in 1166 during Henry II's struggle for power with the church and aristocracy.[2] Initially intended to serve as an instrument for the consolidation of royal power, it operated for almost five hundred years with little change. At the end of the seventeenth century, however, the grand jury began to gain a degree of independence from the crown, which transformed it into a shield for individual liberty against oppression by the state. By 1681, the grand jury was a strong enough institution in its own right to be capable of opposing the will of the monarch, Charles II, by refusing to indict his foremost political enemy, Lord Shaftsbury. The grand jury continued to be an integral part of the British legal system until World War I, when its use was temporarily suspended. The great emotion and paranoia of the war years had resulted in numerous problems caused by run-away grand juries returning wholesale accusations. Reinstated after the war but heavily criticized for inefficiency and wastefulness, the grand jury was abolished by Parliament in 1933, almost eight hundred years after its inception.[3] The grand jury was brought by English settlers to the New World and became part of American common law heritage. The first regular grand jury to sit in the colonies attended the Court of Assistants of the Massachusetts Bay Colony in September 1635. Virginia, founded earlier than Massachusetts, did not seat its first grand jury until 1641. Rhode Island, Connecticut, and the other colonies followed soon after.

Although its duties were patterned after the English juries, there were, from the first, innovations in the colonial juries. In early America, the grand jury served as a kind of ongoing community meeting, acting as a sounding board for judicial and lay opinion on a variety of community and governmental activities. As colonial towns grew and were incorporated, the grand jury became an important instrument for popular participation in municipal, county, and provincial government. By the end of the period, the grand jury was an indispensable part of colonial government.[4]

During the American Revolution, the colonists used the grand jury to harass British efforts in asserting the royal prerogative. In numerous cases, but especially in Boston, the grand jury refused to return true bills in cases against citizens who opposed royal authority. Throughout this period, "grand juries enforced or refused to enforce laws as they saw fit and stood guard against the indiscriminate prosecution of royal officials."[5] Their strong partisan stance evoked reprisals from the British government, which subsequently refused to prosecute cases against British agents and soldiers even though the colonial grand juries had returned true bills.

By 1774, relations between the British government and the grand jury became so bad in Boston that Lord North suspended elective grand juries and began to seat jurors of his own selection. Emotions ran highest in Boston, but similar strife was to occur between British officials and American grand juries in every colony by the opening of the war.

Because of its crucial role in opposing British control the grand jury was retained by every state following American independence. As an institution, it was held in high esteem by postrevolutionary Americans, and its existence was guaranteed when it was written into the federal Constitution as part of the Fifth Amendment. In the early years of the Republic, the federal grand jury was a center of controversy and political disputes. The local grand juries in the states, however, enjoyed such widespread popularity that the new state constitutions and updated old ones all guaranteed the continued existence of the institution.

In the first half of the nineteenth century, a wave of political, legal, and social reforms prevailed. It affected the grand jury as well as all legal institutions in the United States and England. Reformers wanted to limit and restrict the wide powers of inquest that had been a traditional part of the grand jury, believing that they posed too great a threat to individual freedoms and rights. Beginning in Louisiana in 1821, legal changes were made to restrict acess to the grand jury by outside influences. Initially the length and content of statements that could be made to the grand jury by the judges or court were restricted. Eventually the access of public officials to inquests and the deliberations of the jury were also limited.

The reformers also sought alternative methods of presenting cases to court, methods that were more reasonable and efficient than indictment by the grand jury. Since the powers of the prosecuting attorney were expanding during this same period, the possibility of filing cases in court by a prosecutor's bill of information was given serious consideration.

In a landmark case testing the necessity for grand jury indictment, the Vermont courts held in the 1838 case of *State* v. *Keyes,* that the Fifth Amendment only applied to federal cases and that the states could make their own decisions as to the best method of presenting criminal cases.[6] The *Keyes* decision added impetus to the movement for an alternative accusatory process—filing by information. Opposition to the grand jury gained momentum prior to the Civil War. The most common complaints were that the powers of the grand jury to conduct investigations were undemocratic and that jury services and costs were highly burdensome. Oregon, in its 1850 constitutional convention, almost succeeded in abolishing the grand jury. Michigan experienced a similar attempt in its legislature in 1859.

The momentum turned into a full-scale movement after the Civil War, when efforts to abolish the grand jury reached almost epidemic proportions all across the country. Opponents labelled the grand jury a "relic," a "time-waster," a process "unfit for an enlightened age." Intense criticism focused on the cloak of secrecy that surrounded grand jury proceedings and on its potential use of unbridled powers for corrupt purposes. In 1884, the abolition movement received a substantial boost when the Supreme Court in *Hurtado* v. *California* echoed the sentiments of *Keyes* a half-century earlier by holding that the Fourteenth Amendment, read with the Fifth, did not require the use of the grand jury indictment in the state prosecution of crimes.[7] Rather, the court held, due process of law included any system of prosecution that preserved liberty and justice.

Between 1860 and 1920 most states west of the Mississippi River abolished the use of grand jury for indictment of crimes, substituting the prosecutor's information. Although many of these states retained provision for a grand jury, in the West the "great inquest" became an exceptional rather than a regular part of the criminal law process. This was not without a certain irony. The most outstanding contribution of the grand jury during this expansionary period was its effectiveness in dealing with commercial swindles, business mismanagements, and monopolies in the "era of big business." Ironically, those states hardest hit by many of these commerical illegalities were the western states, which suffered through numerous land and railroad swindles. Because most of them had abolished the regular grand jury, they were ill-equipped to deal with these problems, lacking an effective method for investigating allegations of wrong-doings. Nevertheless the use of grand juries to expose public corruption gained substantial support in the reform movements of the early 1900s. The most dramatic examples were reported by social reformers like Lincoln Steffans, who described the political corruption in St. Louis, Minneapolis, Pittsburgh, Philadelphia, Chicago, and New York.[8]

In the period between the two world wars, a curious dichotomy of opinion about the grand jury existed. Among the American voting public its prestige rose sharply. This expression of confidence derived from the favorable publicity received by numerous grand juries over their ability to protect the public interest. On the other hand, while the public supported the continued powers and use of the institution, legal scholars and government commissions called for its abolition. Influential reports by legal scholars Raymond Moley and Wayne Morse and by the prestigious Wickersham Commission cast doubts on the effectiveness of a continued use of a grand jury.

Their criticisms were undercut, however, by the startling successes of the grand jury during the 1930s. The most spectacular occurred in 1935 when a grand jury investigating corruption in New York City broke with the New York prosecutor and continued its investigation under the leadership of the jury foreman. When that jury reached an impasse, it petitioned the governor of the state to discharge the panel and to seat an extraordinary grand jury to continue its work. The governor agreed and appointed a special prosecutor, Thomas Dewey, to work with the new panel. This celebrated law enforcement effort pumped new life into the grand jury system.

As a result of the New York experience, grand juries in other jurisdictions began to assert themselves. In 1937, the Philadelphia grand jury indicted the city's mayor twice within a year. Investigations of official corruption in government followed within the same year in Miami, Florida, Buffalo, New York, and Greensboro, North Carolina.

Public officials who tried to undermine the grand jury at this time found themselves opposed by strong public sentiment in behalf of the institution. In 1938, Pennsylvania public officials frightened by the work of the grand jury in Philadelphia attempted to enact legislation to limit the powers of the grand jury. The result was a strong countermovement to reinforce those powers. New York, reacting to the Pennsylvania situation, subsequently added teeth to its grand jury system and made it the most powerful and thorough inquest in the country. Washington State enacted legislation in 1941 requiring that at least one grand jury be empaneled in each county each year even though Washington generally did not require cases to be filed by indictment. In 1943, Missouri passed a law dictating that the powers of the grand jury to investigate official corruption could never be suspended.

By the advent of World War II, these actions, along with the final decision by the New York State constitutional convention to reaffirm the use of the grand jury, effectively brought an end to the movement to abolish the grand jury. The situation since that time has not changed substantially. The public continues to view the grand jury's investigative powers with increased favor—citing successes like the Watergate investigation as the predominant justification. Yet the professionals continue to disagree, arguing for the use of information and preliminary hearings. In 1973, the National Advisory Commission on Criminal Justice Standards and Goals (NAC) summarized the professional's position: "Grand jury indictment should not be required in any criminal prosecution. . . . The grand jury should remain available for investigation and charging in exceptional cases."[9]

## Composition and Term of the Grand Jury

At present, all states have some type of grand jury system. Even those states that do not proceed by indictment have retained grand juries with investigatory or supervisory capacities. Twenty-four states still require the use of an indictment for felony prosecutions or capital crimes. Thirty-three allow for the use of either indictment or information, although most of these rely heavily on the prosecutor's information. Eighteen states use the grand jury indictment process exclusively. Several states still require indictment for serious misdemeanors.

The composition of grand juries varies widely through the fifty-one jurisdictions in the United States. No state has a grand jury with more than twenty-three members; forty-two states provide for twelve or more jurors. Within these limits further size variations are permitted. Thirty states have designated a fixed number of jurors for the panel. The remaining permit selection within a range for jury size. For example, Maine, Maryland, and Massachusetts may have a grand jury with a minimum of sixteen members up to a maximum of twenty-three. Table 5-1 summarizes the frequency distribution of the maximum sizes permitted by the states. Eight states have grand juries composed of fewer than twelve jurors. Virginia, for example, has five to seven members on its panel; South Dakota, six to eight; Indiana has only six; Utah has five to seven; Oregon has seven; Ohio has nine; North Dakota has eight to eleven; and Montana has eleven. Delaware requires fifteen jurors in its most populous county, only ten for the more rural areas. Michigan, whose grand jury normally consists of sixteen to twenty-three members has a special provision, enacted in 1917, that allows a judge to serve as a one-man grand jury in special circumstances. He is limited to a 6-month term as a grand jury, is prohibited from publishing a report, and is not allowed to hear the trial of any accused whom he indicts. The judge has the regular powers of the Michigan grand jury, including its contempt powers and ability to subpoena and call witnesses as part of an investigation.

Unanimous consent by the grand jurors is not usually required to gain indictment. In thirty-one of the thirty-three states whose grand juries have more than twelve members, a concurrence of at least twelve jurors is required to return an indictment. (Delaware and Michigan are exceptions.) In those states where twelve jurors sit regularly, the concurrence of eight members to return a true bill is required, except for Iowa, which requires

Table 5-1
Distribution of Maximum Grand Jury Size Allowed by States

| Maximum Grand Jury Size | Number of States |
|---|---|
| 23 | 14 |
| 20 | 1 |
| 19 | 1 |
| 18 | 7 |
| 17 | 4 |
| 16 | 5 |
| 15 | 2 |
| 12 | 9 |
| 11 | 2 |
| 9 | 1 |
| 8 | 1 |
| 7 | 3 |
| 6 | 1 |

only seven. Tennessee is the only state that requires unanimous consent of all the twelve members of its panel to return an indictment. In the eight states with less than twelve members on a panel, the most common and lowest number needed for returning an indictment is five.

It is difficult to generalize about the structure and size of grand juries because of these wide variations. In fact, in its commentary about grand juries the National District Attorneys Association (NDAA), reached this conclusion after examining the pros and cons of grand jury usage and its changing function: "The Task Force's adoption of a position favoring continued use of the grand jury in investigative and indicting roles is made with an awareness of the views of the various proponents and opponents of the grand jury concept. . . . All these factors make it difficult or impossible to adopt any useful standards on the scope of the grand jury's indictment and investigating functions. Instead, those matters are left for resolution to the individual jurisdictions."[10]

There are also several distinct procedures used to select jurors that reflect the different uses or purposes of the grand jury. Selection by lottery attempts to insure randomness or representativeness. Discretionary selection attempts to achieve other more selective goals. These are traditionally the two basic methods of selecting members for the grand jury. The most common method, and the one first employed in the colonial America, was to draw names by lot from a public list. The juries have traditionally been filled from voter registration lists or tax rolls. However, in recent years, with the development of computerized selection capacity and under pressure from the courts, lists have been generated or created from a variety of sources to guarantee fuller participation by all segments of the population.

A second method is discretionary selection by an official or set of officials at court. This method has come under increasing attack for being prone to abuse and discrimination, and the panels so formed have often been challenged. In several jurisdictions, such as Miami, Florida, and Chicago, Illinois, this method has been used in the past to form so-called blue-ribbon panels, but modern court decisions and more enlightened court administration procedures have minimized the use of this method.

In 1964, of the fifty-one state jurisdictions within the United States (including the District of Columbia) all but eight drew their juries by lot. Six states—Arkansas, Illinois, Maine, Nevada, Texas, and Virginia—persisted in selecting their panels through the exercise of discretion. Two states, Colorado and Nebraska, combined the two methods, choosing forty to fifty panel members by lot and then narrowing down to the final number by discretionary choice. Since 1964, several of these states have adjusted their procedures. Illinois, for example, developed a lottery system in 1965, and Arkansas, Maine, and Kentucky followed subsequently.

For the vast majority of the states (thirty-four) the term of the grand jury is the same as the term of the court. The remaining terms vary by set times, by discretion of the court, or by the end of business. In three states the length of the grand jury term rests with the discretion of the presiding judge of the court (Alaska, New Jersey, and Pennsylvania). Seven states have grand juries that sit for a 1-year period (California, Delaware, Massachusetts, Michigan, North Carolina, South Carolina, and Virginia). Five states set terms for less than one year: Arizona, 4 months; Georgia, 4 weeks; Illinois, 3 months; Louisiana, 6 months; and Washington, 60 days.

The qualifications required for individuals to serve as members of the grand jury vary slightly from state to state. In general, jurors are required to be:

1. citizens and electors
2. less than 70 years of age
3. of sound mind
4. not disabled or deformed
5. without record of felony conviction
6. in all other ways able to attend and serve on a grand jury

*Presence and Influence of the Prosecutor on the Grand Jury*

In almost every state, it is the general practice for the prosecuting officer to attend the grand jury. In some instances, this is required by law. His primary duties are to advise the members of the grand jury on their rights and powers, to counsel them on points of law and in many states, to present the independent judgment of the jury; however, the prosecutor is not allowed to be present during deliberations by members of the panel or at the time of voting on a matter under investigation. The same rights and responsibilities apply to assistant prosecutors or other law enforcement officers making presentations. In some states, assistant counsel retained by the state to assist the prosecutor may have the same privileges, but these rights do not extend to private prosecutors or counsel retained by victims, witnesses, or other outside interests.

The exceptions to this general procedure are the states of North Carolina and Connecticut, where the prosecutor does not attend the grand jury at any stage of its proceedings. The jurors form their opinions and make their decisions independent of his participation. Florida has a procedure whereby the grand jury may hire a special counsel to advise it.

A primary criticism of the grand jury system is that the jurors rely too heavily on the advice of the prosecutor and can form their opinions only on the basis of the evidence that he provides. The grand jury is often alleged to be a de facto "rubber stamp" for the wishes of the prosecutor. Critics cite the statistically low "no bill" rates in many American jurisdictions as proof, and some opponents have even called the grand jury an "administrative tool of the prosecutor," which shields his exercise of discretionary power from public scrutiny.[11] Because of the prosecutor's control of the witnesses and information submitted to the grand jury, critics claim that the grand jurors respond with a "passive acceptance of anything which seems to bear the semblance of approval,"[12] seemingly confident that the prosecutor would not present the case if he did not have good reason to believe that the accused was guilty.

There is at least a strong theoretical basis for these criticisms. First, most jurors are untrained or inexperienced in the law and rely entirely on the prosecutor's interpretations and presentation of the evidence. They rarely have the opportunity to obtain independent counsel and seldom require additional testimony or evidence; nor do the jurors, in most states hear any presentation of the defendant's case.

Even in those states where the prosecutor is prohibited from attending grand jury investigations the grand jury remains dependent on the prosecutor. Although it holds independent hearings and makes its independent decisions on the case, the prosecutor exerts special influences on the process. In many ways he controls the flow of information into the grand jury room, although he is not physically present. He prepares the forms for the bills of indictment and provides the grand jury with bills of particulars and affidavits. He even, at times, advises on points of law, although he performs this duty in writing rather than in person. While the relationship is subtle, it may be as effective as direct participation, since the prosecuting attorney is still the principal provider of evidence and information to the grand jury. He learns very quickly what information is most beneficial in obtaining the decision the prosecution desires.

## The Preliminary Hearing

The purpose of the preliminary hearing is to allow an independent magistrate to determine whether there is enough evidence for a reasonable man to believe that a crime has been committed and that the accused may have committed it. The probable cause standard is less burdensome than the reasonable doubt standard necessary to convict at trial. In addition to deciding whether there is probable cause to proceed to trial, the preliminary hearing also serves to determine whether there is probable cause to detain the suspect in light of the Fourth Amendment prohibitions against the restraint of liberty.

No constitutional right exists for such a hearing. The Supreme Court in

*Gerstein* v. *Pugh* held that a probable cause hearing is not required unless the defendant is likely to have his liberty restrained, and then it is only required to make a magisterial determination of whether there is sufficient cause to deprive the subject of his liberty. In some states, the preliminary hearing process is mandated by constitution, whereas in others it is created by statute. If a state constitution or statute requires a preliminary hearing as the basis for a prosecutor's information, a court may not proceed to trial against an accused unless he has had a preliminary hearing or has waived his privilege to one. Although the right to procedural due process can be satisfied by either the use of the grand jury or the use of the preliminary hearing, if specific legislation or constitutional provisions do not affirm the use of preliminary hearings as an accusatory process, it cannot be used exclusively.

The preliminary hearing to determine probable cause did not exist at common law where the grand jury indictment served as the instrument of accusation. A type of preliminary hearing first appeared in England during the reign of William and Mary as a simple magisterial inquiry into the possibility that a crime had been committed. By and large, however, the development of the preliminary hearing as an integral part of the accusatory process is an American legal phenomenon.

A Vermont court case in 1836 affirmed the use of a preliminary hearing in lieu of grand jury indictment in that state and initiated a trend whereby some older states and most newer ones adopted the information-preliminary hearing procedures as the primary method of criminal accusation.[13] Many older states on the eastern seaboard and in the South inherited, developed, and retained the strong grand jury system. But the tendency among the newer states in the Union was to adopt the information-preliminary hearing process.

Nowhere, however, was the grand jury system completely abandoned. All states provide for some type of grand jury, but the degree to which it is relied on diminishes as one moves west. Twenty-five states now permit prosecution by information in all cases. In some of these states, there is latitude for prosecutors to use either the grand jury indictment procedure or the information-preliminary hearing procedure. In a few states, and for some crimes, the prosecution may use both methods in processing cases. There is clearly no discernible use pattern at present other than the geographic one. Most likely the accusatory process is still changing.

Although there are great procedural differences between the indictment and information processes, they have the same powers of accusation. Legal scholar Samuel Dash has written that the grand jury and the preliminary hearing perform identical functions.[14] Some court cases have attempted to differentiate between these accusatory processes holding that the grand jury was primarily accusatory and the preliminary hearing essentially custodial.[15] In spite of these opinions, modern legal scholars have tended to minimize the differences.[16] Whether emanating from a grand jury deliberation or a magistrate preliminary hearing, the standard is employed to produce the same result—the binding over of the accused to the court of general jurisdiction for trial. The similarity has resulted in the development of hybrid institutions such as Michigan's, where a magistrate can operate as a one-man jury.

Most state procedures for preliminary hearing bear little resemblance to the federal procedure for determining probable cause.[17] Since the primary accusatory process in the federal procedure is indictment by the grand jury, prosecution by information exists basically for the benefit of those accused who might wish to expedite the proceedings. In these cases, the accused can waive prosecution by indictment and proceed to trial. The trial court then considers both the question of probable cause and of guilt, and the preliminary hearing becomes unnecessary. In general, there is little use of the preliminary hearing process in federal courts. A federal judge in Michigan's eastern district remarked that he had never conducted a preliminary hearing in his court and has never heard of one being conducted by any other judge.[18] Professor Irving Younger of Cornell School of Law could not recall one in New York's Southern District.

> If the defendant says that he does not wish to waive a preliminary hearing, the commissioner will set the hearing down for a date five or six months hence. If possible, the prosecutor will simply obtain an indictment before the date for the preliminary hearing; the hearing then becomes moot. If for whatever reason, the prosecutor cannot obtain an indictment within that time, he postpones the hearing. He may then obtain an indictment before the new date. If he fails to do so, he will adjourn the hearing again, and so on.[19]

Despite the fact that it is rarely used, the federal preliminary hearing is a model procedure—so much so that its basic format has been copied by a number of states. Among the states, four basic models are followed—the federal, the California, the American Law Institute, and the Rhode Island.[20] Each can be distinguished by its requirements in the following areas:

1.  the number of appearances that the procedure requires
2.  the time limits imposed, if any
3.  the degree of participation by the defense and prosecution
4.  the necessity for questioning and cross-examining witnesses
5.  the amount and type of evidence required

Three of the four procedures are concerned with determining possible cause both to restrain liberty and to proceed to trial. The fourth method is concerned only with the restraint of liberty issue.

*The California Model*

The California model procedure developed in a state that allows prosecution to commence either by indictment or information. This procedure requires two separate appearances. The first occurs promptly after arrest, when the defendant is informed of his rights, has his bail determined, and is assigned counsel if necesary.

The second appearance occurs "within a reasonable" time, usually about one week although no specific time limit is established. A reasonable number of postponements are allowed. At the second hearing, both the defense and prosecution are present, both sides can present witnesses and crossexamine. Hearsay evidence is not allowed, and "sufficient cause" to stand trial is the standard. If the judge endorses the complaint, the prosecution has 15 days to file a bill of information.

In this procedure, the determination of probable cause to detain is made in the first, nonadversarial appearance, and the determination of probable cause to proceed to trial is made at the second, and adversarial procedure.

*The Federal Model*

The federal model was developed for the federal system of prosecution in which most major crimes are prosecuted on indictment of the federal Grand Jury. The federal model follows along much the same lines as the California model, but imposes tighter time restrictions on the process.

Again, two appearances are used. At the first appearance, the suspect is brought before the magistrate without delay, is advised of his rights, is assigned counsel if necessary. In most cases, bail is fixed. This first appearance also begins to toll the strict limits of 10 days (if the defendant is in custody) or 20 days (if he is not in custody) during which the preliminary hearing must occur. These limits are strictly enforced and are only relaxed for good cause shown.

At the preliminary hearing, the defendant and his attorney may be present, may crossexamine witnesses, and may introduce evidence. However, under the federal model, hearsay evidence may also be admitted if it is credible and it is shown that a proper foundation will be laid at trial. Whereas the federal model is like the California model, it is more restrictive in its time requirements. However, it has its advantages because it is less burdensome to the prosecutor in evidentiary matters and is a more flexible procedure.

## The American Law Institute Model Code

The model code procedure is more extensive than either of the two preceding models. At first appearance, which must occur within 24 hours of arrest, the defendant is informed of his rights and asked if he needs to have counsel assigned. The case is then adjourned until the defendant has obtained counsel and is prepared to proceed on the first question, which is for "reasonable cause" to believe that the defendant has committed the crime.

At this second appearance, the defendant is allowed to make a statement, and, in special circumstances, to submit evidence to the court. If the court finds there is reasonable cause to believe that the defendant has committed the crime in question, it then must order him detained or fix bail. Before making the release determination, the session is adjourned for 2 days if the defendant is in custody, longer if he is not. At the continuation of these adjourned sessions, the defendant can now bring forward written and testimonial evidence. Hearsay is allowed under the same restraints as in the federal model. If probable cause is determined at this stage, the court will inform the defendant of his rights to a preliminary hearing. At this stage, only the probable cause to detain the accused has been determined.

The preliminary hearing, held within 10 days (if the suspect is in custody) or 30 days (if he is not), is a full-scale, adversarial hearing, a minitrial in which all the rules of evidence apply except that hearsay is allowed as before. Determination of probable cause at this stage indicates the belief of the court that the defendant should go to trial.

This model, although not yet widely adopted, is favored by the defense bar and considered burdensome by the prosecution.

## The Rhode Island Model

The Rhode Island model was developed for those states that do not require a magisterial determination of probable cause for trial prior to the filing of an information but only to determine whether probable cause exists to restrict the liberty of the suspect. This model is designed to satisfy the minimum requirements of the procedure dictated by the Supreme Court in *Gerstein* v. *Pugh*.

The process is extremely simple. The prosecution files its information with the court, attaching all exhibits and affadavits that it is relying on to prove probable cause. The defendant has 10 days in which to move for dismissal of the charges. If the defendant makes this motion, the prosecution must depend on the strength of the attachments made to the bill of information. If the motion is granted, and the charges dismissed, the prosecutor is prohibited from moving again on the same accusation. If the motion is denied, the court finds probably cause to restrict the liberty of the accused.

The *Gerstein* v. *Pugh* decision may have a profound effect on the ultimate structure and function of the preliminary hearing process, an impact that has just begun to be felt. The Supreme Court dictated that while the prosecutor's decision to initiate prosecution was not reviewable, the prosecutor could not, by use of the information process, totally bypass a probable cause determination of a magistrate. The Court held that an accused was entitled to a determination of probable cause by an independent third party when the issue was denial of liberty. *Gerstein* fell far short of requiring a full-blown adversarial procedure in all cases, as was originally requested by the defendants. Yet it has placed some additional constraints on the American system of prosecution. The Court, in reaching its decision, seemed to be weighing both the rights of the individual and the impact of a more extensive procedural requirement on the criminal justice system. The *Gerstein* decision was a flexible alternative, in this sense, designed to accommodate both interests. Individual rights are now protected by a guaranteed review in the courts to determine probable cause, and the prosecution is spared the overwhelming burden of having to participate in a completely adversarial and evidentiary hearing in all cases.

*Gerstein* already has had impact on various jurisdictions around the country in two ways. First, it has forced many states, such as Florida, to revise preliminary hearing procedures and to provide a more timely probable cause examination than had been required before. In Florida, prior to *Gerstein*, a defendant could be held for as long as 30 days before a probable cause hearing, simply on the discretionary decision of the prosecutor. A similar rule in Wyoming is also in doubt in light of the *Gerstein* decision. State court decisions such as those in Iowa, holding that the filing of the information vitiated the need for a preliminary hearing, are now questionable. Laws and court rules, such as those in South Carolina that require the accused to bear the burden of requesting a timely preliminary hearing, may also be invalid. Automatic and timely preliminary hearings seem to be the acceptable procedure for probable cause determinations.[21]

Second, the *Gerstein* decision may extend the same rights to a timely hearing on probable cause to those accused of misdemeanor violations as well as those accused of felonies. The issue raised in *Gerstein* was not the severity of the offense but the fact that the liberty of the accused was restrained without proper determination of probable cause. It may follow that any such restraint, regardless of seriousness of the crime, would suffer from the same defects as those addressed in the *Gerstein* case. Commentators have pointed out that some states, like Maryland, that do not provide the right to preliminary hearing in misdemeanor cases may have to adjust their procedures.[22]

The impact of the preliminary hearing on the prosecution varies with the rules in each jurisdiction that determine the complexity, timeliness, and extent of the probable cause hearing. Justice Powell, writing the Court's decision in *Gerstein*, said "we recognize that state systems of criminal procedure vary widely. There is no single preferred pretrial procedure and the nature of the probable cause determination usually will be shaped to accord with a State's pretrial procedure viewed as a whole."[23] The Court, in *Gerstein*, did not attempt to impose rigid standards for probable cause hearings but, instead, issued requirements for the minimum type of hearing that must be held to restrain the liberty of an arrestee prior to trial.

## Typical Operations

Before one can really examine the effects of grand juries and preliminary hearings on the prosecution, one must analyze their various combinations and uses in different prosecutive circumstances. The accusatory process is initiated by the decision to charge and prosecute and ends when an accusatory instrument (either an information or an indictment) is filed with the court. To best understand the flow, one must focus on the processing of the case rather than the defendant. At the first appearance hearing, the defendant is advised of the offense and his rights and is either incarcerated or granted bail or some form of conditional release. After this first appearance hearing, the case is prepared for either a preliminary hearing or grand jury review. The path the case follows next determines the differences among various accusatory systems.

In its simplest form, the accusatory phase of the criminal justice system addresses two issues: (1) Is there probable cause to restrict the liberty of the defendant? (2) Under the circumstances, would a reasonable man believe that the defendant committed the crime? If there is probable cause to believe both have occurred, then a formal accusation in form of a written instrument is leveled and the defendant arraigned on the charges. The standard of evidence at this stage is purposefully much lower than the burden "beyond a reasonable doubt" that the prosecutor must bear at trial. The accusatory process demands fewer hard facts and a less compelling production of evidence. In certain jurisdictions even credible hearsay may be admissible in the accusatory stage.

Since there is no single accusatory system, no uniform grand jury procedure or standard preliminary hearing process, the development of the accusatory system, its composition, and its use vary widely from state to state. Notwithstanding, there are four basic patterns that seem to have merged by which one can evaluate their relative strengths and merits.

*Arrest to Grand Jury Presentation*

The simplest and oldest accusatory process operating in the United States is direct presentation to the grand jury. The facts of the case are provided to the grand jury by the prosecutor and/or the police. The grand jury has the option to: return a bill of indictment; return a "no true bill"; or refer the case back to a lower court for prosecution at a reduced level (usually as a misdemeanor). In this process, there is no prior court hearing. The decision-making power of the grand jury may serve one of two possible functions: as a case review and screening activity in lieu of prosecutorial review or as final confirmation or denial of the prosecutor's interpretation and intended disposition of the case. In either capacity, the grand jury, not the prosecutor, is responsible for the final accusation. In sensitive cases that are highly publicized or political and where the accusation is highly controversial this deferral of accusatory responsibility to the grand jury is beneficial to the prosecutor. Consequently the prosecutor can use the grand jury in many instances to protect himself from criticism, since the indictment process implies citizen ratification for the prosecutor's intended course of action.

*Arrest to Preliminary Hearing to Grand Jury*

This procedure requires a probable cause hearing prior to a grand jury indictment. In this accusatory schema, a preliminary hearing is held to determine whether a crime was committed and whether there is probable cause that the defendant committed it. If so found, the case is bound over for grand jury deliberation.

It is probably safe to assume that the existence of this basically redundant process is a result of the existence of two-tiered court systems rather than something deliberately planned. As such, it reflects the coalescence of two court systems for processing felony cases. The lower (usually county) court system generally has primary jurisdiction over all misdemeanors, county ordinance violations, and traffic cases. It also holds probable cause hearings for felonies. For purposes of determining bail and providing for defense counsel representation, it offers a decentralized, readily available intake point for all cases (including felonies). Yet few of these courts have jurisdiction over felony prosecutions or trials; as a result they must be bound over to the higher (felony) court for disposition at that level.

Historically, many county magistrates or justices of the peace were not lawyers and conducted their business in courts that were not "courts of record." As a result, the adjudication of felony cases was reserved by the higher court (usually a circuit or district court). If these higher courts operated with a grand jury, one can envision how this environment for redundancy was created. A preliminary hearing in a lower court would result in a bindover to the higher court's grand jury section. This procedure, while existing in many areas, is not an acceptable one. Standard 4.4 of the NAC emphatically states that "If a grand jury indictment is issued in a particular case, no preliminary hearing should be held in the case."[24] If the concept of two court systems processing the same cases through the two accusatory phases seems less than rational, imagine the confusion engendered when two prosecutive systems (county and district attorneys) support these systems. But that is another story.

## Optimal Use of Accusatory Procedures

Thirty-three states permit the use of either indictment or information. Often, where both are available, the method of formal accusation used in each case depends on how the facts fit prespecified conditions, set by policy or statute. This means that under some conditions, a case will go through a preliminary hearing and will be charged by a bill of information, whereas other cases will be presented to the grand jury for indictment.

The processing decision may be based on formal or informal rules. For example, in Polk County (Des Monies) Iowa, property crimes were filed by information after a probable cause hearing was held and crimes against the person were sent to the grand jury for indictment. In Louisiana, all crimes, except capital crimes, are processed by information arising from the preliminary hearing. Capital crimes are filed after a grand jury indictment. In at least six states, either the constitution or state legislation mandate the prosecution of certain types of crimes (usually capital crimes) by indictment.

## Arrest to Preliminary Hearing

Finally, many jurisdictions have abolished the use of grand juries for the normal accusatory process, reserving their use only for special circumstances, such as investigations of public corruption. In these jurisdictions, a finding of probable cause at the preliminary hearing results in a filing of an information. This procedure is prevalent in the West where the grand jury tradition was never really strong or well rooted, but it has also made inroads in the more traditional court systems of the East and Midwest. Strongest support has been given to this change by a number of commissions and studies. The NAC states boldly, in standard 4.4, "grand jury indictment should not be required in any criminal prosecution . . ." and reaffirms its position in standard 4.8: "arraignment should be eliminated as a formal step in criminal prosecution. The initial charging document, as amended at the preliminary hearing, should serve as the formal charging document for trial.''[25] Other support has been voiced by the Advisory Commission on Inter-governmental Relations[26] and the American Bar Association.[27]

As has been seen, there are numerous practical advantages to the use of the information/hearing procedure at the accusatory stage. The *Gerstein* decision and the subsequent development of the Rhode Island model of procedure demonstrate that individual rights can be justly and adequately protected through a less demanding form of hearing. With worsening economic conditions, states have become more amenable to moving from more expensive and/or redundant processing types to less costly, more efficient ones.

## Altering the Accusatory Process

The arrest-to-grand jury-indictment and arrest-to-preliminary-hearing processes are basically very simple. Disregarding any arguments about which process is preferable, the important point is that neither procedure leaves much opportunity for process manipulation. Both are simple and direct methods for obtaining an accusatory instrument. On the other hand, the accusatory procedures that are either redundant or permit a choice of use are ripe for alteration and modification. An even larger array of strategies and maneuvers are produced when the two procedures are combined. As a general rule, an increase in the number of process steps increases the number of ways the process can be modified to meet special needs. The redundancy of the preliminary hearing bindover to a grand jury, or the availability of dual accusatory routes, creates a natural environment for process manipulation.

### Waiver of Grand Jury Indictment

When an accusatory system utilizes both preliminary hearing and grand jury, the redundancy may be corrected by a waiver of one of the two process steps. A waiver—the intentional relinquishment by the defense of a constitutional or statutory right to a process step—must be agreed to by the state and sanctioned by the court in many jurisdictions. Even though the defendant is waiving what are usually thought of as his own rights, in many instances, courts have held that the state has interests to be protected also. A criticism often levied is that an excessive use of waivers reflects abuse of the processing system and is always detrimental to the defendant. In fact, however, waiver occurs often because it offers incentives and benefits to all parties.

There are a number of legitimate reasons that would induct a defendant to waive grand jury indictment or a prosecutor to consent to such a waiver. Efficiency is among the foremost. An NAC standard states, in part: "If an existing requirement of indictment cannot be removed immediately, provision should be made for the waiver of indictment by the accused. Prosecutors should develop procedures that encourage and facilitate such waivers."[28]

Waiver of grand jury indictment has as its primary advantage the fact that it speeds the case to its disposition. A defendant might want to waive when a plea has already been negotiated and will be consummated as soon as the arraignment is held. Frequently, the state favors waivers for reasons of efficiency. Waivers reduce workload. Fewer cases must be presented to the grand jury, and fewer indictments must be prepared. As a result, in heavily backlogged courts, where this option is available, requesting a waiver may become one more incentive offered by the defense in plea negotiations.

### Waiver of Preliminary Hearing

When the preliminary hearing is waived and a grand jury indictment is sought, the incentives can be attributed to a variety of factors; again cost is the most common reason. For example, where defense counsel are court appointed and the fee for the case is set, each court appearance increases the case's cost. Any reduction in the number of court appearances, therefore, represents savings.

Additionally, the nature of the case itself may make a waiver of preliminary hearing more desirable. Where open hearings may be potentially embarassing to the accused because they involve such offenses as sexual crimes, embezzlement, or narcotics use the secrecy of the grand jury room is appealing. In cases involving informants or undercover investigations, the waiver of an open preliminary hearing prolongs keeping the "cover" of the persons involved, and the time bought is valuable.

From the prosecutor's perspective, such waiver requests have definite managerial benefits (reducing workload) or potential strategic benefits (buying time to develop a series of similar cases or to protect the identity of an informant). This latter advantage may only be temporary. As the NAC standard directed, "In such cases [where no preliminary hearing is held] the prosecutor should disclose to the defense all the testimony before the grand jury directly relating to the charges contained in the indictment returned against the defendant."[29]

There are, of course, other dimensions to the use of waivers. Some prosecutors favor bypassing the preliminary hearing to maintain the secrecy of the accusatory process and thereby strengthen the prosecutor's control over this part of the system. Others find fault because it minimizes accountability to the public. In some jurisdictions the defense uses the waiver as a delaying tactic. One example of the refinement of this tactic is when the defendant states at arraignment that he did not understand what he signed when he waived preliminary hearing, and therefore he now requests such a hearing. With an overloaded lower court, a granting of this request results in scheduling his preliminary hearing many months later.

From a management view, the expected benefit from waivers is a reduction in the number of steps in the accusatory process. They are justified by participants in the justice system on the grounds that they speed up the process. This is not necessarily true. As illustrated earlier and noted in the work of Taylor, the elimination of a process step does not automatically reduce elapsed process time:

> The time for processing felony defendants in County Court appears excessive when the number of events and the court time required for these events is considered. The event that requires the most court time and most preparation by counsel is the preliminary hearing. Yet a comparison of the elapsed time for defendants who have a preliminary hearing with those who waive the hearing shows the latter group on the average take about the same time (6.7 weeks) as those who have a preliminary hearing (6.9 weeks).[30]

*Rearranging the Processing Schedule*

Clearly, the best operational justification for using waivers is that they eliminate essentially duplicative process steps, although this does not necessarily guarantee reductions in processing time. One should also recognize that the use of waivers can indicate either an attempt to adjust to criminal justice system inconsistencies and/or inefficiencies or to adjust the special characteristics of a case to the accusatory mechanisms. Since waivers require at a minimum the acquiescence of the defendant, the prosecutor does not have complete control over this tactic. A more certain flow can be achieved by rearranging the process result and changing the order of accusatory hearings. This is possible because the prosecutor schedules the flow of cases into the grand jury. Thus, if a request for a waiver of preliminary hearing is desirable but not forthcoming or if other justifying circumstances prevail, the prosecutor is able to schedule a grand jury hearing on the case before the preliminary hearing is held. Once a grand jury indictment has been handed down, it precludes the need for probable cause hearing.

There are a number of reasons for this deliberate rearrangement of the accusatory process. Some stem from the prosecutor's personal preference for secret indictments. Others may reflect an unfavorable assessment of the quality of the lower court's ability to determine probable cause, or a desire to circumvent a specific magistrate who is considered incompetent, unqualified, or philosophically at odds with prosecutorial policy. Since the prosecutor exercises control over the grand jury through his presentation of evidence, he can control the amount of time spent in the accusatory stage. This power is particularly important when there are cases not suited to preliminary hearings. For example, it is far easier to let the grand jury examine complicated cases (such as those involving worthless checks or fraud) which require the testimony of a large number of witnesses and consume a lot of time. Using a preliminary hearing for these exceptional cases not only disrupts normal processing times but also limits the ability of the prosecutor to clarify complicated cases, evidence, or issues. This latter point is most crucial.

The fact that this type of accusatory process can be altered highlights its basic redundant and duplicative functions. Unlike waivers, however, this alteration of the process contains the seeds of conflict, because the normal process can be disrupted unilaterally by the prosecutor. It does not require agreement with other parties in the court system nor court sanction even though the defense may actually prefer a preliminary hearing with testimony transcribed and witness testimony subject to impeachment. Thus, because the preferences of all parties may not be in accord, when used, conflict is frequently found.

## The Grand Jury Original

Finally, the prosecutor has the power to obtain a grand jury indictment after a case has been dismissed at preliminary hearing for lack of probable cause. Since jeopardy does not attach until a trial jury has been empaneled and/or until the first witness is sworn in at a trial, this is an allowable procedure and is used in many instances for legitimate purposes. For example, if an arrest was not made on the scene or the evidence not thoroughly developed before preliminary hearing, the case might be dismissed at preliminary hearing. Yet, with additional time and investigation a more complete development of the evidence could be obtained and presented to the grand jury for indictment. When the status of the case changes after arrest or after the preliminary hearing, the use of the grand jury to reinstitute the case is justifiable. For example, if a credit card case was dismissed for lack of evidence at the preliminary hearing, and the state subsequently discovered that the defendant was operating a ring of credit card frauds and was assured that the victim would appear at trial, he could go forward with a grand jury indictment or file an information directly with the court.

Other factors affect the decision of which accusatory route to follow, and one is the type of hearsay permitted. If credible hearsay is limited at preliminary hearings, there is increased pressure to go the grand jury. In a stolen credit card case for example, the magistrate at the preliminary hearing may refuse to accept an affadavit from an out-of-state witness as credible hearsay and insist on the witness' appearance. If the witness is not present, the case is dismissed. The prosecutor, having contacted the witness and receiving assurances of his appearance at the trial, believes the case still warrants prosecution. He, therefore, uses the affadavit as credible hearsay in a grand jury session and proceeds to obtain an indictment.

Controversy results when this authority is used because of differences in opinion, philosophy, or policy between the court and the prosecutor. The exercise of prosecutorial discretion to resolve these differences raises the question of whether the authority of the prosecutor should be used to overturn undesirable judicial findings by "end-running" the case through the grand jury. Since both accusatory routes are legitimately available, the circumstances under which they are used need to be identified before evaluations or judgments are made.

**The Controversial Grand Jury**

Institutions become targets for attack when their functions can be performed by others. Sometimes, just the belief that this capability exists is enough to support attack. Because two accusatory processes exist, the existence and purpose of the grand jury has been debated for the past 200 years with no clear resolution. If anything the public has waivered between support for or condemnation of the grand jury in uneven and unpredictable cycles. Critics favor abolishment following the English example.[31] Advocates staunchly defend its continued existence on the grounds that "it protects citizens from inquisitional conduct on the part of government officials," provides a vehicle for citizen participation in government and insulates the charging process from political considerations.[32] In reality, the results have been compromises, revisions, and modifications of the institutions.

There are, in addition, the real issues of secrecy, investigation, and immunity to be considered. The impact of these issues is poorly understood by the general public. Although public attention is often focused on prosecutorial control of the grand jury and its potential for being abused, a more critical issue is the ability of the grand jury to conduct secret investigations and grant immunity.

A major question facing the criminal justice system is whether the need for secrecy is sufficient to justify the continued existence of the grand jury. When one compares the grand jury process with the preliminary hearing process, the differentiating factor is secrecy. Grand jury operations are conducted in secret, and the prosecutor schedules the state's witnesses and interprets the law and evidence to the jury. Defense counsel is rarely present, and, until the indictment is handed up, the accuser is often unknown. The decision belongs to the grand jury.

Not so with the open, court-conducted probable cause hearing. Here testimony is presented by both sides. The state's witnesses and accusers are known, the defendant is represented by counsel, and the finding belongs to the court.

The questions are whether:

1. The charging of an individual with a crime should result from a laymen's decision based on a one-sided, prosecution-oriented presentation of evidence.

2. The charge should result from the court's finding of probable cause after hearing a narrow presentation of the facts from both sides, prosecution and defense.

The choice should be made in light of the expectations and demands of the public since changing the operations of the accusatory process has marginal effect on the operations of the justice system. A decision to abolish the grand jury as the charging vehicle could add another processing step to existing court procedures if preliminary hearings are not already being held on a regular basis. Under these conditions, the volume of additional work, the type of hearing, and the court resources needed to conduct them would have to be considered.

In addition to the courts, adding probable cause hearings has an effect on the defense component. Unlike grand jury proceedings, probable cause hearings require defense representation and participation prior to arraignment and, therefore, increase defense work activity. If the defense delivery system depends on court-appointed lawyers, additional expenses may be incurred as well. Probable cause hearings are not entirely detrimental to the defense, however. Open court hearings tend to produce additional information and a better assessment of the strength of the state's case, particularly where discovery is not a common practice. It also provides the defense with strategic advantages such as the ability to impeach witness testimony at a later trial stage.

In general, despite the extra work, the preliminary hearing is preferred by defense counsel as the method of accusation. They argue that the grand jury no longer provides the type of independent protection that it was once designed to provide. Defense lawyers suggest that preliminary hearings should involve a greater degree of participation from the defense. Since they posit that the possible deprivation of liberty and the seriousness of placing a man in jeopardy of criminal trial warrants a complex, adversarial hearing on the issue of probable cause, their arguments have had considerable effect in the development of state statutes and procedures.

The prosecutor on the other hand, views preliminary hearings with mixed emotion. Although he has in effect lost control of the accusatory process, he no longer has the operational burden of adapting his organization to the demands of a grand jury. With respect to case processing, probable cause hearings add little to the workload if they seek only probable cause and do not act as "mini trials." Where the more demanding forms of preliminary hearing exist, prosecutors often object to the long, involved, adversarial hearings as giving "two bites at the apple" to the accused. The prosecution has to bear the burden of proving its case twice, albeit the degree of proof is less burdensome at the preliminary hearing stage. This gives the accused an opportunity to escape justice on a technicality rather than on the merits of the case.

Although all the participants in the justice system would be affected in one way or another by removing the grand jury from the accusatory process, none of the effects appears powerful enough to preclude moves in this direction. In fact the move to limit the grand jury function (as called for in 1973 by the NAC) appears to be underway. Impetus toward this change may also be found in emerging public awareness of the justice system and a changing set of public expectations. As the public demand for openness and accountability increases, and the prosecutors themselves adopt stricter standards with respect to their relations with the grand jury, the need for secrecy in the accusatory process becomes less and less justifiable.[33]

The elimination of secret accusatory proceedings, however, does not provide sufficient reason to abolish grand juries in toto. Grand juries perform two functions: accusatory and investigative. Unless this latter function can be eliminated, transferred elsewhere, or retained independent of the accusatory process, the abolition of the grand jury would result in the loss of an effective means of controlling public corruption or system abuse. The NAC recognized these investigative powers and the need for their preservation, concluding its standard on the grand jury functions by stating that: "The grand jury should remain available for investigation and charging in exceptional cases."[34]

The investigative effectiveness of the grand jury results from two powers: (1) the authority to issue subpoenas, and (2) the power to grant immunity. As long as these powers are vested solely with the grand jury, attempts to abolish the institution are subject to failure. Only if alternative institutions are granted these powers can changes be made. This is not unrealistic. Some jurisdictions (California and Florida, for example) have vested the power to subpoena with prosecutors. In Florida, this is called an "office subpoena." The clerk of the court issues a subpoena at the request of the prosecution and sworn statements are taken by the state.

Contracts of immunity may also be obtained in Florida based on statutory authority that allows the court to grant immunity based on a contract between the individual and the prosecutor. It is interesting to note that when the prosecutor assumes this funtion it is with court sanction and approval, a significant departure from the autonomous authority exercised by the grand jury. Three states have established one-man grand jury procedures to supplement the investigative function. In Michigan, judges of the Superior Court may order an "investigation" *sua sponte* or on a motion of the state's attorney. Connecticut has a similar procedure, and in Kansas a state or local prosecuting official may move a district court to conduct an "inquisition into any matter." Although it is clear that the powers can be transferred to other components of the criminal justice system, the basic question of whether they should be remains.

Few want to eliminate these investigative tools. The public as well as legal practitioners recognize that society needs the capability of conducting sensitive investigations, particularly those concerning the corruption of public officials. Opponents to the transfer of this power to the prosecutor express disapproval by asking "who prosecutes the prosecutor?" Yet where judicial sanctions exist for using these powers, the question appears inconsequential.

Whereas the controversy over the grand jury's secrecy, investigatory role and power to grant immunity are debated in the academic and legal environments, in the routine world of criminal justice the controversy is more practical. It debates the operational incentives, second-shot review, better scheduling, and citizen input. Those prosecutors who continue to resist elimination of the grand jury as an accusatory vehicle do so because they like the grand jury process and its operational benefits.

In an adversarial system of justice, accusation by secret proceedings gives the prosecutor the advantage over the defense. Since discovery procedures are often minimal or nonexistent in criminal cases, the prosecutor does not have to reveal his evidence, witnesses, tactics, or strategies. Under these conditions, he believes his case is stronger and the chance of convicting the defendant is greater. However, this very advantage may be a detriment to the speedy processing of cases. If discovery is minimized and the incentives strong enough, one may find the defense delaying the process after indictment by an excessive use of motions to reveal that which could have been revealed automatically through probable cause hearings.

Some prosecutors view the grand jury as a means of getting a second shot at case review or screening. When an arrest is made on the scene, the time lapse between arrest and grand jury presentment provides this opportunity. That which may have passed unnoticed at the initial review may be revealed in the grand jury examination. Testimony that was not available previously may be subpoened and time can be used to strengthen the evidence and gather additional witnesses. This period of time also presents further opportunity to pursue plea negotiations.

By controlling the case flow through the grand jury, work can be performed more efficiently with fewer delays. Each presentation can be regulated by the amount of time spent on it, thereby producing economies that are difficult to obtain at a preliminary hearing.

Lastly, since the prosecutor is usually the elected official of his community, the grand jury expresses the community's norms and values. Even charging policies may be adjusted if the grand jury expresses hesitation or opposition to indicting certain types of crimes. Although rare, run-away grand juries also serve as powerful vehicles to express a community's changing value system.

Despite all these operational benefits to the prosecutor, the case for maintaining the grand jury accusatory system is unconvincing. No empirical proof exists that shows that the secrecy of grand jury actions and investigations results in higher conviction rates. Little documented evidence exists about the added benefits that might be derived from having another review opportunity that could not be attained from a well-organized screening or intake unit. And grand juries can, at times, be as prone to delay and backlog as any other process step in the system.

Sometimes the structure of the grand jury accusatory process creates inconveniences, supporting the call for its abolition. The nature, composition, and timing of the grand jury may be an impediment to prosecution if it represents too narrow a segment of the community, meets irregularly or for too short a period of time. Additionally, where dual systems operate, not only is there a functional redundancy but also extra work is required to schedule witnesses, allocate office manpower, and maintain paperwork and records. The increased costs and opportunities for delay may be substantial in some jurisdictions.

In summary, if there are substantive issues involved in the grand jury controversy they are not necessarily lodged in the procedural or structural aspects, but rather in the public's expectations about the following.

1. a charging system based on secret, one-sided testimony heard by a grand jury or based on open presentations under judicial control in a probable cause hearing

2. the investigative power exemplified by the power to issue subpoenas and the power to grant immunity held either by the grand jury, the prosecutor, or some combination of the two

3. the maintenance of redundant systems when both probable cause and a grand jury presentation exist in the same court system

With scant regard for these policy issues, the majority of prosecutors work within their own system, griping about court delay or witness scheduling problems, adjusting the system to meet operational needs and working always toward the best acceptable case disposition. With the demands of the daily working environment, they rarely have the luxury to be able to argue these issues even though the type of accusatory process differentiates one prosecutor's office from another.

## The Effect of Grand Juries on Prosecutive Systems

The strongest differentiating effects of the two accusatory processes are evident in the attitudinal, functional, and structural responses of the prosecutor's office. These responses give rise to certain operating and management procedures that are supported by the specific accusatory environments. The road to success in one environment may not be at all feasible in another. A point needing serious consideration is that changes in procedures or transfers of operations from one office to another should not be undertaken without considering the structure of the accusatory process.

Prosecutorial attitudes are rather simple to classify and understand when they are considered in the abstract. But it is far more difficult to explain them in a working environment. This is because attitudes reflect both the personality and the policy of the prosecutor and his response to the environment, and separating personal response fromm environmental ones is not an easy task. However, some clues appear if prosecutors offices are differentiated by their accusatory process and examined for attitudinal differences or expected behavior. One can expect prosecutorial attitudes to be compatible with the characteristics of the accusatory process. If we let the adversarial system of justice assume the characteristics of a poker game both in style and operation, we can find a prosecutor who plays his game close to his chest, bluffing and raising the ante until he has to show; a prosecutor who folds rather than call defense counsel's bluff; and a prosecutor who calls and lays his cards on the table.

Lacking adequate research in this area, one can only hypothesize about the extent to which the prosecutor's style is colored by the accusatory system. Grand juries encourage and support secrecy and caution—the hand played close to the chest. On the other hand, preliminary hearings, even if conducted in their narrowest sense, encourage and support openness, discovery, and accountability—the cards are laid down, the facts are assessed, the winner declared. The effects of these types of accusatory processes or discovery, plea bargaining, and pretrial conferences can be reduced. One would expect these practices to flourish in the open environment of preliminary hearings; in contrast, the secrecy of the grand jury process should increase the number of motions filed by the defense as they seek to discover the facts should increase with grand jury usage.

This is not meant to imply that discovery and other positive attitudes toward openness and accountability operate only in accusatory systems that use a preliminary hearing to determine probable cause. Rather it is stated in this fashion to draw attention to the power of the accusatory process. Still, it is not absolute. The personality and policy of the prosecutor also contributes. A good example of openness within a traditional grand jury system exists in the Bronx District Attorney's office. When the present District Attorney took office, he stated his intention to implement discovery. Although almost unanimously warned that taking such a step would result in a drastically reduced conviction rate, he implemented an open file policy without suffering adverse results.

In addition to influencing the attitude of prosecutors, the accusatory process generates operational procedures that range from simple to complicated. The direct routes from arrest-to-grand-jury and arrest-to-preliminary-hearing require the least complicated procedures.

Adding other process steps makes procedures more complicated, since each step requires its own operating tasks. As a result, the redundant, accusatory systems produce different and more complicated operating procedures than do the simpler systems; at the same time they increase the probability of system breakdown.

The processing system of Dade County (Miami), Florida, is typical of redundant accusatory systems. The felony case is reviewed by an assistant state's attorney assigned to a magistrate court that holds probable cause hearing. A complaint/affidavit is prepared in the prosecutor's office, and is presented at the preliminary hearing by the assistant along with testimony of the arresting officer and necessary witnesses. To reach this step, the office has also prepared and typed the complaint and affidavits, notified the witnesses of their appearance dates, prepared and mailed subpoenas, and set up case files and records.

If probable cause is found, the assistant again reviews the case, interviews witnesses for grand jury, schedules grand jury presentation, notifies the necessary witnesses of appearance dates, prepares witness lists, obtains evidence and reports, and finally presents the case to the grand jury. Upon indictment, the indictment is prepared by the assistant, typed by the clerical personnel, reviewed for accuracy and completeness by another assistant, and filed in the court with copies to the prosecutor's file. The witness notification and subpoena process is repeated, the arraignment is set, negotiations between defense counsel and the assistant are held to determine whether a plea is possible, and the final documents prepared for the arraignment date. Although these may not be all the operations that are conducted in this process all the time, they demonstrate the numerous steps involved and point to reasons why the type of accusatory route has a significant effect on the operations of the prosecutor.

Finally the impact of these routes can be seen in structural terms as well as operational ones. The inclusion of the grand jury in the accusatory system results in the creation and maintenance of a separate organizational entity. This entity, by its very nature, requires secure space, bailiffs or marshalls to guard the space, training and orientation facilities, maintenance of lists of eligible jurors, and the creation and updating of selection procedures for panels. Sometimes, transportation facilities are also necessary. None of these is required by preliminary hearings. In short, a new organizational entity is created when a grand jury is utilized that must be supported both by the prosecutor and the court.

Once established, the grand jury affects the court's operating system as well as the prosecutor's in both caseflow and case-processing time. The grand jury interrupts a flow of cases through a court. In some court systems, all cases proceed through the grand jury. In others, only those meeting special conditions are routed there.

In both circumstances, the effect is to remove cases temporarily from the court-controlled system and place the responsibility for their processing in another agency's hands. This interruption poses both management and operational hazards.

The propensity for the grand jury to increase case-processing time is ever present. A study of the Bronx District Attorney's office in 1972 showed that of the 522 matters scheduled for grand jury action in a 2-week period, 199, or 38 percent, were not heard on the date scheduled.[35] Quite simply the extra processing step of the grand jury adds extra delay time to the system that is ultimately attributable to prosecutorial resources rather than judicial. The fact that slippage can occur between the courts and the prosecution simply illustrates the principle that at each transfer point in a process, the chance for error or loss exists, and the need for administrative controls is magnified. Clearly, the use and function of the grand jury as an accusatory vehicle needs careful consideration before decisions to change are undertaken. Their effect on prosecution as well as the justice system is too powerful to be ignored.

## Notes

1. *Gerstein* v. *Pugh*, 420 U.S. 103, 93 S.Ct. 854 (1975).

2. John Spain, "The Grand Jury, Past and Present: A Survey," 2 American Criminal Law Quarterly 117 (196).

3. R.M. Calkins, "Abolition of the Grand Jury in Illinois," 1966 University of Illinois Law Forum 423 (1966).

4. Richard Younger, *The People's Panel: The Grand Jury in the United States, 1643-1941* (Providence, R.I.: Brown University Press, 1963), p. 20.

5. Ibid., p. 17.

6. 8 Vermont 57 (1836).

7. 110 U.S. 516 (1884).

8. See, for example, Lincoln Steffans, *The Shame of the Cities* (New York: Hill and Wange, 1904).

9. National Advisory Commission on Criminal Justice Standards and Goals (NAC), *Courts* (Washington, D.C.: U.S. Government Printing Office, 1973), p. 74

10. National District Attorneys Association (NDAA), *National Prosecutor's Standards* (Preliminary Draft, 1976), p. 720.

11. James Shannon, "Grand Jury: True Tribunal of the People or Administrative Agency of the Prosecutor?" 2 New Mexico Law Review 141, 142 (1972).

12. M.P. Antell, "The Modern Grand Jury: Beknighted Super Government," 51 ABA Journal 153, 154 (1965).

13. State v. Keyes, 8 Vermont 57 (1836).

14. Samuel Dash, "The Indicting Grand Jury: A Critical Stage?" 10 American Criminal Law Review 807 (1972).

15. See People v. Kent, 54 Ill.2d 161, 295 N.E. 710 (1972).

16. See John C. Robinson, Jr., "The Determination of Probable Cause in Illinois—Grand Jury or Preliminary Hearing?" 7 Loyola Law Journal 931 (1976).

17. See 21 American Jurisprudence 2d, "Criminal Law §444" (Rochester, N.Y.: Lawyers Cooperative Publishing Company, 1965), p. 447.

18. Quoted in "Note: Probable Cause at the Initial Appearance in Warrantless Arrests," 45 Southern California Law Review 1154 (1972).

19. Ibid., pp. 1128, 1131, and n. 11.

20. The framework for these models were developed in D. Grossman, "The Grand Jury: Its Evolution and Alternatives. A National Survey," 2 Criminal Justice Quarterly 114 (1974).

21. "Note: Pretrial Detention in Maryland: The Aftermath of Gerstein v. Pugh," 5 University of Baltimore Law Review 322 (1976). See also and compare other commentary: 51 Washington Law Review 425 (1976) (questioning whether Gerstein v. Pugh is a correct interpretation of the Fourteenth Amendment); 10 Valparaiso University Law Review 216 (1975) (emphasizing Gerstein's Fourth Amendment focus); 6 Golden Gate Law Review 39 (1975) (disappointment with Court's failure to fully consider Fourteenth Amendment issues); 7 Loyola Law Journal 901 (1976) (analyzes decision in terms of possible system impact).

22. Ibid.

23. 420 U.S. 103, 122 (1975).

24. NAC, *Courts*, p. 74

25. Ibid., pp. 74, 87.

26. Advisory Commission on Inter-governmental Relations, *State-Local*

*Relations in the Criminal Justice System* (Washington, D.C., 1971), p. 51.

27. American Bar Association Project on Standards for Criminal Justice, *Standards Relating to the Administration of Criminal Justice* (New York: The American Bar Association, 1974), "Discovery and Procedures before Trial," sec. 1.1(b), p. 253.

28. NAC, *Courts*, p. 74

29. Ibid.

30. Jean G. Taylor et al., *Comparison of Counsel for Felony Defendants* (Arlington, Virg.: Institute for Defense Analyses, and Springfield, Virg.: National Technical Information Service, 1972), pp. A-29, A-31.

31. See Committee on Criminal Courts, Law and Procedures and Committee on Federal Courts, "Strengthening of the Role of the Federal Grand Jury: Analysis and Recommendations," 29 Association of the New York Bar 516 (1974).

32. Younger, *People's Panel*, p. 20.

33. National District Attorneys Association (NDAA), *National Prosecution Standards* Chicago: National District Attorneys Association, 1977), pp. 182-184.

34. NAC, *Courts*, p. 74.

35. Joan E. Jacoby, *Snapshot-Spin Around: A Technique to Measure Capacity in a Prosecutor's Office* (Washington, D.C.: National Center for Prosecution Management, 1973), p. 5.

# 6 Toward Trials and Dispositions—The Concluding Stage

## Introduction

Once a case has been accepted for prosecution and the accusatory phase has been completed, the focus of work shifts from evaluating the case for acceptance to evaluating it for disposition. Involved in this concluding stage are a number of activities: (1) case assignment, (2) trial preparation, (3) court appearances, and, at times, (4) sentence recommendations. Case assignment begins after the defendant has been formally accused through a bill of information or indictment and may occur in two ways. Many offices use an assembly-line or process organizational model that transmits cases to trial divisions or to specialized units formed to try specialized types of crime. In other jurisdictions, where cases are individually docketed to a judge or assigned to a courtroom, the assignment may start earlier in the process—at the point where judge or courtroom is first identified—and usually the case remains with the assistant through disposition or even into post-conviction areas. In this trial-team organizational model, the start point can be defined functionally and begins after the accusatory phase is complete.

Trial preparation is the most work-intensive activity for the assistant prosecutor. It encompasses interviewing witnesses, amassing the evidence, sorting out the facts, and evaluating case strength and defense strategies. It involves legal research, the preparation of briefs, and responses to motions. It is in this phase of prosecution that the maximum use of legal training and skills is demanded of the assistant. All the work undertaken in preparing for trial is done within a framework of expected dispositions and the use of appropriate strategies to achieve these dispositions.

These expectations are not unlimited. They are constrained by a number of external factors including the type of defense counsel representation—whose importance and effect has been described in chapter 3—the organization of the court, the court's continuance policy, and the prosecutor's ability to affect some aspects of sentencing.

When a case is scheduled for a court appearance, either trial or a motions hearings, the work activity of the assistant intensifies. He must be sure that the witnesses required for a hearing are notified and available, that the case file and paperwork is complete, and that he is prepared to anticipate the actions of the defense counsel. Although ideally he approaches each scheduled court date with a case ready for trial, he knows that the greater likelihood is for the case to be continued. The continuance policy of the court is probably the single most important factor affecting the successful disposition of cases. Excessive continuances not only increase the work of the prosecutor but also, as will be seen, seriously diminish his capacity to bring the case to a successful disposition. They are the simplest and purest indicators of delay.

Once a case is resolved, the final prosecutorial activity in this concluding phase occurs after conviction if the prosecutor has the ability to make sentence recommendations and if, in fact, he chooses to exercise that option. In making a sentence recommendation the assistant considers factors that were not necessarily at issue during the trial or relevant at the time a plea was negotiated. Of major import is the previous record of the defendant. This is considered along with the crime and extent of injury inflicted. Not all prosecutors have or use this power; but where the prosecutor is involved in all activities, from the setting of the charge to recommendation of a sentence that relates to the seriousness of the charge, then the prosecutive function has come full circle.

Although the activities involved in the concluding stage of trial preparation and case disposition remain essentially the same, the case-processing systems used by prosecutors vary substantially in form and structure. Much of the difference can be attributed to the policy of the prosecutor. But, policy notwithstanding, the process is also seriously affected by external factors as well. These are the subject for examination here. The differences in trial processing systems are due to three factors: (1) the effect of the continuance policy on delay in the trial-processing phase; (2) the organization of the court and the court workgroups, and (3) the influence of the prosecutor on sentencing.

Of the three factors beyond the prosecutor's control, the amount of delay and the factors contributing to delay that are beyond his control are the most important. Once the dimensions of delay have been identified and the need for accountability fixed, then it is possible to look at the other two factors, the structure of the court and its workgroups and the influence of the prosecutor on sentencing.

## Continuances and Their Effect on Case Delay

Almost without exception, delay in case processing has been pronounced the number one enemy of the American criminal justice system. Its destructive effects on the individual, society, and the criminal justice system have been widely documented and dilatory practices unanimously condemned.

The whole development of the concept of speedy trial has been based on the traditional doctrine of the presumption of innocence—that an individual has a right to have the charges brought against him resolved quickly, since failure to do so causes great injury to the innocent. The state has the responsibility to do so as quickly as possible under jeopardy of having charges dismissed. The accused individual may suffer severely because of delay. If jailed, pending trial, the defendant is subjected to the same environment as the convicted. The brutalizing effect of jail on individuals has been graphically discussed by politicians, scientists, and inmates.[1] The economic loss of income, and sometimes even jobs, not only affects the accused but also may work undue hardship on the family as it is forced to endure prolonged separations and, at times, to rely on public assistance for support. The social costs are enormous.

In sum, the negative effects of jailing the accused are so powerful that a wide range of release alternatives have been developed and adopted to counteract these effects to some degree. Most are directed toward pretrial release programs—bail, bond, personal recognizance, or third-party supervision. Yet the stigma of being accused still clouds the defendant's activities even when he is out on release. Although not deprived of his liberty, he may still suffer the loss of employment, family pride, and reputation. The longer the situation exists, the more prolonged and adverse are its effects on the individual.

To the extent that delay in case processing exists, it blocks society from reaching its goals of reducing crime and providing safe living conditions for its members. Katz has identified three objectives in the criminal justice system that affect the quality of society and noted that their effectiveness is reduced as delays in case processing increase.[2] Briefly stated, they are: (1) to remove certain criminals from society for its own protection; (2) to incarcerate certain criminals thereby deterring others from engaging in the same conduct; and (3) to rehabilitate some criminals before they can resume their places in society.

It is obvious that if a guilty person is released, the time between arrest and trial constitutes a risk to society. The extent to which criminals commit additional crimes while on release has been the subject of many studies. One of the forerunners conducted by the National Bureau of Standards in 1968 estimated that in Washington, D.C., 11 percent of the defendants out on bail were rearrested.[3] Other studies also confirm these risks with percentages reported ranging from as high as 32 percent found in 1976 to a low of 20 percent found in 1973.[4] The additional losses to society in personal injury or property loss inflicted by the conduct of some released defendants while awaiting trial may, at times, be significant.

Delay in processing also has a direct relationship with conviction and incarceration that is independent of release status. As time elapses in the processing of a case, witnesses are less likely to reappear, memories begin to fade, strong evidence tends to weaken. Societal protections may be jeopardized just as much by case delays that result in the defendant "walking" because of a witness no-show, for example, as it might be by having the defendant released pending trial.

Deterrence has been mentioned as a goal of criminal justice. Its effectiveness, too, may be reduced by case-processing delay. Katz points out that one reason for the apparent failure of this theory to gain acceptance may be not the invalidity of the theory but rather the length of time before punishment is imposed.[5] Punishment to be effective as a deterrent should follow the wrongful act closely. Deterrence is not likely to operate when others contemplating a crime know what they have, first, a good chance of not being caught and, even if apprehended, have perhaps even a better chance of not being convicted or of not being held to account for a long period of time.

Both deterrence and rehabilitation (the third goal of the criminal justice system) if at all workable should be attempted in an environment where the punishment for the crime is "swift, sure and certain." As Katz states: "rehabilitation is most effective when begun as close as possible to the criminal activity which necessitates the treatment. It is least effective when postponed so that the wrongdoer is scarely able to relate the treatment to his wrongful act."[6]

A substantial part of the failure of the justice system to reduce crime and provide protection to the public can be attributed to the effects of delay. Society's burdens are not measured only in terms of personal injury and property loss or damage but also include large public financial supports. The criminal justice system is financially supported by society's tax monies. Delays in processing overburden an already costly system and place new demands on more expenditure of funds. For pretrial detention alone, the National Advisory Commission concluded from its surveys on the costs of pretrial detention that "projecting such figures on a national basis and allowing for lower costs and crime rates in smaller communities, pre-trial detention expenses probably exceed $100 million per year."[7] To the extent that the length of time in pretrial detention and all other processing steps can be reduced, savings to society should potentially accrue.

The criminal justice system cannot escape adverse effects where there is delay. More than anything else, delay erodes the strength of the case, is a major contributor to congestion, and degrades the overall quality of justice. The major effect of delay is to encourage "witness no-shows." As the National District Attorneys Association (NDAA) recognized and emphasized in their commentary, "Witnesses are a vital cog upon which the judicial system heavily relies in its search for justice. As the case stretches on, multiple court appearances by witnesses may be required. Often where a last minute continuance is obtained, the witnesses' appearances will be for naught, their sacrifices wasted. Eventually, both witnesses and complainants may lose interest and cease to appear."[8] Not only are the effects clearly manifested by witness no-shows, but, as the period between the incident and trial lengthens, witnesses who are still available may lose credibility as their memory weakens. Even the collection and storage of evidence presents additional risks. Human error or poor operating procedures are more likely to cause the loss or destruction of important evidence as times increases. All these effects lead to a single result: as delays in case processing increase, the probability of obtaining an adjudication on the case's merits decreases.

The interaction of delay and congestion undermines the criminal justice system and the public's image and confidence in their system of justice. In jurisdictions operating under overloaded conditions, complaints about case backlogs, large pending dockets, and lack of speedy trial are indicators that congestion is pervasive. Where such conditions thrive, delay cannot be tolerated. Hurried attempts to move dockets may result in hasty actions that would not be considered under less congested circumstances. As one Assistant District Attorney in New York City observed to the Vera Institute on Justice staff about his actions: "Sometimes there's intimidation, a bribe or a scare to put off the complaining witness. I just don't have time to find out—the drive is just to clear the calendar."[9]

If the negative effects of delay are so strong to the accused, society, and the justice system itself, then one must question why delay is still rampant in criminal justice systems. One must wonder why in seeking its goals of crime reduction and public protection, society has failed to heed the expertise of Chief Justice Burger when he stated: "The most simple and most obvious remedy is to give the courts the manpower and tools . . . to try criminal cases within sixty days after indictment and then see what happens. I predict it would be to sharply reduce the crime rate."[10] The resolution of this apparent contradiction between the unanimously expressed desire to reduce delay and the inability to do it can be found in the workings of the criminal justice system itself.

Delay in case processing is a difficult problem to approach because there are no uniformly recognized methods for defining delay. Methods of measuring time in process are inconsistent among the numerous jurisdictions, perceptions vary, and as a result case delay in one court system may not constitute delay in another system. The first goal to be attained in any attack on this pernicious problem is the development of a standard method of defining delay. This lack of standard definition has arisen because delay is not, in all cases, a destructive factor to all actors within the system. As has been seen earlier, there are occasions where case delay can work, at least temporarily, to the advantage of a defense attorney or to  judge with a crowded docket, although the long-time effect is disastrous to the system as a whole. The concept of delay is often tempered by the exigencies of daily working conditions. Even the programs designed to control or reduce delay, such as the implementation of speedy trial rules, need examination within the context of the realities of the criminal justice world.

Delay in many criminal justice systems is not entirely a reflection of society's neglect or indifference. We have seen that delay is counterproductive to society's goals, and we assume that it is also counterproductive to the individual, whether jailed or released, because of the stigma of being accused of a crime. But is this assumption correct? When the effects of delay are examined from the different perspectives of each of the actors in the criminal justice system and with respect to the expectations of the different organizational components of the system, it becomes evident that there is no absolute. Delay may or may not be an advantage. The conflicting goals operating in our adversary system of justice are never so manifest as when we examine this issue.

For the defendant facing trial, delay in case processing is generally more beneficial than detrimental. This is especially valid if he is not innocent but, in fact, guilty, and has had a previous record. This type of person constitutes a rather large percentage of all those arrested. Recent studies show that in a typical jurisdiction from 62 to 79 percent of persons arrested were previously known to the police.[11]

The primary issue for the defendant regarding delay rests on his release status. If detained, the generally inhumane environment of the jail coupled with a loss of freedom compels the defendant to seek release and, failing that, to demand either quick dispositions or a speedy trial. The court ordinarily gives precedent to "jail" cases, giving them priority over "bail" cases.

However, defendants in jail do not always demand a speedy trial. There are circumstances where delay is more attractive than immediate disposition. Since the operative reality is that the state's case will tend to erode over time, thereby increasing the chances for a dismissal of the case, the defendant may be willing to gamble. This may occur frequently if the defendant has a long record or has committed a very serious crime. If the state's case is strong, it may not be willing to bargain. Facing a long sentence on conviction, the defendant's better course is to delay the trial as long as possible hoping the case will fall apart. Even under less severe conditions, the gamble may be worthwhile if the court's sentencing policy is to credit the defendant with "time served." (Time served pending trial is subtracted from the sentence after conviction.) In addition, delay is particularly attractive if during the course of the wait a plea can be negotiated or probation avoided.

Even the released defendant may desire delay. The simple fact is that, if the accused is guilty, there are few benefits to be derived from seeking a fast case disposition. The defendant's liberty is not restrained. His actions are mostly unsupervised, and he is free to pursue his usual interests whatever they might be. Additionally, from his viewpoint the free time on the streets may be used more profitably. He can outwait the opposition and wear down either the witnesses or the prosecution. For each continuance gained, the defendant has a better chance of walking.

It would seem reasonable to expect the defense counsel to be attuned to the desires of the defendant, and, for the most part, this is true. As we have seen, the priorities of defense counsel shift from obtaining an early and quick disposition (dismissal) to an acceptable plea negotiation (again the earlier the better) and, finally, in lieu of all else, the longest processing time as possible. If an acceptable disposition cannot be negotiated with the state quickly, or if the defendant will not plead to the original charge, then with only the option of a trial left, delay becomes an effective strategy. Sometimes this strategy will result in wearing down witnesses or undermining their credibility so that the prosecutor will be affected and will produce an acceptable offer.

In addition to these reasons, defense counsel may also support delaying tactics for their own personal benefit. This is common for two purposes: to collect fees and to avoid incurring losses. The NDAA addressed the former condition in its commentary on speedy trial standards: "One of the most disturbing examples of . . . delay is utilization by defense counsel of continuances to collect money owed them by clients."[12] NDAA cites Banfield's study of Cook County, which rationalized these practices.[13] The defense counsel believed that fees would be difficult to collect once the case was concluded, especially if the conclusion was not a satisfactory one for the defendant. Katz reports in his study that this practice is widespread and even reports delays that were granted so that defendants out on bail could continue working and thereby pay the attorney's fee.[14] Eisenstein and Jacob recognized the practice in Chicago's circuit court by noting that "both judges and prosecutors, often tried to help retained regulars collect their fees."[15]

Finally for those defense counsel retained privately or court appointed, the fee set is usually based on the work activity of the counsel in disposing of the case before trial. The costs of a trial may be more than the costs of this one case. If the counsel is a regular, he usually cannot afford to absent himself from his other clients and be tied up in a trial. As Eisenstein and Jacob recorded in their study of Baltimore, where cases were "paneled" out to private attorneys, a "complicated mixture of incentives" arose.

> When they were paid by the defendant, they had to handle all aspects of the case efficiently. If they consistently spent more time in preparation and courtroom appearances than the defendants could pay for, their ability to earn a good living was destroyed. . . . However, when attorneys represented indigent defendants assigned by public defenders, they had no problems getting paid. The defender footed the bill. . . . Protracted jury trials remained unattractive, although panel attorneys received at least something for their courtroom time. Guilty pleas were not much more attractive than brief bench trials, and perhaps they were less so because guilty pleas might produce less billable preparation time.[16]

Thus, at times, delaying techniques employed by the defense counsel are strongly influenced by the type of financial arrangement under which they are being reimbursed and may vary substantially according to whether they are court appointed, privately retained, or public defenders.

To look at delay from the court's perspective with any clarity, one must first define the perspective as either an organizational structure, an individual courtroom setting, or the policy, personality, and qualificaitons of an individual judge.

By far, the most important factor affecting the ability of the court to control the flow of cases is what Eisenstein and Jacob call the "norm of individual autonomy" for judges.[17] This means that the court is comprised of a set of judges who, as some more cynical critics observe, "report only to God." The manifestation of autonomy in judges is mirrored by a lack of centralized management and administrative controls, a consensus approach to organization, and an inability to control sentencing differentials or increase uniformity in case processing. Within the relatively autonomous environment of this type of court system, the chances of producing an efficient and manageable system of case processing are greatly reduced. As Katz noted: "Traditionally, judges have played little or no management or supervisory role in the control of their courts, and in the speed at which cases are processed."[18] The exceptions stand out as shining examples, they are so few.

Given this principle of independence and autonomy, it is not surprising to see court organization marked by little centralized power. Eisenstein's and Jacob's description of the authority of Detroit's presiding judge is hardly unique: a judge whose influence depends on the resources available to the position, the good will of his colleagues who elected him, and his ability to form a consensus through voluntary cooperation in matters normally left to the prerogative for the individual judges.[19] Under these circumstances, the opportunity to utilize organizational control over judicial actions that affect case delay are extremely limited.

As a result, most of the pressure for reducing delay in the court has been generated from external forces, most notably the prosecution and defense. On the whole, the goals of the defendant and defense counsel most often conform with those of the prosecution for speedy dispositions, although, as previously enumerated, they will diverge on occasion. The overwhelming push is for speedy dispositions.

The individual judge sitting in a courtroom and the assistant prosecutor assigned there cooperate to process a routine work flow on a daily basis, although each views the process differently. For the prosecutor, every delay reduces his chances for a successful disposition. The judge, on the other hand, wants to move the docket, which may consist of pleas, trials, motions, and motions for continuances. Granting motions for continuances is the quickest way to move a docket. Unlike a motion to suppress or for discovery, which may require arguments from both sides, continuances can be granted with little or no discussion. Unlike taking a plea, which may require the reading of the charges and questioning, continuances can be processed quickly. They avoid the consequences of making decisions and in toto represent an immediately advantageous means for moving a large docket. In a court crowded by a large docket before a judge less than eager to work long hours, continuances mean the docket can be called and ended while the day is still young. Under these conditions the judge has more incentives to continue a case than to bring it to disposition.

Where sanctions are invoked to counteract these pressures, they often take the form of peer group pressure or work record comparisons. For the latter, the organization of the court must be considered. There is a limited opportunity to make comparisons in the process, assembly-line court model where the functions of each courtroom vary, some handling arraignments, others preliminary examinations, still others motions or trials. Comparison becomes more feasible in the integrated trial team model, where individual docketing or assignment to a single court permits workload comparison and strict accountability.

Thus, delay in court disposition assumes different dimensions depending on the unit of court affected: the court as a whole, the courtroom workgroup, or an individual judge. Court delay is more affected by external pressures exerted by outsiders or other components of the system further removed, like the media and the electorate, than it is by internal sanctions. This is simply because, as Banfield noted, "Judges whose schedules are too full are more likely to be liberal in granting continuances requested by parties than they otherwise would be."[20]

Within this milieu of criminal justice actors, sanctions, and incentives, only the prosecutor is consistently disadvantaged by case-processing delay. Because this delay has such a powerful impact on his ability to prosecute successfully he must anticipate the defense strategies, evaluate the judge's proclivities, and be ready to respond to maintain his advantage. Yet unless he controls the docket or case scheduling, his power is limited.

Any examination of delay from the participants' perspective demonstrates that the incentives for delay in case processing vary widely according to the goals and measures of success for the participants in the process. One needs to recognize that there is no simple, single-purpose goal operating in the system to "reduce delay in case processing." Not only is this not a universally accepted goal, but its meaning is as vague as its measurement.

One cannot hope to achieve reductions in case delay or evaluate its impact on prosecution without first being able to define and measure its dimensions. The chief mechanism for delay is a motion for continuance. When granted, it results in the postponement of the scheduled court appearance and necessitates the rescheduling of the case at some later date.

The power of the continuance to diminish the witness' willingness to testify is well documented. The latest analysis of the Washington, D.C., PROMIS data shows that in 1974, 30 percent of the approximately fifteen thousand cases prosecuted were dismissed or nolled, and, in perhaps 25 percent, the reason cited was for "witness-no-show." Add to that figure the unknown number of cases lost or reduced because the witnesses' memories dim and the dimensions of the problem can be better understood. The second effect of a continuance is the required rescheduling of the case. For each postponement and rescheduling, the chances of mistakes occurring are increased. Some cases are simply lost. The file folders may be misplaced, and, if the paperwork management controls are deficient, they may even disappear. Some cases involve so many participants that establishing a mutually convenient date may in itself prove difficult. Nevertheless, the need for a mechanism to continue a case is essential. It cannot be eliminated for it serves many legitimate purposes.

The most important reason for a continuance is to assure a fair hearing. For the defense it provides additional time to vindicate the defendant or to provide an adequate defense. The increased number of procedural rights afforded the defendant have also increased the number of justifications for motions for continuance. The requirement for defense representation now extends earlier and earlier in the process in misdemeanor trials and in preliminary hearings, and full exercise of the right to consult with counsel may delay the hearing in many cases. After this, the defendant's counsel can make pretrial motions, motions to suppress or dismiss; he may ask for time to find missing witnesses, to collect evidence, to have mental competency examination, to extend an investigation, or to perform additional legal research. All may be used to legitimately request a continuance.

Although the prosecutor may also seek continuances for many of the same reasons, it is not with the same force. The prosecution bears a stiffer burden in preparing for trial. Delays requested by the state seldom are given the same consideration by the court as those requested by defense counsel. Yet the system must make allowances for the unavoidable and the unexpected whether it is caused by human negligence or extraordinary circumstances. The quest for reduction of delay cannot be allowed to impinge on the interest of all actors in a fair hearing that may require a continuance or postponement.[21]

Since delay may be a defense tactic—and often a powerful one in negotiating a successful plea bargain or in gaining a dismissal because a witness did not show—its use raises certain ethical ambiguities. When continuances are excessive, the defense may be stepping over the fine line between a necessary tactic and abuse of the system. The clearest distinction appears when one differentiates between delay that serves the interest of the defendant and that which serves the personal interests of the defense attorney.[22]

It is this latter category that deserves more than just the ethical sanctions of the defense bar and bar associations and calls for tighter controls by the court. Too often continuances are requested to enable the defense counsel to collect his fee,[23] or to provide a means of avoiding time-consuming and financially unrewarding trials.[24] With motivations such as these, the interests of neither the defendant nor the system are served.

Continuances not only provide the defense with a tactical advantage in wearing down the state, but they also debilitate a prosecutor's effort to bring the case to a swift and certain disposition. Despite his attempts to reduce the number of continuances in a case, the prosecutor is generally powerless to do so. He may oppose the motion, he may cite the number of continuances already granted to the defense in the case as an indication of abuse, he may even confer privately with the judge to impress on him the gravity or precariousness of the case's status. But his influence is limited. If he controls the docket, he may be able to mitigate some of the effects of the continuance by controlling the rescheduling of the case. Generally, though, the court decides and controls this issue.

One of the most important controls imposed to reduce some of the debilitating effects of delay are the speedy trial rules of a jurisdiction. The right to speedy trial is established by the U.S. Constitution's Sixth Amendment. It states in part, "In all criminal prosecutions, the accused shall enjoy the right to a speedy and public trial." Many of the states have enacted similar legislation but usually without a specific definition of what constitutes "speedy." This task has been left to the courts.

As the law developed, there was a general unwillingness to impose a specific time limit during which trial must be commenced. In 1967, in *Klopfer* v. *North Carolina* the Court held that the federal right to speedy trial was to be applied to the states through the Fourteenth Amendment.[25] Five years later, in *Barker* v. *Wingo*,[26] they still refuse to impose time limits on the definition, holding that "to do so would be to engage in legislative, rather than adjudicatory activity."[27] Instead they defined the concept of speedy trial as the relationship between the defendant's assertion or demand for a speedy trial, the length of the delay, the reason for the delay, and the prejudice to the defendant.[28] As they stated, "Courts still must engage in a difficult and sensitive balancing process" to determine whether a violation has occurred.[29]

At the local level the implementation of speedy trial rules has been far from uniform. The modern trend is for the speedy trial deadline to be expressed in terms of a period of days or months. This position is supported by the American Bar Association.[30] The time period may differ depending on the seriousness of the crime charged, whether felony or misdemeanor.[31] Some states impose shorter time limits if the defendant has been denied pretrial release.[32] Most speedy trial rules have provisions for tolling the calendar. The least explicit rules merely provide that the time can be extended by the court "for good cause."[33] The most explicit can be found in Ohio, whose speedy trial provision lists eight major categories of exceptions.[34]

The state bears the burden of ensuring that the defendant receives a trial within the time frame stipulated by the speedy trial rule. The running of time begins in some jurisdictions at arrest, in others when a formal accusation is made or at arraignment. There are provisions in most speedy trial rules for the tolling of its running. After speedy time starts running, most delays or continuances, except those that are specifically requested by the defendant, will be counted against the prosecution. Failure to bring the defendant to trial, even if that failure is caused by court backlog or some other reason beyond the control of the prosecutor, will still be counted against him. If the defendant does not get to trial within the allotted time, the case against him must be dismissed.

In deciding whether delay will be charged to the prosecution, states have keyed on the issue of whether speedy trial rules should include sanctions against trial court congestion. In some states, trial court congestion is excepted from delay that may be held against the state.[35] Other states have avoided the problem by requiring that the prosecution be "ready" for trial within a certain period.[36] Although such rules encourage prompt case preparation by the government and minimize requests for continuances by the state, they place no sanctions on the defense and may do little to reduce court delay or congestion.

The overriding effects of continuances on the prosecutor are negative. He is generally powerless to counteract delay. Speedy trial rules increase the need for quick case preparation yet require accommodations to the defense to avoid the time limits imposed under speedy trial rules. The court yields great power and influence in determining the speed at which a case moves through the criminal process.

## Court Organizations and Work Groups

If the court wields such great power in controlling and reducing delay, the logical questions seem to be why does it grant unnecessary motions for continuances and why does it fail to reduce delay? A partial answer to these two questions may be found in the structure and capacity of the court. There are many legitimate reasons for delay and the system's inability to reduce delay. Foremost is a simple lack of resources. Despite all the latest trends to increase the level of funding, many court, prosecution, and defense systems are understaffed, underequipped, and barely able to cope with the present volume of cases. Delay in these systems merely aggravates an existing problematical area. As NDAA noted: "Shortage of resources may be the most critical problem of all. The fact is, that the system has not grown to meet the challenge of rising criminal activity. Especially in urban jurisdictions, there is a shortage of courtrooms and judges sufficient to try even the small percentage of cases which actually are taken to trial. The result is a growing case backlog."[37] The lack of resources is not entirely an urban characteristic. We have seen that even in the more rural areas of the United States, the lack of flexibility in the smaller prosecutors' offices and court systems leaves little margin for emergencies or increased crime. The solo prosecutor working with three magistrate courts, for example, has limited capacity to absorb increase in workload. Continuing in this discussion, NDAA says: "These judicial problems are often compounded by a lack of sufficient prosecutorial personnel, and the public defender services may be similarly overburdened. Overload may extend to the private defense bar as well. . . . The overloading of the system may also contribute indirectly to the large number of abusive and unnecessary continuances plaguing the criminal trial process."[38]

The increasingly complex procedures employed in the criminal trial process as mandated by statute and court rule also contribute to the ineffectiveness of the court in reducing delay. An underlying factor that produces more work effort and requires more time is the expanded use of motions. The need to ensure a fair hearing must not be minimized. Yet the extent to which the court may adapt or change its procedures to minimize these negative effects is under scrutiny. Katz calls for a reduction in duplicative processes and a dispensing of unnecessary stages that no longer have validity. He views court delay as a product of tradition that requires broad and fundamental changes. He states: "The American way has been to increase steps rather than refine or dispense with stages that no longer fulfill a valid purpose. . . . The system has been receptive to expansion at various levels but has been extremely reluctant to relieve itself of unnecessary procedures that have firm historical roots. . . . It is society's inability to confront this reality which has contributed to the problem of court delay today."[39]

Whereas Katz's indictment may be generally true and valid, a more specific explanation of the problem can be found through examination of the organization of the court and the effects of this organizational structure on the trial process. The organizational characteristics of the court tend to foster the autonomous authority of the court; this increases the opportunity for inconsistency and a lack of uniformity in procedures and values within a courtroom, and it provides little opportunity for proper management and administrative and planning controls.

To understand the inability of the courts to make changes in structure or to exert control over its members, it is necessary to view this organization from three perspectives: the organization of the court, the courtroom work group, and the individual judge. Formal organizations may be approached and examined in several different ways, but these three components seem most significant for this analysis and must not be viewed independently but rather as interrelated and interdependent forces.

When formal organizations are examined with the individual as the unit of analysis, the examination necessarily focuses on psychological factors and work roles. The motivation of the individual to contribute to the organization and his ability to work effectively become the basis for the study or organizational psychology or business psychology.[40] A major study area within this type of organizational analysis focuses on the personality of the worker and the effect of personality on his work behavior. Whereas the personality of the judges, coupled with an organization setting that gives them great autonomy, has a direct effect on the courtroom, it will not be examined in depth here. We will merely note that in most court systems there exists a wide range of personalities, motivations, and definitions of job satisfaction. Given this diversity we will examine the extent to which the formal organization and the work group shape the individual judges behavior.

Eisenstein and Jacob have produced the most detailed study on the small work group, one that is cited extensively in this discussion.[41] In organizational sociology, the small work group merits special interest with regard to group cohesion, relationships within the group, and group ability to operate harmoniously within the larger, formal organization.

A group "personality" has been labeled "syntality" by Cattell.[42] As a reflection of the personality of the group, researchers have noted that syntality is more than just the sum of the individual personalities within the group. The work group assumes its own identity with its own attributes. It may be efficient or apathetic, erratic or routinized in its behavior. But it reflects a unique group attitude. The group acts and the group thinks in its own identifiable way. To the extent that it has its own identity, sociologists have termed this "reification." This type of organizational analysis of the work group assumes significant importance in the judicial system. Unlike some work groups in business or industry, which may have weak or amorphous impact in their social context such as in assembly-line processes or small family businesses, the courtroom work group has an effect on the entire criminal justice system.

The formal organization as a unit of analysis is also important in our examination of the ability of the court to affect the prosecutor's case processing and dispositional achievement because of its limited ability to control the work groups and the individual judges. Formal organizations have unique qualities and characteristics in much the same sense as individuals and work groups have characteristic attributes. Organizations can be characterized by size, "the centralization of authority and decisionmaking power, the specialization of tasks and the functional complexity of task interrelationship and the proportionate size of the administrative component."[43]

Sociologists have developed models that indicate some differences between types of formal organizations and serve as a classification system to provide greater insight into the problems of the organizations.[44] Within limits they can be used to provide an organizational perspective for the courts. The court system can best be described as a type of organization referred to as "the professional model."[45] The professional model has been described as an organization composed of professionals dealing with problematic events that require training in specialized schools, developing complex skills and special knowledge, and exercising internalized control mechanisms.[46] The professional model, in contrast to the bureaucratic model, tends to operate with specialists in specific functions under a hierarchial structure within a system of formal rules. The effects of this type of organization have been documented by researchers and social scientists. "Professionals are likely to reject bureaucratic rules because they perceive themselves as capable of establishing a more functional set of behavioral expectations. They resist standards of bureaucratic organizations because, reflecting a cosmopolitan orientation, they adhere to the standards created by the abstract professional aggregate on a national scale" (for example, the American Medical Association, the American Bar Association, and the American Psychological Association).[47] The professionals antipathy toward bureaucratic controls and supervision is well known. The formal organization of this type finds it exceedingly hard to impose adequate management and administrative controls on its members or work groups. One researcher explained the difficulties that occur this way. "Professionals will be able to operate in organizations more effectively by applying greater expertise with respect to task knowledge and social skills. On the other hand, professionals are increasingly likely to resist or reject various bureaucratic rules, resist or reject bureaucratic standards, resist bureaucratic supervision and reflect only conditional loyalty to the bureaucracy."[48]

This model applies well to the court system, where the organization consists primarily of professionals (judges) who operate within a tradition of autonomy of judicial opinion. The members tend to support the continued existence of an organization with little centralization of authority and little control over procedures. Thus, from the formal organization's perspective, one can expect little initiative toward central control. The organization operates in such a collegial fashion. There may not even be a presiding or chief judge. Even where such a position exists, it tends to be more ornamental than functional. The group's proclivities are to maintain independence and to avoid implementing change, making improvements, or enforcing and monitoring consistency or uniformity in decision-making procedures. Eisenstein's and Jacob's description of judicial organization in Baltimore supports the principles of this type of model.

> The judges of the Supreme Bench held weekly meetings at which the chief judge, appointed by the governor, presided. The judicial or organization was not strong, and the powers of the chief judge were limited . . . he pre-

sided over the weekly meetings, reserved to himself . . . the right to authorize postponements of cases scheduled for trial (a power formerly exercised by trial judges individually) and sought to install a computerized record-keeping system.[49]

Since central authority is weak and lacks the necessary cohesion that one would look for in a more bureaucratic model, any change that occurs most likely results from peer pressure, not hierarchial mandate. Within the confines of the collegial atmosphere, actions that affect the overall court system do occur. For example, in Baltimore despite the lack of centralized power, decisions were made (usually more collegially than not) that affected the operations of the court. Work was distributed to the courtrooms, a clerk's Case Assignment Office was established with the responsibility for assigning cases to trial courtrooms, and even though there was divisiveness among the judges, the court did change and operate. This type of formal oranization is not necessarily bad. But it inherently limits the extent of change that can occur within its structure and distributes power and authority among the courtroom work groups.

The courtroom work group is by far the dominant factor in the prosecutor's trial and disposition phase. The relatively routinized procedures leading up to trial are not so strongly dependent on the courtroom work group. Arraignments, motions, and to a lesser extent, probable cause hearings tend to operate independent of the syntality of the work group. However, once the accusatory process has been completed and the case is assigned for trial, courtroom work groups dominate further procceedings.

The courtroom work group exhibits a cohesiveness that may stand in stark contrast to the generally weak formal organizations of the court and at times in conflict with the norms of equal justice. It is within these work groups that the individual attitudes, as units of organizational analysis, can be placed in perspective and contrasted to the syntality of the group. Courroom work groups assume some characteristics of formal organizations. They exhibit authority relationships; they display influence relationships that modify authority; they share common goals; they have specialized roles but contribute to a single process; they use a variety of work techniques, engage in a variety of tasks, and have different degrees of stability and familiarity.[50]

Because they may evolve into semiautonomous work groups, they cause the prosecutor to respond to the trial process in ways that are compatible to the specific work group. Yet conflicts arise because uniformity and consistency of decisions and actions among these groups are difficult to attain. Eisenstein and Jacob make a significant distinction between the goals external to the work group and those that are internal. Those falling in the latter category deal with having to "do the work." To do the work, there is a need to maintain group cohesion and thereby reduce uncertainty. As the work group participants become more and more familiar with each other's work patterns, and their actions be more predictable, a more orderly and efficient pattern for doing the work can be established.

The external goals are those of the sponsoring organizations participating in the work group, primarily, the court, prosecutor, defense counsel. It is not inconceivable that the totals of the office of the prosecutor may be subverted to meet the goals of the work group.

The expressed goal imposed by the external environment is to do justice. All the principal participants are attorneys, and are bound to that goal by their professional training. The ambiguity and disagreement contained in the notion of justice in society are mirrored in the varying perspectives of work group members. For the defense, doing justice may mean either obtaining an acquittal or a mild sentence for its clients, or forcing the prosecution to prove its cases. . . . The prosecution often sees doing justice in terms of its conviction rates. . . . Judges generally see this goal as requiring impartial behavior, although their definition of impartiality often favors the defense or the prosecution. Thus, surface agreement within the courtroom organization on the goal of "doing justice" often engenders behavioral conflict.[51]

Since the task of the work group is to process the work, it calls for goals and behavior less conflicting and less adversarial. There must be some compromise reached between cooperation and cohesiveness of the work group and the clear policy prerogatives of formal sponsoring organizations. The description of the Detroit prosecutor's policy for no reduced pleas after the pretrial conference points up the power of the court to subvert the policy and subvert it on a selective basis, namely courtroom by courtroom. The no reduced plea policy was intended to preserve the validity of the pretrial conference, where a plea negotiation was offered the defense. If this was not accepted, then the case would be tried on the original charge (hence the terminology, no reduced plea). The second purpose was to take to court a pure trial docket, one that the court would know was going to trial for a specified charge. "The willingness of judges to accept a plea bargain a defendant had rejected thirty days earlier created obvious pressures on the assistant prosecutors assigned to their courtroom. Judicial pressure produced a strong incentive for trial attorneys to undercut office policies. The administrative staff was fully aware of these pressures and sought to counteract them."[52]

The interaction of the participants in the courtroom work group, the shift of power and influence among the members, and the relative autonomy of these groups in relation to their sponsoring organizations, are clearly shown in the Eisenstein and Jacob study. What is most important about this study is that with a courtroom work group perspective, some of the reasons for inconsistencies in decision making are clarified and the paradox of a court creating rather than reducing delay is made sensible. The norm of individual autonomy for the judges not only allows for the emergence of different personalities, policies, and procedures among the judges but also tends to restrict the role played by a presiding judge in management, administration, or policy making.[53]

Because the court relies on specialization in the professional area of law, the formal organization takes on the characteristics of the professional model. Collegial in nature, resistant to bureaucratic and supervisory controls, there is little opportunity or expressed desire for a hierarchy. Unlike the prosecutor who has direct control over his professional staff (he generally can hire and fire them) the judges generally operate in a less controlled environment, which in turn works against increasing judicial centralization or direction. As a result, the courtroom work group emerges as the dominant force, operating with three primary components, the court, prosecution, and defense. As a separate entity it may indeed be in conflict with the formal court organization's policies, but there is little incentive and few sanctions to change this reality for the sake of uniformity or consistency.

Court delay can be explained by this phenomenon. The court grants necessary motions for continuances because it is in the interest of the courtroom work group to keep working relationships smooth and move the cases along. Because the courtroom work group exists almost autonomously within a weak formal organization that exercises little centralized control, power, or direction, the ability of the court to move to reduce delay by controlling the individual courtrooms is extremely limited. Even if one judge refused to grant continuances, the policy would be generally ineffective unless all the other judges would agree to conform to the same policy.

Jacob[54] makes the distinction between the adversary process that assumes the innocence of the defendant and "operates under the simplifying assumption that conflicts are two-sided or can be presented in the framework of a two-sided dispute"[55] and a dispositional process that assumes that most defendants are guilty and the goal is "not to discover the truth or separate the innocent from the guilty. Rather, the objective is to determine appropriate treatment of the defendant."[56] As Jacob further notes in this discussion: "The operating characteristics of the dispositional process differ markedly from those of the adversary process. Perhaps the most prominent difference is that defense and prosecuting attorneys alike are allies rather than adversaries. . . . Both have an overwhelming concern to maintain a smooth flow of cases and to prevent a breakdown in the decisional process."[57]

The distinction between these two models can be more easily understood when one considers how they can coexist in our system of justice. The formal organization previously discussed can be viewed as more a representation of the adversary process, whereas the courtroom work group takes on more of the characteristics of the dispositional process. Yet, elements of both models can be found to exist in most courtroom proceedings.

If the negotiation and collaborative characteristics of the courtroom are taken into consideration, not only can we understand some of the elements of court delay and its relationship to continuances, but we also may gain insight into the final step in the trial process, the sentencing.

## Sentencing

A case is finally disposed of when the judge passes sentence. In an adversary system of justice one assumes that this action by the court is taken in an impartial manner after considering facts and information provided by the defense counsel, prosecutor, and the presentence investigation (usually prepared by the probation department, an arm of the court).

Sentencing and the prosecutor's sentence recommendations generally are inextricably intertwined. Not all prosecutors participate in the sentencing process, and not necessarily all the time. The NCPM survey reported that 90 percent of the prosecutors stated that they had the right to make recommendations at both misdemeanor and felony sentencings but that only 70 percent made recommendations more than half the time in felony cases, and only 44 percent made recommendations consistently (90 percent of the time or more). The prosecutor's use of sentence recommendations as a final action in the trial process generally can be attributed to three factors. It may be an integral part of the prosecutor's use of plea bargaining as a dispositional vehicle; it may be based on the court's reluctance to make sentencing decisions without prosecutorial input; or it may be the result of prosecutorial policy.

### Plea Bargaining and Sentence Recommendation

The expected sentence guides the entire range of activities found in the criminal case process, from acceptance for prosecution to plea negotiations through trial, from trial through incarceration and pardon or parole. The overriding consideration is the uncertainty regarding the possible penalty that might be imposed for conviction. In many courtrooms the need to process the workload with minimum effort is most easily achieved by obtaining a guilty plea from the defendant or failing this, dismissing the case. If a defendant insists on a trial, he is usually penalized upon being found guilty by receiving a harsher sentence. As Alschuler pointed out, the underlying reason for the more severe sentence is that the trials subvert the dispositional process.[58]

As a result, the influence of the prosecutor's ability to make sentence recommendations is felt long before a case ever enters the courtroom. In many cases the ability of the prosecutor to influence the sentencing process will determine if the case ever gets to trial. The ability to make specific sentence recommendations to the court is a tool that the prosecuting attorney can and often does use in negotiation with the accused for a plea of guilty.

Plea bargaining may be defined in terms of a simple bilateral contract as the acceptance by the defendant is a criminal action of an offer made by the prosecutor to plead guilty to a criminal charge for a consideration.[59] The bilateral contract concept is most apt because "plea bargaining flourishes because its benefits are bilateral, accruing to the prosecution as well as to the defense."[60]

The benefits to the prosecution are simple and straightforward. A plea of guilty saves valuable attorney time, prevents lengthy litigation in cases where there is overwhelming evidence for conviction, prevents needless case delay and case backlog, and saves substantial amounts of money for the taxpayer. It also saves the prosecution the risk of having to go to trial with cases they may lose. The benefits for the defendant are also substantial if that defendant has indeed committed the crime and is fairly certain that he will be unable to raise a reasonable defense. A guilty plea affords some hope of more lenient treatment than is prescribed by strict application of the law. A serious offense can be reduced by the prosecutor who may choose to charge the defendant with a lesser included offense.

Not all prosecutors want to recommend sentences. Some do not because the traditional separation between the judicial process and prosecution has clearly defined this as being a judicial function, some because their personal policy opposes making recommendations. Some courts, however, insist that the prosecutor recommend at sentencing. This may be because the judge simply does not want to make such a decision independently; or, at times, it may be used by the court to reduce any criticism of its sentence decision by buttressing it with the support of the prosecutor.

As the legislative trend today begins to reflect the public's harsher attitude toward crime and criminals, the power of the prosecutor in the postconviction area will increase. The legislation of mandatory minimums, flat sentencing, and determinant sentencing can only accord extra power to the prosecution. By the careful selection of charges the prosecutor not only controls the sentencing outcomes if the defendant is found guilty but also gains more power in negotiating pleas. Clearly, the trials-to-disposition phase needs further study and exploration beyond the legal perspective. The organization structure of the court, its docketing procedures and continuance policies, the case assignment practices of the prosecutor, and the trial strategies available or permitted are additional areas of interest as they affect the function and performance of this component in the criminal justice system.

The external environment changes significantly as the prosecution moves from charging to accusation, trials, and dispositions. These changes should be recognized and included in any consideration of prosecution from a functional approach.

## Notes

1. See Lewis R. Katz et al., *Justice Is the Crime: Pretrial Delay in Felony Cases* (Cleveland, Ohio: Case Western Reserve University Press, 1972), p. 54.

2. Ibid.

3. J.W. Locke et al., *Compilation and Use of Criminal Court Data in Relation to Pre-Trial Release of Defendants: Pilot Study*, National Bureau of Standards Technical Note 535 (Washington, D.C.: National Bureau of Standards, 1970), pp. 1-2.

4. Ibid., p. 15. See, also, *Report to the Judicial Council Committee to Study the Operation of the Bail Reform Act in the District of Columbia*, 2d ed. (Washington, D.C.: 1969). (Available through the National Criminal Justice Reference Service). See also, n. 11, p. 11.

5. Katz, *Justice Is the Crime*, n. 1, p. 53.

6. Ibid., n. 1, p. 55.

7. National Advisory Commission on Criminal Justice Standards and Goals (NAC), *Courts* (Washington, D.C.: U.S. Government Printing Office, 1973), p. 38.

8. National District Attorneys Association (NDAA), *National Prosecution Standards* (Chicago: National District Attorneys Association, 1977), p. 197.

9. The Vera Institute, *Felony Arrests: Their Prosecution and Disposition in New York City Courts* (New York: Vera Institute of Justice, 1977), p. 69.

10. Warren G. Burger, "The State of the Judiciary, 1970," 56 American Bar Association Journal, 929, 932 (1970).

11. Institute for Law and Social Research, *Curbing the Repeat Offender: A Strategy for Prosecutors*, PROMIS Research Project Publication #3 (Washington, D.C.: Law Enforcement Assistance Administration, 1977), p. 15; 79 percent is for all offenses, 62 percent for felonies only; 51 percent of those arrested had been arrested in the past 5 years, and 11 percent had had ten or more previous arrests.

12. NDAA, *National Prosecution Standards*, p. 198.

13. Laura Banfield and C. David Anderson, "Continuances in Cook County Criminal Courts," 35 University of Chicago Law Review 259, 262 (1968).

14. Katz, *Justice Is the Crime*, n. 1, p. 77.

15. James Eisenstein and Herbert Jacob, *Felony Justice: An Organizational Analysis of Criminal Courts* (Boston: Little, Brown, 1977), p. 109.

16. Ibid., pp. 89-90.

17. Ibid., p. 144.

18. Katz, *Justice Is the Crime*, n. 1, p. 82.

19. Eisenstein and Jacob, *Felony Justice*, pp. 144-145.

20. Banfield and Anderson, "Continuances," n. 3, p. 266.

21. Ibid., n. 3, p. 264.

22. NDAA, *National Prosecution Standards*, p. 198.

23. Katz, *Justice Is the Crime*, n. 1, p. 77.

24. Ibid., n. 1, p. 77.

25. Klopfer v. North Carolina, 386 U.S. 213 (1967).

26. Barker v. Wingo, 407 U.S. 514 (1972).

27. Ibid., p. 530.

28. Ibid., pp. 530-531.

29. Ibid., p. 533.

30. The American Bar Association, *Standards for Criminal Justice: Speedy Trial* (New York: The American Bar Association, 1968), approved draft.

31. California Penal Code sec. 1382 (West, 1970); Florida Statutes sec. 3.191(a) (1) (1968); Ohio Revised Code sec. 2945.71 (1971).

32. New York Code of Criminal Procedure sec. 30.20.1 (McKinney, 1971).

33. Arizona Rules of Criminal Procedure, Rule 236; California Penal Code sec. 1382 (West, 1970).

34. Ohio Revised Code sec. 2945.71 (1971).

35. Arkansas Statutes Annotated sec. 1710 (1947).

36. New York Code of Criminal Procedure sec. 30.30 (McKinney, 1971).

37. NDAA, *National Prosecution Standards*, p. 197.

38. Ibid.

39. Katz, *Justice Is the Crime*, n. 1, pp. 32-33.

40. Bernard M. Bass, *Organizational Psychology* (Boston: Allyn and Bacon, 1965); A.P. Quinn and R.L. Kahn, "Organizational Psychology," *Annual Review of Psychology* 18 (1967):437-466.

41. Eisenstein and Jacob, *Felony Justice*.

42. Raymond B. Cattell, "Concepts and Methods for Measuring Leadership in Terms of Group Syntality," *Human Relations* 4 (1951):161-184.

43. Dean J. Champion, *The Sociology of Organizations* (New York: McGraw-Hill, 1975), p. 8.

44. Ibid., pp. 24-63.

45. Ibid.

46. Richard W. Scott, "Professionals in Bureaucracies: Areas of Conflict," in *Professionalization*, ed. H.M. Vollmer and D.L. Mills (Englewood Cliffs, N.J.: Prentice-Hall, 1966).

47. Champion, *Sociology of Organizations*, p. 52.

48. Scott, "Professionals in Bureaucracies," pp. 268-269.

49. Eisenstein and Jacob, *Felony Justice*, p. 79.

50. Ibid., p. 20.

51. Ibid., pp. 26-27.

52. Ibid., p. 152.

53. Ibid., p. 144.

54. Herbert Jacob, *Urban Justice: Law and Order in American Cities* (Englewood Cliffs, N.J.: Prentice-Hall, 1973); Herbert L. Packer, *The Limits of the Criminal Sanction* (Palo Alto, Calif.: Stanford University Press, 1968).

55. Jacob, *Urban Justice*, p. 99.

56. Ibid., p. 101.

57. Ibid., p. 102.

58. Albert W. Alschuler, "The Prosecutor's Role in Plea Bargaining," 36 University of Chicago Law Review 50-112 (1968).

59. Joan E. Jacoby and Edward C. Ratledge, "A Feasibility Study for a Cost Analysis of Plea Bargaining" (Paper, 1976).

60. Henry B. Rothblatt, "Bargaining Strategy," *Trial*, 9 (1973):20.

# Part III
# Internalizing the Prosecutive
# Function

# 7

# Internalizing the Prosecutive Function

## Policy and Prosecution

We have explored in some broad measure how parts of the external world affect prosecution and constrain the function in varying ways. Now it is time to turn inward and examine the world which the prosecutor controls. It is a world of policy, of discretionary decision making, and of great power. The power emanates from the almost unreviewable authority of the prosecutor to make decisions that profoundly affect the lives of individuals and the community. It is also a world that is misinterpreted and misunderstood by the public.

The discretionary power of the prosecutor has repeatedly been the focus of analysis and debate since the 1920s. At that time, as discussed in chapter 2, many studies were instituted in various cities and states that had become increasingly troubled by the rise in the crime rate that the United States experienced after World War I. Within the context of new technology, increased economic expectations, a growing population, expansionary immigration, prohibition, and other changes in societal and moral outlooks, these studies attempted to define the state of criminal justice and assess its abilities to cope with the additional stresses of that turbulent period. At the heart of the studies was the question of discretionary justice: "The law is written by legislators, interpreted occasionally by appellate courts, but applied by countless individuals each acting largely for himself. How it is applied outweighs in importance its enactment or its interpretation."[1]

The "how" in the application of prosecutorial discretion is still the subject of concern and study, fifty years or so later. The ambivalence toward autonomous prosecutorial decision making has not been resolved. Indeed the increased complexity of our society has placed additional demand and pressures not only on the prosecutor but also on the criminal justice system, thereby strengthening ambivalent attitudes. Many of the more recent examinations allude to these complexities, both within the criminal justice process and within our changing society. The study decision-making practices and procedures in a modern, courtroom working environment,[2] within a political environment,[3] in small towns and middle America,[4] or in an urban environment.[5] They focus on the ethical and legal considerations of individualized justice,[6] abuse, corruption, and ethical considerations,[7] the need for discovery,[8] and the perils of delay.[9]

All studies, those conducted 50 years ago as well as those done more recently, have proceeded under the same two basic assumptions: (1) the prosecutor's discretionary power is the overriding important variable no matter what perspective is used in the study, and (2) the decision-making power extends beyond the office itself into a larger processing system.

For the average citizen, the term discretionary justice raises a red flag; it often denotes an uneven and unfair application of justice, and the uncontrolled wielding of accusatory power by the prosecuting attorney. But for the professional studying the nature and effects of discretionary justice, the term is far less threatening and raises interesting questions about the way in which the prosecutor operates within the criminal justice system, and the effect that his decision-making power has on the system, on individual defendants within the system, and on the community in which he is operating. Researchers are most interested in developing ways of describing and measuring the prosecutor's policy and his performance.

Early efforts directed toward developing measurement tools focused on individual offices. Even though individual offices are important units of study, especially if one desires to develop methods of comparison across jurisdictions, the early studies and their results suffered somewhat from parochialism. The conclusions reached from studying a single office generally could not be applied to any other jurisdiction because researchers had not yet developed a sufficiently broad wide theoretical framework for describing the effects of different environments and different policies on the various measures.

Prosecutorial policy is broadly defined as a course of action adopted by the district attorney in enforcing the law and performing his or her duties. Recent evaluations of pretrial screening programs have indicated the influence of prosecutorial policy in generating certain dispositional patterns, in selecting strategies to obtain results, and in structuring organizational resources to achieve the goals of the office.[10]

Most of the existing studies, although tremendously valuable in their ability to identify the more significant variables operating in the prosecutor's environments, are inadequate to produce performance measures that can be used for comparative evaluation because the measures have been derived independent of policy considerations. The majority of studies today tend to either describe offices or prosecutive processes, to explore the dimensions of prosecution from different functional perspectives, or to analyze according to different process points. As such, these studies represent a variety of methodologies and academic subject areas.

Management and systems analysis has become the dominant methodological approach to prosecution, not only because it provides operational benefits to the prosecutor in the form of improved procedures and tools, but also because it is so eminently suitable to a process that is as interactive as prosecution is. Management analysis can highlight work relationships and place process or decision points within their operating perspective. This approach has probably yielded more understanding and knowledge about prosecution than any other methodological technique.

The social sciences have also contributed substantially to present knowledge because of their focus on work roles and individual perception as well as demography, population, and other external social forces that affect crime and, ultimately, prosecution.

Political science and public administration have recently focused increased attention on criminal justice, in general, and prosecution, in particular. These disciplines have also added dimensions and perspective to the study of the prosecutor. The prosecutor is a locally elected official in the majority of jurisdictions, enmeshed in a political environment, and political scientists have become fascinated with the power and influence he wields. Also of great interest are the public administration aspects of the prosecutor's office, which demonstrate the power of organization and resource allocation to affect the performance level of this public official.

What is missing in most of these methodological or subject area approaches to prosecution is a conceptual framework that can use these local descriptive findings and interpret them, in terms of national or societal effects. The need for policy analysis is clear. Unless the diversity that exists throughout the United States can be explained in terms of policy choices, unless the performance of a prosecutor can be measured in terms of how well the policy is working or whether one office is implementing a policy better than another, there will simply be a continuation of the development of the same research products that have been produced since 1968.

Within this decade, information has been gathered to enable researchers to integrate past products into a foundation that can tackle the difficult questions of (1) explaining and accounting for diversity in prosecutive systems, and (2) measuring and evaluating prosecutorial performance and its impact on the criminal justice system and local government.

**Prosecutorial Policy within a Conceptual Frame**

An adequate analysis of the prosecutive process and function must take into consideration the following factors:

1. the external constraints of the prosecutor's environment, or those aspects of the criminal justice system that limit or determine the bounds in which the prosecutor will function;

2. the prosecutor's perception of his role and his selection of a policy to follow for dealing with crime and prosecution;

3. the resources available to him in terms of personnel, finances, space, and equipment and his control over their utilization; and

4. prosecutorial strategies available such as discovery, plea bargaining, diversion, sentence recommendation, and so forth.

The conceptual framework for a policy perspective assumes that the local environment affects prosecutorial policy: that it shapes and colors the policy of the prosecutor and his perception of his role and that it constrains the extent to which he may select policies not acceptable to the community he represents. It also assumes that the prosecutor's policy is implemented through an organizational structure that allocates resources in the office and develops management and operational controls to ensure the implementation of policy.

Policy may be implemented by the use of various prosecutorial strategies that do not vary substantially from one jurisdiction to another. (However, in some states, statutes, constitution, or court rule may preclude the use of some of these strategies.) Some strategies are more consisteent for implementing a specific policy than others. Thus their use implies the existence of a selection process.

The dispositions that result from the implementation of a policy will, when considered in the aggregate, produce a dispositional pattern that is distinctive to that policy. Because of this, if one knows the policy of the prosecutor, one should expect a pattern of dispositions consistent with that policy.

Underlying all these statements is a basic, although controversial, assumption that the prosecutive function is a rational process and that all patterns of behavior, even those that seem inconsistent at first glance, can be substantially explained and interpreted if placed within a proper perspective.

The conceptual framework recognizes the effect of the environment on prosecutorial policy as discussed in part II. However, the focus of this section will be on the internal factors under prosecutorial control that can be used to implement the policy selected. This includes the organization and management of the office. These determine the prosecutor's ability to control and monitor the decision makers who attempt to implement policy by selecting specific actions intended to yield certain dispositions.

## A Policy Typology

Research on the effects of prosecutorial policy began in earnest in 1975 when the Law Enforcement Assistance Administration (LEAA) as part of a national evaluation program awarded a grant to the Bureau of Social Science Research in Washington, D.C., to conduct a Phase I Evaluation of Pretrial Screening Projects.[11] The primary purpose of the grant was to decide whether a full national evaluation of these projects was feasible. The

Bureau conducted an extensive 15-month study of the subject, which included an exhaustive examination of the issues and literature and through observation and interviewing in nineteen different prosecutor's offices throughout the country. The study concluded that a national evaluation was conceptually possible but not desirable until further research could be conducted, especially on the effects of prosecutorial policy.

In conducting its site visits, the study team was able to detect a distinct influence of individual policy decisions on office performance—an influence that was manifest in distinctive patterns of disposition, allocation of resources, and use of strategies. The research team began to realize that the effects of policy colored the offices' performances to such a degree that a national evaluation or cross-jurisdictional comparison of any sort would be deceiving unless the evaluation construct could effectively take into account the influence of these policy choices.

The results of this study were published in 1976 and were greeted favorably in criminal justice research circles.[12] The evaluation approach suggested by the study, a policy-based approach, recognized the individual discretion of the elected district attorney and sought to account for his particular choices in measuring performance without attempting to dictate choices to him, or to impose values on the decisions that he made. One commentator noted:

> The material developed . . . offers a major breakthrough in the development and understanding of case screening. . . . The typology . . . sets forth a methodology for evaluating screening mechanisms in operation in a given office to determine whether those devised are fulfilling the purposes for which the prosecutor adopted them. Nowhere does [the study] seek to dictate a policy to prosecutors, instead they recognize that there are many possible policies form which a prosecutor may choose one or more. Their role was not to evaluate or criticize those policies but to develop measures which would enable a prosecutor to determine whether his or her policies are being serviced. The typology deals with four of the policies and provides tools for measurement at each stage of the criminal process.[13]

The purposes of part III are to (1) summarize the findings of this study, (2) show that the identification of policy is a primary requirement in evaluating prosecution, (3) illustrate how differing strategies and allocation patterns are needed to support different policies, and (4) finally, indicate the policy choices available and some of their effects on local government budgets.

The last item is becoming increasingly important. Recent trends in local government funding raise questions about the type of prosecutorial services that communities can afford. More and more, the prosecutor is being financially pressured to be highly selective in the type of case he prosecutes and the way in which that prosecution should proceed. As a result, policy criteria have to be stated so that sound decisions can be made.

The prosecutor is feeling the tug of two opposing trends. On the one hand, rising crime, demands for improved legal processes, and increased and more expert legal defense increase the need for larger and better-paid prosecutorial staffs.[14] On the other hand, pressure to reduce governmental costs means that the prosecutor must learn to operate more efficiently with the staff he has available. More lawyers to process more work is one answer, but it is not feasible in light of current public pressure from the taxpayer. More likely, the solution lies in the prosecutor exercising increased discretion in selecting those cases that enter the court system.

Additional pressures threaten with the current trend away from plea bargaining. Several states are examining the possibility of abolishing the practice of plea negotiation altogether and one, Alaska, is already experimenting with its abolition. Individual prosecutors have also attempted to eliminate the practice by policy decision within their office. New Orleans, Kalamazoo, Portland, and Boulder have all experimented with this change within the past few years. Abolition of plea bargaining, of course, raises additional pressures on the staff of the prosecutor and has great impact on other portions of the criminal justice system. Court capacity must be increased to meet trial needs, alternatives to adjudication have to be developed, better methods of case processing and screening have to be developed. Again, of all these alternatives, only increased efficiency within the prosecutor's office will assist in this change without radically increasing the amount of resources that local government must commit to criminal prosecution. The average community may be able to afford a tough prosecutor, but it cannot afford a sloppy or inefficient one.

It is clear from this example as well as from many others that the effects of prosecutorial policy changes are not limited only to the office of the district attorney. Their impact can be measured by the adjustments that become necessary in the other segments of the system—the police departments, the defender's office, the courts, and, perhaps most dramatically, the correction facilities. This phenomenon suggests another possible area of measurement that could prove extremely valuable to the criminal justice system. Additional information about the impact of prosecutorial policy on other system members may allow for better planning among all system members. When a policy change is being considered in prosecution, for example, further research may allow planners to anticipate the resultant future needs of corrections as a result of that change. A different change in policy may well indicate the need for new or altered treatment programs. This predictive power can be turned into a highly effective planning and management tool and can be used to test performance when attempting to find solutions for some of the problems that occur within the system as a whole.

With this rationale in mind, we now will examine four "ideal" policies that are likely to be found in one form or another in prosecutor's offices. The effects of each policy will be discussed in terms of anticipated case disposition rates and strategy use. Resource allocation patterns that suport each policy will be briefly examined.

*Prosecutorial Policies*

No matter what the external environment or a prosecutor's perception of his discretionary authority, the prosecutor operates with a policy (usually either the one for which he was elected or the one inherited) and implements the policy by various strategies. One might expect the policies of the 3,000 District Attorneys to vary widely given the different characteristics of jurisdictions they serve. However, research and observation to date have indicated that generalized classifications can be delineated. The four discussed here have all been observd operating in almost "pure" form in offices throughout the United States. The differences due to policy were so clear that the abstraction of these operations into policy models was not a difficult task.

The four examples presented are therefore discussed as ideals or models. They are not necessarily exhaustive nor mutually exclusive. Other policies may exist that result in different treatment modes and disposition patterns. In some offices a mix of these policies exists. For the purpose of this presentation, however, the policy types have been abstracted and presented as pure types. The policies have been given the abbreviated descriptive titles of legal sufficiency, system efficiency, defendant rehabilitation, and trial sufficiency.

**Legal Sufficiency Policy.** Some prosecutors believe that if any case is legally sufficient (that is, if the elements of the case are present), then it is their responsibility to charge and prosecute. For example, in a breaking and entering case, if there was evidence of forcible entry, an entry without the permission of the owner, and if the person arrested was found to have in his possession items belonging to the victim, the case is prosecuted because it is legally sufficient. The elements of the case are present. However, what on the surface seems to be a prosecutable crime may be lost because of constitutional questions, for example, an illegal search and seizure. Implementing this policy at the charging level requires only an examination for legal defects. If the basis for a charge is not legally sufficient, either additional investigation could be ordered or the case would be rejected. The legal sufficiency policy is most prevalent in the lower, misdemeanor courts processing large volumes. Here cases are routinely but quickly examined for obvious defects prior to court appearance. This is usually the extent of screening that a case receives. As a result, overloads occur, plea bargaining is encouraged to reduce the volume, and with scant case preparation time, dismissal and acquittal rates tend to be high. (See table 7-1).

**System Efficiency Policy.** Another prevalent policy can be labelled "system efficiency." It aims for the speedy and early disposition of cases by any means possible. Time to disposition and the place in the court process where disposition occurs are measures of success in addition to favorable dispositions.

The same breaking and entering case which would have proceeded to a trial phase under a legal sufficiency policy would never have done so under a system efficiency policy, because the efficient procedures established at intake and review would have spotted any potential constitutional or evidentiary questions. Even had the case been accepted, its likelihood of going all the way through the process to trial would be slight; a more probable outcome would be disposition by plea, nolle, or dismissal.

The existence of the system efficiency policy usually indicates a backlogged court and an overworked prosecutor's office with limited resources. Of necessity, system efficiency places initial emphasis on pretrial screening. Qualified assistants are used at this level to insure that weak cases are removed from the system at the earliest possible opportunity.

Under these conditions, any other methods of case disposal, in addition to pretrial screening, that can be found will be used. The prosecutor may ac-

**Table 7-1**
**Legal Sufficiency Policy: Expected Frequency of Dispositions**

| Disposition Universe (Numeric Base for Rates) | Disposition | Frequency |
|---|---|---|
| Cases presented | Reject for prosecution | Low |
| | Accept for prosecution | High |
| | Divert—non CJS | Not predictable |
| | Refer—other CJS | High |
| Cases accepted | Dismiss at preliminary hearing | High |
| | Bound over | Minimize |
| | Plea to reduced charge | Maximize |
| | Plea as charged | Low |
| Cases bound over | No true bill (grand jury only) | High |
| Trials | Guilty—trial | Low |
| | Acquittal—trial | Low |
| | Dismissed—trial (insufficient evidence) | High |

tively search for additional avenues of case disposition. Cases will be examined for possibility of plea bargaining. To achieve this, overcharging may be used. Extensive use will be made of community resources, other agency resources, and diversion programs so that cases may be kept out of the criminal justice system. Charges will be broken down for handling in the lower courts, if possible, or modified and referred to another court in a different jurisdiction (for example, a county case referred to municipal court). All the court's resources and the prosecutor's authority will be combined to hasten the disposition of the case. Particular emphasis will be placed on the disposal of the case prior to a bindover to the higher court or grand jury. (See table 7-2.)

**Defendant Rehabilitation Policy.** A third approach, based on a policy of rehabilitating the defendant, utilizes some of the elements of the early and speedy disposition policy but should not be confused with it. Under this policy, the prosecutor believes that the most effective treatment for the vast majority of defendants who pass through his office is anything but processing them through the criminal justice system. To use our breaking and entering case again, as an example, if the defendant was a first offender or had a drug problem and restitution was made to the victim, he might very well be placed in a pretrial diversion program or, if none is available, with the court's concurrence he could be given a sentence of probation without verdict. Under this policy, the charging and prosecution decision depends pri-

**Table 7-2**
**System Efficiency Policy: Expected Frequency of Dispositions**

| Disposition Universe (Numeric Base for Rates) | Disposition | Frequency |
| --- | --- | --- |
| Cases presented | Reject for prosecution | Not predictable |
| | Accept for prosecution | Not predictable |
| | Divert—non CJS | Maximize |
| | Refer—other CJS | Maximize |
| Cases accepted | Dismiss at preliminary hearing | Low |
| | Bound over | Minimize |
| | Plea to reduced charge | Maximize |
| | Plea as charged | Low |
| Cases bound over | No true bill (grand jury only) | Not predictable |
| Trials | Guilty—trial | High |
| | Acquittal—trial | Low |
| | Dismissal—trial (insufficient evidence) | Low |

marily on the past history of the defendant and secondarily on the offense that he was alleged to have committed. Thus, the goal is the early diversion of many defendants from the criminal justice system coupled with serious prosecution of cases allowed into the system. There is vigorous prosecution of this latter category, especially if the defendant's history includes prior convictions with no evidence of rehabilitation. Offices using this policy tend to rely heavily on the resources in the community as well as in the criminal justice system to move eligible defendants out of the judicial and correctional systems. A close cooperation with the court often ensues, particularly in using the sentence recommendation power of the prosecutor to ensure consistency in the recommended treatment plan for the defendant. (See table 7-3.)

**Trial Sufficiency Policy.** The fourth policy, less commonly used, is trial sufficiency. This policy dictates that a case be accepted only if the prosecutor is willing to have it judged on its merits and expects a conviction. Under these circumstances, the prosecutor views his charging responsibility as being of paramount importance. If a decision was made to charge the defendant of our hypothetical breaking-and-entering case, and again if the constitutional question of the search was overcome, the defendant would be charged with the felony and a conviction expected at this level. Under this policy, once the charge is set it is difficult to change. To implement this policy, good police reporting is required, since the initial charge closes out

Table 7-3
Defendant Rehabilitation Policy: Expected Frequency of Dispositions

| Disposition Universe (Numeric Base for Rates) | Disposition | Frequency |
|---|---|---|
| | Reject for prosecution | Not predictable |
| Cases | Accept for prosecution | Minimize |
| presented | Divert—non CJS | Maximize |
| | Refer—other CJS | High |
| | Dismiss at preliminary hearing | Low |
| Cases | Bound over | High |
| accepted | Plea to reduced charge | Not predictable |
| | Plea as charged | Not predictable |
| Cases bound over | No true bill (grand jury only) | Low |
| | Guilty—trial | High |
| Trials | Acquittal—trial | Low |
| | Dismissed—trial (insufficient evidence) | Low |

most options. It also requires alternatives to prosecution, since not all cases will be prosecuted. Most importantly, it requires high court capacity, since each case accepted is expected to go to trial. Finally, this policy, as compared to the others, mandates the tightest management control in the office to ensure that the initial charge is proper and, once made, not changed. (See table 7-4.)

## A Charging Typology

Using the policies just described, it is possible to develop models that demonstrate how the prosecutive functions differ with the adoption of the various policies. A comparison of these models illustrates the impact of policy decisions. Unless policy is taken into account, it is not possible to evaluate prosecutorial effectiveness and dispositional data.

Table 7-5 lists goals and predicted outcomes for each of the four policies previously discussed. The goals are disposition outcomes that should be maximized or minimized for each policy. Because of the interrelatedness of the prosecutorial process, once these goals are established other outcomes are expected to occur with either a high frequency and a low frequency, or with some unpredictable outcome that is independent of the policy. The high and low frequencies listed do not have specific numerical values. They are relative highs or lows, depending on the universe specified for each dis-

**Table 7-4**
**Trial Sufficiency Policy: Expected Frequency of Dispositions**

| Disposition Universe (Numeric Base for Rates) | Disposition | Frequency |
|---|---|---|
| Cases presented | Reject for prosecution | High |
| | Accept for prosecution | Low |
| | Divert—non CJS | Not predictable |
| | Refer—other CJS | Not predictable |
| Cases accepted | Dismiss at preliminary hearing | Minimize |
| | Bound over | High |
| | Plea to reduced charge | Minimize |
| | Plea as charged | High |
| Cases bound over | No true bill (grand jury only) | Low |
| Trials | Guilty—trial | Maximize |
| | Acquittal—trial | Low |
| | Dismissed—trial (insufficient evidence) | Minimize |

The American Prosecutor: A Search for Identity

**Table 7-5**
**Expected Frequency of Selected Dispositions as a Function of Policy**

| Disposition Universe (Numeric Base for Rates) | Dispositions | Policies | | | |
|---|---|---|---|---|---|
| | | Legal Sufficiency | System Efficiency | Defendant Rehabilitation | Trial Sufficiency |
| Cases presented | 1. Reject for prosecution | L | N | N | H |
| | 2. Accept for prosecution | H | N | Mn | L |
| | 3. Divert–non CJS | N | Mx | Mx | N |
| | 4. Refer–other CJS | H | Mx | H | N |
| Cases accepted | 5. Dismiss at preliminary hearing | H | L | L | Mn |
| | 6. Bound over | Mn | Mn | H | H |
| | 7. Plea to reduced charge | Mx | Mx | N | Mn |
| | 8. Plea as charged | L | L | N | H |
| Cases bound over | 9. No true bill (grand jury only) | H | N | L | L |
| Trials | 10. Guilty–trial | L | H | H | Mx |
| | 11. Acquittal–trial | L | L | L | L |
| | 12. Dismissed–trial (insufficient evidence) | H | L | L | Mn |

Goals: Mx–Maximize this disposition; Mn–Minimize this disposition. Expected Outcomes: H–high frequency; L–low frequency; N–not predictable.

position. The designation of what is high or low will vary somewhat in each prosecutor's office. Whether specific number values can be generated that have nationwide applicability is yet to be determined.

For any single disposition in table 7-5, the expected values may change drastically depending on the policy being used. For example, the number of cases dismissed at preliminary hearing or a probable cause hearing should be high under the legal sufficiency policy because cases receive only routine screening for obvious defects. Other more serious defects may not be noticed until a later processing point is reached. Use of this policy suggests reliance on the courts to determine legal sufficiency rather than on the prosecutor. On the other hand, the low dismissal rate expected for the system efficiency policy and the defendant rehabilitation policy may be attributed to relatively few cases being processed through a preliminary hearing. Under system efficiency, the tendency is to screen first then "break it down and plead it," thereby producing fewer cases at preliminary hearing. Those cases that do survive are better prepared and are likely to be nonpleadable. The same pattern occurs for the defendant rehabilitation policy but for different reasons. All less serious defendants and cases are handled by informal means, with the remaining cases, comprising the most serious defendants, being vigorously prosecuted. Finally, the trial sufficiency policy, which anticipates trial and conviction, mandates that dismissals be minimized, since, if one occurs, it is a direct reflection on the quality of the intake division's decision and may point up errors on their part.

Not all dispositions by dismissal are adverse measures of prosecutorial performance. As already mentioned, a dismissal of additional charges may occur after a conviction has been obtained for the most serious charge. In other instances, the case may be dismissed because the complaining witness refused to prosecute, the police officer failed to show, or the defendant was placed in a medical or health treatment facility. The dismissals that are used to evaluate the performance of the prosecutor should be limited to those that reflect insufficient case review or lack of adequate preparation. Generally, they can be classified as "dismissed—insufficient evidence." This is a relatively frequent occurrence under the legal sufficiency policy, since only cursory review is made of a case; it is relatively infrequent under the system efficiency and defendant rehabilitation policies, since both actively seek methods of dispositions other than court hearings or trials. All dispositions considered a purified dismissal rate (which attributes responsibility to the proper participant in the system) as the most sensitive indicator of prosecutor performance and the most accurate in measuring the effect of the charging policy.

Not only does a comparison of policies demonstrate that prosecutorial performance varies with respect to the policy of the office, but it shows why policy must be determined before performance can be evaluated within an office. Table 7-5 shows that expected distributions of outcomes are consistent with certain policies. For example, the trial sufficiency policy, that of ensuring that the initial charge is correct and the case will result in conviction, logically will result in a high rejection rate at intake; an indeterminate number of referrals to other criminal justice systems (for example, a municiple court); a minimizing of dismissals both at the probable cause hearing and at the trial level; a high frequency of bindovers resulting in trial; a minimizing of plea bargains; high rates of pleas to the original charge; and, correspondingly, a maximizing of convictions.

Under the system efficiency policy (which emphasizes early and speedy disposition of cases) an evaluator should measure success or failure in terms of the number of persons diverted from the criminal justice system; the number of cases referred to other court systems; the number of cases disposed of by a plea bargain; and the number of cases bound over (the latter should be minimal). "Time in process" statistics, especially during the court phase at which disposition occurs, are also essential to the evaluation of this policy.

Use of the typology thus permits the examination of prosecutorial performance within a rational and logical system. Since the relative frequency and pattern of dispositions will vary according to the policies being pursued by prosecutors, any evaluation must take this into account. The pattern of dispositions is expected to vary across policies. Once policy is taken into account the pattern of dispositions should be regular and interpretable as prosecutors strive to maximize undesirable dispositions of their cases according to consistent policy choices.

**Strategies to Implement Policy**

Just as certain policies generate specific outcome patterns, so too do they foster the use of certain strategies. Strategies can be defined for the purpose of this discussion as the methods used to achieve policy goals. At least three major strategies are immediately identifiable: plea negotiation, discovery, and diversion. This section will explore how a prosecutor chooses and uses them to attain his policy objectives.

*Plea Negotiation*

One of the most important strategies available for case disposition is that of plea negotiation or plea bargaining. Its use or prohibition is highly controversial and has generated volatile discussion, but its role as a strategy to implement policy has been generally ignored. An attempt to abolish plea bargaining by 1978 was incorporated into the National Advisory Commission on Criminal Justice Standards and Goals.[15] This recommendtion generated so much discussion, controversy, and argument that plea bargaining dominated all other criminal justice issues at the national conference that promulgated the standards. Whether a plea to a reduced charge as a result of plea bargain is an acceptable form of case disposition is a social policy question beyond the scope of this discussion. However, plea bargaining, as a means of implementing policy in an office is a crucial area of research and inquiry. Although not all plea negotiations result in the disposition of a "plea to reduced charge," for simplicity it will be treated as such here.

Plea negotiation, as a means of case disposition, is consistent with both the legal sufficiency and system efficiency policies. Having little preparation and review time, trial assistants working under a legal sufficiency system will tend to accept pleas to reduced charges as a means of either correcting a charging mistake or minimizing the time required for more substantive case preparation. Under the early and speedy disposition policy of system efficiency, plea negotiation is the primary means of disposing of cases, because it leads to the fastest and least costly conclusion. If a defendant rehabilitation policy is in effect, it is difficult to predict whether plea bargaining will be used because the policy permits either option. Whether the more serious cases are allowed to plead to a reduced charge is a function of court capacity as well as prosecutorial policy. Under the trial sufficiency policy, on the other hand, plea bargaining is minimized, since the initial premises for accepting a case for prosecution are that it is properly charged, is capable of being sustained in a trial, and is likely to produce a conviction. Plea bargaining, therefore, contradicts the primary goals of this policy.

*Discovery*

Discovery is the procedure whereby the prosecutor opens his case file to defense counsel revealing the evidence and the strength of the case. Where discovery does not exist, the defense counsel is usually limited to that information that has been filed in the court (usually the accusatory instrument) and that which he may glean from his client or from witnesses suggested by the client. In some jurisdictions, the defense counsel does not even see a copy of the arrest report until it is entered as evidence, nor does he know what witnesses will be called by the state prior to the trial.[16]

The most commonly expressed opposition to discovery is based on the prosecutor's fear that exposing his case to defense scrutiny will jeopardize his chances of winning. This fear is often justified where the review and charging process is nonexistent or weak. Whether case weakness is a function of the resources and experience of the police department or a result of prosecutorial policy must be determined before an evaluation of the use of discovery as a strategy could be made.

Conceptually, the degree to which voluntary discovery is used should vary according to the policy being followed by the prosecutor. Under a legal sufficiency model, discovery is not likely to be a viable prosecutorial strategy precisely because the policy tends to result in processing weaker cases. On the other hand, since the use of discovery should induce a high rate of disposition by pleas—either to the original or a reduced charge—one would expect to find this strategy operating in both the system efficiency model and the trial sufficiency model. The defendant rehabilitation policy illustrates the multipurpose characteristics of strategies. Discovery for enhancing a plea disposition is not mandated by this policy, since it is not necessarily relevant to the outcomes sought under this policy. However, discovery to assure the diversion of a defendant to a proper treatment program might be essential to a rehabilitation policy.

*Diversion*

Diversion is the third strategy commonly available to prosecution. Like plea negotiation, diversion is often erroneously considered a disposition. In reality, it is a strategy that results in a disposition of a case. Diversion, as a strategy, refers a case to somewhere outside the formal court-processing system and avoids formal court disposition. A case may be diverted from the criminal justice system to alternative treatment programs: the drug abuser, for example, to Treatment Alternatives to Street Crime (TASC), or the first offender to an employment program. (When a case is transferred from one part of the criminal justice system to another, it is called "a referral" to distinguish it from the treatment function inherent in informal diversion programs.)

Diversion from the criminal justice system to treatment programs such as educational training or medical treatment programs is a strategy that can be used under all policies, but often for different reasons. The legal sufficiency model accepts a high proportion of marginal cases relative to the other policies, and diversion may serve as an acceptable alternative for case disposal in an overloaded court system. The system efficiency model produces strong incentives to use diversion as a way to speed up the system and reduce workload. For the defendant rehabilitation policy, diversion is a legitimate and necessary treatment option. The trial sufficiency model does not necessarily need a diversionary exit; since its intake decision is essentially binary in nature (trial or no action), the use of diversion is more a matter of individual preference than system pressure.

When cases are referred to another court or jurisdiction, the reasons for this decision may be due to one or more of the following factors: (1) the police charges may not be accurate reflections of the prosecution charges (this is particularly true if police tend to overcharge); (2) referral to another court may be a technique to reduce workload; (3) pleas in the lower court may be the result of a bargain where lesser charges mean lesser sentences.

Table 7-6 summarizes how these three strategies are likely to be used by an office to implement policy. Since the ultimate goal of the prosecutive function is case disposition, how the case is disposed of by using these strategies and others is clearly a reflection of the policy of the office.

### Resource Allocation Concepts

No matter what policy is being implemented, work has to be distributed in a rational manner if desired outcomes are to be attained. Many resource allocation options that theoretically could be available to the prosecutor may, in actuality, be precluded by the external environment. For example, it is difficult to organize an office on a trial team concept (wherein one or two assistants handle a case all the way from charging, through trial to disposition) without a court docketing system geared to support it. Successful trial teams flourish when cases are assigned by the clerk of the court to a specific judge or a specific courtroom or when the prosecutor controls the docket.

Most prosecutive resource allocation plans are primarily responses to the external environment. From an evaluation focus, one must account for resource allocation responses due to the characteristics of police, defense, and courts before a valid critique of any operation can be made. But critiques are

**Table 7-6**
**Expected Use of Strategies to Implement Policy**

| | Strategies | | | |
|---|---|---|---|---|
| Policy | Discovery | Plea Negotiation | Referral (Other CJS) | Diversion (Non CJS) |
| Legal sufficiency | Not predictable | Yes | Yes | Yes |
| System efficiency | Yes | Yes | Yes | Yes |
| Defendant rehabilitation | Yes, to expedite treatment | Not predictable | Yes | Yes |
| Trial sufficiency | Yes, to ensure adjudication | No | Yes | Not predictable |

possible. After the exogenous factors have been identified and their constraints determined, one can evaluate resource allocation patterns with respect to their consistency with the policy and priorities of the prosecutor. Just as different policies require a rational implementation of strategies, so too do the goals of the office establish rational resource allocation patterns. This section briefly examines some of the ways resources can be distributed to ensure consistency with policy. It focuses only on those areas under the prosecutor's control—charging, case assignment and trial preparation, and sentence recommendation—while recognizing the importance of external factors. Table 7-7 summarizes these distributions with regard to these three areas and the policy model.

The timing and completeness of police reporting is essential to the charging process. Equally important are the qualifications of the person making the charging decision. Table 7-7 shows that the experience level of the charging assistant may vary according to the policy of the office. For example, if the policy of the office is to examine cases only for legal sufficiency, as is the common practice in misdemeanor courts, then it is not necessary to use the most experienced assistant. The newest staff attorneys,

**Table 7-7**
**Expected Patterns of Resource Allocations by Type of Policy**

| | Resource Allocation Needs | | | |
| | Charging | | Case Preparation for Trial | Sentence Recommendation |
| Policy | Minimum Qualifications for Charging | Personnel Needed to Review Charges | Trial Experience Necessary | Personnel Needed for Sentence Recommendations |
|---|---|---|---|---|
| Legal sufficiency | Paralegal; 3rd-year law students; new assistants | Yes | Minimal | None |
| System efficiency | Trial and criminal justice system experience | Not necessary | Minimal | None, unless basis for plea bargain |
| Defendant rehabilitation | Trial and social work background | Not necessary | Moderate | Yes, to ensure consistency with treatment |
| Trial sufficiency | Extensive trial experience | Yes | Extensive | Yes, to ensure consistency with charge |

or even third-year law students, are capable of examining a case for the elements, with minimal review of their decisions by junior assistants.

In contrast, the system efficiency policy requires that the charging decision be made with respect to a speedy and early disposition. Thus, the charging assistant should have enough trial experience to know what is negotiable, enough system experience to know what can be diverted, referred elsewhere (either to another court or other noncriminal justice programs), or tried. There is little need for internal review of these charging decisions, since either the case is sent elsewhere or the charge is capable of being changed by the plea-bargaining process. Satisfaction is guaranteed as long as speedy dispositions are occurring and "garbage" cases are not being allowed to clog the system.

Similarly, the defendant rehabilitation policy requires minimal review of the charging decision. Since the goal is to divert the treatable defendant from the system and to prosecute the recidivist who would not be eligible for diversion, the charging assistant must not only have trial experience but should have training in some type of social work. The delicate decision of whom to prosecute and whom to divert offers potential danger for an elected prosecutor. A defendant released to a community treatment program always presents a certain level of risk. The prosecutor must feel confident that his decision maker is competent, experienced, and attuned to the prosecutor's own philosophy. Since the operators of the diversion programs can accept or reject the referral, the need for a review function in the prosecutor's office is minimal.

Finally, under a trial sufficiency policy the most experienced trial lawyers must be used to make the charging decision. There is little deviation allowed once the charging decision is made. The strategy is set; the case will go to trial, and a conviction is expected. As a minimum, therefore, the charging decision can be made by an experienced assistant; optimally, it will also be reviewed by another experienced assistant, thereby reducing any chance of error.

Not only does the allocation of personnel to the intake process vary according to policy, but so too does the assignment of personnel for the case preparation and trial process. The legal sufficiency and system efficiency policies both move the cases after charging to assistants, who first attempt to strike a bargain and, failing this, prepare the case or transfer this task to other assistants. Since the goal is to minimize trials, it is not necessary that the assistants have extensive trial experience. Under these conditions, it is interesting to question whether staff characteristics (young, inexperienced assistants and a high turnover rate) create a policy to accommodate to this environment or whether the policy creates and supports the existence of this environment.

The defendant rehabilitation policy can sustain a mixture in personnel.

Inexperienced assistants may handle misdemeanor court, and monitor diversion programs, if they are under prosecutor control, or try un-complicated felony cases. Since the cases accepted for prosecution are carefully examined, their assignment to assistants is based on the trial needs. Complex cases are given to the more experienced assistants. A similar strategy would apply under a trial sufficiency policy, although a major difference will be found in the control placed on the assistant's discretionary authority. Under this policy, winning trials is paramount in importance, changing charges or dismissals are practically prohibited.

The prosecutor's option of making recommendations at sentencing is only minimally employed under the legal sufficiency and system efficiency concepts, since so few cases are expected to be disposed of by trial and since the majority will be disposed of by plea negotiations. For the defendant rehabilitation and trial sufficiency policies, on the other hand, sentence recommendations are used extensively, since, for the former, they ensure both treatment consistent with the needs of the defendant and punishment consistent with the charge brought against the accused.

Although this discussion merely highlights, in the briefest form, various patterns of work distribution, it does suggest the validity of evaluating resource allocation patterns in light of the policy and priorities of the office. Consistency of resource allocations with goals is obviously the critical factor. Just as it makes little sense to assign third-year law students at intake to determine whether a case can be bargained, so too it is unreasonable to use experienced lawyers simply to determine if the elements are present.


**Conclusion**

Policy has a critical impact on dispositions, prosecutorial strategies, and resource allocation patterns. Valid evaluations of the performance of the prosecutor, and even more broadly, of all criminal justice activity, must first seek to determine what the prosecutor is attempting to do; second, assess how well he is doing it; and third, see whether the community agrees with him. Ultimately, the public makes its own evaluation at the ballot box. Unfortunately, the real issues are not well analyzed and presented to the public. One benefit derived from policy analysis is to better rationalize and understand the real limits and potentials of the prosecutor's power and to provide a fair perspective from which to assess his effectiveness.

The following three chapters present case studies of three prosecutors' offices that have clearly defined although different policies with regard to prosecution. They have been included here for two reasons: first, to illustrate the differences due to policy that occur in the operations of an office; and, second, to show that there are special requirements or strategies relevant to each of the policies. All these offices have successfully implemented a prosecutorial policy in a manner that is rational and consistent. They closely conform to the pure forms listed in the typology. The reader will quickly note that without a policy perspective, that is, without a systematic understanding of what the prosecutor was attempting to do, a comparison of these three offices would only produce confused images.

**Notes**

1. Newman F. Baker and Earl H. DeLong, "The Prosecuting Attorney—Provisions of Organizing the Office," 23 Journal of Criminal Law and Criminology 926 (1933).

2. James Eisenstein and Herbert Jacobs, *Felony Justice: An Organizational Analysis of Criminal Courts* (Boston: Little, Brown, 1977).

3. George F. Cole, *The Politics of Prosecution: The Decision to Prosecute* (Ann Arbor, Mich.: Xerox University Microfilms, 1968).

4. David W. Neubauer, *Criminal Justice in Middle America* (Morristown, New Jersey: General Learning Press, 1974).

5. The Vera Institute, *Felony Arrests: Their Prosecution and Disposition in New York City Courts* (New York: Vera Institute of Justice, 1977).

6. Frank W. Miller, *Prosecution: The Decision to Charge a Suspect with a Crime* (Boston: Little, Brown, 1969).

7. The American Bar Association, Project for Standards on Criminal Justice, *Standards Relating to the Prosecution Function and the Defense Function* (New York: American Bar Association, 1971).

8. Brian A. Grosman, *The Prosecutor* (Toronto: The University of Toronto Press, 1969).

9. Lewis R. Katz et al., *Justice Is the Crime: Pretrial Delay in Felony Cases* (Cleveland, Ohio: Case Western Reserve University Press, 1972).

10. This section relies heavily on Joan E. Jacoby, *The Prosecutor's Charging Decision: A Policy Perspective* (Washington, D.C.: Law Enforcement Assistance Administration, 1977), pp. 13-32.

11. Joan E. Jacoby, *Pretrial Screening in Perspective, A National Evaluation Program Phase I Report*, ser. A, no. 2 (Washington, D.C.: Law Enforcement Assistance Administration, 1976).

12. Jacoby, *Pretrial Screening*, pp. 61-79.

13. Lewis R. Katz, preface, ibid., pp. vii-viii.

14. See, for example, Argersinger v. Hamlin, 407 U.S. 25 (1972).

15. National Advisory Commission on Criminal Justice Standards and Goals, *Courts* (Washington, D.C.: U.S. Government Printing Office, 1973), p. 46.

16. See Grosman, *The Prosecutor* for an excellent discussion advocating abolishing this practice and implementing discovery in criminal proceedings.

# 8 Orleans Parish District Attorney's Office

## The Setting

Orleans Parish is a large metropolitan seaport area, centered around the city of New Orleans, which has a population of more than 560,000, 45 percent of which is black. The local labor force is predominated by blue-collar and service-related jobs, reflecting the domination of the shipping industry as the primary employer.

The crime rate in New Orleans is relatively low compared with cities in its same population range. The city rated below nineteen other cities in its size category and is below the national average in all but one of the eight major classes of crime listed by the FBI index. Statistics for 1976 show that New Orleans' local crime problems concentrate in two offense categories—larceny thefts and forcible rapes.

The New Orleans Police Department processes about 95 percent of all the cases that come to the attention of the District Attorney's Office. In 1977 the department had a strength of 1,521 sworn officers supported by nearly 500 civilian personnel. The quality of the work provided by the department is considered to be very good, although naturally there is individual variation among officers. On the whole the relationship between the police and the District Attorney is a positive one with regular weekly meetings between the top echelons of both agencies. Twenty-two officers from the force are detailed to the prosecutor's office to serve as office investigators. They are in addition to the eleven investigators that the District Attorney has full-time on his staff. There are a number of smaller police agencies who add incrementally to the office's work load: the Bridge Police, the Levee Board Police, the Harbor Police, Wildlife and Fisheries, the State Police, and a detachment of Armed Forces Police. The sheriff for Orleans Parish acts as a court officer rather than a police agency administrator. His primary responsibility is to administer the parish prison, the local jail.

The court system is a unified one: total jurisdiction over all criminal cases, both felonies and misdemeanors, is exerted by a single court—the Criminal District Court. The Magistrates section of the court conducts first appearances and preliminary hearings and holds trials in misdemeanor cases. The Magistrates section is staffed by a single elected magistrate and three appointed commissioners to assist him. The District Court consists of ten elected judges. There is a presiding judge but few centralized procedures and little centralized control.

Indigent defense in the parish is available from three sources: a court-funded program of public defenders, a court-appointed list of private attorneys, and two university law school clinic programs (Tulane and Loyola). The most important of these is the Orleans Indigent Defender Program (OIDP), which employs twenty-two attorneys and has its own investigative staff. The assistant public defenders are young—with 2 to 3 years experience on the average—and, in general, paid less than the District Attorney's assistants. (They average about $12,000 per year.) The program is attractive, however, because it offers an opportunity for extensive trial experience and because a civil practice is also permitted. In overload situations, or in cases with multiple defendants, the court will appoint a private attorney from a list compiled by the bar association. Assigned counsel are not paid because funds were never appropriated by the state. The prevailing philosophy is that these services are a part of the lawyers' responsibilities. About ten to fifteen attorneys regularly receive these appointments.

There is no public bail agency in New Orleans. Bail is handled by private commercial agencies. Bond setting occurs in Magistrate's Court at the initial appearance, where the Assistant District Attorney in attendance generally makes a recommendation for the maximum amount allowable. Bail on a misdemeanor ranges from $250 to $2,500. A class three felony, the least serious felony, generally receives a bond of $5,000 to $35,000, whereas a class two felony may be bonded as high as $75,000. There is no bond available in capital cases.

As an alternative to bail, there is a recognizance release program for first offenders involved in nonviolent crimes. A pretrial diversion program is also run by the office for first offenders and especially those involved in crimes of possession of small amounts of marijuana.

Detention facilities are maintained primarily at the parish prison, although the police department also has a lockup. Convicted defendants serve their sentence at the parish prison if it is less than 5 years. Defendants with longer sentences are sent to the Louisiana State Penitentiary at Angola. This presently is a problem, since the court is under a Federal Court order banning an increase in Angola's population. As a result the parish prisons have had to accept many felons who normally would serve their time in Angola. The Orleans Parish prison was overcrowded with 560 convicted felons in March 1977. This led to an increase in transfers between the two facilities—the sheriff sending "dangerous" defendants to Angola and receiving in exchange a prisoner with a less serious crime record.

## The District Attorney

Harry Connick was elected in April 1974 as District Attorney of Orleans Parish. At the time, he was the only prosecutor in Louisiana who was elected for a 4-year term, all the rest having been elected to serve 6 years. This has subsequently been remedied by the state legislature, which extended his present term through August 1978, when he will stand for a regular election and a term of 6 years.

One of the unique attributes of the prosecutor's office in Orleans Parish is the willingness of the District Attorney to be publicly explicit in his policy pronouncements. Even while running for election Connick clearly outlined the path that his office would follow including the controversial one of reducing plea bargaining. Most importantly, however, is the fact that he has implemented thorough measures to ensure the consistent enforcement of his policy throughout the office.

The charging policy of the office, put simply, is one of trial sufficiency. The District Attorney will prosecute to the fullest extent those cases that he deems strong enough to obtain a conviction (with the exception of certain specific nonviolent first offenses). All other cases not meeting these standards are not accepted.

For all its clarity in statement there are several elements that complicate the implementation of this policy. First and foremost is the pressure that it puts on an early screening system. Since the District Attorney will accept for prosecution only those cases for which there is a reasonable chance of successful prosecution, the first decisions made in the screening division need experienced attorneys and careful review. Although certain types of cases are reviewed later by specialized crime units—for example, economic crimes, consumer fraud, juvenile crimes—all cases are submitted to this initial screening unit. Evidence is reviewed, interviews are conducted with arresting officers, complainants, witnesses, and victims. The office mandate is to charge accurately and to charge all crimes that have been committed with the goal of obtaining conviction in a trial court. This mandate precludes overcharging and adding charges for the purposes of inducing a plea to a single charge. The test for the screening assistant is whether the case has been accurately and comprehensively charged; and the basis for evaluating this decision is its disposition. A conviction is a success, an acquittal or dismissal is a failure. This early screening and the charging decision lay the framework for all other process steps in the office. As stated in the office's 1975 Annual Report: "These policies—swift prosecution, limited plea bargaining, and multiple billing—form the basis of our fight to make every criminal pay dearly for the crimes he commits."

Although there is no formal speedy trial rule in the court, the District Attorney has set one for the office. Once the charges have been established, a conviction should be obtained within 60 days. To do this, office resources and procedures are geared to move a case as quickly as possible, and in most cases, the 60-day goal is met. Early in 1973 there were 350 open cases in the courts backlog; today there are less than 180. Because the office accepts only the best cases for prosecution, there is a limited need for plea bargaining. When Connick took office, 85 percent of all cases were being plea bargained. Now, less than 10 percent of all cases are the result of a negotiated plea of guilty. When these pleas are negotiated, they are done so within strict review and approval procedures. Multiple ''billing''—the practice of listing all charges on an indictment or information—is a result of a Habitual Offenders Act sponsored by the District Attorney and passed by the legislature. The act allows a prosecutor to multiple bill a defendant thereby (according to a formula) doubling, tripling, or even quadrupling the sentence if he is convicted. The office places special emphasis on the recidivist and has developed two programs to deal with him. The first is the Career Criminal Bureau, a tracking and trial unit that concentrates its resources exclusively on repeat violators. The second is the office's Post-Conviction Tracking Unit, which extends the office's activity beyond the trial disposition stage into postconviction. This unit receives notification of all requests for parole and pardon, reviews the closed cases that appear to be serious, and decides whether the office should oppose the application for parole, pardon, or early release. If the decision to oppose is made, testimony is prepared for the hearing boards.

Whereas the office is stern in its prosecution of the serious or repeat offender, it has also developed less harsh treatment alternatives. A diversion program is available for felony offenders who are residents of Orleans Parish, involved in a nonviolent offense (no weapons) and in cases of theft and forgery, if restitution is made. Felony offenders are specifically tapped because felony convictions are not expungable and the stigma sets up barriers to employment, economic parity, and other associated problems. Generally cases involving drugs are not divertable, although deferred prosecution is sometimes used for a misdemeanor marijuana possession arrest.

## Office of the District Attorney

### Size, Organization, Tenure, and Experience

The District Attorney's staff includes sixty-one full-time attorneys and thirty-three investigators. The overall supervision is provided by the District Attorney himself and his First Assistant. The office is organized into divisions, bureaus, and units that reflect both a two-tiered court structure and an individual court-docketing system. The major office activities are located in the Screening Division, the Magistrates Division, two Trial Divisions, and the Career Criminal Bureau. There are other bureaus and units that deal with specific types of crime, and these will be discussed later in this chapter.

The attorney staff in the office is traditionally young, generally having less than 3 years experience. Newly hired assistants are employed with the understanding that they will spend 3 years with the office. Turnover, therefore, is relatively steady; few remain with the office for more than the 3 years. The most experienced assistants are given status as Chiefs of Screening, Trial Divisions, the Career Criminal Division, or are assigned to the Screening Division. The less experienced assistants may be found in the Magistrate Division or Trial Divisions.

The Screening Division is manned by nine Assistant District Attorneys and four investigators. One of the attorneys serves as the Division Chief, and the others are assigned to handle intake according to generic types of crimes: one each for armed robberies, homicide and rape, narcotics, and vice; and four for general duty. The assistant who reviews murder and rape cases also takes them through the grand jury, since the District Attorney by law must seek indictments on capital cases (murder, rape, and kidnapping). The assistant assigned to vice cases also supervises Magistrates Court and acts as Training Officer for the office. Incoming cases are assigned to those screening assistants with responsibility for specific crimes or to the general screening assistant who has duty for that day. Each screening assistant also has some trial work, usually limited to a trial or two per month.

The Magistrates Division is responsible for first appearance misdemeanor trials and preliminary hearings in felony cases. This Division is staffed by the newly hired assistants. They are assigned to specific court sections, and their workload depends on the cases that are docketed into their sections. The division has eight attorneys and four investigators.

The Trial Division is divided in half for better office supervision and control. The two Co-Chiefs of the Trial Division handle the same types of cases differentiated only by the court to which they are assigned. Each Trial Division has approximately ten attorneys working in five courtrooms under the supervision of a Division Chief. The Division is given the largest investigative support capability in the office, with ten investigators permanently assigned to the two divisions. Trial Divisions handle primarily felony trials and some misdemeanor trials (misdemeanors may be removed to the District Court). Both Divisions generally assign two attorneys to each courtroom. A senior trial assistant and a junior assistant usually team up to provide the state's representation in each courtroom. Sometimes, it is difficult to distinguish between senior and junior because of the short tenure.

Trial assistants have generally had some prior experience in the office, starting in the Magistrates Division before being assigned to felony trials.

The blind docket assignment system of the court results in each courtroom assistant handling a variety of cases, although, on occasion, special staffing will be produced for particularly complex or sensitive cases.

The Career Criminal Bureau's duties span the boundaries of the three divisions discussed so far. Once an arrestee has been designated a candidate for career criminal prosecution (having either five felony arrests and/or two felony convictions) the Career Criminal Division assistants take total responsibility. Staffed by nine attorneys and four investigators, the unit works days but maintains a "call" deputy on a 24-hour basis. Assignments to individual attorneys within the unit are for the duration of the case; that deputy is responsible for the case at all stages starting with first appearance.

The other specialized units within the office include: Diversion, Postconviction Tracking, Appellate, Economic and Consumer Fraud, Juvenile, Child Protection, and Child Support Enforcement.

### Jurisdiction and Volume

The District Attorney's jurisdiction is primarily criminal. He has some limited civil duties, mostly in the area of juvenile problems and child support enforcement. The District Attorney's Office also handles appeals to the Louisiana Supreme Court. Table 8-1 shows the distribution of workload, the number of cases handled by the various units during 1975 and 1976.

Of special interest is the number of felony trials conducted in New Orleans since the current administration has been in office. In 1973, the

Table 8-1
Orleans Parish District Attorney's Office Caseload by Unit, 1975-1976

|  |  | 1975 | 1976 |
|---|---|---|---|
| Screening unit | Presented | N/A | 8,982 |
|  | Refused | N/A | 3,919 |
|  | Accepted | 6,300 | 5,063 |
| Trial division (felony trials) |  | 568 | 754 |
| Career criminal bureau |  | N/A | 220 |
| Juvenile division |  |  |  |
| Delinquency petitions |  | 2,331 | 2,607 |
| Cases terminated |  | 2,646 | 2,579 |
| Commitments |  | 194 | 223 |
| Unruly or ungovernable |  | 352 | 550 |
| Neglect cases |  | 613 | 460 |
| Appeals to state supreme court |  | 65 | 150 |

year before Connick came into office, there were 190 jury trials; in 1974, his first year in office that figure leaped to 463, continued to grow in 1975 to 568, and reached a new high with 754.

## Process Steps

### Intake

The clear intention of the office is to make a charging decision as early as possible on all cases. All weak or improper cases are weeded out from the system leaving only those cases with the highest probability of conviction. To do this, police reporting procedures have been streamlined to insure that reports are forwarded to the screening division quickly. At the present time, the assistant receives a complete case including the defendant's criminal history within 72 hours after the arrest. For armed robberies, burglaries, fraud, homicide, rape, and narcotics, the New Orleans Police Department's detective bureau works up the report. In other cases the arresting police officer prepares the arrest and incident reports. Both police and the District Attorney's office share online computer systems so that reports can be transmitted electronically to the District Attorney.

The charging decision does not have to be made immediately. There is no specific speedy trial rule by statute or court rule, although the office has imposed on itself a 60-day rule from time of arrest through trial. In addition by local court rule, the prosecutor must bring his charges within 10 days if the defendant is in custody or have the case dismissed by the court. Normally, all charges are filed within 6 days under present working conditions.

Cases are assigned to the assistants in sets, each assistant has 4 days to review the cases and reach a charging decision before he receives another set of cases. The assistant is given total discretionary power over the charge. Only in the event of a refusal is he required to obtain the Screening Chief's approval. If a decision is made to accept the case, a Screening Action Form is completed, which lists the facts of the case, the witnesses, and evidence available, and the potential problems with the case or tactics that might be used by the defense. The screening assistant also notes a preferred disposition. The Screening Division also houses a five-man victim/witness participation unit. An assistant interviews the witnesses and victims and notes any additional information on the Screening Action Form, which is also placed in the case folder for the trial assistant's future use.

There is a lot of communication with defense counsel in this Division. Many counsel, retained early after the arrest and knowing the charging policy, prefer to meet with assistants before the charge is filed. If there is exculpatory evidence it is preferable to reveal this early, since the information may obviate the need for further processing or make the defendant eligible for diversion.

Defense counsel may suggest mitigating factors, which although not resulting in a decision to reject, may influence the level at which the defendant is charged. Open discussion at this point not only permits the assistant to more accurately assess the case and arrive at a realistic charge, it also strengthens their evaluation of the strength of the case and defense tactics, thereby setting a preferred disposition.

Of the 8,982 cases presented in 1976, 3,919, or 44 percent, were rejected by screening. Certain classes of cases are almost automatically rejected as "not suitable." Many of these are first-offender cases where there is no substantial harm or where restitution has been made. In others, the reasons are associated with the type of crime and their special problems. For example, narcotics and bad searches; robberies and identification; rapes and victim reluctance; and other crimes where the defendant is related to the witness.

At intake, cases are disposed of through five major routes:

1. A refusal to charge.

2. Referral to the felony diversion program. The defendant enters the program for 3-6 months, after which the case is returned to the office for reconsideration. If the defendant has successfully completed the program, the office refuses to prosecute; if not, the screening assistant may institute formal charges. This program is also available for some high misdemeanor cases.

3. Informal mediation in family dispute cases. Where mediation fails, the prosecutor may suggest that the complainant file an affidavit *pro se* with the Municipal Court.

4. Prosecution in Magistrates Court as a misdemeanor rather than a felony with the use of expungement proceedings after a successful probation.

5. Prosecution as a felony.

The way in which the intake unit is specialized has enabled the screening assistants to focus on the particular problems in their area, to become familiar with the case law and procedures in presenting the evidence to the trial court, and to pass this knowledge on to the less experienced trial assistants.

*Accusatory Stage*

Those cases that are accepted by the Screening Division are then assigned to the Magistrates Division, which conducts the preliminary hearings. Most cases are filed by information after a preliminary hearing. The exceptions are capital cases, which must be submitted to the Grand Jury for indictment. In the latter event, these cases bypass the Magistrate Division and are presented to the Grand Jury by the homicide screening assistant.

The probable cause hearing is a short procedure in New Orleans. It is designed to present the *prima facie* case to establish reasonable belief that the crime was committed and that there is a strong likelihood that the defendant committed the crime. Generally the only witness called by the state at this stage of the process is the arresting police officer. Credible hearsay is admissible, and the tenor of the proceeding minimizes adversarial activity at this stage.

Even if the Magistrate fails to find probable cause, the District Attorney is not precluded from proceeding with a prosecution. The State of Louisiana allows the direct filing of information in the District Court. The defendant's liberty could not be restrained, of course, in such a case, but the state could still proceed on the basis of the information filed with sworn affidavits in support. The Supreme Court of Louisiana has upheld this independent power to charge, and the result is certainly consistent with the U.S. Supreme Court's decision in *Gerstein* v. *Pugh*, which held that the requirement of Magisterial review at a probable cause hearing is for the purpose of protecting against undue restriction of liberty, not for the purpose of restricting the prosecutor's power to file criminal informations.

Use of this procedure, however, is extremely rare. The daily reality is that the preliminary hearing is a procedural formality in most cases, with the state expending minimal resources—perhaps 2 or 3 minutes—in establishing a sufficient *prima facie* case so that the defendant can be bound over for trial. In most cases, the Magistrate Court assistant handling the case has had little or no time to prepare. He normally receives the case jackets on the afternoon before the hearing is set. Most of his decisions and actions at this hearing are detailed on the Screening Sheet and the Screening Action Forms prepared by the screening assistants. The cursory review and case preparation is generally sufficient for the procedures mandated by this court hearing. As a result, both the office organization, which assigns the most inexperienced attorneys to this stage, and the office procedures, which allow very little review time, are realistic reflections of the lack of complexity inherent in the preliminary hearings in Orleans Parish.

*Trial to Disposition*

After the preliminary hearing and the filing of information the defendant is arraigned. It is at arraignment that the defense may request a pretrial conference. This conference is optional with the judge of the court to which the case has been assigned and is often a chance for the defense counsel to acquaint his client with the reality of the court proceedings so that they can determine whether they want to pursue a full trial.

Cases are assigned randomly to the courts with each judge getting every tenth case. Every judge also has 1 "free" month a year during which he receives no cases at all. This gives him an opportunity to clear his docket. The system has worked well as evidenced by the fact that during the past year, three judges have cleared their backlogs and reduced their docket to current cases only.

The number of dispositions resulting from trials has increased dramatically with the imposition of a trial sufficient policy and curtailed plea bargaining. The latter produced an initial reaction from the defense to take cases to trial, resulting in an enormous leap from 190 to 463 trials between 1973 and 1974. This upward trend continued in 1976 when 1,069 cases were disposed of by trial. Of these, 471, or 44 percent, were disposed of by jury trials.

Despite these enormous increases in the number of trials, the office has suffered neither from an increased backlog (on the contrary, it has been reduced) nor a poor conviction record. Of the 5,568 cases disposed of in 1976, 6 percent were acquitted, 79 percent convicted, and 15 percent nolled. Within the latter category, 23 percent of the nolles were for reasons clearly favorable to prosecution, occurring either as a result of deferred prosecution or because a conviction was obtained in another case. The reasons for the remainder of the nolles are not clear from the data, whether they are based on factors beyond the prosecutor's control or within it is an obvious area for examination.

Plea bargaining has not been eliminated; rather its use has been restricted and circumscribed by tight management controls. Where negotiations are entered into, they are generally the result of evidentiary or procedural problems that were not initially anticipated. Under these circumstances, a trial assistant may negotiate a plea to a lesser charge after he has obtained the written approval of the Trial Chief or the First Assistant. In 1976 of 3,645 cases disposed of by pleas, 3,445 were pleas to the original charge and 200 (or 5.5 percent) were pleas to a lesser charge.

There are three major contributing reasons for the surprisingly high plea rate in light of this restriction on plea negotiation. The first, of course, stems from the openess of the intake and charging process. The fact that defense counsel are permitted and even encouraged to discuss the case with the experienced screening assistants prior to the filing of the charge not only displays the strengths and weaknesses of the case to both parties but, coupled with the office's policy of not changing a charge once filed, reinforces the defense counsel's understanding of the rules and their relative inflexibility later in the trial stage.

Secondly, there are probably strong incentives for the defense bar to pursue a course of efficiency in disposing cases once they have been accepted for prosecution. The OIDP are allowed a private civil practice in addition to their criminal duties. The court-appointed attorneys are not reimbursed for their services, and the privately retained may indeed seek quick disposals once they could not prevail at the screening step.

Finally, although the office prefers to go to jury trial, the defendant may waive without the state's approval and have the case heard by a judge. This may be a strategic advantage, because the court is almost equally divided in their support of the District Attorney's philosphy. Five of the judges support his minimal plea-bargaining position. Five do not. One would expect that because of this latter group, a larger proportion of pleas to lesser charges would appear as dispositions than it does. With only 200 out of 3,645 cases being disposed of by a plea to a lesser charge, it appears that at least in this area the District Attorney's policy is effective despite differing judge sentiments. The distinction is more likely to be found in other areas, sentencing being the most likely candidate. Although, again, comparative data are not available, it is of interest to note that of the 471 jury trials, 20 percent resulted in acquittals, whereas of the 596 bench trials, 37 percent resulted in acquittals. Of all the acquittals, the overwhelming proportion (70 percent) were a result of a bench trial. Thus, if plea-bargaining incentives are available in the court system, they most likely focus on the sentencing aspects of the process than the charging.

Despite these environmental constraints, it is clear that the dispositional results of the trial stage activity are consistent with the policy of the office. Nolles are minimized, convictions are maximized, and pleas to a reduced charge approach zero (3.6 percent of all dispositions in 1976).

*Postconviction*

As a logical extension of his policy and to ensure that each convicted defendant serves the sentence given him, the District Attorney created a Post-Conviction Tracking Unit, which serves two functions. First, it performs a postprocess review function; second, it is responsible for monitoring parole and pardon hearings for defendants who were convicted on prosecutions instituted by the office.

In its review posture, the closed cases are submitted daily to the unit, which is staffed by one assistant, an investigator and secretarial support. Each case that has been nolled or one in which there is a plea to a reduced charge is especially examined by the assistant for the appropriate approval forms and signatures. Nolles must be approved by either the screening assistant who set the charge or his supervisor, the Chief of Screening. If the approval is not documented in the file, it is returned to the Chiefs of the Trials Divisions to notify them of this procedural violation and to complete the necessary forms. Additionally, the Chief of Screening is notified monthly of all nolles so that he can monitor the quality of the screening assistants charging decisions. This part of the Post-Conviction Tracking Unit's function is vital to the management of the office and the implementation of its policy. It serves as a final check on the consistency of the procedures and their application, and is a mechanism for bringing managerial attention to operational problems or breakdowns.

The Post-Conviction Tracking Unit as it relates to parole and pardon activities is unique to prosecution in the United States. It operates in a supportive state legislative environment, one which requires the Parole and Pardon Boards to inform the District Attorney of applications for parole and pardon. With this authority, the Unit reviews each case on its individual merits to determine whether the office should oppose the application.

The Louisiana Board of Pardons hears about forty applications each month for clemency, commutation of sentence, pardon, and citizenship restoration. By statute, the Board is required to notify the District Attorney and to "afford reasonable opportunity to be heard." Usually, with a month's lead time, the closed cases are pulled, sorted into priority categories that were established in the office, and reviewed. First-class priorities are given to capital cases with life sentences imposed; second class, armed robberies; third class, other crimes; and fourth class, misdemeanors. The latter two classes are rarely reviewed.

If opposition is justified, the District Attorney files a formal letter of opposition to which are attached statements about the nature of the offense, the aggravating circumstances, victim and witness statements, signed confessions, and so forth. The assistant in the Post-Conviction Tracking Unit makes an appearance at the Board of Pardons hearing to justify the stated opposition. Much of this opposition is based on a need to ward off the use of pardons as a means of circumventing no parole situations. (For example, after December 1966, there is no parole for armed robbery.) The second area of the Board of Pardons' authority is the restoration of citizenship rights to persons convicted of a felony. If the defendant has ties to organized crime, these applications are likely to be opposed. Figures for February 1977 showed that of the thirty-seven applications, twenty-three were recommended to be denied, ten were recommended favorably, and two were taken under advisement.

Unlike the Board of Pardons, which conducts public hearings without the defendant's presence and can only present their recommendations to the Governor, the Board of Parole meets with the defendant, reviews a preparole report prepared by the Department of Corrections, and decides at that hearing whether to grant parole or not. If the District Attorney opposes the application, he makes a presentation to the Board. Preparation for this task is comparatively easier than for the Board of Pardons. The assistant basically reviews the preparole reports already compiled by corrections for accuracy and completeness. He does not have to develop a package like the one used for the pardons hearings.

The effectiveness of this activity is partially indicated by the number of applications withdrawn. There has been a tendency since the institution of these procedures for the number of withdrawn applications to increase. In 1976, the District Attorney wrote 270 letters of opposition; fifty-seven inmates were granted parole over opposition, and ninety-three inmates withdrew their applications for the hearing. There appear to be two reasons for this increase in withdrawals. One is based on the perceived power of the District Attorney's opposition by convicts, correctional officers, wardens, and even the prison newspaper. The second is that as the parole date approaches, the time left to serve has decreased to a point where it is more advantageous for the defendant to be released on a good time discharge than to be paroled. In the latter situation, not only is he still under institutional supervision but, if he is convicted on a new offense while on parole, his parole is revoked and the time he has to serve on the new offense runs consecutively from the time remaining from the original offense. To cap it off, parole violators are also designated as career criminals. It should be noted here, however, that before the office had the capacity to track defendants and keep records of their parole status, none of these sanctions were relevant, because it was usually impossible to determine whether the defendant was on parole at the time of his arrest and prosecution. Hence the penalties could not be invoked.

On the other hand, the legislation establishing good time credit is extremely liberal. The formula used to compute good time credit results in about one-half of the sentence or about 25 days a month being credited for good time. The effects of this are illustrated by table 8-2. It is, therefore, far more advantageous in some situations for the defendant to forego parole and seek an early discharge on good time credits or clemency from the Board of Pardons as a means of reducing his sentence and speeding up his release date.

This participation in pardon and parole board hearings has not been observed in other offices, which usually define the end of prosecution by the disposition of the case or, sometimes, by the results of an appellate process. But here in New Orleans, the activities of the Post-Conviction Tracking Unit are a logical extension of the prosecutor's policy and his perception of

Table 8-2
Credit for "Good Time" in Louisiana Penal System

| Sentence Imposed | Minimum Sentence with Maximum Credit for Good Time | | |
|---|---|---|---|
| | Years | Months | Days |
| 10 years | 5 | 5 | 12 |
| 15 years | 8 | 2 | 3 |
| 20 years | 10 | 10 | 24 |
| 30 years | 16 | 4 | 6 |

his prosecutorial responsibilities. As one assistant noted, "We owe our allegiance to the average person on the street. We'll do everything to protect the citizen."

Although the Post-Conviction Tracking Unit operates within the Trial Division, the office also has a separate Appeals Branch. The Chief of Appeals, an assistant with over thirteen years experience, is supported by three assistants. Appeals flow from the criminal District Court to the State Supreme Court. In addition the Appeals Branch handles all federal *habeaus corpus*.

The shift in emphasis of the office from pleas to trials as the major dispositional route has brought about an increased number of appeals as convictions rose and sentences became longer or more incapacitative. Also the active use of the multiple offender statute, which automatically increases the severity of the sentences, has led more defendants to take the appeals route than in the past. Appeals are offered first to the trial assistants who prosecuted the case. If they wish, they are allowed to respond. Most of the time, however, they decline because of their ongoing trial caseload, letting the Appeals Branch assume responsibility. Only the Career Criminal Bureau is an exception, since they handle their cases from intake through appeals.

Despite the time constraints that surround any appellate process (the cases being appealed often are years old) and with few resources, the record of the branch is excellent. The latest statistics show that they are prevailing in about 90 percent of all their appeals.

## Special Programs

One of the few special programs in the office that processes selected cases from intake to disposition is found in the Career Criminal Bureau. (Another program falling within this definitional status is the felony diversion program.) The Career Criminal Bureau (CCB), operational now for only 3 months is staffed by eight assistants (with an expected staff of fourteen to sixteen) and is supported by investigators. They prosecute cases that meet the CCB criteria of five felony arrests or two felony convictions.

Of interest is how the office with an overall trial sufficiency policy adopts a program of selective prosecution that also has the same policy yet differentiates one from the other. The differences are: (1) individual representation (one assistant handles the case from intake through appeals in contrast to the other cases that are assigned to an assistant only after bindover); (2) small caseloads (the assistants carry fewer cases than other trial assistants); and (3) more experience and discretionary power (the assistants are far more experienced than the trial assistants because they must perform the rigorous screening function in addition to their trial duties).

Although still in the early days of its operation, (hence its effect is still indeterminate) the opinion held by the chiefs and supervisors is that the isolation of the career criminal as a subset of the cases further strengthens the policy of the prosecutor and increases the uniformity of its implementation.

## Management Controls and Communication

Prosecution in Orleans Parish is strictly controlled by the executive level policy makers, and, with the exception of screening, assistants in the operational sectors of the office exercise little discretion or autonomy. Policies and procedures are disseminated by both written media and informal meetings or daily contacts between supervisors and staff attorneys. Management and evaluation data are systematically collected at each stage of the process and just as systematically reviewed by the First Assistant. The office has developed a computerized defendant tracking system, which is also able to produce information for assessing the degree to which policy or procedures are being implemented. At the executive level constant attention is given to a series of checks on procedural actions or to dispositions that are sensitive to policy prerogatives.

The importance of this executive level attention is illustrated best by citing the time when the First Assistant noticed that nolles due to witness lack of cooperation were beginning to show an increase on the monthly reports. When they reached a level for concern, he found that the Victim-Witness Bureau and Screening Division assistants were not interviewing all the witnesses as required. "They felt that it was not necessary"; and, in fact, it wasn't to their activities. But the overall effect on the office was detrimental. Executive level involvement is a primary factor in the successful implementation of policy.

In addition to executive review procedures, more formal control mechanisms have been established to ensure consistency in operational decision making throughout the office. Two of the most powerful concern nolles and plea negotiations. If a case has been dismissed in Magistrates Court the Assistant responsible for the case is required to notify the Chief of the Screening Division of this disposition by means of a written memorandum setting out the circumstances surrounding the dismissal. The assistant who set the original charge then must justify to the Chief of the Screening Division why he made the decision that ultimately ended in "failure." Similarly if a trial assistant wants to file a *nolle prosequi*, he must seek the approval of the screening attorney who charged the case of the Chief of Screening in addition to the approval of his own division chief. All dismissal requests (nolles) must be signed off by persons in both the

Trial and Screening Divisions, and must receive final authorization from the First Assistant. The only exception to this rule is in heroin cases, where the rule is even stricter—there, approval of the District Attorney himself must be obtained.

If an assistant desires to reduce a charge for any reason, even if the original charge is obviously the result of an error, he must seek modification approval from his division chief and receive a signoff signature for such a change on the case jacket itself.

In any instance where the original charge is changed or the case is dismissed, signoff authority must be placed in the file folder.

After disposition, all cases are reviewed by the assistant in the Post-Conviction Tracking Unit. If the appropriate approvals are not included in the file, it is returned to the trial assistant or his supervisor for explanation. Additionally, the Co-chiefs of the Trial Division are responsible for conducting trial reviews in all cases in which there is a verdict of acquittal.

Daily operational controls are maintained by the open-door policy of all supervisors to the younger assistants. Even the physical access to the supervisors' offices is designed to facilitate this. Although there is a need for a training activity in the office, there are no resources available to support it. Thus the open-door policy also substitutes for a more formal training function.

The District Attorney publishes and disseminates frequent staff memoranda covering matters that are of concern to the entire office, and, at the present time, a policy manual is in preparation. Staff meetings for supervisory personnel occur every week, and the supervisors attempt to have weekly meetings with their individual staff members.

## Conclusion

From a policy perspective, this office can be used to develop a model for a Trial Sufficient prosecutorial policy. It illustrates not only the constraints imposed by its environment but also how they can be adjusted by appropriate management procedures and operational controls. This policy, more than any other, mandates a management and operating system that controls each of the decision points.

It shows that the District Attorney has a clear perception of his role and objectives and has integrated them into all phases of the prosecution process. As a result, activities and dispositions of the office are consistent with his aims. In adopting a trial sufficient stance, however, he has placed himself and his staff in a working environment that requires a rigorous and controlled operation. It is a working environment that cannot succeed unless the proper management and organizational responses are employed and the proper management and organizational responses are employed and

and the process monitored constantly by the executive level of the office. This is a difficult stance for a prosecutor to take, because it imposes many additional managerial activities on the office than would be found in offices with prosecutorial styles that allow greater autonomy in the decision-making power of the assistants.

To be consistent with a policy of charging accurately and at a level capable of being sustained at trial, a number of activities must take place. In take and screening, as the most important decision point in the process, must be staffed by the most experienced assistants, who are capable of determining an expected disposition at that early process point. Trial experience, therefore, is essential. It is also at this point that the most individual discretion can be permitted. Once the charge is set and, ideally, cannot be changed, wide discretion is not required to bring the case to a successful conclusion.

Since the amount of changes permitted once the charge is set is minimized and the discretion of the trial assistant is, in effect, eliminated, it is possible to assign less experienced assistants to the trial divisions. There they can concentrate on developing skill in trial tactics, and, under proper, experienced supervision, will produce quite acceptable results. As an aside, one could speculate how well this situation would work if experienced assistants, brought up in a tradition of making discretionary decisions, were required to work under these controlled circumstances. One could also speculate as to what the effect would be if the office, instead of operating on a 3-year turnover system, began to develop "career assistants." The fact that it operates so well in implementing the policy raises the question as to whether it is because the policy is implemented so well or the circumstances fit the policy requirements so well. Perhaps the question is moot in light of the fact that the two circumstances have meshed to produce a successfully implemented prosecutorial operation.

The extension of the prosecutor's activities in the postconviction area as expressed in terms of this opposition to paroles and pardons, as well as his effectiveness in introducing new legislation designed to ensure the public's protection through the incapacitation of the defendant, all combine to demonstrate the extent to which a prosecutor's role can have significant impact on other parts of the criminal justice system. This activist position is also consistent with the prosecutor's policy, which extends its influence beyond the limits traditionally assumed by prosecutors who tend to end their activities with dispositions.

Finally, this policy requires that management controls (in the form of review and approval of decisions that may change the original charge) be instituted and carefully maintained. A single loophole or a rule without a feedback mechanism or a review procedure could seriously jeopardize the implementation of the policy. The postconviction review, for example, is the final mechanism that ensures the proper performance of the trial assistants. If deficiencies were noted but not referred back for justification, the effects of this control mechanism would be denigrated. In this respect, the office is a model for how these controls can be instituted and maintained under the most rigorous circumstances and according to the most demanding standards. The value of these management controls is clearly substantiated.

It is important to note that this policy (and others) can only be successfully implemented if it is articulated and supported by the executive level of the office—most importantly the District Attorney himself, followed by his First Assistant and other supervisory personnel. Without their commitment the discretion of the individual assistants would ultimately emerge and even predominate in some of the various process points. The fact that this particular charging policy has such a profound effect on the rest of the prosecution process shows that its dimensions need to be clearly recognized so that the programs or procedures emanating from it are consistent and logical with respect to its goals.

The general consensus within the office is that this policy has resulted in a reduction in case backlog, a speedier process, and increased certainty and even severity of punishment. One would expect that a policy such as this could not operate in a court system that was backlogged or philosophically opposed to this stance, where plea bargaining was espoused as a major solution to backlog and court delay; and accepting marginally strong cases was justified in fear of police outcry. Yet, it happened in New Orleans. The court increased its productivity, thereby reducing its backlog and opening up its dockets for the additional trials; and the prosecutor rejected up to 50 percent of the police-forwarded cases without creating the oft-predicted war.

# 9

## Jackson County Prosecuting Attorney's Office

### The Setting

The Kansas City, Missouri, metropolitan area has experienced phenomenal growth during this century. Its population has tripled since 1900, and, with a current population in excess of 463,000, Kansas City ranks as the twenty-seventh largest city in the United States. Due to its growth, Kansas City has spread geographically so that it sits within the borders of three different counties—Jackson, Clay, and Platte—although most of the city is contained in Jackson County. Jackson is the second most populous county in the state of Missouri, exceeded only by St. Louis County. Jackson County also includes the suburb of Independence, which has grown to a population of nearly 112,000.

The Jackson County Prosecuting Attorney's office works primarily with the Kansas City Police Department and to a lesser extent with the Jackson County Sheriff and seventeen other municipal law enforcement agencies. The criminal court system in Jackson County is two-tiered. The court of general jurisdiction is known as the Circuit Court, which has sixteen judges who all handle both civil and criminal matters. Five courtrooms in the Circuit Court have been designated as criminal courts, and judges are rotated through these five courtrooms on a monthly basis. Each month one of the five criminal judges is designated administrative judge with the duty of assigning cases to the dockets of the other four judges when cases are filed with the court. Aside from this assignment function, the administrative judge also has a criminal docket, albeit a lighter one than the other four. In calendar year 1976, 1,547 defendants were disposed of by the Circuit Court.

The court of limited jurisdiction is the Magistrate's Court, which handles misdemeanor cases, ordinance and traffic violations, and preliminary hearings in felony cases. The Magistrate's Court is not a court of record and so trial *de novo* is available in the Circuit Court on appeal from the judgement of a magistrate. There are seven Magistrate's Courts, four operating in downtown Kansas City and three in outlying areas of the county.

Indigent defense is provided by a public defenders office, which has fifteen full-time attorneys who handle the majority of criminal cases in the jurisdiction. The public defender attorneys' salaries are roughly equivalent to those of the assistant prosecutors; the starting salary is slightly higher, but their maximum earning capacity is slightly lower. In addition, another eight-to-ten private attorneys practice criminal law regularly on a retained basis.

The daily working relationship between the assistants, public defenders, and privately retained attorneys is cordial. The latter are so few in number that they are familiar to the assistants, and their talents and strategies are well known. As a result, there is little uncertainty introduced in this aspect of the courtroom work group. Instead professionalism and efficiency find amenable dispositional environments here.

### The Prosecuting Attorney

Ralph Martin, the Prosecuting Attorney for Jackson County, is currently in the midst of his second 4-year term. Martin has had a long career in public law. He served as a municipal judge in Kansas City for 6 years and was the Public Administrator for 4 years, an elected position that handles probate matters.

Martin brought to the office a thorough understanding of the court system and of the demands that modern courts find placed upon them. During his first term he began to implement procedures that would help the office deal with the realities of an expanding court system. He also tried to widen the scope of the office's influence and to involve it in state and national issues. He was overwhelmingly reelected for his second term and viewed that reelection as a vote of confidence for his efforts to professionalize the office of the Prosecuting Attorney.

Martin inherited an office that had developed over the years a strong sense of professionalism and extensive experience. Twenty years earlier, in 1956, the Prosecuting Attorney for the county and his staff consisted of three part-time positions, each receiving a compensation of less than $5,000 per year. In those days, the docket was small, ranging from a low of 100 cases during the nonairconditioned summer session of court to a high of 250 cases during the fall session. Despite the small caseload, the office regularly engaged in plea bargaining to increase the time available for the private practice of its assistants.

During the period between 1962 and 1967, the county's population grew enormously, and, with it, the size of the office. By 1967, there were fifteen assistants in the office, all of whom still worked part-time. Their compensation rose to a maximum of $7,000 per year. Attorneys within the office were divided into three classes, pay was scaled according to experience. The criminal docket increased dramatically during this period, and its backlog became the major political issue defeating the incumbent prosecutor's quest for reelection. His successor was Joseph Teasdale, who has since been elected governor of the state.

By the time Teasdale assumed office in 1967 the case backlog had worsened. Many of the incumbent assistants, thinking that they would be dismissed by Teasdale, had resigned and left during the period between the election and the start of the new administration. When Teasdale took office, his first imperative was to "keep the docket moving," and that attitude has continued to the present day. For the first 2 years of Teasdale's tenure the positions within the office remained entirely part-time; obtaining full-time status became a focus of Teasdale's early efforts. In 1969 the Prosecuting Attorney's elective term was lengthened to 4 years, and for the first time the position was made full-time. In a gradual process over the next 8 years, both Teasdale and his successor, Ralph Martin, the current Prosecuting Attorney, managed to extend full-time status to the majority of assistants in the office. Today there are twenty-seven assistants in the office; eleven still retain a part-time status.

The Office of the Prosecuting Attorney for Jackson County is a classic example of system efficiency. The primary emphasis is to develop the most advantageous disposition of the case as early as possible in the process and to control the size of the criminal docket by utilizing alternative dispositions to trial. As will be seen, all the organizational and operational procedures within the office are directed to consistently support the goal of swift and early disposition.

System efficiency has long been the mode of operation in Jackson County. When Teasdale first took office in 1967, having just left service with the U.S. Attorney's Office in Kansas City, he brought with him a policy of tough prosecution and a desire to reduce plea bargaining and organize the case processing to ensure the stiffest sentences possible for all defendants who were found guilty at trial. It was not long before he recognized that this particular policy goal flew in the face of the real imperative of reducing an overwhelming case backlog within the time alloted under the statutes. His stance was modified, and the emphasis in the office shifted to management efficiency; however, the desire to be tough was not entirely eliminated. When Ralph Martin was elected, he continued the policy and, responding to staff increases, developed new organizational and procedural techniques to perfect its use. He formalized previously ad hoc procedures that allowed early discovery by defense counsel to induce or facilitate early dispositions in strong state cases. He "front-ended" his office resources by placing strong emphasis on putting sufficient personnel with long experience in the screening function, making case review at intake the single most important decision area in the operations of the office. He brought with him a modern professionalism that extended the role of prosecution beyond the confines of the office into state and national involvement.

Although there has been a strong tradition of system efficiency in this office, tradition alone does not account entirely for the continuation of this policy within the office. A lack of resources coupled with increasing case volume has also made this a realistic policy choice. For the past 4 years, there has been no increase in the office's budget, despite inflation. This circumstance coupled with the traditional acceptance of the need for this policy by the public, media, and criminal justice officials has favorably effected the office's morale. Job satisfaction and dedication among the assistant prosecutors is high despite the lack of pay incentives, poor space, and inadequate support services. Under these circumstances the attitude and demeanor of the office is unexpectedly professional, dedicated, and experienced.

## Office of the Prosecuting Attorney

### Size, Organization, and Experience

In 1977, the office employed sixteen full-time assistants and eleven part-time. With the exception of two part-time and two full-time assistants, who were assigned to the branch office in Independence, the rest were located in the main office in downtown Kansas City. In addition, seven staff investigators, most of whom are retired or ex-policemen, were employed with the primary duties of contacting witnesses or serving subpoenas.

All assistants serve at the pleasure of the prosecutor, and staff assignments are based on the experience level. The overall experience level is high compared with national trends and despite the relatively low salary level that is offered. More than half of the full-time assistants have 4 years or more experience. Most of the part-time assistants have been with the office between 8 and 10 years. The management and executive level attorneys are even more expert; the two chief assistants have 12 and 20 years of experience, respectively.

The salary range of full-time assistants starts at $11,500 for a Class I, or beginning attorney with a maximum of $15,000. Class II attorney salaries range from $15,000 to $20,000; Class III attorneys, those with the highest level of experience, range from $20,000 to a maximum of $26,000. Attorneys who work part-time are paid from $7,200 up to $12,000, the latter for attorneys with 5 or more years of experience. Many attorneys are willing to accept these lower salaries because they can supplement their prosecution income with the proceeds of private practice. It has been estimated that some part-time attorneys have incomes as high as $50,000 a year.

The office is organized on the basis of the military delineation between the operations and administration functions. The Director of Operations supervises the attorney staff and the case-processing functions, including:

intake, the accusatory process, trials, and special actions such as arraignments and extraditions. He also supervises the Child Support Division and the branch office operations.

The Director of Staff supervises all the support services and personnel including: investigators, administrative and secretarial personnel, statistical and record-keeping functions, subpoenas, and the citizen complaints section. The Director of Staff views his role and duties as supportive of the operations of the office. Thus whatever potential areas of conflict over power and control might be present elsewhere, they are minimized here because of this perception.

The organization is bimodal in character. Major emphasis is placed on the intake function called the "Warrant Desk," which has subsumed under its control the accusatory process. The Warrant Desk Officer is in charge of intake and review. He not only performs screening but also supervises the operations of preliminary hearing, grand jury, diversion programs, and the branch offices. This emphasis on controlling all entrances into the office logically supports the organizational placement of the branch offices and the grand jury within the Warrant Desk's purview. Since diversion programs offer the potential for speedy dispositions, their representatives can be found in the Warrant Desk's operational area.

Once past intake and accusation, the second major organizational response is to the trial requirements of cases. The Trial Director, as the recipient of cases bound over from preliminary hearing or sent by grand jury indictment, represents the final sieve of the prosecution function. The Trial Director individually assigns cases to assistants, who take them to their conclusion. Assignments are made with respect to the judge, defense counsel, and the skills of the assistants.

By analyzing the organization through the case-processing stages, it becomes apparent that the office has been designed to afford maximum opportunity for reaching early dispositions. The following sections will follow case flow through the prosecution process in both Kansas City and the Independence branch office.

*Jurisdiction*

The Prosecuting Attorney's jurisdiction is entirely criminal with the single exception of a wife-and-child-support section staffed by four attorneys and three investigators. There is a Court of Appeals to the Circuit Court, but most of the cases are appealed to the state Supreme Court and handled by the Attorney General. The Attorney General has a regional office in Kansas City that provides an opportunity for discussion of cases if needed.

**Process Steps**

*Intake*

In Jackson County, police must receive prosecutorial approval before cases can be filed in the court. This requirement imposed on an already qualified and experienced detective force has resulted in a cooperative and cordial working relationship between the two agencies that centers on the Warrant Desk operations. The center of the intake and review function is staffed by the Warrant Desk attorneys and four part-time attorneys. It operates 7 days a week because Jackson County is under a "20-hour rule," which requires the prosecutor to file charges 20 hours after arrest. Within the 20 hours, the prosecutor is supplied with all the information available at the time. He has the detective's testimony and the investigation report. Because sufficient evidence may not be developed or available in that period of time, the pressure on this decision point also supports active police-prosecutor coordination and liaison. The agencies do not use standardized police reporting forms. As yet the office has not seen any need for introducing standardization. One reason is the low volume of cases coming into the office. As the head of the Warrants Desk stated: "If you have plenty of time to read the report, you can extract what you want." The five to twenty cases coming in each day permit this type of reading. Additionally, the need for standardization is met through the use of the Warrant Desk data sheet. It is this sheet that extracts the information from the various police forms and compiles it into a standardized format for the assistants' use. Thus, the lack in standardization in police reports is corrected by prosecutorial action.

Three general procedures exist for case review at intake.

1. For serious or exceptional cases, such as murder, kidnapping, or rape, the detective calls the Warrant Desk assistant regardless of time of day so that the assistant can go to the scene of the crime and assist in developing and preserving the evidence.

2. For nonexceptional cases, a Warrant Desk assistant usually goes to the Police Department daily to determine: what cases are under investigation; which are ready to be sent over; what is still needed on problem cases. The assistant may recommend that a less serious case be transferred to the City Court rather than Circuit Court or that it be considered for diversion. The result of this procedure is to maximize the opportunity for case review and evaluation. This usually occurs in cases where the defendant has not yet been arrested.

3. Most often, however, the detective brings the case to the prosecutor's Warrant Desk for review and an intake decision. The options available here are many in addition to accepting the case for prosecution. They include: transferring the case to City Court; placing the defendant in a pretrial diver-

sion program; referring the defendant to the military, if appropriate; placing the defendant in a career criminal program; referring the case for Federal prosecution; or rejecting the case outright.

The intensive screening and review function results in many cases being rejected. In the first 4 months of 1977, 358 (28 percent) of the 1,288 cases presented were rejected. The three most common reasons for declining the 374 cases were: (1) There were already other charges filed against the defendant in 21 percent of the cases. (2) Almost one-third of the declinations were based on evidentiary factors: insufficient evidence; illegal arrests or bad search and seizures; lack of complaining witness; or other justifiable or accidental events. (3) In almost 17 percent of the declinations the defendant was placed in pretrial diversion or deferred prosecution programs, or transferred to City Court. The office has no hesitancy in declining cases, and encounters little conflict because declinations are made with the full knowledge of the police department and are perceived as a professional response in a system that puts much emphasis on intake and screening. Additionally the two agencies historically have always understood the distinction between the power of the police to arrest and the power of the prosecutor to file charges.

The ability of the Warrant Desk to profoundly affect the operations of this office is reflected in the operations of diversion programs. The Warrant Desk is located in a controlled-access area, divided into cubicles for the assistants' use. There are two unique features in the Kansas City intake area. First, there is an interview room, where the defendant is brought in the custody of the detective, and, second, there are representatives of three major diversion programs located in or adjacent to the area. Before any charges are placed against a defendant, he is screened for eligibility by the Deferred Prosecution Director. If accepted, he is placed in the informal Deferred Prosecution program, which relies mainly on regular or periodic telephone contacts. Failing this, the defendant is referred to the Pretrial Diversion Program or, if eligible, to the Treatment Alternatives to Street Crime (TASC) program. The chiefs of these programs are located nearby and interview the defendant in the same interview room. By this method, if the defendant is eligible for any of the programs, the charges are disposed of by a formal acknowledgement at the Magistrate Court with little resource expenditure.

If the defendant is not eligible for diversion, then the case is reviewed by the Warrant Desk assistant, and a proper charge is determined. To transmit information or instructions to the preliminary hearing assistant, a Warrant Desk data sheet is prepared for each case and defendant. The data sheet identifies all companion cases pending against the defendant; lists codefendants; notes whether other cases are pending so that a probation revocation hearing can be requested; and summarizes the criminal history of the defendant. Most importantly, the Warrant Desk Officer records his initial impressions from reviewing the case's evidentiary strength and recommends a disposition for the case. If a Warrant Desk Officer feels strongly that a case should be bound over, he so instructs the assistant at preliminary hearing, who otherwise is allowed some discretion in reducing the case to a misdemeanor. A strong statement by the intake review assistant often limits that discretion. Since the trial-experienced reviewing assistants have prior knowledge about the facts of the case, recommendations regarding strategy or ultimate disposition of the case often are made. The importance of the data sheet is that it provides a vehicle for transmitting intake policy and standards to the accusatory process. Since preliminary hearings are brief, averaging only about 10 minutes, the data sheet also serves to recap the major points for the assistant.

In 1975 with Law Enforcement Assistance Administration (LEAA) funding the office expanded the dispositional power of the intake function by establishing a new project called "Implementation of Discovery." Originally supported with LEAA funds, the purpose of this project was to review cases after charging and before the magistrates' hearing (if possible) and to negotiate dispositions. The Implementation of Discovery project removes about twenty-five to thirty cases a month from the docket. It was designed to provide a means for the Public Defender and the prosecutor to discuss matters about the case with an aim of keeping it off the trial docket. After the arrest, two copies of the report were made: one for the prosecutor, the other for the public defender. The Public Defender prior to this project had no knowledge of the facts of the case except what was reported by the defendant and his witnesses.

Within the 6 to 10 days between the filing of the charges and the scheduling of the preliminary hearing, the case is discussed and a number of alternatives to trial are considered. They include a reduction of the charge from a felony to a misdemeanor for a plea; a recommendation for probation or deferred prosecution; a recommendation of sentence time; the dismissal of the charges; and a referral to diversion programs. If any one is mutually agreeable, then the case is handled accordingly.

On the surface, it would appear that this is a redundant process since many of the alternatives have already been considered by the Warrant Desk's review in the course of its making the charging decisions. However, there are major differences. First, its very existence provides an opportunity for the negotiated disposition of cases before the preliminary hearing. Second, it provides another opportunity for review after the 20-hour rule limitation and permits the examination of further evidence and information that may have been developed since the charging decision. Third, it gives the office more time to develop other dispositional procedures in the Magistrate Court in addition to the traditional plea to a misdemeanor. By increasing the number of options available, more dispositions are obtained. The unit uses second and even third attempts at diversion, deferred prosecution, waiver of preliminary hearings and even dismissals as negotiating incentives.

Implementation of Discovery does not review all the cases. Excluded are those cases that involve murder, crimes of violence, rape, bad checks, and tax cases. Also excluded are an overwhelming number of robbery and narcotics sales cases. Robberies are specifically excluded because of an office rule that they cannot be plea bargained.

The number of cases being referred to the Implementation of Discovery Project is being further reduced because of a change in the Public Defender's policy on stipulation. Originally, all cases were referred to the project, but when the Public Defender decided not to stipulate to the evidence at the preliminary hearing—thereby turning it into a minitrial—the prosecutor responded by submitting those cases to the grand jury.

Implementation of Discovery generally reviews cases that can be disposed of by diversion or reduction: property crimes, youthful offenders, minor vandalism, and the like. It often requires restitution within 2 years and if diversion is utilized, it permits the full expungement of the record in 1 year.

The Implementation of Discovery project is an autonomous unit under the general supervision of the Warrant Desk, although it has the authority to change recommendations that the assistant at the Warrant Desk indicated on the data sheet. It may also send cases back to the Warrant Desk if it feels that the charge is inappropriate. Of the 1985 cases reviewed by the unit, 698 or 35 percent were disposed of before preliminary hearing.

The intake process has a dispositional focus unless the case is to be bound over. The recommendations made at the charging level and recorded on the data sheet consider whether a bindover should be sought or whether the case should be disposed of as soon as possible, usually before arraignment at Circuit Court. Bind over is reserved for the more serious crimes or the marginal cases involving notorious or repeat offenders.

Because of the serious nature of the charging process, control mechanisms are much in evidence. A biweekly staff meeting produces complaints from the trial assistants if the quality of the bind overs deteriorates. If there are problems with a particular case, trial assistants often go directly to the Warrant Desk to talk to the charging assistant. Because the office is small and the staff centralized in a relatively small space, communication is informal and extensive.

If a case has been bound over that clearly should have been stopped at intake, on complaint by the trial assistant, the Chief of the Warrant Desk can reassign it to the charging assistant. This has proved to be an effective technique for controlling and maintaining the quality of the charging decisions. Assistants who stray too far from the charging norms receive complaints from defense counsel as well, who are quick to tell the prosecutor that the assistant was wrong or that he filed without reason. Finally, controls are exercised by the court. The relationship between the judges and the prosecutor's office are generally very good, and informal complaints by the Magistrate judges about the quality of the charging decisions are carefully considered. Because a different judge is assigned to arraignment weekly, the quality of the charging decisions are reviewed by all judges, not merely one.

Not all controls are in the communications areas, statistics are also used as a management tool. The office maintains good data that reflect not only the daily dispositions and activities but year-to-date cumulatives as well. The chiefs monitor the statistical reports and recognize the need to investigate when trends appear to change.

### Accusatory

All the intake procedures are directed at the two-pronged effort of disposing of cases as quickly as possible before or by the end of the accusatory process, leaving only a "clean" felony caseload bound over to the Trials Divisions. To achieve this, the accusatory process has been integrated into the intake function and serves as the final processing point for a large number of cases.

Although the Jackson County Prosecuting Attorney has access to two accusatory vehicles, the grand jury and the preliminary hearing, by far, the latter is the preferred and most selected accusatory route. During the calendar year 1976, 1,506 defendants were assigned to the Circuit Court. Of these, 1,178 or 78 percent were presented through the prosecutor's bill of information, which involved either a preliminary hearing for determination of probable cause or a waiver by the defendant of that procedure. Only 223, or 15 percent, came to the Circuit Court as a result of Grand Jury indictment.

**Preliminary Hearing.** In Kansas City, preliminary hearings are held in the Magistrate Court. The proceedings are not totally uniform; the length and specificity of the proceeding are often functions of the individual philosophy of the judge and his determination of the requirements of establishing probable cause to bind over for trial. This is because every 5 weeks one of the five judges is assigned to preliminary hearings.

Preliminary hearings are held 1 day a week on Thursday morning-although they may overflow to Friday. Usually there are sixty to seventy cases scheduled—twenty-five for Thursday morning, twenty-five for the afternoon, and an overflow valve for another twenty-five is reserved for Friday morning. Since most judges want to clear their dockets, even if a victim or witness is not available, they will hear part of the evidence from those present and then delay the rest of the hearing until the remaining witnesses can appear. The goal here is minimize the number of dismissals due to witness no-shows.

Preliminary hearings usually take about 10 minutes per case. It is at this point that a wide range of dispositional outcomes are used. A felony may be reduced to a misdemeanor with a plea or a recommendation to try the case in the Magistrate Court as a misdemeanor. Diversion recommendations may be made if the defense attorney stipulates to the evidence and restitution is agreed on. The case may be dismissed—this occurs in weaker cases where the crime arose from family squabbles or there are identification problems or other evidentiary difficulties. Or as the last resort, the case may be bound over for trial.

The assistant at preliminary hearing has little time for preparation and review, which is why the data sheet assumes an important function. Case files are received by the assistant the Friday or Monday before the preliminary hearing. Witness notices are sent out by mail. And the dispositional processes at the hearing itself are based on informal negotiations between the defense counsel and the assistant.

Plea bargaining is a pervasive operational form. The defense counsel will bargain with the assistant even if the witnesses fail to show and there are other cases pending against their client. Part of this bargaining process is supported by conditions of the local jail. There have been known instances where the defendant has refused an offer to plead to a misdemeanor, preferring instead to waive the preliminary hearing and plead to a felony at arraignment merely to escape the local jail. They feel that 1 year in the jail is worth 2 years at the state penitentiary at Jefferson City.

The skills of plea negotiation are highly tuned in this jurisdiction. What may appear to be an unnecessary reduction in charge may in fact accomplish longer-range objectives. To illustrate, a plea to a misdemeanor with a short jail sentence may be offered to give the prosecutor more time to develop and prepare other pending felony cases against the defendant while he serves his "local time."

The defendant has the right to waive preliminary hearing. In some cases the waiver is used by the defense counsel to prevent the judge from raising the bond. In other cases, it is used to reduce the number of witness appearances and the subsequent frustrations that may cause them not to show at the trial level.

The preliminary hearing then assumes major and often critical importance as a vehicle for moving cases to early and swift dispositions. Even the waiver of preliminary hearings as an accommodation to speeding up the system is important. If stipulations are not to be forthcoming from the defense, or if continuances are wearing out the witnesses, these and other factors can be mitigated because the grand jury can be used instead.

**Grand Jury**. The Jackson County grand jury is appointed for a 6-month term and meets every Friday. The proceedings are conducted in secrecy and are *ex parte*. The state, through an assistant prosecutor, presents its case for probable cause and puts on its primary witnesses, usually the victim of the crime, the police officer, and any eyewitnesses.

In 1978, 223 defendants were indicted by the grand jury. For the 4 months ending April 30, 1977, 211 true bills had been returned and only 3 no true bills. Following the office policy, most grand jury indictments involved serious crimes: 53 percent of the indictments were for narcotics sales and possession; another 15 percent involved murder, manslaughter, or felonius assault; and armed robbery or burglary constituted 14 percent of the indictments the grand jury is also used routinely for murders and sex offenses and for complicated cases that cannot be presented in the ordinary 10-minute preliminary hearing in the Magistrate Court.

Having access to both forms of accusatory processing has given the prosecutor not only flexibility in obtaining either indictments or bind overs as the nature of the case may require but also the ability to use these procedures to gain time for case preparation and indictment. Since the prosecutor has only 20 hours within which a charge must be filed, and since the grand jury only meets once a week, obviously the 20-hour rule cannot be met if a grand jury indictment is sought to protect witnesses or present the more complicated time-consuming cases. In these instances, a complaint is filed within the time limit in Magistrate Court, thereby holding the defendant, and the case is then presented to the grand jury. Once the indictment is handed up, the complaint in the Magistrate Court is dismissed.

There is an additional flexibility inherent in using the grand jury as the accusatory vehicle. The Magistrate Court is restricted to the review of the charges that have been placed and no others. The grand jury, on the other hand, can change and add charges as they deem suitable. In this respect, it becomes a more powerful charging vehicle than the preliminary hearing.

In addition to its accusatory function, the grand jury also has an investigative one. Indictments are usually completed by 1:30 p.m., at which time the grand jury turns into an investigative body focusing on county operations. They have the responsibility to report on all county facilities and public institutions and have the power to subpoena in the performance of these duties. An investigation of the county jail in 1975, for example, resulted in the firing of fifteen employees and several indictments. The major weakness of the grand jury lies in the fact that although they have the power to subpoena, they do not have the power to grant immunity.

The recent increase in obtaining grand jury indictments for narcotics sales rather than proceeding through a preliminary hearing is a direct result of the change in public defender policy. Previously the public defender had stipulated in the evidence in many cases; with the change in policy, the prosecutor was required to establish all facts, including producing the undercover agents, at the public hearing. Rather than do this, the cases were referred to the grand jury.

The accusatory process is ended with the arraignment of the defendant on either an indictment or bill of information. At arraignment, a determination of indigency is made, defense counsel is appointed, and bond is set. The law requires that the indictment or information be read, but this is usually waived, and the defendant enters a formal plea of guilty, not guilty, or not guilty by reasons of mental disease or defect. Most of the defendants plead not guilty at arraignment; pleas of guilty are rare, these having been taken in a separate action. As a result, the arraignment proceedings are quick and essentially act as a bond hearing and a trial date setting. Jury trials are automatically set unless they are waived on the day of trial.

In 1976, 1,406 arraignments were held. Although the assistant prosecutor at arriagnment has the discretion to dispose of cases here, this proceeding is not used for this purpose. The bond-setting function identifies some of the tactical advantages that may ensue from this procedure for both prosecution and defense. By obtaining a high money bond on a career criminal defendant, his location is known to all parties, the 10 percent surety bond—which is the most common type set—can be used as a means of providing the defense counsel with access to his fee, since he can request the fee rights be assigned to him as part of his fee, and even though the defendant may ultimately be placed on probation, he gets a "taste of jail."

## Trials to Disposition

The trials division of the office is under the policy direction of the Director of Operations and headed by a Chief Trial Attorney. Although all the assistants in the office are permitted to try cases and hence may be thought of as under the supervision of the Director of Operations, in practice, only eight full-time assistants and seven part-time ones do so. The part-time assistants are trained and experienced, reflecting 8 to 10 years of practice in prosecution. The full-time assistants have less experience—3 to 7 years on the average.

The organization of the trial division underlines the goals of efficiency in the office: it is simple and direct. Control is maintained informally. The small staff size is easily supervised, and hence policy maintenance is simple. The discretion permitted the trial assistants is, by the nature of the communication in the office, controlled by informal procedures rather than formalized ones.

Case assignment is made by the Director of Operations after reviewing all the files after arraignment. Thirty-five to forty cases a week are reviewed.

This involves reading the complete file, the police report, the Warrant Desk report, the criminal history of the defendant, and any other additional information including the identity of the defense counsel. A computer print-out supported the assignment procedure, since it identifies each assistant, the number of cases currently assigned him, and the number of defendants. With the case in front of him, the Director of Operations goes down the list and selects the appropriate assistant to handle it.

Trials go primarily to the most experienced lawyers, and full-time assistants generally are given preference over the part-time assistants. Newer assistants are given only a few trials a year—perhaps three to five—generally they are the simpler ones. Where possible, and in complicated cases that involve a good deal of preparation time, a new assistant will be assigned to work with the more experienced ones—thus adding a training component to the assignment process. Assignments also consider the defense representation, and assistants are assigned with respect to their ability to handle significant characteristics of the defense and their style of operation. Since there are only eight to ten privately retained counsel and fifteen public defenders, this is not a complicated task.

There is some specialization in the office. One attorney is very good with rape and sex crimes; five others prepare the most complicated or sensitive cases; two lawyers specialize in bad check cases and one on most of the narcotics cases. The office experimented with a trial team concept in which the assistants were supported by investigators and clerical support. Although they liked the results and performance, the LEAA funding ceased and with it the program.

Once a case has been assigned, the trial assistant reviews it within 24 hours after arraignment, prepares a witness list for the investigators, and gets the subpoenas typed. Then they have 3 to 5 weeks to prepare the cases. The office considers a dismissal because of a witness no-show as a key indicator of whether the case was prepared. Additionally, each assistant's performance is reviewed on the basis of his yearly and monthly box score.

The office is opposed to the concept of assigning assistants to courtrooms. They feel that given the underpaid circumstances of the assistants, they would quit if assigned to a judge they couldn't get along with. They also believe that the court would then exert undue influence on who would try the cases because they had control of the docket; as a corollary to this, they also believe that they would lose the benefit of the specialization that has developed from their present assignment procedures.

With an eye toward efficiency and professionalism, little is left to chance in this prosecution process. In fact, it can be best described as anticipatory. If the case is of any consequence, the Director of Operations has already discussed it with the Chief of the Warrants Desk before it is bound over. Often these discussions include the Prosecuting Attorney himself. Once bound over, the Director of Operations anticipates the expected disposition and strategies to achieve it. If there are going to be special problems—for example, discovery—he notes on the file that the trial assistant should see him. If he so desires, he may also "bottom line" the bargain that can be offered in terms of its ultimate disposition.

The trial strategy is to try the marginal cases and "not give the good cases away." The assistant is responsible for the case through its disposition and sometimes even into the postconviction stage, where sentence recommendations may be used. Because of this type of assignment the anticipatory nature of the review and supervisory control and the small size of the office, accountability is high and the trial assistant's performance easily evaluated. Such a system for all its benefits also has a few problems, chief among which is that the assignment procedure can generate scheduling conflicts. With five circuit courts hearing criminal cases at the same time, the simultaneous assignment of assistants to different courtrooms is an ever-present problem. To counteract this, the office rule is to try older cases first and seek continuances on the others. Since the expected disposition has already been bottom lined by the Director of Operations, the choice between what cases should be continued is made less uncertain.

Robbery and assault cases are offered no reductions unless they fall into the "garbage" category—then they are reduced. A Missouri statute calls for a minimum of 5 years and a maximum of 30; the office generally recommends 10 years. The reason why such a hard bargain can be negotiated is that the alternative is even less attractive to the defendant—namely, jury sentencing.

The office also takes a strict stance against serious offenders. The Felony Tracking Unit was established to focus on recidivists and career criminals. The office worked with the Kansas City Police Department to develop two books that identify major criminals involved in bad checks and burglaries. Each of these notebooks contains photos and personal identification of persons who have been convicted of these offenses. The books were distributed to the head of the Warrant Desk, the Chief of Trials, and the Independence office so that if any of these defendants were arrested, they would not "slip through the cracks."

The Office's attitude toward first offenders or youthful offenders is less strict. Defense counsel, the assistant, and the judge will meet in the latter's chambers to discuss the case and negotiate a disposition, which will be stated in court by the judge as "it is my understanding that the prosecutor has agreed to recommend—years, and the court will accept this recommendation."

With the exception of these two classes of offender, the assistants are generally allowed to bring cases to disposition as they choose. This is not truly unbridled discretion. First, the experience of the trial assistants tends to be extensive; second, the office is small enough to include daily communications among the assistants and with the Chief of Trials. There is by its very nature a large amount of informal control exercised.

The type of discovery used in Circuit Court varies substantially from that in Magistrate Court. Formal discovery is based on the first filing principle—whoever files first, the state or the defense, must provide discovery first. Although the prosecutors generally try to file first, they usually do not receive the materials until the day of trial, even though it is supposed to be submitted within 10 days after filing. The private bar is more cooperative in this matter than the public defender.

Discovery is not as informal or open at the trial level as it is at pretrial. This is basically due to the fact that, the cases that end in trial with the exception of murder, tend to be the marginal ones. Both parties prefer not to "show their hand." Thus it is not unusual for the delays in producing discoverable materials.

The strong cases have already been pled out, based on the negotiations directed at sentence recommendations rather than charge reductions. Of the 286 guilty pleas, only 30 were reduced.

Success is measured by the reductions in the number of pending active cases. The backlog is divided into active and inactive cases. The latter are comprised mostly of mental competency cases and *capias*. The active case backlog has been running about 400 a year—a figure that the office would like to reduce to 300. The combination of a goal to reduce the backlog and a willingness to negotiate pleas has produced a pattern of dispositions that is not unexpected. Of the 1,547 cases disposed, 61 percent were by guilty pleas and only 10 percent of these to a reduced charge. Since the office procedure is to negotiate pleas on lesser cases prior to Circuit Court action and to go forward with either the strong cases or those involving serious offenders, the vast majority of pleas at the Circuit Court level reflect the State's strength of case and the reputation of the length of sentences that could be forthcoming from the jury. In this jurisdiction, the jury generally sentences, and their sanctions are traditionally considered more severe than the court-imposed sentences.

The second-largest disposition group in Circuit Court is dismissals. Twenty-eight percent of 441 defendants had cases dismissed at this level. Dismissals are not viewed negatively in this office; in fact, 416 of the 441 dismissals resulted from the dismissal of companion cases after a plea to the original case was entered. Multiple charging at the Warrant Desk is a routine procedure to assist the plea negotiation process as well as to protect the state's case if one of the charges breaks down.

The second major reason for dismissals indicates a serious problem in the office—witness no-shows. Historically, the office has had much difficulty in locating witnesses, even though Circuit Court subpoenas are hand-served by investigators. Under Martin, the investigator's record has improved substantially. He has reduced the all-time high of non-delivered subpoenas from 11 percent to a little less than 1 percent. The problem stems from the poor scheduling of cases and a lack of docket control. The fact that a docket is set for a given day does not mean that the cases will be called in that order. As a result, the investigators are hard put to locate and bring in witnesses with an hour's notice.

Also raising the dismissal rate in this jurisdiction are the dismissals of cases that have successfully completed pretrial diversion (75 of the 441) and for "no-go" cases that cannot be tried—for example, where the defendant, witness, or victim has died. The dismissal rate is not considered to be high but rather a legitimate result of the prosecutor's responsibility to dismiss cases that cannot be proven. Trial assistants generally discuss the decision with the Chief of Trials or the Director of Operations, unless they are the experienced part-timers, who generally are allowed to dismiss cases at their discretion. To keep the docket moving, even the court on occasion has dismissed a case, at which point, the assistant refiles it.

One might expect with such intensive screening, with the extensive use of plea negotiation, and moving the marginal cases forward to trial, that the acquittal rate would be high. On the contrary, with the specialized assignment procedures and the experience of the assistants, only 10 percent of the 1,547 defendants were disposed of by trial and only 3.8 percent of these were acquitted.

*Postconviction*

The office regularly uses the postconviction area to bring dispositions to their desired conclusion. Three major factors affect sentencing and the power of the prosecutor. The first, of course, is the fact that under routine circumstances, the jury sentences—and traditionally sentences severely. Jury sentences can be overruled by the court, but this is rarely the case.

There is an exception to this procedure, however. Missouri has a second offender act that takes sentencing out of the jury's purview and gives it to the court. If a defendant being tried for a felony is found to have another felony conviction in that jurisdiction or another, the prosecutor can file an amended information under the second offender act alleging the prior felony. When this is filed with the court, the judgement of conviction is automatic. The judge can recess the trial, find that the defendant is a second offender and excuse the jury. The court may sentence within an offense range. Sometimes, the assistant may not use the second offender act, chancing that the jury will sentence more severely than the court. The defendant can waive a jury trial at the discretion of the court.

Even though the office engages extensively in making sentence recommendations, it is opposed to recommending probation as part of the plea-bargaining process. This is not always conformed to by the assistants, some of whom may get carried away or have less experience and are coerced by the court to make such a recommendation.

In general, however, the office has adapted to the sentencing procedures in the jurisdiction, has integrated their usefulness as a dispositional strategy into their goals, and has fine-tuned the final phase of the prosecutorial process as efficiently as the first phase.


### Branch Office—Independence, Missouri

Independence, Missouri, is a bedroom community in Jackson County with a population of 120,000. Scattered throughout the rest of Jackson County are another 80,000 residents, bringing the total up to 200,000 outside the central city of Kansas City. Martin would like to open other branch offices in addition to the one at Independence, in the Lake Jacomo area for example, but the County Council has not appropriated funds for this.

Independence is a rapidly growing town, from a population of 12,000 in 1947 it expanded until 1977 its population reached 120,000. Independence is a conservative town and predominately Mormon. This coupled with the fact that there is not much crime there has produced a shared community attitude that crimes committed there should be punished severely. This response is in stark contrast to the relatively tolerant and fatalistic attitude of the citizens in Kansas City.

The office is under the supervision of the Chief of the Warrant Desk and is headed by an assistant who is sensitive to the community's values as well as the goals of the office. Thus cases will be filed that in Kansas City would be considered less serious or important. Where in the city there is a need to prioritize crime and the office's resources, in Independence no such need exists. The head of the office worked at the Warrant Desk for 2½ years prior to his transfer. The relationship between Independence and Kansas City is very good because of this training and association. The Independence chief talks on the phone daily with his boss, the Warrant Desk officer.

The assistants in the Independence office have to represent three Magistrate Courts: the Sixth District is located in Independence; the Seventh District Magistrate rides the circuit between three towns, Lees Summit, Raytown, and Grandview; and the Eighth District is located at Blue Springs. The workload in all these courts is predominately traffic. Unlike the Kansas City office, where no traffic cases are handled unless they are driving under the influence (DUI) cases (traffic is handled by the City Court), in the rest of the county, traffic takes up the largest volume of work. For example, of the 6,355 cases filed in 1976 in Independence, 5,613 or 88 percent were traffic violations. Most of the traffic cases are generated by the Highway Patrol and the county's Sheriff's Patrol. Of the eight Magistrates in the County, five downtown will not accept traffic cases. Therefore all the traffic is distributed among the remaining three County Magistrates in Districts 6, 7, and 8. Last year, the three Magistrates processed a total of 18,563 tickets.

As one of the assistants in the Kansas City office said, "Going to Independence is like going to a foreign county." And well it might seem when they see a jurisdiction that has a totally different crime focus (traffic) and is primarily a Magistrate Court system with a bindover capability to the Circuit Court in Kansas City. The office is small and informal. It deals with seventeen municipal and local law enforcement agencies as opposed to the single one dealt with in Kansas City. The agencies range in quality and professionalism. As a result, there is more emphasis on providing legal assistance and advice than would ever be needed downtown. The assistants will go out of their way to help save some of the more important cases.

There are three secretaries in the office, one assigned to each Magistrate Court. On occasion a Circuit Court criminal division is assigned to Independence, but it does not conduct jury trials. Pleas are taken, and parole and probation revocation hearings are conducted. The three Magistrate Courts hear criminal cases one day a week. The docket tends to be mostly preliminary hearings for felonies, since the other cases are sent to the local city courts. About thirty-five cases are heard in a day in one court. The preliminary hearings are very short.

In Independence the Magistrate Court schedule calls for a preliminary hearing docket on Thursday and a traffic docket Wednesday afternoon. Traffic trials usually last three to five minutes unless they are DUIs, which may run 45 to 60 minutes. Civil cases are then scheduled although they may be interrupted for arraignments. If a felony is reduced to a misdemeanor for a plea, the Magistrate will sentence the defendant immediately unless the defendant's background is unknown. Rarely are presentence investigations requested.

Waivers of preliminary hearings in this branch office typify the potential problems that arise from the separation of the two prosecutive systems and a lack of accountability. When the present branch chief was a member of the downtown staff, he recalled staff meetings when no Independence assistants attended. The Kansas City trial assistants complained about the poor quality of cases sent up from Independence resulting from bad screening, filing, and bindover procedures. Part of the problem was attributed to the fact that often the defense attorneys were not experienced in representing criminal cases. It was easier for them to waive the preliminary hearing and shift the case to Circuit Court with different defense representation. It also gave them time to attend to their civil caseload. As a result, when the present chief was assigned to Independence he warned his assistants to examine all waivers, make sure they were good cases, and be prepared to dismiss and refile them as misdemeanors if necessary.

Contact and communication with the main office is supported by the chief attending every staff meeting held each Friday. Without such contact, the Independence chief feels that he would soon be out of touch with the rules of the office, the current court and defense tactics, charging standards, and the legal interpretation of the statutes. Because of this close communication, the branch office has noticed a shfit in job definition. The assistants, recruited locally with no previous downtown experience, tended to define the end of their work by a bindover decision. The present chief, with an expanded view of his duties, now evaluates the cases with respect to their final dispositions.

As a result, the fine tuning that characterizes the Kansas City office can be seen in Independence, particularly in its most important function—intake.

No longer are bindovers boxed up and mailed to Kansas City. They are reviewed and the questionable ones discussed with the Warrant Desk first.

The problems of operating branch officers and relating their activities to a main office can vary enormously even though the work appears to be simpler and with fewer processing steps. When the activities are integrated with the needs of "downtown," conflicts, complaints, and mistakes are minimized. When they are autonomously administered and operated, the risk of developing distinctly different systems of justice is ever-present. The Jackson County office has lived through both types and opted for the integrated approach.

# 10 Twentieth Judicial District Attorney's Office

## The Setting

Boulder County, Colorado, is a community north of Denver with an immensely bright future. The county seems to have everything to offer its citizens—it is scenic, prosperous, and progressive. Boulder County occupies about 260 square miles—extending west of the continental divide, over the mountains, to 30 miles east into the Eastern Colorado Plateau. It is a cosmopolitan area and a popular recreation spot, easily connected to metropolitan Denver by modern highway. It is also the site of the state's largest institution of higher learning, the University of Colorado.

The population of the county resides largely in eleven municipalities, which account for 81 percent of the local citizenry. Seventy-five percent of the population lives in the three largest towns: Boulder—the county seat and site of the University, Longmont, and Bloomfield. Growth has been steady and rapid in the county over the past few decades with the population increasing at an annual rate of nearly 8 percent during the sixties and nearly 7 percent during the seventies. The heaviest growth has been experienced in the southernmost towns in the county, especially Bloomfield, which has become a bedroom suburb of the expanding Denver area. Bloomfield's annual growth rate is currently 16.4 percent.

Boulder County is attractive because of its natural advantages, beautiful scenery, and beneficent climate, but it is also attractive economically. The median family income for the county is over $11,200 with only a slight part of the population falling below the poverty level and a sizeable proportion of that group being located in the rural sections of the county. The per-capita income is high enough to make the county the most affluent in the state.

The county has a highly homogeneous population—about nineteen out of every twenty citizens are white. The only minority of any significant population are Mexican-Americans. Employment opportunities are available primarily for white-collar positions or in light industry. Boulder, the county seat, and the University provide a wide array of professional, administrative, and clerical jobs and set the base for the county's affluent economy. Unemployment is well below the national average.

The educational level is, as might be expected, also high. The median number of years completed in formal education by a citizen 25 years or older is 14. This, again, clearly reflects the influence of the University and the enterprises that it attracts. There are no military bases within the county and no significant migrant population, outside of the 20,000 students who are now attending the University of Colorado.

The commerce that has been attracted to Boulder County is either light industry or scientific and professional. There are four major aerospace research facilities and two large manufacturers of computer equipment. Head Ski Corporation, a developer and producer of sports equipment, is also located in Boulder as is a major publishing and magazine business.

Because of its relative affluence and high educational level there is not much hard-core crime in Boulder. Compared with 253 other counties of similar size (50,000-100,000), Boulder was slightly higher than the national average in only one crime—larceny theft. Most of the crimes in the county consist of petty offenses such as trespassing and drug crimes. The number one felony is burglary—both residential and commercial. Much of this is attributed to the opportunities presented by the large number of vacation homes that are left vacant for long periods of time. Arrests for negligent and nonnegligent manslaughter tend to occur more in the rural or outlying areas of the county.

Police services in the county are provided by eleven different agencies, which include the county sheriff, the state patrol, eight municipal forces, and the university police. The two largest and most significant are the Boulder County Police with 154 sworn personnel, and the Boulder City Police with 133. Longmont has forty-five sworn officers, and the rest of the forces are much smaller. The major portion of the District Attorney's intake comes from either the sheriff's office or the Boulder County Police.

The statewide Public Defender system has provided the county with a Public Defender, two staff attorneys, an investigator, and law students. The jurisdiction of the Public Defender's office is countywide—the County Court and the District Court. Law students handle misdemeanor defenses, leaving the felony defense representation to the Public Defender and his staff attorneys. The relationship between the Public Defender and the District Attorney is open and informal. Discussion about the fate of the defendant is the main topic of conversation about cases.

Defendants also have access to court-assigned attorneys and privately retained counsel. There is no scarcity of lawyers in Boulder County. In 1976, the District Court reported the following case distribution by type of representation: Public Defender, 176; privately retained, 150; court appointed, 62; and no defense counsel, 3.

Boulder County has a two-tiered court system, both levels having three judges. The court of limited jurisdiction is known as the County Court. It is a court of record and has jurisdiction over civil cases up to $500, misdemeanors, and felony preliminary hearings. The trial court is known as the

District Court and has felony jurisdiction in addition to civil responsibilities. The presiding judge has elected to hear most of the felony criminal cases himself. The presiding judge previously conducted all the preliminary hearings as well, but the recent increase in workload has forced him to delegate these matters to the County Court judges. A second District Court judge handles probate and juvenile matters; the third handles civil proceedings.

Bail service in the county is provided by commercial agencies. However, because there is extensive use of release on recognizance it is not a major factor in Boulder as in other jurisdictions. The District Attorney's policy is to support recognizance release wherever possible, with the exception of cases involving crimes of violence or serious, repeat offenders.

Barely 3 months in existence at the time of this study, the Community Corrections program has the potential for being the single most important influence on the prosecutor's function in this community. This is because its creation will permit the District Attorney to transfer to this agency many of the functions that his office performed either by choice or because there was simply no other agency capable of providing these services. Its ultimate influence will be to allow the prosecutor to change directions or policy, since this agency will free him from providing many previously needed services.

The concept of the Community Corrections program was developed by the Criminal Justice Advisory Committe—a group representing the health department, hospitals, and social services agencies in addition to the criminal justice agencies. When fully staffed, it will perform the following functions:

1. provide diagnostic services including conducting jail interviews for bond recommendations (recommendations were previously made by the District Attorney);

2. operate a felony diversion program for first-time, nonviolent offenders (replacing the prosecutor's use of deferred prosecution and sentencing);

3. operate an alternative community service program whereby the defendants involved in less serious crimes make restitution through community service (a program started by the District Attorney);

4. operate a pretrial release program (filling an obvious gap in the present system); and

5. conduct a volunteer coordination program to solicit volunteer help in many of these services (a program analogous to the victim/witness program operated by the District Attorney).

The local jail in Boulder County is a modern and highly praised correctional facility, which has been cited as an exemplary project by LEAA. Whenever possible, the prosecutor makes use of that facility rather than asking for imposition of a sentence to the state penitentiary. Oftentimes, use of the jail is contingent on a disposition that combines a limited amount of time to be served with a longer period of probation. Time served on a felony, otherwise, must be served in the Colorado State Penitentiary. The District Attorney, because of his unique defendant-oriented policy perspective, prefers to utilize the county jail where possible. Part of this is justified by the community's attitude that the state prisons do little to rehabilitate the defendant. In fact, recent recidivism studies of inmates at both institutions suggest that the state penitentiary is experiencing a two-thirds recidivism rate, whereas the Boulder County jail's rate is much less—somewhere in the area of 8-15 percent. Recidivism rates for defendants whose prosecution or sentencing is deferred is extremely low, 2-3 percent, but no direct causal connection can, of course, be asserted between the treatment mode and the recidivism rate.

## The District Attorney

Alexander Hunter is the District Attorney for the Twentieth District of Colorado, which is contiguous with the boundaries of Boulder County. Hunter graduated from the University of Colorado School of Law in 1963, and from 1965 to 1967 served as an assistant District Attorney under then-prosecutor, now Judge, Rex Scott. Hunter left prosecution in 1967 to enter private practice, which he pursued until 1972. A large amount of his practice during this period was involved with criminal defense, giving him an appreciation of the complexities of the criminal law and its processes from both the state's and the defendant's point of view. In 1972 he ran for District Attorney and narrowly won in a hotly contested campaign revolving around the issue of decriminalization of marijuana. He was unopposed in his campaign for reelection in 1976, setting a new precedent for this traditionally one-term office.

Hunter's predecessor had the reputation of being conservative and hardline in his approach to prosecution. He identified more with the policies of the police department, believing that his function was to prosecute their arrests. When Hunter took office, he brought in all new staff with the exception of one deputy who had coordinated the office's activities with the law enforcement agencies.

Hunter brought with him a different prosecutorial outlook. He gave recognition to the political roots of the office by stating, "We reflect the attitudes and values of the community." He was not far removed from being defense-oriented, taking an individualistic approach to justice—one that recognized the magnitude of the stigma of a felony conviction on a person's record. Furthermore, he renounced the image of closed-door prosecution by opening the charging discussions to the defense as well as the police.

The very fact that he chose to pursue an open door policy with the defense counsel reinforced the style of prosecution that was to emerge. The defendant-oriented approach requires by definition that cases be assessed individually, taking to account not only the facts as presented but the background of the defendant. A good illustration of the extensiveness of this approach involved the case of a 21-year-old soldier, who, after drinking all day, had been arrested for picking a fight with strangers in the snack bar of a local drive-in movie and attacking one with a knife. The incident occurred on Saturday evening. On Monday morning, the question of how to charge the defendant first came under discussion. The choices were to charge him with felony menacing, to drop charges because the military would handle the situation, or to reduce the charge to a misdemeanor so there would be no felony record created. By the end of the week, the decision had yet to be made, and the defendant was out on bail. The time spent on this case during the week was extensive. The office called the commanding officer to discuss his service record and what the military would propose to do. They interviewed his girlfriend and the other participants in the fight and obtained a full picture of not just the circumstances of the incident but the character and problems of the defendant. The final decision to charge the defedant with a felony was based on the total assessment of all the facts.

Before the daily staffing and charging conference was instituted early in Hunter's administration, there was minimal case review prior to the preliminary hearing. Police charges were filed, usually unchanged by the intake deputy, who acted more as a liaison and coordinator between the two offices than a screener. Decisions about the defendant, particularly those with respect to diversion, were made at the trial level by the senior trial assistants. These are not the same assistants who participate in the daily staffing and charging conference. In essence, under present procedures, the same decisions are being made with the same policy reference, although they are being made earlier in the process and by the District Attorney himself.

Sensitivity to the defendant and his needs permeates the actions of the office. Deferred sentencing and deferred prosecution provide important dispositional vehicles to test the rehabilitation of defendants and to avoid the stigmas of convictions. Deferred prosecution is a statutory process where the defendant is supervised by probation, and, on successful completion of the term, the case is dismissed. Deferred sentencing occurs when there is a conviction, but the sentence is deferred until probation is completed.

As the years passed, and with the existence of community corrections, Hunter already is envisioning changes in this area. He feels that he will be reserving the deferred sentence for constructive and rehabilitative purposes and would like to minimize if not eliminate entirely the use of deferred prosecution. Along with these changes, he also feels that the community would like more stable charging with clear accountability of the defendant to the crime, less plea bargaining, and more emphasis on prosecuting recidivists and putting them in the penitentiary.

Despite this harder attack on recidivism, the office nonetheless reflects Hunter's belief, based on his personal experience and his perception of community spirit, that prosecution can involve a strong humanitarian element and that the criminal justice system must, to some degree, be concerned with the rehabilitation or treatment of those persons who have broken the law. Along with this is a basic belief that public confidence in the criminal justice system must be maintained and that confidence has too often been undermined by the public perceptions of the plea-bargaining process.

Defendant rehabilitation exists here because there are so many support systems, volunteers, and facilities available to the defendant. In addition there is a strong community attitude that defendants should serve their sentences locally. There is a belief that a person coming back from the state penitentiary is "bummed out," and they will go to great lengths to avoid such a sentence. Even the more conservative, rural mountain communities have this same ethic. With these supports, the prosecutorial style and policy of the District Attorney operate harmoniously with the public.

**Office of the District Attorney**

*Size, Organization, and Experience*

The office of the District Attorney is small. There are eleven deputies, the District Attorney, and his First Assistant. Additionally, the office employs three investigators and ten support personnel. All positions are full-time, and the deputies serve at the pleasure of the District Attorney.

The office is organized around four main functions, each headed by an experienced Chief Deputy District Attorney and under the general supervision of the Assistant District Attorney and the District Attorney. Being a small office the areas of responsibility are held collegially rather than bureautically. One Chief Deputy is responsible for investigations, mental health, vehicle confiscations, and intake; another, for County Court cases, motor vehicle appeals, and bond; the third, felony for trials; and the fourth, for administration, which has been broadly defined to include many of the peripheral activities of the office such as juvenile, community dialogue, environmental protection, alcohol and drug abuse, and consumer affairs. In addition to these major organizational areas, there is a Nonsupport and Welfare Fraud Division which for all practical purposes is in the Social Services Department of the County; a Check Division—a Witness Unit which is supported by one full-time paraprofessional and volunteers—and the Longmont Branch office. This office does not prosecute cases, it serves as liaison and advisor for the municipal police departments and a convenience to the largely Chicano community. It is staffed by an office manager and two clerical personnel and is visited weekly by a deputy or the District Attorney himself. Citizen meetings are regularly scheduled.

Starting salaries in the office in 1977 are $13,000 for new law school graduates. Most are assigned first to the County Court. Deputies with two or more years of experience are transferred to the District Court, and eventually earn a salary of about $20,000. Deputies with supervisory responsibility earn salaries that range between $24,000 and $27,000.

Staff and attorney turnover has been very low. Generally, the few openings that do occur are when an experienced deputy leaves to enter private practice. Most of the present attorney staff has been with the District Attorney during his entire term of office. This is a new trend. Traditionally, the office experienced high turnover rates—young attorneys staying a year or a year-and-a-half before starting private practice. Since 1976 however, with salary increases, the saturation of the job market, and the changing perception of the role of the prosecutor as a career, the staff is getting older, and turnover at the entry level is lessening. Usually, it is the top felony deputy that receives the offer from the private firms.

The office has five investigators, two of whom were trained at the police academy. They concentrate on rape cases, bad checks, and fraud. One investigator is a Captain detailed from the Boulder Police Department and has extensive experience in investigations. As a unit, the investigators mainly support the intake and felony filing functions of the office.

There is also a Victim Witness Unit supported by one full-time paraprofessional and volunteers. Reflecting the spirit of the office, it has extended its aid deep into the community, by maintaining a network of "underground" contacts supplementing those formally identified in the *Directory of Boulder County Community Resources*. For example, unit members know what locksmith shop will fix an elderly person's locks broken in a burglary. They know how to use the University's clearinghouse to arrange for child care. They bake cookies for witnesses, allay a witness' fears, and even find counseling and therapy services as needed—all reflecting the sense of care and responsibility that exists in the Boulder community.

*Jurisdiction and Volume*

The jurisdiction of the office is both civil and criminal, although its primary focus is criminal. In the years prior to this District Attorney's election, felony filings were averaging about twelve hundred a year. Most of these were drug-related offenses. After Hunter was elected on a platform opposing the prosecution of lesser marijuana cases, the number of felony filings fell to about six hundred. Of these cases, twenty-three resulted in trials in 1977.

About 85 percent of the trials result in a finding of guilty. Of all the cases filed by information in the District Court, only 5 percent were not bound over by the judge presiding at preliminary hearing or were bound over on a lesser charge. This is mainly due to the fact that the County Court is the recipient of the more marginal cases, and the felonies taken in are expected to be reduced to misdemeanors.

The County Court has three divisions. It hears criminal and civil matters and has jurisdiction over misdemeanors and traffic cases. It may also conduct preliminary hearings for felonies. The County Court Division is manned by four deputies who are newly admitted to the bar. They tend to stay two to three years in this division. The Chief of the County Court division doubles also as a felony trial assistant. He carries a felony caseload of five to ten cases in addition to his supervisory duties over the lower court.

The docket in County Court varies from one with no criminal trials to one with twenty to thirty trials in addition to motions and preliminary hearings. For the norm however, a more typical calendar consists of twelve pretrials, twelve trials, and one or two motions. Usually the morning in court is focused on first appearances, summonses, and complaints, and the afternoon session focuses on first appearances for returnees on summonses or arrests.

County Court procedures leave time for negotiation. After the first appearance, where the defendant is formally charged, a pretrial conference is scheduled for 1 or 2 months later. At this conference, if the defendant is represented by counsel, plea negotiations proceed. About 50 percent of the cases are disposed of here by this type of activity. If a disposition is not reached, a hearing motion is set, usually about a month later. Motions are rarely used in this lower court and usually within 1 or 2 months after the pretrial or the motions setting, the case is set for trial. Most of the pleas are taken at the trial level. The last week of each month in two divisions is set aside for jury trials. Most of these are traffic cases where the defendant, because of his past record, has nothing to lose in hoping for an acquittal or criminal misdemeanors such as aggravated assault where there are bad feelings on both sides. Trials generally last 1 day; usually two to five are set each day.

Most of the convictions in County Court result in probation. If the defendant is given a jail sentence, he may apply for probation. There are few appeals from County Court to District Court, averaging fifteen to twenty-five a year. The County Court deputy handles his own appellate caseload.

The District Attorney must appeal if a statute has been declared unconstitutional. He may initiate an appeal on a dismissal. The Attorney General handles most of the postconviction appeals to either the Court of Appeals or the Supreme Court. The District Attorney may take some if he wishes, but this rarely happens. In fact in 1976, the office took none.

Juvenile crimes fall within the jurisdiction of the office. In 1976, juvenile arrests were made for 253 thefts, 34 burglaries, 27 drug-related offenses, 16 vandalism, 12 assaults, 6 rapes, and 2 robberies. The policy of the District Attorney and the Court is to keep juveniles in the community. Ninety percent of the cases are given 2 years probation with parental supervision. Some children are sent to detention homes or community-based facilities such as group homes. Two years after the juvenile has completed probation, his record is expunged. The filing policy is consistent with the adult charging decisions. The approach is defendant-oriented; the parents are present during the discussion, or, if not, an attorney is appointed. There have been no jury trials in the last 4.5 years. Juvenile filings are down. In 1976, 600 filings were made, this year, only about 400 were made.

**Process Steps**

*Intake*

The investigators are extensively involved in the intake process. Felony cases may be brought directly to the Charging Deputy, who, after a brief review, sends them to the investigators for the development of any additional information. Alternatively, felony cases may be submitted directly to the investigators. The transmission routes are not standardized. Thus, from 7:15 to 7:30 each morning an investigator calls all the courts to get the jail list for onsite arrests and for those felonies that are in custody because of warrants. The Boulder Police Department may send over a complaint field report by a courier, but these do not generally have criminal histories attached. If the complaint field report is not sent over, the investigator calls the detective for the information and collects it from his oral report. A criminal history record check is made from the Sheriff's computer and the case reports compiled.

If the investigators cannot complete the reports in time for the 24-hour bond hearing, they complete a District Attorneys Defendant Information (DADI) form. This form goes to the intake deputy with the investigator's recommendation for a charge and includes any other relevant comments. The investigator may sit in on the charging conference, but this is not routine. Most often, they are unaware of the ultimate charge on the case or its subsequent disposition.

In addition to handling the intake, investigators process the citizen complaints that are referred from the police departments or result from walk-ins. If they recommend that criminal charges be filed, the information and recommendation is forwarded to the intake deputy. The investigators also have their own caseload, which consists primarily of those cases that are complicated, such as embezzlements, or sensitive, such as police brutality.

The actual charging decision is made at the screening and charging conference. Most cases are reviewed at the conference on the day after the arrest. State law requires that charges be filed with the court within 72 hours; however, the District Court for Boulder County made this requirement even more restrictive, ruling that charges must be filed within 24 hours. Extensions to the filing deadline may be obtained if the defense counsel assigned to the case will waive the requirement. If it is to their advantage so that mitigating facts or exculpatory evidence can be gathered prior to the conference, they will waive.

The daily screening and charging conference is attended by all members of the prosecutor's staff who are not scheduled in court at the time of the meeting. It is open to police officers or representatives from the various police forces who are involved in the case—generally there is representation from at least the two larger forces in the County, the Sheriff's department and the Boulder Police. Arresting officers may be present to discuss a specific case, or the department may send a single representative to handle all cases. All defense counsel are invited to attend, but, in practice, only the representatives of the Public Defender's office appear. At times a representative of other agencies interested in a case, especially the Community Corrections, which operates pretrial diversion programs, will also attend.

For obvious reasons of confidentiality, defense counsel only sit in on those portions of the conference that directly affect his or her client. When defense counsel is present to add input on his client's case, however, there is little inhibition of the general discussion. Although Colorado law contains no specific provisions for this type of case disclosure the District Attorney has adopted an office policy of plenary discovery of the state's case to the defense attorney at this point. The policy is based on the belief that full disclosure lays a solid ground for gathering all information about a case so that a fair and just disposition can be reached as soon as possible. Defense counsel are asked to participate because the state wants to be aware of any mitigating circumstances that might exist that would justify the use of alternative forms of adjudication. Although the public defender can act as a strong advocate for his client at this point in obtaining a reduction in the charge, or by informing the state of the reasons that he feels diversion would be appropriate, this input is weighed against the opinions of law enforcement officials, before the final decision is made. Where there is no ample justification for reduction, or where the justification seems unsupported by fact, there will be no reduction, and the state elects to proceed with formal adjudication on the charges.

Each morning, approximately five to ten cases are discussed and reviewed. The presentation of the facts is made initially and informally by the arresting police agency. Then, a long serious discussion follows. Although the final charging decision for every case rests with the District Attorney himself, the discussion and subsequent decision-making process tends more to reflect a consensus of the persons who are present at the meeting. At times radically different opinions are held about the type of disposition warranted or about the question of going forward with a case. Even though they are still in an investigative stage and not yet ready for prosecution, some cases are brought forward for discussion with the police at these meetings. For example, the District Attorney and the police may discuss a case where there is ongoing investigation of a criminal suspect—involved with gambling or sale of narcotics—to evaluate the strength of the evidence at the current state of the investigation. The possibility of proceeding with the evidence available, the types of charges that could be brought, and the likelihood of successful prosecution are all subjected to review. The status of the whole case is discussed, and strategies that would be most effective in continuing the investigation if the present amount of evidence is insufficient or unconvincing are proper subjects at this conference.

Unlike many other states, the prosecutor does not have total discretion in refusing to file a case. Colorado has enacted a statute that has been incorporated in the criminal code, allowing a judge to compel the prosecutor to go forward on a case. If the judge receives an affadavit from a citizen alleging the commission of a crime, and alleging as well that the prosecutor has been unjustified in refusing to bring criminal charges against the perpetrator, the judge can require the District Attorney to appear before him to explain his refusal. If, in the judge's estimation, the refusal was unwarranted, he may order the prosecutor to file an information in the case or may appoint a special prosecutor to do so.

*Accusatory*

First appearance occurs in the County Court within 24 hours of arrest unless the right to that appearance has been waived by defense counsel. In many cases the defendant is either indigent or has not yet obtained counsel, in which case the office proceeds within the limits of the 24-hour court rule. At first appearance the charge is read to the defendant, and the court inquires about the defendant's financial status and his need for counsel. The defendant's constitutional rights are explained to him.

Formal charges may be filed with either the County Court or the District Court; in the former the instrument used is called a "felony criminal complaint," and in the latter it is a bill of information. Felonies sent to County Court for filing are generally considered to be of lesser quality than those filed in District Court, and plea negotiations or reductions in charges are expected. For those filed in the District Court, a formal arraignment is held usually within a few days after the first appearance. At that time, the formal complaint on which the prosecution will proceed is read, and a date is set for preliminary hearing.

At the District Court level, preliminary hearings by statute and rule must held within 30 days. They usually occur within a week or two after arraignment. If the defendant is on bail, the time limit is usually waived if the defense is negotiating for a reduction in the charge or for diversion. During this interim period, the defendant can be presented as surrounded by supports, friends, relatives, treatment programs, employment counseling and so forth—all designed to convince the District Attorney that the defendant is a good diversion candidate.

Preliminary hearings are rarely waived. If they are it is because the defense counsel had negotiated a disposition and wants the case settled quickly or because the crime is a sensitive one such as rape. Normally, however, preliminary hearings are conducted under tightly controlled time limitations—in a single-judge court this is essential. The state produces its witnesses and presents the key elements of its case; the defense is present and may explain its defense but cross-examination of the state's witnesses is rare. The victim is generally brought forward because the District Attorney feels that the state has an "obligation to the aggrieved" to show him that the system responds to his complaints. Preliminary hearings for burglaries take about 30 minutes; for rape, hours; and for murder, a day or less.

If the judge at preliminary hearing rules that there is insufficient cause to bind the case over for trial, the case is dismissed unless the prosecutor feels that there has been an injustice, at which time he can elect to present the case to the grand jury and seek to obtain an indictment.

Colorado has a grand jury system, although it is not used as the primary accusatory vehicle. In Boulder, it meets eight to ten times a year, usually one evening a week from 7-11 P.M. During the last term, in 1977, for example, it examined a police shooting, a complicated robbery that involved providing immunity, and it initiated a probe of a county commissioner.

If the case is bound over, the court determines whether the defense intends to file motions. In two-thirds of the cases, motions hearings are set. This provides the defense counsel with about a two-week delay, during which time he continues to negotiate with the deputy for a satisfactory disposition. The remaining third are immediately set for trial.

### Trials to Disposition

Once the arraignment is held, the 6-months rule goes into affect. A trial date must be set within this time period. Due to the small felony caseload, the low number of serious or violent offenses in Boulder, there are very few criminal trials, although that number has been increasing and a more crowded trial docket may result in the future. For the present, there are still few enough cases so that all trials can be heard by a single judge. In 1977, twenty-three trials were conducted.

Presently, the trial date is set within 60-90 days after the preliminary hearing. Motions are set 14 to 21 days prior to the trial date. In a single-judge court, most of the technical and procedural matters are settled informally and reflect the preferences of the judge. As the only judge conducting trials, his influence on the way in which the prosecution and defense conduct the case is substantial. Unlike courts with many judges, where the power of the judiciary becomes diffused, here the locus is singular and constant. Thus the relationships that have developed are dispositional in nature, and although differences of opinions may occur naturally in the course of a case they are resolved informally and usually outside of the courtroom before being formalized through the court process. The mutual respect for the duties and obligations of each office is manifested by the discussions, advice, and perspectives offered by the many actors in the process. Clearly in the single-judge court, the protocols and rules vary substantially from those operating in large urban courts. The extensive examination of the cases with respect, first, to the defendant's situation, then, to the law is supported by the very existence of this court situation and the low caseload.

*Postconviction*

Since the interactions with the court are extensive and informal and the policy of the District Attorney is to dispose of a defendant rather than a case, it is not surprising to find the office involved in postconviction activities. They range from sentence recommendations to expungements and include a host of considerations, all of which are defendant-oriented.

Operating within a one-man court situation, the District Attorney is encouraged by the dispositional nature of the proceedings to make sentence recommendations. The office does not sentence bargain as matter of policy; however, in certain cases it will either recommend probation or stand mute. There are, of course, few defendants sentenced to prison. the three to five probation officers each carry caseloads of 100 to 150, with most cases running 2 years at the maximum and averaging 1 year. Given the volume of crime in this jurisdiction, this is quite a caseload. In 1977 Colorado formalized the expungement process, modelling the law after the practice followed in Boulder. Under the law, expungement of a defendant's record is allowed 7 years after release from probation or jail for a felony offense and 5 years after a misdemeanor. Before 1977, the Boulder District Attorney, relying on Colorado case law, had instituted a vigorous program of initiating expungements. Under his program a defendant receiving a deferred sentence or probation could ask for expungement. All the paper work, including the stipulation for expungement, was prepared and executed by the District Attorney's office. Thereafter the defendant signed the stipulation and an appropriate court order was entered. The District Attorney's office also developed instructions for other agencies as to the processing of expungements. These instructions were sent to the local police departments, sheriff's office, and the Colorado Criminal History computer service, and the FBI. It is interesting to note that most of the counties in the state had never handled expungements prior to the passage of the state law. Yet in 1976, the office in Boulder processed two hundred expungements, and over a 4-year period had handled four hundred. The majority of the expungements were for misdemeanors; only 5 percent were felonies.

A motion to expunge is optional. As a result of the office's activity in this area, rules and guidelines also emerged. Expungements are not supported if there is a pattern of crimes in the history of the defendant or if the evidence strongly indicates that the defendant committed the crime. With these as a guide, each case is reviewed individually. The office feels that expungements should be requested by an individual for a specific purpose.

The office has little activity in the parole and pardon aspects of the postconviction process. There is a state board of parole appointed by the Governor. But the office has had little luck in obtaining a list of parole applications. At the time of this study, they were attempting to have such a list sent to the Colorado District Attorneys Association. They have been even more disappointed in the area of pardons, since this activity is under the Governor's authority, and information about who applied for pardons and who were granted them is not available.

Finally, in the area of appeals, the Attorney General has the general responsibility to handle all appeals. An individual prosecutor's office may take the case if they desire, but this is infrequent. However, the District Attorney must appeal if a statute is found unconstitutional.

**Special Programs**

The reach of this prosecutor's office beyond the narrowly defined limits of trial dispositions into the postconviction area is infrequently observed throughout the United States. However, it is entirely consistent with the policy stance of the prosecutor and extends his power into areas beyond the traditional. Another extension of the prosecutor's policy and an indication of the responsiveness of the community to this policy is the prosecutor's initiation of a Community Dialogue Program. The District Attorney meets weekly with a group of eight to twelve citizens who are somewhat randomly selected to reflect different politics, education, and economic status. The purpose of these meetings is to discuss the types of cases that are coming in for prosecution and to have a dialogue with the citizens about what the community wants to do for these defendants or what it wishes it could do. The types of cases discussed include a wide range of topics—from possession of marijuana and drunken drivers to burglaries. In addition to discussing crime, other grievances emerge that sometimes moves the office into areas of peripheral interest to them but of major interest to the community. For example, a survey of medical fees was conducted based on the grievances of the community.

The program over the past 3 years has permitted the District Attorney to meet with approximately five thousand people. A good 15 to 20 percent of the persons selected are community leaders. Others are selected from groups lists that include union groups, teachers, members of the League of Women Voters, student groups, and others who can speak for the community and engage in dialogue.

## Management Controls and Communication

The small size of the Boulder County operation makes management control extremely simple; there need not be much elaboration on so obvious a point. The entire staff occupies a single suite of offices, which is small enough to put all members of the staff within a few steps of one another and to permit constant and daily contact with each other (the exception to this is the Longmont Branch office, but, as has been mentioned, there are no decision makers assigned to that office, only persons with limited clerical responsibilities). Lines of authority are very informal and the four executives in the office, the District Attorney, his First Assistant, the Chief of the District Court Division, and the Charging Deputy, are continuously accessible to anyone in the office. In fact, the entire staff meets on a daily basis during the Staffing and Charging Conference, and even the most junior member of the professional staff has an opportunity to observe the office's primary decision-making process firsthand. Even better, he or she has an opportunity to be a part of that process.

Assignment of duties to personnel is informal. There is a certain amount of separation of administrative from operational duties, but it is minimal in comparison to the other offices studied. Record keeping is manual. No elaborate or complex method of case tracking exists; indeed, there is no need for such.

All staff are aware of the general policy directions of the prosecutor. As a result deviations from this policy are rigidly controlled. If the District

Attorney wants to make an exception, it is duly noted on the case jacket at the time of the screening conference. There are few enough cases in the system and enough contact by the staff that almost everyone can be aware of all the business in the office at any time.

The style and organization of the office is well-suited to the caseload demands of the jurisdiction. Still, there are indications that this style and policy may soon have to be modified as the caseload increases. The recent boom in cases that are going to trial makes it less and less possible for all cases to be considered and evaluated by the entire staff. The more cases that go to court, the less possible it becomes for all members of the staff to attend the daily staffing and screening conferences. Increases in workload at the trial level will inevitably stretch the lines of communication and strain this present method for transferring policy.

There have also been some marginal side effects on office management practices. Since the beginning of the year there has been more difficulty in case tracking through all the preliminary stages, and the office has begun to investigate the possibility of obtaining a minicomputer to help keep track of scheduling problems. These scheduling problems may also occur in the District Court Division as the presiding judge begins to ship some of his work to other judges, especially responsibility for preliminary hearings.

Whether the defendant-oriented policy can be sustained with growth is a question of more than passing interest. The District Attorney could envision its implementation in large urban areas only if the charging decisions were delegated down to small organizational units. Even then his hesitancy in predicting its success under these circumstances was illuminating. It may be that this approach to prosecution in pure form can only be found in the smaller towns of the United States and that to observe it in the larger jurisdictions, one has to focus on its institutionalized form—diversion.

Of immense value is the scope of prosecutorial influence that has 'een revealed in the study of this jurisdiction. The community activities, the community's resources, and the use of the postconviction area to continue to reinforce the prosecution process are significant. Clearly the extension and the power of prosecutorial policy to influence the quality of justice are given dimension and scope in Boulder.

**Part IV
The Search for Identity:
Issues and Findings**

# 11

# The Search for Identity: Issues and Findings

## Origins and Development of the American Prosecutor

Despite the lack of knowledge and sometime confusion surrounding the origin of the prosecutor and the prosecutive function in our system of criminal justice, the prosecutor is actually a rational entity performing a totally rational function. He is, in fact, logically derived and historically consistent.

His origins may be traced to a number of different cultures as well as a variety of governmental structures and criminal justice systems. These disparate influences were combined into a unique American form by the geography of the New World, the character of its inhabitants, and the triumph of local governmental autonomy. Roots developed in colonial America have given sustenance over the past 300 years to the form and function of prosecution as it is known today.

The structure of our present criminal justice system was drawn from several long-established European models, primarily the English, Spanish, French, and Dutch. Yet none of these systems of justice could remain intact when transferred to a country that was typified by its vastness and isolation. European forms had been based on a centralized government, a concept ill-suited to the American wilderness. Hybrid systems soon developed, because localism and the desire for autonomy not only were powerful goals for the early settlers, they were also goals both practical and attainable. After the Revolution, local authority dominated the federal prerogative, and most communities never released their grip on the local criminal justice system despite attempts at strengthening control by the states or federal agencies. The issue still is very much alive 200 years later.

In those early days of the formation of the criminal justice system, the prosecutor was not an important figure. In fact, when defined in his own terms as a locally elected official, he was barely recognizable after the Revolution. His role was local, but much of his prosecuting function was performed by the elected sheriff and coroner. Prosecuting crimes was then considered a part of the law enforcement activities in a community. A grand jury was simply a group of citizens whose primary purposes were to control excesses in law enforcement and to advise the community on the standards that it expected to be maintained. The few written references to the prosecutor in the period after the Revolution and the signing of the Constitution indicate that he was only a minor local court functionary.

It was not until the 1800s and the era of Jacksonian democracy, when a major expansion of the franchise occurred and the number of locally elected offices increased, that the prosecutor began to move toward a position of independent and substantial power. Concomitantly, a movement defining the police role as an executive function, subject to the control of the locally elected officials, provided the opportunity for the transfer of most actual prosecutorial powers and activities from the police to the prosecutor. As Jacksonian democracy swept the country in the 1830s, the prosecutor rode the coat-tails of the judges to elective status. Even today, it is only in those states where judges never gained elective status that the prosecutor is still an appointed official. By the onset of the Civil War, the prosecutor was complete; he was local, elected, and an official.

Officialdom and autonomy came gradually. The doctrine of unreviewable discetionary power imbued in the prosecutor developed as a parallel to judicial power, and the courts were the prime movers and supporters of this access to authority. Just as the separation of the police function from prosecution transferred power to the prosecutor, the court, when it lost its minor functionary through the elective process, furthered the prosecutor's separation and growth by upholding the unreviewability of his discretionary powers. The early American goals of separation of powers and an adversary system of justice providing checks and balances within a local democracy were supported by these transfers of power. And the separation between the three components—police, prosecutor, and courts—continues today as society becomes more complex and the procedures surrounding criminal prosecutions requires greater specialization and professionalization.

Thus the prosecutor and the prosecutive function developed in a manner consistent with the development of our nation. As a result, the prosecutor today is uniquely American and uniquely derived. He has no exact counterpart anywhere in the world. Straddling many arenas, the political, legislative, executive, and judicial, he often projects a confused image, creating controversy that stubbornly defies easy solution or clarification. The dispute revolves primarily around his locally elected status and his discretionary power.

The control and accountability won by early Americans over their local jurisdictions and the resultant responsibility for locally implementing state laws are often at variance with the goal of an equitable distribution of prosecution services and/or financial support throughout a state. Other frequent disputes center on consistency in applying state laws at the local level; on control and removal procedures other than through the elective process; and on the means for standardization, or perhaps more importantly, the opportunity for comparative evaluations. Yet another dimension is added to the issues of consistency and standardization by the discretionary power embodied in the prosecutor, which, if not present, would permit simpler solutions.

At the heart of discussions on these issues is the dilemma of what to do with a product of our democracy that was created and empowered to reflect local norms and values so that it could be held accountable by the local jurisdiction but is now often being criticized for using these very powers in exercising its duties. Arguments for some sort of statewide support and control are powerful. They probably will increase in intensity as the larger urban areas, drained of their own financial resources, begin petitioning the state for help. Smaller, more rural areas with insufficient tax bases to support a proper level of prosecution may soon join them. Daniel Skoler has produced an excellent discussion of these issues that need not be duplicated here.[1] However, if the issues of control, supervision, coordination, or administration of the delivery of prosecution services on a state level are addressed, the political reality and impact of the locally elected prosecutor, the existence of variations in community standards and values, and the inherent discretionary power of the office must be considered. Starting from this base, it then appears that consideration should first be given to developing minimums, baselines, ranges, and acceptable levels of performance, so that the tradition of local autonomy and control can continue to coexist within a wider (state) universe.

There is an obvious and critical need to develop an ability to compare performance in criminal justice, a need that is being increasingly recognized by the public through media coverage of the famous, infamous, and ordinary aspects of the criminal justice system. As a result of this extension of public knowledge and sensitivity, one can expect to see a more informed voter demanding more consistency in the application of justice but not relinquishing its control over the prosecutor through local elections.

As one traces the development and growth of the prosecutor over 300 years, it seems clear that in our modern, sophisticated, and increasingly communicative democracy, there is a need for comparative accountability that takes into consideration local variations while striving for consistency and uniformity in implementing the laws of the state. It is also apparent that the economic supports for prosecution need readjustment. With disparities among local jurisdictional tax bases affecting the delivery of prosecution services, state supplements to establish at least a minimally adequate base of support become essential. If legal and judicial procedures continue to multiply both in number and in complexity, and if the justice system becomes even more institutionalized and formal, one can expect the prosecutive function to be colored by the same events.

**Population and Prosecution**

Although the prosecutor sprang from the rich soil of diverse cultural experiences to a position of great power and influence, he projects a single stereotype—that of the urban prosecutor battling big city crime with unfettered discretionary power. In reality most prosecutors operate in rural or small-town environments that are relatively crimefree. Much of a prosecutor's exercise of power is constrained by an external environment over which he has little control but to which he must respond, adapt, and, sometimes in the face of overwhelming odds, perform his duties. Consideration must be given to these external environmental factors and their special effects on prosecution if the results of research and study are to avoid parochialism or produce conclusions applicable to only certain parts of the prosecution process. Attempts to improve the system through constructive and reformed change may fail if our ability to compare and evaluate performance is so impaired. As a result, it is crucial that the function of prosecution be examined within the constraints of an external environment.

Preliminary research has shown that within this environment the most significant factor affecting the prosecutive process is the population characteristics of the jurisdiction represented. Of the approximately 3,000 local prosecutors, three-fourths work in small offices staffed with fewer than four assistants and almost 40 percent operate alone. Prosecution in America takes place predominantly in small towns or rural areas. With few crimes to process in these communities, prosecutors characteristically either have a private practice in addition to their public duties or they handle civil matters for the local governing body. Numbers not withstanding, since crime is an urban phenomenon, it is not surprising to see the stereotype emerge of the urban, big-city prosecutor.

Increasing size leads to increasing crime. Thus the size of a jurisdiction presents a relatively reliable indicator of the volume of work handled by the prosecutor's office. Additionally, the demographic characteristics of the jurisdiction indicate the type of work being forwarded to the prosecutor's office; a community peopled by a lower socioeconomic class can usually be expected to produce more armed robberies and crimes of personal violence than can affluent communities where property crimes, such as burglaries, are more typical. But it is the density of the population that creates special workload effects. The urban ghetto mixes poverty, unemployment, drugs, and robberies into an unending flow of defendants charged with an array of crimes through overcrowded courts. Rural communities on the other hand, cope with the unceasing "driving under the influence" and simple property crimes but rarely see violence or armed robbery. The suburban communities, an aftermath of World War II, have now come of age presenting yet another population group, somewhere between the two extremes and creating a relatively new phenomenon, the suburban prosecutor. Flexible because he developed in a growth environment that produced relatively homogeneous communities, the suburban prosecutor responds to a fixed crime pattern and serves as an accurate barometer of community values and standards.

What this means is that the effect of population size and demographic characteristics is so powerful that it raises separate and distinct issues for these different groups of prosecutors. These issues are so different that they must be acknowledged if the role of the prosecutor is to be examined or if system standards are to be developed.

The rural prosecutor with a low caseload, part-time criminal prosecution duties (partially compensated, supplemented by civil responsibilities, or both) representing a jurisdiction with a limited tax base faces two basic issues: (1) potential conflict of interest and (2) lack of system flexibility. The first is a constant fear that pervades all parts of the legal profession feeding off the uncertainty involved in the changing status of a case from civil to criminal or to the possibility of criminal corruption of the jurisdiction's governing officers whom the prosecutor advises. An unexpected change of a divorce matter into criminal assault or the investigation of a commissioner's handling of contracts present conflict-of-interest issues that are rarely known to larger jurisdictions.

Where one-man offices exist (and almost 40 percent of prosecutor's offices are in this category) the personal health and availability of the prosecutor becomes a major factor in the functioning of the criminal justice system. Unexpected illnesses or emergencies that preclude his participation in a criminal proceeding demonstrate the system's inflexibility and show how prone to damage it is. Even in the smaller offices with a few assistants, the justice system cannot tolerate complicated crimes, exceptional cases, or lengthy investigations. Under these circumstances, there exists an obvious need for access to relief.

The urban prosecutor, on the other hand, rarely has to cope with these problematic issues. His commitment to prosecution is full-time, and, with some exceptions, civil and criminal responsibilities are generally separated. He has numerous resources to shift to pressure points as emergencies arise. Yet it is these very resources that are of primary concern. The issues confronting the prosecutor in large offices are size related. They focus on reducing the workload, allocating resources, and processing cases uniformly.

Since most of the large offices face ever-increasing workoads without proportional increases in funding levels, a major concern is the development and use of various methods to reduce caseloads. This is immediately apparent in the recent emphasis on programs devoted to screening, diversion, and other alternatives to adjudication, as well as the use of such strategies as plea bargaining, discovery, and deferred prosecution. One suspects that these may be embraced more for their efficacy in reducing workload than for their effectiveness as proper dispositions.

In a large office, organization and the allocation of resources to various parts of the prosecutive process are crucial issues. Yet few prosecutors have had management and organization training. The concept that sound management is a necessity for high-quality performance has received little emphasis in the past among most attorneys. Only recently has the court administrator analogue found its way into prosecution. But even here, little attention has been given to promoting a systematic inquiry into which organizational model is most suited for a given court structure, police intake procedure, or prosecutorial policy. Tradition reigns.

The final and perhaps most important issue to face the urban prosecutor is that of uniformity and consistency in decision making. As authority to make decisions about the processing and disposition of cases is delegated farther and farther away from the elected prosecutor, the probability of inconsistencies within an office increases. Discretionary justice under these noncontrolled situations may indeed produce inequitable justice. Yet the collegial nature of the organization assumes that each assistant is capable of making a decision that is uniform and consistent with that of the prosecutor and the other assistants. This may well be the most important issue facing a urban prosecutor, but it is usually not recognized as such. When it is, one soon finds that tools and techniques for supporting consistency and uniformity are not readily available.

The suburban prosecutor is our newest product, displacing the rural prosecutor with the development of suburbia and moving, often quickly, to the brink of being an urban prosecutor. The suburban prosecutor has grown up in a changing environment, coped with that change, and, as a result, tends to be more flexible than his brothers. The issues facing the suburban prosecutor obviously are change related; resulting from increasing land development, population growth, and a concomitant increasing tax base. What distinguishes the suburban prosecutor today from his urban counterpart is the homogeneity of suburbia and its ample resources. This produces a fertile environment for experimentation and evaluation within a relatively controlled environment. The suburban prosecutor, as a result, presently offers a rare opportunity to test and evaluate the effect of changes in the criminal justice system.

Living in a favorable environment supportive of modern technology, the suburban prosecutors should emerge as the leaders in the prosecution world. Unencumbered by tradition, they view the role of the prosecutor with new eyes, capable of placing it in more modern perspective and translating their observations into new forms and structures for prosecution.

## The Effect of Defense Systems on Prosecution

In a long series of cases, starting with *Powell* v. *Alabama*[2] in 1932 and culminating with *Argersinger* v. *Hamlin*[3] in 1972, the U.S. Supreme Court extended the defendant's right to counsel from a narrow federal court requirement to practically all state and local misdemeanor prosecutions. While the Court defined the rights of the accused, rich or poor, to representation by counsel at trial, it also considered the various processing steps in the criminal justice system and made decisions that specified these same rights at "critical stages" of the criminal process. The right to counsel was guaranteed at police investigations, police questioning, postindictment police line-ups, preliminary hearings, on appeal, and at probation revocation proceedings.

These holdings did not, however, immediately or necessarily assure that all defendants would receive aggressive or even adequate, defense representation or even that a model defense delivery system could be designed to achieve these goals. What they did assure was the prosecutor's attendance or involvement at a number of critical stages that previously were ignored. They also resulted in the development of more complex procedures at these processing steps. By extending the right to counsel over such a wide segment of the justice system, the U.S. Supreme Court became a major force in placing bounds on the prosecutive function. Not only did these court rulings add to the workload of the prosecutor and define procedural limits for each stage, but, over the years, they slowly opened up the prosecutive function to public scrutiny as more and more of the court hearings were placed on record.

Although the effects of the Supreme Court rulings on the prosecutor are relatively clear-cut, the same cannot be said for the effects of defense systems created largely by these same rulings. In this largely unexplored area, insights may be derived from the few case studies available. But the formal systematic studies of the defense-prosecution interactions and their effects have yet to be produced. The examination undertaken here has done little more than identify some of the key areas for investigation and highlight what some of the issues may be. Conceptually, the prosecution-defense interaction and its effect on the prosecutor should be examined from the following perspectives: (1) the type of defense delivery system utilized and its organizational implications for prosecution; (2) the quality and characteristics of the defense counsel; (3) the size of the pool normally available for criminal defense work; and (4) the prosecutor's perception of his role.

Before starting such an examination, one must first recognize that there are relatively few criminal defense lawyers providing indigent defense services. In 1966, out of 313,000 lawyers licensed nationally, only about 2,500-5,000 could be considered criminal lawyers. Yet 2,750 counties in the United States were appointing lawyers from the private bar to provide these services. Obviously, with a shortage of criminal lawyers, the delivery of defense services assumes critical importance. However, to this day, no ideal system has been identified; the wide diversity that exists in operational and structural types substantiates this conclusion as each jurisdiction seeks its own solution.

The two basic organizational forms in common use are the defender organization and the assigned counsel system. These, coupled with the privately retained counsel system handle, in various combinations, the criminal caseload in a jurisdiction. Disregarding funding sources and the degree of autonomy permitted in each system, the public defender organization has, like its counterpart the prosecutor's office, a single mission—to provide defense services to indigents within the jurisdiction. Operating primarily in those urban areas that can economically support such formal organizations, they are few in number (only 650 in 1974) but handle the largest proportion of the criminal caseload.

The assigned counsel system can be found more frequently in the less populated areas of the country: counsel appointed by the trial court from a list of all private lawyers, those with criminal case experience, those expressing interest in handling these cases (usually the younger, less experienced attorney), or other combinations. The available talent and the selection procedures used obviously affect the type of defense representation and raises serious questions about quality, adequacy, and control. Even though these are significant issues for the defense sector, their ultimate effect on the prosecutor can be seen in two ways. First from an organizational view, the existence of a defender organization with policy, structure, and procedures presents a known form to the prosecutor. There is a chief, who can centralize direction and control, work that can be processed in a routine and ongoing fashion, and procedures between the two agencies that can be established and regulated. From an organizational perspective, it appears easier for the prosecutor to deal with a public defender organization than the individuals representing assigned counsel or privately retained. The latter, lacking such an organizational structure, presents an amorphous form if issues of policy, control, and authority need resolution.

Theoretically this may be a valid observation, but its validity is denigrated by the quality and characteristics of the defense bar that may operate independent of the power of the formal organization. It has been observed in some jurisdictions using both a public defender organization and privately retained counsel that a distinction can be made between the youthful and relatively inexperienced public defender's staff and the more experienced and competent private criminal defense bar. Conversely, the qualifications of the privately retained, "lawyer-regulars" who eke a miserable existence from the corridors of the courthouse have been too often exposed and condemned to be ignored as a reality. Thus, unless the quality and the experience in the defense systems are known, it is almost impossible to predict a system effect on prosecution. One can only conclude that the prosecutor will adapt and adjust to whatever quality is offered. Although the formal organization may produce benefits to prosecution by its very existence, the quality of the defense staff shapes the extent of these benefits.

Also characteristic of the defense delivery system is its economics. In the assigned counsel and privately retained counsel forms, and to a lesser extent in the defender organization, the amount of money available is restricted either by appropriation in the latter case or by compensation rates imposed by the state or the court. This has produced a priority dispositional ladder that is characterized by the time involved and the cost incurred. The ranking preferred by most counsel is in order of economic desirability: (1) dropping the charge or dismissal early in the process; (2) alternative dispositions to adjudication, for example, diversion to treatment programs; (3) plea bargains; (4) acquittal; and (5) reversals on appeal.

The economic motivations of the defense counsel systems must be considered in understanding the prosecutorial response to caseload. The incentives for early disposition are strong in all systems and reinforced where the defense systems are court assigned or privately retained. One would expect to find policies and practices that support such aims prevalent under these circumstances. The public defender, although sensitive to this dispositional ranking, views it more as a measure of efficiency and program effectiveness than cost. The cutting edge between the two basic forms of defense systems is that the defender organization can afford to put up a vigorous defense challenge, the court-appointed attorney cannot.

The size of the criminal defense bar in a local jurisdiction is important not from a numerical sense but from its ability to be known by the prosecutor. Regardless of type of system used, it is important to determine the extent to which defense counsel are known to the prosecutor. With knowledge comes a predictive ability and a reduction of uncertainty. This means that if a small number of criminal lawyers regularly handle defense work, the prosecutor becomes familiar with their defense style and tactics, thus making his prosecutorial strategy more predetermined and permitting him more reliability in predicting the outcome of the case. As Eisenstein and Jacob pointed out, the certainty and predictability associated with the courtroom workgroup regulars had a strong effect on selecting the dispositional process for case resolution rather than the adversary process.[4] Extending this implication to the degree to which the defense attorneys are known to the prosecutor results in an assumption that the prosecutor prefers to work with regularly assigned defense counsel because the dispositional uncertainty attached to each case is minimized and the prosecution strategy selected is based in part on the ability to predict defense tactics. Where uncertainty exists, it seems reasonable that the adversary position is more logically the one selected.

Finally, although the type and characteristics of the defense system clearly affect the prosecutor, the reverse is also true. The prosecutor's perception of his role and his policy determines the extent to which the dispositional process is carried out, as well as the efficiencies and effectiveness of procedures. The professional prosecutor, self-assured, confident of his role, with a clearly defined policy should be more capable of organizing around and adapting to the defense characteristics than the prosecutor with little self-perception of his changing role. To the extent that the overall objectives of the prosecutor meet those of the defense sector, good relations between the two systems should exist. Where conflicting value systems exist, for example, attitudes toward drug possession, rehabilitation versus punishment, and so forth, one can expect to find less communication and cooperation.

## Intake

The intake process illustrates the gate-keeping function of the prosecutor. Optimally, an efficient and effective intake process is one in which all relevant information reaches the prosecutor as quickly as possible after an arrest or criminal event. In this way, all the facts of the case can be reviewed and analyzed prior to a charging decision or the initiation of any court proceeding. The culmination of this review process is the charging decision, which represents the first implementation of prosecutorial policy. The quality of the decisions that are made here sets the course for justice in a community; consequently, there is a need for timely, accurate, and complete information.

Little systematic attention has been given to the intake process in studies of prosecution, because of the overwhelming power of its end point, the charging decision. Separating the charging decision (which legitimately falls under prosecutorial control) from the remainder of the intake process (over which the prosecutor has limited control) reveals other noteworthy issues and findings. It lays bare the largest part of the interaction between police and prosecutor, clarifies certain confusions that abound in the definitions of each agency's responsibilities, and presents some, as yet, untested assumptions. The area is worthy of further study and examination, since the prosecutor's ability to prosecute successfully and with a quality performance is directly dependent on the groundwork laid by police.

From our examination of how the intake procedures affect the prosecutor, two major areas of importance have been identified. The first concerns the amount of information made available to the prosecutor; the second concerns the timing of the charging decision. Both of these areas point to the symbiotic relationships existing among police, prosecutors, and courts and demonstrate the need for careful planning in these areas of interaction, taking into account the abilities and policies of the agencies.

To study the more observable effects of police case preparation one must consider the quality of police reporting. Additionally, one can also assume that the more information a prosecutor receives, the higher will be the quality of his charging decision. Thus the effect of various routes taken by the police in transmitting the case to the prosecutor may be postulated independent of the quality. Where the arresting police officer brings the case directly to the prosecutor, one can expect only minimal facts about the offense and circumstances of the arrest. Often the information is hastily collected, unverified, and generally incomplete, particularly with respect to the criminal history of the accused.

In contrast, a case that has been turned over to the detective force for preparation prior to prosecutorial review should be more valuable. The contents may include not only the basic facts but supplemental witness testimony, depositions, a listing of the physical evidence, a Miranda warning, search warrants, and other documents necessary to prosecution.

Differences in the type of case preparation point up not only the value of continuous police training in preparing reports and gathering evidence but also the need to develop a standard for police performance that includes their ability to meet a prosecutor's informational needs. To the extent that the law enforcement agencies recognize the ongoing needs of the system after an arrest, the chances of the prosecutor's receiving well-prepared cases at intake are proportionately increased. This is especially critical in the smaller jurisdictions, where the training of law enforcement officers is not subsidized as much as in urban areas, and detective forces are nonexistent. It is in these jurisdictions that the maintenance of a continuing dialogue between the prosecutor and police is most pressing.

To counteract deficiencies in police work, some prosecutors place inordinate reliance on their own investigators. Investigators have been used variously to substitute for untrained or ineffectual police, to supplement police reporting by performing essentially detective functions, and to assist in case preparation for trial. Ideally, the last of these is the logical role for a prosecutor's investigators—namely, the development of the evidentiary strength of a case for disposition by trial. Use of investigators in lieu of appropriate police activity signals the existence of some deficiency in the intake process.

Another significant factor in this phase of prosecution is the amount of time that elapses between arrest and the charging decision. In most jurisdictions, there exists some form of court mandate that orders the defendant to be brought before a court "without undue delay," a phrase widely interpreted to mean within a 24-hour period. At this hearing the defendant is notified of the police charges and his rights, including the right to remain silent, the right to be represented by counsel, the right to a preliminary hearing, and the possibility of release on bail. The confusion that exists between the necessity for a speedy first appearance and the filing of a prosecutor's charge produces a quiet culprit impeding the effectiveness of the intake process. The quick timing requirements for a first appearance need not be the same as those for the prosecutor's charging decision. In jurisdictions where the two events are separated by time, the defendant's rights are accorded him "without undue delay," and the prosecutor still has the opportunity to make well-informed and responsible decisions. The need to "fix mistakes" later in court is diminished. If such a distinction is made between the first appearance and the probable cause hearing, it will separate the requirement for immediately reviewing a justification for restricting a person's liberty from the prosecutor's charging decision.

Of all the prosecutorial stages, the intake process is the one that should be conducted deliberately within realistic time limits. Even though, extensive case preparation may create delay and by separating the first appearance from the filing of the accusatory instrument may increase the time lapse between these two steps, the result favors a more responsible charging decision. If the prosecutor is to assume a more responsible attitude toward charging, it has to be with the recognition that, as the first prosecutorial decision, it not only reflects the policy of the office but also sets the quality of its future work. Careful case preparation by the police should be supplemented by prosecutorial review before filing and adequate time between arrest, first appearance, and the charging decision.

The previous discussion has assumed prosecutorial review of the facts before the charging decision. This, of course, is not always the case. In some jurisdictions, structural barriers exist to hinder prosecutorial review. Where police file complaints in the court without the prosecutor's review or knowledge, where police act as prosecutors in the lower (misdemeanor) courts, or where bifurcated court and prosecutive systems exist, the opportunity for the prosecutor to participate in the intake process and produce a charging decision for which he can be held accountable is diminished, if not precluded. The very existence of these impediments points up the fact that even today the role of the prosecutor remains obscure in some parts of the country.

**The Accusatory Process**

The accusatory process, beginning with the prosecutor's decision to charge and ending with the arraignment of the defendant on the charges, affects both the future of the individual defendant and the overall operation of the criminal justice system. The procedures used in this period have widely different effects for prosecution—some beneficial, others debilitating.

There are two major forms of criminal accusation in the United States, the grand jury indictment and the prosecutor's bill of information, which presents probable cause and must be upheld by the court at a preliminary hearing.

Within these two general categories, four basic accusatory operations are observable in local criminal justice systems. From arrest to arraignment, they may briefly be described as follows: (1) arrest to grand jury for indictment; (2) arrest to preliminary hearing for bindover to grand jury for indictment; (3) arrest to grand jury for indictment or arrest to preliminary hearing on a bill of information, a combination of (1) and (2); and (4) arrest to preliminary hearing to a bill of information. The effect of these different accusatory processes on prosecution is basically two-fold. Some can be used effectively by the prosecutor as strategies to produce desired dispositions. Conversely, others can create barriers to effective and efficient prosecution at this stage in the system.

The study of the accusatory process also illuminates the changing role of the grand jury in our modern and mobile society. From its historical function of community standard setting, the grand jury has evolved into a multijurisdictional institution that has importance on an exceptional rather than a routine basis. The routine, daily use of a grand jury indictment as the means of accusation is a tradition still maintained by most of the states that comprised the original thirteen colonies. Normally, the grand jury "rubber stamps" the prosecutor's recommendations, and because of this it provides an indirect benefit to the prosecutor. Its existence provides the prosecutor with an avenue for rejecting sensitive cases or making decisions that may be publicly unpalatable. On a more critical note, it also may be used by a prosecutor to evade his responsibility for screening and review. For all the criticism of the grand jury system, it nevertheless provides some real system benefits. One of these is that it enables a prosecutor to take as much time as necessary in presenting complicated or sensitive cases—cases that would be too time consuming for a routine preliminary hearing procedure, too complicated for an untrained magistrate, or too expensive if formal court testimony had to be taken instead of hearsay or depositions.

There is little rationale or justification for the redundant accusatory process that exists in the many jurisdictions where, after a preliminary hearing, the defendant is bound over for grand jury indictment. Most likely this situation was produced by the coalescence of two court systems, each conducting its own accusatory process. Where it occurs, the prosecutor is given additional but unnecessary opportunity to manipulate the accusatory process. In addition the dual systems reduce accountability for actions while fostering opportunities for system breakdowns and management inefficiencies.

Optimal use of the accusatory function occurs when the prosecutor may have access to either the grand jury or the preliminary hearing, but not both sequentially as described in the redundant process. Because a choice can be made, rules governing the use of each must be established. Where possible selection of the accusatory route should be based on factors that extend beyond the crime-specific; for instance, grand juries should be reserved for sensitive, complicated, or exceptional circumstances, allowing the majority of cases to be processed by an open preliminary hearing. Adoption of this format tends to overcome the reservations of the critics of the grand jury and yet satisfy the prosecutor's need for time and, sometimes, secrecy. Still opportunity for prosecutorial manipulation of unfavorable court decisions is present, thereby requiring careful stipulation of the rules for grand jury usage and public accountability.

Many jurisdictions have done just this by eliminating the use of grand juries in the normal accusatory process, reserving them for only the most exceptional circumstances. These systems, introduced during the expansionary days of our frontier, can be found more frequently as one moves westward. Filings are made on a bill of information after a finding of probable cause. The support given to using this accusatory process (most recently as a result of the *Gerstein* v. *Pugh* decision) has had a direct effect on increasing the use of discovery, creating an environment for responsible prosecutorial charging and accountability, and, sometimes, increasing the prosecutor's efficiency in the court.[5] The last is not always predictable, particularly when some courts interpret the probable cause hearing to be a minitrial or when the prosecutor and defense use it for other purposes not related to determining probable cause (plea bargaining or discovery).

The variations in the form of preliminary hearings show the need for giving priority attention to the definition of the scope and limits for probable cause hearings. Even today four models can be found in the states—the federal, the California, the American Law Institute, and the Rhode Island. Their operations support the criticism of a lack of clarity or uniformity in the purpose of the preliminary hearing. Three of the four procedures are concerned with determining probable cause both with respect to restraining liberty and procceeding to trial. The fourth method (Rhode Island) is concerned only with the restraint of liberty issue.

Favorable court decisions expanding the authority of preliminary hearings, coupled with an increasingly mobile and more complex society, have reduced the justification for local grand juries to an exceptional basis. But abolition will not come about at the local level unless the powers of the grand jury can be transferred to alternative institutions. At issue are the power to subpoena witnesses and the power to grant immunity. Where this transfer has occurred (Florida and California are examples) the power to issue subpoenas has been vested in the prosecutor. In some states contracts of immunity may also be obtained by the prosecutor from the court. One should note that as the traditional autonomous powers of the grand jury to subpoena and grant immunity are transferred to the prosecutor, autonomy gives way to court sanction and approval.

A contemporary examination of grand jury use can be placed in a more legitimate perspective if its local role is distinguished from its multijurisdictional one. At the local level the powers of investigation and immunity are probably quite properly vested in the local prosecutor. However, this does not necessarily apply to the role of the multidistrict or statewide grand jury. An almost indisputable need currently exists for a vehicle empowered to conduct investigations on criminal conduct that spans a number of local jurisdictions, one having the broad accusatory responsibilities necessary in this increasingly complex and mobile society. The current call for "special statewide prosecutors" only partially responds to this real need for a statewide or multidistrict investigatory and accusatory body. Structure of this body whether a grand jury, a prosecutor, an Attorney General, or other variation is an appropriate area for public decision making.

Three basic and substantive issues emerge from the examination of the accusatory process. They are best viewed as choices that should be based on the public's expectations about: (1) whether to have a charging system based on secret, one-sided testimony heard by a grand jury, or based on open presentations under judicial control in a probable cause hearing; (2) whether to vest the investigative power exemplified by the authority to issue subpoenas and the power to grant immunity either in the grand jury, the prosecutor, or some combination of the two; and (3) whether to maintain redundant accusatory systems or to simplify the process steps to include one but not both. In this unique aspect of the prosecutive and court process, the issues are truly public ones, based on the fundamental expectations of the public about democracy and justice.

**Toward Trials and Dispositions:**
**The Concluding Process**

Following the accusatory process, the prosecution focus is shifted from charging to case disposition. Ideally, a disposition is achieved in a manner that is consistent with the policy of the prosecutor's office, which establishes a bottom line for each case. How dispositions are obtained may vary for each case according to a number of circumstances, not the least of which is the courtroom environment and the composition of the courtroom work group. This process stage is usually the most work-intensive, since it anticipates the possibility of a trial. Case review, evaluation, assignment, trial preparation, court appearances, and, sometimes, postconviction activities are all included.

In opposition to this environment of anticipated activity stands the number one enemy of prosecution—court delay, operationally defined here as continuances. Much delay in our court system arises legitimately, engendered by a fundamental lack of resources capable of processing the workload. In many jurisdictions experiencing increasing workloads, the courts and associated activities of defense and prosecution simply have not been able to keep pace. The focus here is not on unavoidable delay but on how delay is used as an effective defense strategy and why it is tolerated by the court. Through this examination the Achilles heel of prosecution is exposed.

From the prosecutor's perspective, every delay threatens the evidentiary strength of the case, resulting in less confident witnesses, dimmed memories, or loss of evidence. Victims and witnesses involved in a criminal event, the criminal justice system, as a whole, and the prosecution, in particular, all suffer. Not so the defendant, defense counsel, and, at times, the court; delay tends to favor them. It may be tolerated and even encouraged because of the immediate benefits of reduced workload pressure or because there are few sanctions against the process.

For a large number of defendants, especially those with prior criminal records, release on bail is almost as satisfactory a status as having their case dismissed or acquitted. Defense counsel may deliberately seek delay as a strategy to accomplish various ends: to bring mitigating or circumstantial evidence to the prosecutor's attention; to show that the defendant is remorseful and is taking steps to correct prior mistakes or prevent future ones; to leave more opportunity to plea negotiation; to provide more opportunity to collect his fee; and, of course, to hope for a weakening of the evidentiary strength of the prosecutor's case. Consequently the call for swift and speedy trials rarely comes from the lips of the defendant or his counsel. On the contrary, the demand for jury trial is often made only because the larger dockets result in slow processing times and long defendant queues.

If delay threatens the quality of the adversarial justice process and gives lop-sided advantage to the defendant at the expense of the victim, witness, and prosecutor, why do the courts tolerate and even abet delay by granting motions for continuances? The key to this question lies in the organizational structure of the courts and the mode of operation in the courtroom.

Formal court organization and informal courtroom work groups constitute barriers to improvement or change. The formal organizational structure is more properly classified as professional than bureaucratic. Its collegial arrangement lacks centralized direction and control, provides minimal external or internal sanctions against its members, and disperses power almost equally among the peer group. With this organizational configuration it is not surprising to find many courts incapable of employing fundamental management improvement techniques leading to efficient case processing. The limits to which the courts can absorb the basic features of a bureaucratic model while retaining a collegial relationship is clearly at issue, affecting not only internal but also systemic efficiency.

As it is, the formal organization fosters the norms of local autonomy that operate in the courtroom work group. Using a statistical analogy, one would expect to find in a court system more variance among the courtrooms than within a single court. But it is within these courtrooms that the work of the prosecutor culminates, and the operation of these courtroom work groups has a powerful effect on his activity.

Unlike the stereotyped adversarial courtroom drama, justice is meted out in terms of a dispositional process rather than an adversarial one. As Packer so clearly observed, in the dispositional mode the defendant is assumed to be guilty, leaving the work group with the sole task of reaching a satisfactory disposition through collaboration and negotiation.[6] This is a far cry from the norms of the formal organizations, which assume that the defendant is innocent until, through confrontation, the truth emerges. Yet it suggests an explanation for why the court tolerates delay.

The more informally constituted courtroom work group needs to move the day's docket, and continuances are a swift, simple, and legitimate means of doing just that. In fact, as a means of quickly moving from case to case, it is even more efficient than accepting a guilty plea. Within the work group there are few court sanctions or incentives available to reduce this daily dispositional practice, and as has been noted the formal organization is not structured to alter this pattern.

In this single stage, the prosecutor operates with the least power and authority. He can only thinly protest to the court about its excessive continuances; for if the ordinary dispositional mode of operation is upset, the alternative effects of operating with an adversarial one are almost too terrible to contemplate. Moreover, given the relatively autonomous position of the judges within the formal court organization, court delay emerges more as a product of the personal philosophy and work ethic of an individual judge than a procedure amenable to management change. Paradoxically in this one stage where the early presentation of the strongest evidence is essential to prosecution, the prosecutor is incapable of counteracting the debilitating effects of delay.

The organization of the court may be limited in its ability to deal with the problems of court delay; nevertheless, it has a powerful influence on the prosecutor's organization. Its docketing and case-processing practices almost totally define the limits within which prosecutorial manpower is assigned. Two basic forms of manpower allocation exist: the process or assembly-line organization and the trial team or integrated organization. The form used creates different results. If the court follows a practice of individual docketing, the courtroom work groups are relatively stable, and maximum system accountability is achieved. Where cases are processed assembly-line fashion, from one step to another, according to a master calendar assignment system the ability to hold specific individuals or work groups accountable for their actions is greatly reduced.

Finally, although the prosecutor's control over the disposition of the case is gradually shifted to the court as the trial approaches and is ultimately lost upon disposition, his influence may still be felt after the conviction, as evident in the use of sentence recommendation. The wide variation among jurisdictions in utilizing this procedure, and even among courtrooms in a judicial system, indicates that this is another area poorly defined and worthy of interaction research.

Making recommendations at sentencing may be a response the court demands or desires. Some judges want to have all perspectives on the case in front of them before sentencing. Others may want to evade the sentencing responsibility by relying on the prosecutor's recommendation. Alternatively, the prosecutor may make recommendations as a matter of policy, believing that the state has a duty and right to recommend; or he may not recommend, believing that the state has rested its case. He may even utilize recommendation as part of a plea-bargaining strategy, either recommending an agreed-on sentence or standing mute. Where the prosecutor is precluded from participating in this activity, whether by court rule or statute, his inability to affect the sentencing limits the scope of his function. The issue is at what point does the prosecutorial function end? As has been seen in New Orleans and Boulder it may extend far past the appellate level, encompassing parole, pardons, and expungement activities. The very arguments applied for extending law enforcement goals into the prosecutive function may be applied here to argue for extending the prosecutive function past conviction to protecting the community through participation in sentencing and postconviction activities.

An examination of the external constraints faced by the prosecutor reveals that they may be divided into two broad categories: those that apply to an external universe of populations, represented by the characteristics of the population served, its size, density, and complexity and those that apply to the various stages of the prosecution process from intake to postconviction activities. Within this world of constraints, the role of the prosecutor is shaped, and the limits of his activity and power are defined.

The issues that surface in the examination of external constraints on the prosecutor are particularly significant because they are either interactive or responsive in nature. Thus changes or shifts in the police function, the accusatory process, or the court may have profound effects on the prosecutive function. However, so little work has been done in the analysis of these interactions that the total effects are unknown, and even the marginal ones are uncertain. As a result, it is dangerous to apply universally any specific findings from one location to all others. One thing is certain: there exists more diversity than uniformity in our local systems of justice; these heterogeneous environments and practices produce more dissimilar issues and effects than similar ones.

## Prosecutorial Policy—Internalizing Control

No matter what his external environment or how his discretionary authority is perceived, the prosecutor operates with a policy (either one for which he was elected or one he inherited), which is implemented through various strategies. Policy is defined here as a specific course of action chosen from a range of possible actions. Recent evaluations of pretrial screening programs have indicated the power of prosecutorial policy in developing certain dispositional patterns. This involves the selective use of particular strategies to obtain expected results and the structuring of the organization and resources to be consistent with the policy and goals of the office.

Four distinct policies have been identified to date, each producing profoundly different dispositional patterns.[7] Attempts to explain the function of the prosecutor without accounting for these differences in approach and objective would yield less than satisfactory results. Policy is the single most important aspect of prosecution over which the prosecutor has complete control, and therefore, the need for policy analysis is clear. Much of the diversity that exists throughout the United States in similarly constituted offices can be explained in terms of policy choices. Thus the performance of a prosecutor should be measured through an examination and comparative analysis of policy, its implementation, and its effectiveness. Unless prosecutorial policy can be used as a basis for grouping and studying offices, criminal justice planners will not be able to transcend viewing prosecution at a local level and consider issues having national or societal impact. It has already been demonstrated that there are issues arising from a prosecutor's external constraints (such as what type of state support or accusatory systems are needed or wanted). These must now be considered in light of varying prosecutorial policies and the new issues that might also arise as a result of adopting another policy.

The local environment, especially the population size and demographic characteristics of the jurisdiction, affects prosecutorial policy. It shapes and colors the policy of the prosecutor and his perception of his role and influences the extent to which he selects policies not acceptable to the community he represents. It does not, however, appear to dictate the policy adopted.

Case studies show that the prosecutor's policy is implemented through an organizational structure that allocates the office's resources and develops appropriate management and operational controls. Where policy is not transmitted through the proper, organizational vehicle or supported by proper management techniques, there is wide variation in action decisions (exemplified by "assistant shopping") and little accountability.

In each of the offices examined, essentially the same set of strategies were available: discovery, plea bargaining, diversion, and other alternatives to adjudication, with only slight variation in access depending on state laws and court rules. Of all the strategies available, the prosecutors generally selected those that were most consistent with the implementation of their own policy. As a result, the aggregate dispositions flowing from the implementation of policy produced patterns that were distinctive to the policy. Thus, if one knows the policy of the prosecutor, one should expect dispositional patterns that are consistent with it. Or, stated in another way, one should not evaluate a prosecutor's dispositional performance unless one knows what the prosecutor is attempting to do.

The three offices participating in this study were selected because they were operating successfully, although each had different and easily identifiable policies. One incorporated a trial sufficiency policy—in which cases accepted for prosecution were charged at a level capable of being sustained on conviction. A minimum of plea bargains or dismissals resulted. The second had a system efficiency policy whereby cases brought to the prosecutor were disposed of as quickly and as early in the process as possible. A reduction in the size of the docket was a goal resulting in few bindovers for felony prosecution and extensive plea negotiation. In the third office, a defendant rehabilitation policy was observed. Cases were processed with an emphasis on their effect on the defendant and his future well-being. Acceptance of cases into the formal criminal justice system was discouraged in favor of the use of diversion and other alternatives. An indepth examination of each of the offices was conducted to determine if the policy framework outlined was sufficient and if any inconsistencies or defects could be found in implementing policy and, most importantly, to identify the ingredients that seemed to produce successful models.

The findings confirmed some assumptions and added dimension to others. Environment, indeed, supports prosecutorial policy. For example, the defendant-oriented policy operated successfully in part, because it was in a young, professional, affluent, civic-minded, and college-oriented community. Whether this same policy could be implemented in urban ghetto areas or in a conservative, blue-collar environment is questionable. It appears that some of these prosecutorial policies might be more environmentally dependent than others.

Policy is derived from a number of sources. In one office, policy was formulated by the newly elected prosecutor, who had extensive prior experience in prosecution; in another, the 20-year-old policy of the office was inherited and retained; in the third, the policy was created out of whole cloth but strongly colored by the prosecutor's previous experience as defense counsel. Regardless of source, two facts were obvious. The elective status of the prosecutor and the practice of having the assistants "serve at the pleasure" of the prosecutor combined to facilitate implementation of policy.

As the prosecutor and the office matured (each prosecutor studied was serving a second term) the process became more responsible and cohesive. Emphasis on gimmicks used for public appeal were downplayed, and the serious but more subtle refinements to prosecution were increased. As the prosecutor and his staff became more knowledgeable about the intricacies and workings of the criminal justice system, they were better able to organize the offices, select appropriate strategies, and identify areas for improvement.

The strict management controls and accountability procedures established by the trial sufficiency office to reduce plea bargaining and dismissals and to increase convictions on the original charge are examples of effective prosecutorial policy and organizational implementation.

Whereas some strategies are clearly inconsistent with some of the policies (such as plea bargaining and trial sufficiency), they are directly supportive to others. The system efficiency model produces an almost perfect, front-ended anticipatory system of prosecution. Its organization focuses on the intake division and encourages wide availability of alternatives for early case disposition, such as screening, diversion programs, discovery, and prosecutor-police teamwork. This broad assortment of strategies combines to produce the early disposition of most cases with the few serious cases that remain being handled by a small cadre of experienced trial attorneys.

Despite differences in policy, all three offices were organized so that the trial assistant's handling of the case and ultimate disposition was controlled by the policy. The trial sufficiency office carefully supervised inexperienced trial assistants in the choice of strategies and in the disposition process. Little discretion was permitted by the time the case reached the trial process stage. In the system efficiency model, each process step anticipated the needs of the next. As a result information or advice that might be needed by the next assistant was carefully documented and transmitted, thereby achieving maximum efficiency throughout the entire process. Discretionary decisions were allowed, and minimal supervision of the experienced trial assistants was exercised. In the defendant-oriented system, the small office size and the light caseload gave the staff opportunity to discuss each case and its bottom line. Strategies most likely to bring about the desired effect on the defendant could be explored by the assistants. This policy required the maintenance or close liaison with the community, law enforcement agencies, and the court. Once a consensus was reached about the desired outcome, the trial assistants operated independent of supervision.

If one were to attempt to sort out the common elements among these successful, but distinctly different, prosecutorial policies, three trends seem to emerge: an increasing professionalism in the approach to prosecution; an increasing extension of the prosecution function over the criminal justice system; and an increasing expansion of the role of the prosecutor into the external environment.

In each of these offices the maturation of the prosecutor led toward an increasing desire to professionalize prosecution. Illustrative of the obvious change in attitudes toward the charging process were remarks such as "we're not going to shotgun charges anymore" or "I don't want to fix mistakes later." For whatever reason—simple maturation, the effects of inflation, the result of better publicity for screening programs, or simply the existence of overcrowded jails—the prosecutors recognized the need for proper charging and its impact on the other process stages. This concern went well beyond the original justifications used to establish screening units (to "get rid of the garbage") to a desire for increased accuracy in the charging function.

A surprising dimension added during this study was the extension of the prosecutive function into the postconviction area of the justice system. This activity may always have been present but obscured by the emphasis traditionally placed on the intake and trial stages of prosecution. The creation of a postconviction tracking unit in the trial sufficiency office that reviews applicants for parole and pardon and, when deemed appropriate, recommends against a release decision, is one example of how a prosecutor attempts to protect the community from dangerous criminals by ensuring that the sentence they received is served. In this same postconviction area, the defendant-oriented prosecutor actively engages in expungements to restore the defendant to society by wiping out the stigma of an arrest and criminal conviction. It is significant that in both of these offices, serious attention was given to using all activities that could extend the impact of their policy as far as possible throughout the system.

Finally, the study found that in all of these offices, each prosecutor had a clear perception of the power and extent of his role. No longer confined merely to operations of the office, these prosecutors have become leaders in developing legislation and even in proposing constitutional amendments to improve deficiencies in the system. Their interest in the community, its values, and expected levels of performance was obvious. It was typified in one office by a community dialogue program and in another, by branch offices maintained for citizen and police relief. Any parochialism or isolation that might have been in existence was erased through their active involvement in state and national professional associations, their work as consultants providing technical assistance to other prosecutors, and their participation in advisory board meetings and policy-making groups. If one were to chart the prosecutor's growth and expansion from the minor court functionary of the 1800s to his status in 1977, these offices would provide good examples of how extensively the role and function of the American prosecutor has developed.

## Conclusion

In retrospect, one has to ask what this study has shown. Perhaps most importantly, it spotlights the fact that the prosecutor and the prosecutive function have been for the past 200 years victims of discrimination by stereotype and that, once the stereotypes are shattered, very little substantive knowledge of their activities remains. Not only is it difficult to extend our findings to all prosecutors based on what little we know, but it is even more frightening to realize the dimensions of what we do not know. We do not know, in any documented fashion, the effect of the external environment on the prosecutor or vice versa. From a prosecutor's perspective no systematic study has been made of these highly interactive areas. Nor would we know what to do with the results if they were available. Even now, we barely distinguish between one office and another, judging all in terms of either inadequate measures or measures that do not take into account the policy and goals of an office. After all these years, we are still incapable of comparing the performances between offices and have never, as a result, been able to extend our knowledge substantively into the predictive and planning areas.

The diversity that exists in the real world of prosecution demands more than urban stereotypes and media images of the "man with the black hat" ruthlessly pursuing the innocent defendant. The American prosecutor has grown up in the various locales and jurisdictions across the nation. If his role and function are to have any coherent meaning beyond this local level, then an amalgamation of our current knowledge expanded by the collection of additional information and data is clearly mandated.

This examination of the American prosecutor presents clearer insights into the choices that are available to the public including the role of law enforcement agencies vis à vis the prosecutor, the abolition of grand juries at the local level, and the expanded utility of discovery and preliminary hearings, sanctions against judges who foster and tolerate unnecessary delay, and the choice of prosecutorial policy—hard-line, tolerant, minimally sufficient, or defendant oriented. The public, through the elective process, created the prosecutor, and the courts endowed him with great power. Today, we need more than a fearful stereotype of uncontrollable power. We need the ability to make informed decisions about the prosecutorial process, to select that which is compatible with our view of the role of prosecution in a justice system, and to establish accountability for discretionary decisions.

## Notes

1. Daniel L. Skoler, *Organizing the Non-System* (Lexington, Mass.: Lexington Books, D.C. Heath, 1977), chap. 5.

2. 287 U.S. 45 (1932).

3. 407 U.S. 25 (1972).

4. James Eisenstein and Herbert Jacob, *Felony Justice: An Organizational Analysis of Criminal Courts* (Boston, Mass.: Little, Brown, 1977).

5. 420 U.S. 103 (1975).

6. Herbert L. Packer, *The Limits of Criminal Sanction* (Palo Alto, Calif.: Stanford University Press, 1968).

7. Joan E. Jacoby, *The Prosecutor's Charging Decision: A Policy Perspective* (Washington, D.C.: U.S. Government Printing Office, 1977).

# Table of Cases

# Name Index

Alschuler, Albert W., 187
American Bar Association, 57, 96, 99, 114, 117, 128, 154, 179
Advisory Commission on Inter-governmental Relations, 64, 154
American Medical Association, 183
American Psychological Association, 183

Baker, Newman, 28, 31, 33
Baker, Newman and Earl Delong, 34
Banfield, Laura, 175, 177
Bentham, Jeremy, 9
Bettman, Charles, 31
Blumberg, Abraham, 95, 97, 102, 103, 115
Bordua, David, J., 113
Bureau of Social Science Research, 198, 199
Burger, Warren G., 173

Calvert, William, 15
Campbell, Douglass, 17
Cattell, Raymond B., 182
Chadwick, Edwin, 9
Charles 11, 138
Cole, George F., 116
Coloquhoun, Patrick, 9, 10
Connick, Harry, 219-220

Dash, Samuel, 146
Davidson, Franklin C., 31
Delong, Earl, 33
De Tocqueville, Alexis, 28
Dewey, Thomas E., 140
Duke of York, 14

Eisenstein, James and Herbert Jacob, 103, 175, 176, 182, 184, 185, 281
Evans, William, 35

Friedman, Laurence, 5

Grosman, Brian, 5, 114, 116, 117

Henry II, 138
Hunter, Alexander, 258-260

Jackson, Andrew, 25, 37
Jacob, Herbert, 186

Katz, Lewis R., 114, 116, 117, 125, 129, 171, 172, 176, 181
Kress, Jack, 5, 6, 7

LaFave, Wayne, 123

Law Enforcement Assistance Administration, 99, 198, 242
Lee, Richard, 13
Leonard, Robert F. and Joel B. Saxe, 121
Ligda, Paul, 91
Lloyd, David, 15

MacDonald, Austin, 32, 33
Morten, Frank, 4
Martin, Ralph, 236, 238, 250, 252
Miller, Justin, 32
Miller, Frank W., 114, 116, 117
Missouri Crime Survey, 3, 31
Moley, Raymond, 32, 140
Montesquieu, Charles Louis, 26
Morgan, Robert B. and C. Edward Alexander, 64
Morse, Wayne, 140

National Bureau of Standards, 171
National Advisory Commission on Criminal Justice Standards and Goals, 90, 110, 114, 122, 128, 141, 153, 155, 160, 172, 209
National Center For Prosecution Management, 54, 56, 58, 63, 75, 85, 108, 113, 118, 119, 129, 187
National Prosecution Standards, 120
National District Attorneys Association, 53, 54, 58, 59, 62, 65, 108, 120, 128, 143, 172, 175, 180, 181
National Association of Attorney Generals, 4, 28, 36, 53, 54, 57, 58, 71

Orfield, Lester, 33

Packer, Herbert L., 289
Peel, Sir Robert, 9
Pitkin, William, 10
Pound, Roscoe, 25, 31
Powell, Lewis F., 151
The President's Crime Commission on Law Enforcement and The Administration of Justice, 52, 160, 61, 113
Puttkammer, Ernst, 32

Quinlin, William B., 33, 35
Quinney, Richard, 72

Reiss, Albert J., 113, 131

Scott, Rex, 258
Shaftsbury, Lord, 130

298

# Subject Index

300

# About the Author

**Joan E. Jacoby** has been a research associate at the Bureau of Social Science Research in Washington, D.C., since 1975, directing national programs of research in prosecution and criminal justice. Before this appointment, she was the executive director of the National Center for Prosecution Management, a nonprofit corporation that provided management and technical assistance to prosecutors nationwide in addition to conducting research on the prosecutive role and function.

From 1968 to 1972, she was the director of the office of Crime Analysis in the District of Columbia Government. Prior to this apointment, she was a statistician in the Management Office of the District Government. She received the B.A. in sociology from Boston University and the M.A. in statistics from The American University. Because of her criminal justice experience, she was appointed a member of the National Advisory Commission on Criminal Justice Standards and Goals' Advisory Task Force on Information Systems and Statistics and a consultant to the Court Task Force. She was also a member of Project Search's Task Force on Computerized Criminal Histories and Task Force Standardized Crime Reporting Systems.

Ms. Jacoby has lectured at Catholic, American, and Georgetown Universities, the National College of District Attorneys, the Institute for Court Management, and meetings of the National Association of Attorneys General. She has served as a consultant to the Alaska Judicial Council, the Criminal Justice Coordinating Council in New York City, the American University Courts Technical Assistance Program, and LEAA. She has written numerous articles in the fields of automation, management information system, and prosecutorial research.